Mary Shelley:
An Annotated Bibliography

Garland Reference Library of the Humanities (Vol. 22)

Mary Shelley:
An Annotated Bibliography

W. H. Lyles

Garland Publishing, Inc., New York & London

1975

Library of Congress Cataloging in Publication Data

Lyles, W   H
    Mary Shelley, an annotated bibliography.

    (Garland reference library of the humanities ;
no. 22)
    1. Shelley, Mary Wollstonecraft Godwin, 1797-
1851--Bibliography. I. Title.
Z8815.2.L93   [PR5398]   823'.7   75-17713
ISBN 0-8240-9993-1

TO

PATRICIA RYAN LYLES
Shakespearean scholar, &c.

THIS VOLUME

Is respectfully inscribed

BY

THE AUTHOR

CONTENTS

CONTENTS

CONTENTS

CONTENTS

Appendices

PREFACE

The past few decades have seen a resurgence of interest in Mary Wollstonecraft Shelley (1797-1851), the author of *Frankenstein,* wife and editor of Shelley, daughter of William Godwin and Mary Wollstonecraft—usually in that order. I have tried to follow that priority in the present bibliography, but making the important additions of her other works, the novels *Valperga, The Last Man, The Fortunes of Perkin Warbeck, Lodore,* and *Falkner,* and her stories, articles and reviews, biographies, travel works, and poems. All are necessary to gain a perspective on this major writer; if many of these have been neglected (only her two major novels and a handful of stories are currently in print), it is hoped that the present work may stimulate contemporary editions, so that by 1980 scholars may have access to the entire Mary Shelley canon.

This bibliography is divided into two basic sections, listing works by and about Mary Shelley. Part I lists all known writings of the author, including some doubtful ones (preceded by a question mark); the second, all works of importance commenting in some detail upon her in a biographical or critical light. I should emphasize that a list of all editions of Mary Shelley's works is not the major reason for the bibliography: I have tried to be as complete as possible when listing editions of *Frankenstein,* for example (though I am aware that I may have missed a Japanese or Chinese edition along the way), but I am somewhat more concerned about providing an index, from 1817 to the present, of all known works concerning Mary Shelley. The majority of these items are annotated, but for those few which I have been unable to locate I have preceded the item by an asterisk (*).

I should also emphasize that the second part presents a selective list; that is, biographers and critics of Shelley who

xiii

merely mention Mary in passing, without giving any new information concerning her life or works, are not included. Nor are those works which merely quote from her journal or letters, unless an editorial remark is present or unless the quotaton marks the first publication of the journal extract or the letter. I have also omitted superficial accounts of her life after 1900, such as the endless repetitive examinations of her elopement with Shelley. However, the seminal sources of Shelley biography, applying as well to Mary Shelley, are carefully annotated: Thomas Medwin's *Life of Percy Bysshe Shelley* (1847), Thomas Jefferson Hogg's *The Life of Percy Bysshe Shelley* (1858), Lady Jane Shelley's *Shelley Memorials* (1859), Edward John Trelawny's *Recollections of the Last Days of Shelley and Byron* (1858)—revised in 1878 as *Records of Shelley, Byron, and the Author*—and Thomas Love Peacock's *Memoirs of Shelley* (1860). Other works not included here are those which peripherally mention Mary Shelley as her husband's editor—unless critical comments of some depth are present, as they are in Charles H. Taylor's study.

Criticism of Mary Shelley's works has largely centered about *Frankenstein,* all of which is included, as are a few works examining the myth generated by the novel and extended to other media, particularly that of film. However, since criticism of her other five novels and of her other works is scarce, I have been at pains to include all such references, including those which devote only a sentence or two to Mary Shelley. These last, if the item concerning Mary Shelley is quoted in full, are marked at the end of the quotation by a dagger (†).

Part I. Works by Mary Shelley

Within each category, the listing is chronological, the annotation containing any extraneous publication information ("The Library of Literature"), mention of the byline (anonymous or "The Author of 'Frankenstein' ")—unless it is one of the variations of Mary Wollstonecraft Shelley—or any other pertinent information, including for rare items those libraries possessing the work. Cross-references

PREFACE

within Part I are made without a preceding number in boldface; that is, "See also B5a" for a work within Part I, but "See also IIA176" for an item in Part II. Whenever the potential for confusion exists within a single paragraph of the annotation, I have preceded cross-references with boldface numbers.

Journal & Letters. This is a selective listing; rather than repeat items in both parts of the bibliography which contain both editorial comment and a letter or journal extract, I have listed these items in Part II. A complete list of all material concerning the letters or the journal may be found in the Index.

Novels. All known editions are included, although *Frankenstein* presents a special problem in that it has been reprinted so often and in both English and foreign editions. Editions in languages using non-Roman alphabets have been transliterated, most from the entries in the annual bibliographies of the *Keats-Shelley Journal.* In some cases, I suspect inaccuracies in the transliteration (the Urdu-language edition of *Frankenstein,* for example); however, I have had to rely on foreign correspondents and on the *Keats-Shelley Journal* for much of this information.

Stories. The majority of Mary Shelley's stories are reprinted in Richard Garnett's 1891 collection, but since occasional variations exist between the stories' original publication and Garnett's versions, I have listed these items separately.

Poems. Unless the poem is reprinted in a revised version, notice of reprinting is given in the annotation of the main item.

Travel Works. Notice is made of only one reprinting of *History of a Six Weeks' Tour,* since that work is contained in most editions of Shelley's prose. Such listings would be superfluous, I feel, in a bibliography of Mary Shelley.

Biographies. Contents of the five volumes are given, with mention of those essays generally attributed to Mary Shelley.

Articles and Reviews. Included are several doubtful items. All works, whether a review or the "Memoirs of Godwin" in *Caleb Williams,* are included in this category.

Edited Works. Only the first edition is given for Mary Shelley's edition of Shelley's *Posthumous Poems* (1824), the first and second for the *Poetical Works* (which include the 1824 volume), and the first for *Essays, Letters from Abroad, Translations and Fragments.* However, I have included the most accessible edition of Shelley's poems (the modern Oxford edition) and the 1889 edition of Shelley's complete works which contains Mary's notes. Other editorial work attributed to Mary Shelley is included, even though Trelawny bitterly denied that she had any hand in his *Adventures of a Younger Son.* Following the lead of several other critics, including Elizabeth Nitchie, I have been inclined to disregard his statements.

Part II. Works about Mary Shelley

The arrangement here is alphabetical. Generally, the same guidelines followed in Part I apply here also, with the following additions:

Books. Whenever possible, I have cited the first edition of the work as the main entry, noting reprintings and facsimile reprintings following the annotation. Multivolume sets (such as the works of Lord Byron) are listed as one item, and separated within by the individual volumes.

Periodicals. For those periodicals (especially 19th-century ones) which have a counterpart with a similar title, I have given the full title, and occasionally the place of publication: *The Eclectic Review of Foreign Literature* (N.Y.). Also, certain groups of letters in the *Times Literary Supplement* are listed as one item, the responses listed chronologically following the original letter. The only abbreviation used in this section is *PMLA.*

Reviews. Only those reviews giving full publication information are included here. For others (including notices of the publication of one of Mary Shelley's novels), see the Index for listing in the relevant section. The order here conforms to that in Part I, although those few items reviewing Mary Shelley's journal or collected letters appear in "Periodicals" and are cross-referenced in Part I.

PREFACE

Graduate Research. Whenever appropriate, I have given page numbers, and *Dissertation Abstracts* listing in brackets following the title, school, and date.

Foreign Items. Included here are only those works in languages other than English. For English-language items published in a non-English-speaking country, see the appropriate section elsewhere in Part II. Several items have not been translated, and are marked, as are all items which I have not seen or translated, with an asterisk.

Mary Shelley in Fiction. This is a selective list, included mainly as a supplement. Several of these works, particularly Catherine Dodd's *Eagle Feather,* are often noted as "biographies" of Mary Shelley.

In addition, several contemplated works are not yet ready for inclusion in this bibliography. The present author plans for publication sometime in the late 1970's a work examining the myth generated by *Frankenstein,* a work similar in scope to Donald F. Glut's *The Frankenstein Legend,* though somewhat more critical, and to Christopher Small's *Ariel Like a Harpy,* but considering the film versions of the novel in detail. Paula Feldman, of the University of South Carolina, is preparing a new and complete edition of Mary Shelley's journal, a revised version of her dissertation. Charles E. Robinson, of the University of Delaware, is readying a collected edition of Mary Shelley's shorter fiction; Betty T. Bennett, of the State University of New York at Stony Brook, a complete edition of Mary Shelley's letters; and Alice Green Fredman, of Columbia University, a critical biography.

Appendices

I. MARY SHELLEY'S WORKS, CHRONOLOGICALLY ARRANGED. Only dates and titles are given, with cross-references to Part I.

II. THE LEGEND OF GEORGE OF FRANKENSTEIN. This essay, last printed in English in 1892, is here reprinted in full.

III. THEATRICAL, FILM, AND TELEVISION VER-
SIONS OF FRANKENSTEIN. For the theatrical versions, I
have reproduced information on cast and plot, whenever that
information was available. For several of these items I express
my gratitude to Elizabeth Nitchie's "The Stage History of
Frankenstein," to which I have occasionally referred the reader
for more information. For film versions, I have given all cast
and credits I have been able to locate, listings for the most part
made from personal viewings of the films; I have also briefly
noted the plot of the more important films, and cross-
referenced to Donald F. Glut's *The Frankenstein Legend* for
those readers wishing further information. I should emphasize
that this represents a selective listing: well over a hundred film
adaptations exist, but the majority of these feature a character
from Mary Shelley's novel in a very small role, often only a
"walk-on." For a complete list of films such as these, see Walt
Lee's *Reference Guide to Fantastic Films* (Los Angeles:
Chelsea-Lee Books, 1972).

The television adaptations present special difficulties.
Tracking down information regarding shows in the early
fifties, the era of live television, is often more difficult than
locating out-of-print 19th-century works. Nevertheless, I have
given all pertinent information available.

IV. SELLING PRICES FOR SELECTED WORKS BY
AND ABOUT MARY SHELLEY, CULLED FROM BOOK
AUCTION RECORDS AND CATALOGUES OF SEC-
ONDHAND BOOKDEALERS. In addition to these two
sources, I have included several offers made privately to the
present author. Such information lends an interesting
perspective to the history of Mary Shelley's works.

As with any bibliography, I owe a special debt to those
works preceding mine. Besides the usual sources of
information and the brief bibliographies in the biographical
and critical studies of Mary Shelley and her husband, I am
indebted to the annotated bibliographies of the *Keats-Shelley
Journal* (although 1970 is the last year wholly covered by the
latest of those) and to the appended bibliography in Jean de

PREFACE

Palacio's *Mary Shelley dans son oeuvre*. Although I did not discover the latter work until the bulk of my research was completed, I owe to it many of the items in the "Reviews" section of Part II. My order, however, differs considerably from de Palacio's: I have fully annotated many works which he considers briefly or not at all, and I have included in the "Periodicals" section many works which he lists as reviews.

The majority of the items in this bibliography proved readily accessible in public libraries. For those that did not, I have the following to thank: the staff of the Stack and Reader Division at the Library of Congress; the staffs of the General Reference Room, Humanities Reference Room, and Interlibrary Loan at McKeldin Library of the University of Maryland; the staff of the Sterling Library at Yale, especially one anonymous member of the Information desks who allowed me access to Yale's dissertation records; the staff of the Bodleian Library, Oxford, particularly that of Duke Humfrey's Library and the Photocopy Service; Janet K. Moss, of the Information Service, Reading Room, British Library; Jean M. Sykes, Assistant Librarian at the University of Liverpool; Marianne Bahmann, of the University Archives at Stanford University; the General Research and Humanities Division of the New York Public Library; D. M. Torbet, of the City Library of Dundee, Scotland, who in addition to supplying me with two photocopies I had requested also included one of which I had no previous knowledge—a very pleasing surprise; the Boston Public Library; *Kirkus Reviews;* the *Eastern Daily Press; Aloft* magazine, of National Airlines; the Central English Library of Zurich; the Public Library of Christchurch, New Zealand; and the American University in Cairo, Egypt.

In addition, I am indebted to the following: Nancy Porter, of the University of Nebraska Press, for providing reviews of *The Last Man;* Carolyn Paton, of Oxford University Press, for reviews of *Frankenstein;* Patty Barker, of Bobbs-Merrill; the University of Oklahoma Press; Donald H. Reiman, of the Pforzheimer Library, for suggesting sources; Burton R. Pollin, for a list of his relevant publications; James Rieger, for information concerning his works; Frederick L. Jones, Jr., for

PREFACE

informing me that his late father's works were at Furman University, Greenville, S.C., and J. Glen Clayton of that institution for providing me with a bibliography of Professor Jones; Paula Feldman, for information concerning her forthcoming edition of Mary Shelley's journal and of other contemplated works concerning Mary Shelley; Lady Mander, for details concerning her biography of Mary Shelley; Christopher Lee, for noting the forthcoming inclusion of a Mary Shelley story in an anthology edited by him; Henry H. Heins, bibliographer of Edgar Rice Burroughs, for putting me on the track of two items touching upon Mary Shelley; Morris D. Rosenberg, of the Washington *Post,* for putting me in contact with Andrew Glaze, British Travel Authority, who supplied information concerning the original appearance of Edmund Allens' article on Sherlock Holmes; and Editions Klincksieck, Paris, for information concerning Jean de Palacio's work.

For translations, I thank James Gallagher, Joseph Markel, Marsha Seabreeze, and Frank Pierce. I am also grateful to students and associates at the University of Maryland for noting recent relevant publications, and in particular to Dr. Jackson Bryer for guiding this project from beginning to end.

Special thanks must go to my wife, Patricia Ryan Lyles, for *not* typing the manuscript, but for providing numerous other services of a decidedly non-secretarial nature, including a great deal of intelligent criticism, not all of which I heeded.

I should add that despite the mention of sources of this bibliography, any omissions or errors, including matters of judgment, are mine alone.

W. H. LYLES

Silver Spring, Md.
March 23, 1975

N.B. The abbreviation "MS" is used throughout the text to designate both "Mary Shelley" and "Mary Shelley's."

PART I

WORKS BY MARY SHELLEY

A JOURNAL & LETTERS

A1   *Mary Shelley's Journal*. Frederick L[afayette] Jones, ed. Norman,
      Okla.: University of Oklahoma Press, 1947.
          Contains the major portion of MS journal (approximately eighty
      per cent) in the Bodleian, previously published in large amounts
      only in *Shelley and Mary* [cf. IIA16]. Covers periods from 1814 to
      1844, with a large gap from May 14, 1815 to July 20, 1816 (lost),
      and lacks the entire years of 1825, 1835, 1836, 1837, 1841, and
      1844, and portions of 1826, 1827, 1828, 1829, 1830, 1831, 1832,
      1833, 1834, 1838, 1839, and 1840. For a more complete version, see
      the dissertation by Paula Feldman [IID6] and the note on its in-
      tended publication.
          Also contains Preface by Frederick L. Jones [cf. IIA223]; edi-
      torial notes throughout the text; "Other Textual Notes" (pp. 211-
      212); list of "Lost or Unprinted Letters by Shelley and Mary"
      (213-215); "References to Shelley's Works" (216-217); "Shelley's
      Reading" (218-231), covering also the reading of MS; and adequate
      Index.
          See also IIA6, A8, A10, A174, A382, B18, B248.

A2   *Letters of Mary W. Shelley (Mostly Unpublished)*. [Henry Howard
      Harper, ed.] Boston: Printed only for Members of the Bibliophile
      Society [Norwood, Mass.: The Plimpton Press], 1918.
          Contains 35 letters to Leigh and Marianne Hunt, from 1817 to
      1844, most printed in full; and portions of MS journal for October
      21, 1838.
          Also contains Introduction by Henry H. Harper [cf. IIA188],
      and editorial notes and comments.
          See also II189.

A3   "The Letters of Mary Shelley in the Bodleian Collection," *The
      Bodleian Quarterly Record*, 6 (3rd Quarter 1929), 51-59 [52-59].
          Seven letters to Maria Gisborne (June 15, July 2, and December
      1818; Feb. 19, April 26, April 27, and May 30, 1819).
          Also contains an Introductory Note by R[eginald] H[arrison]
      H[ill] [cf. IIB119].
          Continued in A4, A5, A6.

A4   "The Letters of Mary Shelley in the Bodleian Collection," *The
      Bodleian Quarterly Record*, 6 (4th Quarter 1929), 79-86.
          Continuation of A3. Six letters, one to Emilia Curran (Sept.
      18, 1819), and five to Maria Gisborne (Oct. 5, November?, Dec. 1,

December, and October 13 or 14, 1819).
Continued in A5, A6.

A5   "The Letters of Mary W. Shelley in the Bodleian Library (*continued*),"
The Bodleian Quarterly Record, 8 (Spring 1937), 297-310, 360-371
[298-310, 360-371].
    22 letters, 18 to Maria Gisborne (Jan. 18, March 8-10, March 14,
March 22, March 26, March 31, April 13, June 18, July 7, Sept. 25,
Dec. 16-24, and Dec. 29, 1820; Feb. 21 and April 15, 1821; Sept. 17-
20, Nov. 6, and Nov. 22, 1822), two to Amelia Curran (Jan 19, 1820;
May 14, 1821), and two to John Gisborne (April 4 and December 1820).
Also contains an Introductory Note by Frederick L. Jones [cf.
IIB133].
    Continued in A6.

A6   "Letters of Mary W. Shelley in the Bodleian Library (*continued*),"
The Bodleian Quarterly Record, 8 (Autumn 1937), 412-420.
    Ten letters, four to Leigh Hunt (July 30, 1823; June 6, 1842;
Dec. 23, 1844; June 10, 1847), one to the Editor of a Periodical
(ca. October 1826), one to Mrs. Bartlett (May 19, 1827), two to
Charles Ollier (Jan. 14, 1830; March 18, 1833), one to Marianne
Hunt (Nov. 21, 1843), and one to Leigh and Marianne Hunt (Jan. 9,
1845).
    Conclusion of the series begun by A3 and continued in A4, A5.

A7   *The Letters of Mary W. Shelley.* Frederick L[afayette] Jones, ed.
2 vols. Norman, Okla.: University of Oklahoma Press, 1944.
    A collection of 705 letters, printed in full or in part, des-
cribed or summarized, or mention of date and addressee, covering
the periods from 1814 to 1850.
    Vol. I contains 311 letters, covering the periods from October
25, 1814 to June 27, 1828. 268 are printed in full, 23 in part,
3 described or summarized, and 17 with mention of date and addressee. Letters addressed to: The Authorities at Via Reggio,
Mrs. Bartlett, Christie Baxter, William T. Baxter, Isabel Booth,
Sir John Bowring, Byron, Thomas Campbell, Claire Clairmont, Charles
Cowden Clarke, Henry Colburn, Amelia Curran, An Editor, John Gis-
borne, Maria Gisborne, John and Maria Gisborne, Godwin, John
Hanson, J. A. Hessey, Hogg, Louisa Holcroft, Mrs. R. B. Hoppner,
Leigh Hunt, Marianne Hunt, Leigh and Marianne Hunt, Victor Jacque-
mont, Thomas Forbes Kelsall, Mary Lamb, Thomas Medwin, Prosper
Mérimée, John Murray, Vincent Novello, Mrs. Vincent Novello, Robert
Dale Owen, John Parke, John Howard Payne, Thomas Love Peacock,
George W. Portman, Bryan Waller Procter (?), Capt. Daniel Roberts,
Mrs. Saunders, Shelley, Sir Timothy Shelley, Sophie Stacey, John
Taafe, Mrs. Thomas, Trelawny, Alaric A. Watts, William Whitton,
Jane Williams, and unknown. Also contains Preface [cf. IIA224],
Acknowledgements, List of Letters in Vol. I, note on sources of
"The Letters Previously Printed," Editor's Introduction [cf.
IIA224], and editorial notes throughout the text by Frederick L.
Jones.
    Vol. II contains 394 letters, covering the periods from June 28,

1828 to September 8, 1850. 364 are printed in full, 19 in part, 7 described or summarized, and four with mention of date and addressee. Letters addressed to: Alexander Berry, Mrs. Alexander Berry, Mr. Blewitt (?), Sir John Bowring, Edward Bulwer, Nerina Mason Cini, Claire Clairmont, Henry Colburn, W. Galignani, Monsieur Galloni (?), Maria Gisborne, John Gregson, Mr. Halford, Marianna Hammond, Mary Hays, Abraham Hayward, William Hazlitt, Jr., Hogg, Thomas Hookham, Richard Monckton Milnes, Lord Houghton, J. C. Hudson, Leigh Hunt, Marianne Hunt, Douglas Jerrold, Maria Jane Jewsbury, Mrs. Jones, James Kenney, Alexander Knox, Walter Savage Landor, George Henry Lewes, Mrs. Manners-Sutton, Gideon Algernon Mantell (?), Thomas Medwin, Mr. Mignot, Mrs. Milner-Gibson, Thomas Moore, Lady Morgan, Edward Moxon, John Murray, Mary Peacock Nicolls, Charles Ollier, Robert Dale Owen, John Howard Payne, Mary Peacock, Cyrus Redding, Frederic Mansel Reynolds, Charles Robinson, Henry Crabb Robinson, Gabriele Rossetti, Sir Walter Scott, Richard Rothwell, Mrs. Stanhope, Sir Timothy Shelley, Mr. Touchet, Augusta Trelawny, Trelawny, Alaric A. Watts, William Whitton, Jane Williams (Hogg), Everina Wollstonecraft, and unknown. Included also is a reproduction of a pencil sketch of Shelley by MS. Also contains List of Letters in Vol. II; Appendix I, "Other Mary Shelley Letters" (43 untraced letters and sets of letters); Appendix II, "Mary Shelley, John Howard Payne and Washington Irving" [cf. IIA224]; Appendix III, "Mary Shelley's Second Defense of Velluti" [cf. H18]; Appendix IV, "Mary Shelley's Last Illness and Death" (letters by Percy Florence Shelley and Lady Jane Shelley); Appendix V, "Owners of the Original Letters"; Appendix VI, "Table of Correspondents"; Index; and editorial notes throughout by Frederick L. Jones.

A new edition of Mary Shelley's letters is planned by Betty T. Bennett of the State University of New York at Stony Brook.

See also IIB72.

A8   *My Best Mary. The Selected Letters of Mary Wollstonecraft Shelley.* Muriel Spark and Derek Stanford, eds. London: Allan Wingate, 1953.

Contains 118 letters, addressed to Sir John Bowring, Byron, Claire Clairmont, Amelia Curran, Maria Gisborne, Abraham Hayward, Hogg, Mrs. R. B. Hoppner, Leigh Hunt, Marianne Hunt, Alexander Knox, Thomas Medwin, Prosper Mérimée, Thomas Moore, John Murray, Vincent Novello, John Howard Payne, Thomas Love Peacock, Charles Robinson, Joseph Severn, Shelley, Trelawny, Augusta Trelawny, Jane Williams, and unknown.

Also contains Introduction [cf. IIA398] and editorial notes throughout the text by Muriel Spark and Derek Stanford.

Also published, N.Y.: Roy Publishers, 1953. Facsimile reprint of London ed.: Folcroft, Pa.: Folcroft Library Editions, 1972.

A9   Frederick L. Jones. "Mary Shelley to Maria Gisborne: New Letters, 1818-1822," *Studies in Philology*, 52 (January 1955), 39-74.

27 letters (May 25, 1818 to Jan. 18, 1822), presented and edited by Frederick L. Jones.

See also IIB138.

B NOVELS

a) *Frankenstein; Or, The Modern Prometheus*

Bla   *Frankenstein; Or, The Modern Prometheus*. 3 vols. London: Printed for Lackington, Hughes, Harding, Mayor, & Jones, 1818.

Anonymous. Published in January, although a few copies may have been distributed in December 1817 [cf. IIB255]. Contains the Preface by Percy Bysshe Shelley (uncredited).

Copies at the Library of Congress, British Library, Bodleian, Yale, and Pierpont Morgan Library (the "Mrs. Thomas Copy").

For reviews, see IIC1-C9. For descriptive bibliography, see A79, A284, A445. See also A154, B145, B156.

B2a   *Frankenstein, ou le Prométhée moderne*. 3 vols. J[ules] S[aladin], trans. Paris: Corréard, 1821.

By Mme. Shelly [*sic*]. The first translation in any language.

Copies at the Bibliothéque Nationale, British Library, Bodleian, and Yale.

For other French-language editions, see B37a, B43a, B59a, B60a, B92a, B93a, B98a, B113a, B116a, B127a, B128a. See also IIA116.

B3a   *Frankenstein; Or, The Modern Prometheus*. 2 vols. London: Printed for G. and W. B. Whittaker, 1823.

Reprinting of Bla, using the same plates—arranged by Godwin to capitalize on the popularity of the theatrical *Frankensteins*. "A new edition."

Copies at the British Library and Yale.

For descriptive bibliography, see IIA284.

B4a   *Frankenstein; or, The Modern Prometheus*. London: Henry Colburn and Richard Bentley/Edinburgh: Bell and Bradfute/Dublin: Cumming, 1831.

One-volume revised edition, the standard text for most future editions, with an Introduction by "M.W.S." explaining the circumstances of the novel's composition and crediting the 1818 Preface to Shelley. No. 9 in the Standard Novels series.

Copies at the Library of Congress, British Library, Bodleian, and Yale.

B5a   Second edition of B4a, 1832.

Copies at Johns Hopkins University, Princeton, University of Chicago, University of Illinois, University of Pennsylvania, and Yale.

B6a   *Frankenstein; or, The Modern Prometheus.* 2 vols. Philadelphia:
      Carey, Lea & Blanchard, 1833.
             By Mary W. Shelly [*sic*].   Pirated edition of the 1818 text.
      Copies at Harvard, University of Illinois, and Yale.
      For reviews, see IIC10, C11.   See also B145.

B7a   Third edition of B4a, 1839.
      Copy at Boston Public Library.

B8a   *Frankenstein; or, The Modern Prometheus.* N.Y.: Henry G. Daggers,
      1845.
             By Mrs. Mary W. Shelley.   The 1818 text.   New Library of Stan-
      dard Novels, No. 1.
      Copy at the Library of Congress.

B9a   *Frankenstein; or, The Modern Prometheus.*   London: Thomas Hodgson
      [1847].
             The Parlour Library, Vol. 144.
      Copy at the Library of Congress.
             For reprinting, see B11a.   Other reprintings may exist, but I
      have seen no editions that differ from these two.

B10a Fourth edition of B4a, 1849.
             By the author of "The last man."   Introduction signed M. W. S.
      Copy at the Library of Congress.
      See also IIA377.

B11a Second edition of B9a [ca. 1855].
             Copies at the Boston Public Library (carded as "[186-?]") and
      the British Library, and in the present author's collection.
             See note at B9a concerning other editions.

B12a *Frankenstein; or, The Modern Prometheus.*   Boston: Sever, Francis &
      Co., 1869.
             Copies at Boston Public Library, Harvard, New York Public
      Library, State University of Iowa, University of California at
      Berkeley, and Yale.
             For review, see IIC12 [and A354].

B13a *Frankenstein; or, The Modern Prometheus.*   London: Milner [ca. 1870].
             The Cottage Library.

B14a *Frankenstein or The Modern Prometheus.*   London: Routledge and Sons,
      1882.
             Copy at the British Library.
             For reprintings, see B17a, B18a, B21a, B26a, B31a.

B15a *Frankenstein; or, The Modern Prometheus.*   N.Y.: J. W. Lovell [1882].
             By Mary Wolstonecraft [*sic*] Shelley.   Lovell's Library, No. 5.
      The 1818 text.
             Copies at the Library of Congress, Harvard, and Yale.

B16a Frankenstein; Or, The Modern Prometheus. N.Y.: George Munro [1883].
Seaside Library, Vol. 76, No. 1538. Extremely small print; 34
pages only.
Copy at the Library of Congress.

B17a Frankenstein or the Modern Prometheus. London: George Routledge
and Sons, 1886.
New format of B14a. Routledge's World Library, No. 25. Introduction by the Rev. H[ugh] R[eginald] Haweis [cf. IIA195].
Copies at the British Library and the Bodleian.

B18a Frankenstein, or The Modern Prometheus. London: George Routledge
and Sons, 1888.
New format of B17a. Routledge's Pocket Library, Vol. 31.
For reprintings, with variations in title, see B21a, B26a,
B31a. Other dates may exist for this 317-page edition (I have two
slightly different editions in my collection), but I have been
able to date only these four.
Copies at Bryn Mawr, Harvard, and University of Virginia.

*B19a Frankenstein; or, The Modern Prometheus. Chicago, N.Y.: Belford,
Clarke & Company [189-?].
Copy at University of Illinois.

B20a Frankenstein; or, The Modern Prometheus. N.Y.: H. M. Caldwell Co.
[189-?].
By Shelley.

B21a Frankenstein; or, The Modern Prometheus. London: George Routledge
& Sons/N.Y.: E. P. Dutton [1891?].
Copy at the London Library.

*B22a Frankenstein, or The Modern Prometheus. N.Y.: Home Book Co. [1893].
The Premium Library.
Copy at Harvard.

B23a Frankenstein. London: Gibbings and Company/Philadelphia: J. B.
Lippincott, 1897.
Copies at the London Library, Princeton, University of Chicago,
University of Cincinnati, and University of North Carolina.

*B24a Frankenstein; or, The Modern Prometheus. London: Downey, 1897.
Listed in The English Catalogue of Books, Jan. 1890-Dec. 1897
(Vol. V, p. 894), as published in July.

B25a Frankenstein; or, The Modern Prometheus. N.Y.: Home Book Co.
[1898?].
Possibly using the same plates as B22a, but I have not seen the
latter.
Copy at University of Virginia.

B26a Frankenstein, or The Modern Prometheus. N.Y.: Routledge, 1899.

*B27a   *Frankenstein, or The Modern Prometheus.*   Chicago: Donohue, Henneberry & Co. [18—?].
       Copy at Harvard.

B28a   *Frankenstein; or, The Modern Prometheus.*   Chicago: Homewood Publishing Company [19—?].
       Oxford and Homewood Series.

B29a   *Frankenstein, or The Modern Prometheus.*   N.Y.: The Mershon Co. [190-?].

B30a   *Frankenstein; or, the Modern Prometheus.*   N.Y.: James Pott & Co., 1901.
       The "Gem" Classics.
       For review, see IIc13.

B31a   *Frankenstein.*   London: George Routledge & Sons [ca. 1911].

*B32a   *Frankenstein.*   H. Widtmann, trans.   1912.
       Publisher unknown.   Source: *Internationale Bibliographie der Zeitschriftenliteratur, Abtetlung C.*
       First German-language translation; for others, see B62a, B94a, B123a, B133a.

B33a   *Frankenstein, or the Modern Prometheus.*   London, Toronto: J. M. Dent & Sons/N.Y.: E. P. Dutton, 1912.
       Everyman's Library, No. 616, published in September, with an anonymous Introduction [cf. IIA216].
       For reprintings, see B35a, B39a, B40a, B45a, B56a, B64a, B65a; new format begins with B75a.

*B34a   *"Frankenstein," il Prometeo moderne.*   Danton M. Fonzo, trans. N.Y., 1914.
       By Mary Woolestencraft [sic] Shelley.
       In the Card Catalogue at the Library of Congress, but searches by the present author have failed to uncover it, to determine publisher and format.
       For other Italian-language translations, see B55a, B66a, B107a.

B35a   Reprinting of B33a, 1922.
       Cornell cards this as "[1921]."

B36a   *Frankenstein, or the Modern Prometheus.*   Boston: Cornhill, 1922.
       Copy at the Enoch Pratt Library.

*B37a   *Frankenstein, ou le Prométhée moderne.*   G. d'Hargest, trans.   Paris: La Renaissance du livre, 1922.
       Introduction by G. d'Hargest [cf. IIE18].
       Listed in the catalogue of the Bibliothéque Nationale, tome 172, p. 11.

B38a   *Frankenstein; or, The Modern Prometheus.*   N.Y.: Brentano's [1923].
       The Lotus Library.
       Copies at Harvard and New York Public Library.

B39a   Reprinting of B33a, 1927.

B40a   Reprinting of B33a [1930].
       Copies at Pennsylvania State Teachers College and Swarthmore
       College.

B41d   *Frankenstein or the Modern Prometheus.*   London: Readers Library
       Publishing Co. [1932].

B42a   *Frankenstein {Or, The Modern Prometheus}.*   N.Y.: Illustrated
       Editions Company, 1932.
       The 1818 text.   Illustrated by Nino Carbe.   Some copies printed
       as "Deluxe editions."
       Copies at Cornell, Free Library of Philadelphia, Harvard,
       Haverford College, New York Public Library, University of Illinois,
       University of Virginia, and in the present author's collection.
       Illustrations also in B63a.

*B43a *Frankenstein.*   Paris: Editions cosmopolites, 1932.
       In the catalogue of the Bibliothéque Nationale, tome 172, p. 11,
       which lists a subtitle, "Superproduction Universal-Film," and an
       alternate subtitle, "Scenario et adaptation de Robert Florey, d'après
       l'œuvre de Mrs. Percy Bysshe Shelley," and notes that it is part of
       the "Collection du lecteur, No. 91 [96, on title]."   Florey was
       originally responsible for the screenplay of the 1931 film version
       of *Frankenstein,* but was not mentioned in the film's credits.   This
       work seems to be a tie-in with the release of the film.
       See also B44a.

B44a   *Frankenstein or, The Modern Prometheus.   Illustrated with scenes
       from the Universal Photoplay.*   N.Y.: Grosset & Dunlap [ca. 1932].
       Contains an anonymous Introduction [cf. IIA216], and six
       photographic stills from the 1931 film.
       Copy in the present author's collection; although not a par-
       ticularly rare item, it is seldom found in secondhand bookdealers'
       shops, and I know of no copies at libraries.
       See also B43a.

B45a   Reprinting of B33a, 1933.

B46a   *Frankenstein, or the Modern Prometheus.*   N.Y.: Harrison Smith and
       Robert Haas, 1934.
       With engravings on wood by Lynd Ward.
       Also published as B47a.
       For review, see IIC15.

B47a   *Frankenstein, or the Modern Prometheus.* Toronto: George J. McLeod,
        1934.
            With engravings on wood by Lynd Ward.
            Also published as B46a.

B48a   *Frankenstein or the Modern Prometheus.* N.Y.: The Limited Editions
        Club, 1934.
            With an Introduction by Edmund Lester Pearson [cf. IIA327] and
        illustrations by Everett Henry.
            See also B67a.

B49a   *Frankenstein; or, the Modern Prometheus.* N.Y.: Books, Inc. [ca.
        1937].
            The 1818 text. Duo-tone Classics; The World's Popular Classics;
        Art-type edition.
            For reprintings, with various formats, see B50a, B54a.

B50a   Reprinting of B49a [ca. 1937].
            The 1818 text. Registered Guild Library.

B51a   *Frankenstein.* In *Horror Omnibus, containing two complete novels:
        Dracula, by Bram Stoker; Frankenstein, by Mary W. Skelley* [*sic*].
        N.Y.: Grosset & Dunlap [1939].
            The two novels separately paginated.
            For reprinting, see B154a.

B52a   "The Birth of Frankenstein." In Geoffrey Grigson, comp. *The Ro-
        mantics: An Anthology chosen by Geoffrey Grigson.* London: George
        Routledge & Sons, 1942, pp. 247-249 [Item 299].
            Portion of the 1831 Introduction.
            Reprinted, 1943, 1945, 1947.

*B53a   *Frankenstein (Or, The Modern Prometheus).* N.Y.: Editions for the
        Armed Services, Inc. A Non-Profit Organization Established by the
        Council on Books in Wartime [ca. 1942].
            Overseas Edition, No. 909.
            de Palacio [IIE1, p. 648, Item 11] notes that this edition
        "follows the 1818 text (possibly incorrect)."

B54a   Reprinting of B49a [1943?].
            The 1818 text. The World's Popular Classics; Art-type edition.

*B55a   *Frankenstein.* Ranieri Cochetti, trans. Rome: Donatello de Luigi,
        1944.
            Romanzo nero, v.n. 1. With "Introduzione" by Ranieri Cochetti
        [cf. IIE8].
            In the card catalogue of the Library of Congress, but searches
        by the present author have failed to uncover it.

B56a   Reprinting of B33a [1945].

- 11 -

B57a   *Frankenstein*. Rafael Giménez, trans. Buenos Aires: Edit. Octrosa, 1945.
      For other Spanish-language editions, see B61a, B79a, B106a, B112a, B126a.

B58a   *Frankenstein*. Adapted by Ruth A. Roche. Classics Illustrated, No. 26. N.Y.: Classics Illustrated, Gilberton Company, December 1945.
      Comic-book adaptation, following the novel closely. Biographical sketch entitled "Mary Shelley" after text [cf. IIA270].
      For re issue, see B135a.

B59a   *Frankenstein*. Henry Langon, trans. [Brussels:] Le Scribe, 1946.
      Copy at the Library of Congress.

B60a   *Frankenstein*. Hannah Betjeman, trans. Ambilly: Impr. Presses de Savoie, 1947.
      Editions de Richer.
      For other editions using this translation, see B92a, B98a, B116a, B127a.

B61a   *Frankenstein*. Laura Marazul, trans. Buenos Aires: Edit. Lautaro, 1947.

B62a   *Frankenstein*. Elisab. Lacroix, trans. Hamburg: Johannes Angelus Keune, 1948.

B63a   *Frankenstein; or, The Modern Prometheus*. Garden City, N.Y.: Halcyon House [1949?].
      Illustrated Library; uses the Nino Carbe illustrations from B42a.

B64a   Reprinting of B33a [1949].

B65a   Reprinting of B33a, 1951.

*B66a   *Frankenstein ovvero il prometeo moderne*. B. Tasso, trans. Milan: Rizzoli, 1952.
      Source: Annual Bibliography of the *Keats-Shelley Journal*.

B67a   *Frankenstein or the Modern Prometheus*. N.Y.: Heritage Press, 1953.
      Same format as B48a.

*B68a   *Frankenstein*. Giichi Shishido, trans. Tokyo: Nihon Shuppan Kyôdô Kabushiki-Gaisha, 1953.
      Source: Annual Bibliography of the *Keats-Shelley Journal*.
      For other Japanese-language editions, see B77a, B118a, B147a.

B69a   *Frankenstein*. Nripendra Krishna Chattopadhyay, trans. Calcutta: Deva Sahitya Kutin, 1955.
      Text in Bengali.

B70a   "The Monster's Mate is Destroyed." In Raymond Wright, ed. *Prose of the Romantic Period 1780-1830*. Vol. IV of *The Pelican Book of English Prose*. Kenneth Alott, ed. Harmondsworth, Middlesex: Penguin Books, 1956, pp. 190-192.
Exoerpt from Chapter XX of the 1831 edition.

B71a   *Frankenstein*. N.Y.: Pyramid Books, 1957.
Published in October; the first paperback edition of the novel (with the possible exception of B53a).
For reprintings, see B81a, B87a, B95a, B96a, B97a, B100a, B102a, B103a.

*B72a   *Frankenstein*. Caio Jardim, trans. São Paulo: Ed. Universitária, 1957.
Text in Portugese. Source: Annual Bibliography of the *Keats-Shelley Journal*.

B73a   "I Am the Fallen Angel." In Howard E. Hugo, ed. *The Romantic Reader*. N.Y.: Viking Press, 1957, pp. 276-280.
Excerpt from Chapter X of the 1831 edition.

*B74a   *Frankenstein*. H. Goldmann, trans. Poznań [Posen, Poland]: Wydawnictwa Pozańskie, 1958.
Source: Annual Bibliography of the *Keats-Shelley Journal*.

B75a   *Frankenstein*. London: J. M. Dent & Sons/N.Y.: E. P. Dutton, 1959. Everyman's Library, No. 616; new format of B33a. Published in January.
Reprinted in paperback, B82a.

*B76a   *Frankenstein*. Cairo: al-Dāral-Qawmiyyah lel-Tibāʿah wa al-Nashr, 1959.
Text in Arabic. Source: Annual Bibliography of the *Keats-Shelley Journal*.

B77a   *Frankenstein*. Taro Shioya, trans. Tokyo: Kodan-sha, 1959.

*B78a   *Pretamanushyan*. M. R. Narayana Pilla, trans. Kozhikode: P. K. bros., 1959.
Text in Malayalam. Source: Annual Bibliography of the *Keats-Shelley Journal*, verified by the present author in correspondence with the Anthonian Store, Kuala Lumpur.

*B79a   *El Doctor Frankenstein o El moderno Prometeo*. Antonio Gobernado, trans. Madrid: Aguilar, 1959.
Source: Annual Bibliography of the *Keats-Shelley Journal*.

B80a   *Frankenstein*. Monica Stolpe, trans. Stockholm: Christofers, 1959.
A possible earlier printing date is 1954, which may have stimulated the articles, IIE50, E55.
For reviews, see IIE63-E67.

B81a Reprinting of B71a, 1959.
Published in February.

B82a Reprinting of B75a, 1960.
"Everyman Paperbacks."

B83a *Frankenstein*. Garden City, N.Y.: Doubleday, 1960.
A Dolphin Book.
Also published as B84a.

B84a *Frankenstein*. London. Mayflower Books, 1960.
Published in September.
Also published as B83a.

*B85a *Frankenštajn ili moderni Prometej*. Slavka Stevović, trans.
Belgrade: Mlado pokolenje, 1960.
Source: Annual Bibliography of the *Keats-Shelley Journal*.

B86a *Frankenstein*. Mazharul Haq Alui, trans. Lucknow: Nasim Book Depot
[1960?].
Text in Urdu.

B87a Reprinting of B71a, 1960.
Published in February.

B88a *Frankenstein or The Modern Prometheus*. N.Y.: Collier Books/London:
Collier-Macmillan, 1961.
Reprinted four times, but B111a is the only one I have seen.

B89a *Frankenstein [or, The Modern Prometheus]*. N.Y.: Airmont Books,
1963.
Contains Introduction by Mary M. Threapleton [cf. IIA414].
Copyright page notes that this edition published simultaneously,
Toronto: The Ryerson Press, but I have not verified that it exists
as a separate edition.

B90a *Frankenstein*. London: J. M. Dent & Sons/N.Y.: E. P. Dutton, 1963.
New format of B75a; Everyman's Library, No. 616. Contains
Introduction by Robert E. Dowse and D. J. Palmer [cf. IIA128].
For reprintings, see B100a, B144a.

*B91a *Frankenstein*. London: Transworld Publishers, 1964.
A Corgi Book. Cover printed in Glut [IIA4, p. 18].

B92a *Frankenstein*. Hannah Betjeman, trans. Lausanne: Editions Recontre,
1964.
Préface [cf. IIE4] and filmography by Michel Boujut; illustrations by Christian Broutin.
For the same format, see B98a, B116a, B127a.

*B93a *Frankenstein.* Joe Ceurvost, trans. [Belgium:] Verviers, Gérard, 1964.
Contains Préface by Jacques Bergier [cf. IIE2].
Listed in the catalogue of the Bibliothéque Nationale, Supplement, tome 9, p. 572.

*B94a *Frankenstein oder Der Neue Prometheus.* 1964.
German translation. Source: Annual Bibliography of the *Keats-Shelley Journal*; does not give publication information.

B95a Reprinting of B71a, 1964.
Published in February.

B96a Reprinting of B71a, 1964.
Published in June.

B97a Reprinting of B71a, 1964.
Published in September.

B98a *Frankenstein.* Hannah Betjeman, trans. Paris: Union Générale d'Editions, 1965.
Same format as B92a.

B99a *Frankenstein, ili Sovremenyi Promethei.* Z. Aleksandrova, trans. Moscow: Khudozhestvennaia literatura, 1965.
Foreword and Notes by A[nna] A[rkad'evna] Elistratova [cf. IIE13].
For review, see IIE68.
Copy at the Library of Congress.

B100a Reprinting of B90a, 1965.

B101a *Frankenstein (or, the Modern Prometheus).* N.Y.: Dell Publishing Co., 1965.
The Laurel-Leaf Library. Published in March.
For reprintings, see B121a, B131a, B136a, B137a, B140a, B141a, B148a.

B102a Reprinting of B71a, 1965.
Published in August.

B103a Reprinting of B71a, 1965.
Published in September.

B104a *Frankenstein Or, The Modern Prometheus.* N.Y.: The New American Library, 1965.
A Signet Classic. Published in December. Contains Afterword by Harold Bloom [cf. IIA60]. "A Note on the Text" (p. 224) mentions that the text was taken from the 1831 edition at the Carl H. Pforzheimer Library.
For reprinting, see B109a.

*B105a *Frankenstein.* Tomáš Korbař, trans. Prague: Prace, 1966.
"Knižnice Románové novinsky" [New Novels Library], Vol. 159.
Source: Annual Bibliography of the *Keats-Shelley Journal.*
For other Czech-language editions, see B124a, B125a.

*B106a *El Doctor Frankenstein.* Antonio Gobernado, trans. Madrid: Aguilar,
1966.
Source: Annual Bibliography of the *Keats-Shelley Journal.*

*B107a *Frankenstein.* Elisabetta Bützeberger, trans. Milan: Corno, 1966.
Source: Annual Bibliography of the *Keats-Shelley Journal.*

B108a *Frankenstein.* Kirsten Diemer, trans. Copenhagen: Biilmann &
Eriksen, 1966.
Flagermus-bog nr. 4. The 1818 text.

B109a Reprinting of B104a, 1966.

B110a "The Recalcitrant Robot." In I[drisyn] O[liver] Evans, ed.
Science Fiction Through the Ages I. London: Panther Books, 1966,
pp. 104-116.
Excerpt from the 1831 edition.

B111a Reprinting of B88a, 1967.

*B112a *Frankenstein o el moderno Prometeo.* Jorge Ferreiro, trans. Mexico
City: Novaro, 1967.
Source: Annual Bibliography of the *Keats-Shelley Journal.*

*B113a *Frankenstein.* Eugène Rocart and Georges Cuvelier, trans. Paris:
Les Editions de La Renaissance, "Club Géant," 1967.
Contains "Au Pays des Monstres," by Hubert Juin [cf. IIE23].
Source: Annual Bibliography of the *Keats-Shelley Journal.*

B114a *Frankenstein.* N.Y.; London; Richmond Hill, Ontario: Scholastic
Book Services, 1967.
Published in April.

B115a *Frankenstein or The Modern Prometheus.* N.Y., Toronto, London:
Bantam Books, 1967.
A Bantam Pathfinder edition; published in June. Contains
"Introduction: Mary's Monster," by Robert Donald Spector [cf.
IIA399].
Copyright page mentions 2nd and 3rd printings, but not dates.

B116a Reprinting of B92a, 1968.

*B117a *Het monster van Frankenstein.* Else Hoog, trans. Utrecht: Bruna,
1968.
Source: Annual Bibliography of the *Keats-Shelley Journal.*

B118a *Frankenstein*. Yamamoto Masaki, trans. Tokyo: Kadokawa Shoten, 1968.

B119a *Frankenstein*. In Peter Fairclough, ed. *Three Gothic Novels*. Harmondsworth, Middlesex: Penguin Books, 1968, pp. 256-497.
The Penguin English Library; included with Horace Walpole's *The Castle of Otranto* and William Beckford's *Vathek*. Contains "Introductory Essay" by Mario Praz [cf. IIA340], and Notes to the novel by Peter Fairclough [cf. IIA140]. Front cover reproduces a detail from Henry Fuseli's "The Nightmare."
Reprinted, B129a, B138a, B142a.

B120a *Frankenstein*. Adapted by Dale Carlson. N.Y.: Golden Press, 1968.
A Golden Book.
For review, see IIC16.

B121a Reprinting of B101a, 1968.
Published in October.

B122a *Frankenstein or The Modern Prometheus*. M[ichael] J[oseph] Kennedy, ed. London, Oxford, N.Y.: Oxford University Press, 1969.
Oxford English Novels series. Contains Introduction, "Note on the Text," "A Chronology of Mary Shelley," three Appendices, and Textual and Explanatory Notes by M. J. Kennedy [cf. IIA227].
Reprinted in paperback, B132a.
For reviews, see IIC17-C25.

*B123a *Frankenstein*. K. B. Leder and Gert Leetz, trans. Vienna: Buchgemeinschaft Donauland, 1969.
Source: Annual Bibliography of the *Keats-Shelley Journal*.

*B124a *Frankenstein*. Tomáš Korbař, trans. Prague: Lìdové Nakladatelstvi, 1969.
Source: Annual Bibliography of the *Keats-Shelley Journal*.

*B125a *Frankenstein, čiže moderný Prometeus*. Pavel Vilikovský, trans. Bratislava: Tatran, 1969.
Source: Annual Bibliography of the *Keats-Shelley Journal*.

*B126a *Frankenstein, El Moderno Prometeo*. E. Fariñas, trans. Barcelona: Ferma, 1969.
Source: Annual Bibliography of the *Keats-Shelley Journal*.

B127a *Frankenstein*. Hannah Betjeman, trans. [Levallois-Perret:] Distributed by Cercle du Bibliophile [1969?].
Les Chefs d'œuvre. Same format as B92a.

*B128a *Frankenstein*. Adapted and Abridged by Marilyn Gillet. Paris: Hachette, 1970.
Facts and Fiction in Easy English Series. Source: Annual Bibliography of the *Keats-Shelley Journal*.

B129a Reprinting of B119a, 1970.

*B130a *Frankenstein: oder der neue Prometheus*. Friedrich Polakovics, trans. Munich: Carl Hanser Verlag, 1970.
　　　Contains "Nachwort" by Hermann Ebeling [cf. IIE11]. Source: Annual Bibliography of the *Keats-Shelley Journal*.
　　　See also B133a.

B131a Reprinting of B101a, 1970.
　　　Published in May.

B132a Reprinting of B122a, 1971.
　　　Paperback edition.

*B133a *Frankenstein*. Friedrich Polakovics, trans. Berlin: Darmstadt/ Vienna: Deutsche Buch-Gemeinschaft, 1971.
　　　Same format as B130a. Source: Annual Bibliography of *Keats- Shelley Journal*.

B134a "The Making of a Monster." In Seon Manley and Gogo Lewis, eds. *Ladies of Horror. Two Centuries of Supernatural Stories by the Gentle Sex*. N.Y.: Lothrop, Lee & Shepard, 1971, pp. 13-30.
　　　Excerpts from the 1831 edition.
　　　See also IIA267.

B135a Re-issue of B58a, Spring 1971.

B136a Reprinting of B101a, 1971.
　　　Published in May.

B137a Reprinting of B101a, 1971.
　　　Published in September.

B138a Reprinting of B119a, 1972.

B139a "The Monster's Lost Paradise." In Roy Huss and T. J. Ross, eds. *Focus on the Horror Film*. A Spectrum Book. Englewood Cliffs, N.J.: Prentice-Hall, 1972, pp. 69-74.
　　　Excerpts from the 1831 edition.

B140a Reprinting of B101a, 1972.
　　　Published in May.

B141a Reprinting of B101a, 1972.
　　　Published in October.

B142a Reprinting of B119a, 1973.

B143a *Frankenstein (or, the Modern Prometheus)*. In Bram Stoker. *Dracula; and Mary Shelley. Frankenstein (or, the Modern Prometheus)*. Garden City, N.Y.: Doubleday, 1973, pp. 425-655.
　　　Some copies published as part of the International Collectors Library, no date on title page.

B144a Reprinting of B90a, 1973.

B145a *Frankenstein.* Adapted by Otto O. Binder. West Haven, Conn.:
Pendulum Press, 1973.
Now Age Books. Comic-book format, illustrated by Nardo Cruz.
For elementary-school children. Study Guide also issued with the
edition, containing questions about the novel.

B146a *Frankenstein sau Prometeul Modern.* Adriana Călinescu, trans.
Bucharest: Editura Albatros (Fantastic Club), 1973.
Text in Romanian. Contains "Postfață" by Mircea Ivănescu
[cf. IIE22].

B147a *Frankenstein.* Kozaburo Yano, trans. Tokyo: Asahi Sonorama
[1973].
Adaptation "for Boys and Girls." With illustrations.

B148a Reprinting of B101a, 1973.

B149a *Frankenstein or The Modern Prometheus (The 1818 Text).* James
Rieger, ed. Indianapolis, N.Y.: Bobbs-Merrill, 1974.
The Library of Literature. The 1818 text, noting also MS autograph variants in her annotated copy of the 1818 edition, given by
her to Mrs. Thomas and now in the Pierpont Morgan Library. Contains
Acknowledgements, Introduction, Selected Bibliography, Note on the
Text, and three Appendices by James Rieger [cf. IIA356]. Appendix
A is the 1831 Introduction; Appendix B a collation of the 1818 and
1831 texts; Appendix C prints Lord Byron's "A Fragment" and Polidori's *The Vampyre.* Also reproduces in facsimile four pages from
the Thomas copy (pp. 1, 3, 19, 44).
Rieger notes that "All modern editions have followed the [1831
text]" (p. xliii), but see B8a, B15a, B42a, B49a, B50a, B54a.

B150a *Frankenstein.* Monica Stolpe, trans. [Stockholm:] Delta Förlags AB,
1974.
Contains "Inledning" [cf. IIE21] and Prefatory Note by Boris
Karloff [E24].

B151a *Frankenstein.* In Jack C. Wolf and Barbara H. Wolf, eds. *Ghosts,
Castles, and Victims: Studies in Gothic Terror.* A Fawcett Crest
Book. Greenwich, Conn.: Fawcett Publications, 1974, pp. 288-306.
Excerpts from Chapters XXIII and XXIV of the 1831 edition.

B152a "The Monster Lives!" In Peter Haining, ed. *The Monster Makers.*
London: Victor Gollancz, 1974, pp. 17-24.
Excerpt from Chapter V of the 1831 edition. Illustration by
David Smee.

B153a *Frankenstein.* N.Y., Boston: Books, Inc., n.d.
Contains biographical sketch of MS [cf. IIA274]. The World's
Popular Classics.

B154a *Frankenstein.* In Mary Shelley. *Frankenstein* [and] Bram Stoker.
       Dracula. *The Horror Omnibus.* *Containing Two Complete Novels.*
       N.Y.: Grosset & Dunlap, n.d.
              Separately paginated. Contains anonymous Introduction
       [cf. IIA216]. Variant reprinting of B51a.

       b) Valperga

B1b   *Valperga: Or, the Life and Adventures of Castruccio, Prince of
       Lucca.* 3 vols. London: Printed for G. and W. B. Whittaker, 1823.
              By the Author of "Frankenstein." Some editorial work by
       Godwin, the extent of which is uncertain.
              Copies at the Library of Congress, British Library, Bodleian,
       Boston Public Library, Duke, Harvard, Huntington Library, Princeton,
       University of Michigan, University of North Carolina, and University
       of Virginia.
              Xerographic copy available from University Microfilms, Ann
       Arbor, Michigan (order no. OP56292).
              For descriptive bibliography, see IIA445. See also A177,
       A247, B34, B58, B77, B151, B241.
              For reviews, see IIC26-C38.

       c) The Last Man

B1c   *The Last Man.* 3 vols. London: Henry Colburn, 1826.
              By the Author of Frankenstein.
              Copies at the Library of Congress, British Library, Bodleian,
       Duke, and Yale.
              For descriptive bibliography, see IIA445. See also B21, B25,
       B45, B122, B128, B129, B130, B131, B165, B166, B167, B226, B227,
       B228, B347, B352.
              For reviews, see IIC39-C43.
              For reprinting, see B2c.

B2c   Second edition of B1c, 1826.
              Differs only from B1c in that "Second Edition" appears on the
       title pages of the three volumes.
              Copies at the Library of Congress, British Library, Bodleian,
       Harvard, Princeton, University of Illinois, University of Michigan,
       University of Virginia, and Yale.

B3c   *The Last Man.* Paris: Published by A. and W. Galignani, 1826.
              Copies at the Bibliothéque Nationale and University of North
       Carolina.

B4c   *The Last Man.* 2 vols. Philadelphia: Carey, Lea & Blanchard, 1833.
              Copies at Boston Public Library, Harvard, University of North
       Carolina, and Yale.
              For review, see IIC44.

B5c   "Appendix. The Last Man—An Abridged Version." In Muriel Spark.
Child of Light: A Reassessment of Mary Wollstonecraft Shelley.
Hadleigh, Essex: Tower Bridge, 1951, pp. 195-230.
     Part extracts, part editorial comments and summation.
See also IB6c; IIA20.

B6c   *The Last Man. A Novel in Three Books by Mary Shelley.* Author of
'Frankenstein.' London: The Falcon Press [1954].
     Contains Editor's Foreword by Muriel Spark [cf. IIA397]. The
complete text of the novel.
     A handwritten note by A. Muirhead in the Bodleian copy (256 e.
16843) states that a half-dozen proof copies of this book were in
existence when The Falcon Press ceased publication; this copy,
bound at the Bodleian, is one of those.

B7c   *The Last Man.* Hugh J. Luke, Jr., ed. Lincoln, Neb.: University of
Nebraska Press, 1965.
     Contains Introduction, "Mary Shelley: A Brief Chronology," and
Note on the Text by Hugh J. Luke, Jr. [cf. IIA253].
     For reviews, see IIC45-C54.

B8c   "From The Last Man." In Joan Goulianos, ed. *by a Woman writt.*
Literature from Six Centuries By and About Women. Baltimore:
Penguin Books, 1974, pp. 188-197.
     Excerpt from Vol. III, Chapter X.
     *First published, Indianapolis: Bobbs-Merrill, 1973.
See also IIA174.

d) The Fortunes of Perkin Warbeck

B1d   *The Fortunes of Perkin Warbeck, A Romance.* 3 vols. London: Henry
Colburn and Richard Bentley, 1830.
     By the Author of "Frankenstein."
     For descriptive bibliography, see IIA445. See also B22, B98,
B99, B230, B231, B236.
     Copies at the Library of Congress, British Library, Bodleian,
Harvard, and Yale.
     For reviews, see IIC55-C63.

B2d   *The Fortunes of Perkin Warbeck, A Romance.* 2 vols. Philadelphia:
Carey, Lea & Blanchard, 1834.
     By the author of "Frankenstein."
     Copy at Harvard.

B3d   *The Fortunes of Perkin Warbeck. A Romance.* London, N.Y.: G.
Routledge & Co., 1857.
     By the Author of "Frankenstein."
     Copy in the present author's collection.

e) Lodore

B1e   *Lodore.* 3 vols. London: Richard Bentley, 1835.
        By the Author of "Frankenstein." One or more copies printed
"1834."
        Copies at the Library of Congress, British Library, Bodleian,
Harvard, Huntington Library, Indiana University, University of
Michigan, and Yale.
        For descriptive bibliography, see IIA445. See also B52, B100,
B101, B132, B229.
        For reviews, see IIc64-c83.

B2e   *Lodore.* N.Y.: Wallis & Newell, 1835.
        Franklin Library. By the Author of "Frankenstein."
        Copies at the Library of Congress, Harvard, and Yale.
        For reprinting, see B5e.

B3e   *Lodore.* Paris: Published by A. and W. Galignani, 1835.
        Printed in Brussels; see IIB19.

*B4e   *Lodore.* London: Bernard, 1844.
        In the card catalogue of The National Union Catalogue in progress
at the Library of Congress, as at Miami University (Oxford, Ohio).

B5e   Reprinting of B2e, 1846.

B6e   *The Beautiful Widow.* Philadelphia: T. B. Peterson & Bros. [ca.
1865].
        By Mrs. Percy B. Shelley.
        Copies at Florida State University, Harvard, and University of
Pennsylvania.

*B7e   *The Beautiful Widow.* N.Y., 1893.
        In the card catalogue of The National Union Catalogue in progress
at the Library of Congress, as at Lehigh University (Bethlehem, Pennsylvania).

f) Falkner

B1f   *Falkner. A Novel.* 3 vols. London: Saunders and Otley, 1837.
        By The Author of "Frankenstein."
        Copies at the Library of Congress, British Library, Bodleian,
Boston Public Library, Harvard, Huntington Library, University of
North Carolina, University of Virginia, and Yale.
        For descriptive bibliography, see IIA445. See also B2.
        For reviews, see IIc84-c95.

B2f   *Falkner.* N.Y.: Harper & Brothers, 1837.
        Copies at the Library of Congress and University of Virginia.

g)   Mathilda

B1g   *Mathilda*.   Elizabeth Nitchie, ed.   Chapel Hill, N.C.: University of
      North Carolina Press [1959].
          Contains Preface, Introduction, and Notes by Elizabeth Nitchie
      [cf. IIA305], and the text of the rough draft, *The Fields of Fancy*.
      For reviews, see IIc96-C103.
      Also published as B2g.

B2g   *Mathilda*.   Elizabeth Nitchie, ed.   *Studies in Philology*, Extra
      Series, No. 3 (October 1959).
          Same format as B1g [cf. IIB247 for editorial work].

C DRAMAS

a) *Proserpine*

*Cla   "Proserpine, a Mythological Drama in Two Acts." In *The Winter's
Wreath.* 1832 [1831], pp. 1-20.
　　　Identified by Sylva Norman in IIA310 (pp. 91-93), who notes
variations from the Bodleian manuscript, upon which Koszul based
his version [C2a].

C2a   "Proserpine. A Drama in Two Acts." In *Proserpine & Midas. Two
unpublished Mythological Dramas by Mary Shelley.* A[ndré] [Henri]
Koszul, ed. London: Humphrey Milford, 1922, pp. 3-44.
　　　Two sections are Shelley's work: the fable of Arethusa (pp. 10-
15), first published in *Posthumous Poems*, as "Arethusa"; and the
Invocation to Ceres (p. 18), first published in the *Poetical Works*,
as "Song of Proserpine. While gathering flowers on the plain of
Enna."
　　　For reviews, see IIC104-C106. For Koszul's Introduction, see
IIA237. See also ICla.
　　　Facsimile reprint: Folcroft, Pa.: Folcroft Library Editions,
1974.

b) *Midas*

Clb   "Midas." In *Proserpine & Midas. Two unpublished Mythological
Dramas by Mary Shelley.* A[ndré] [Henri] Koszul, ed. London:
Humphrey Milford, 1922, pp. 45-89.
　　　Sylva Norman, in IIA310 (pp. 92-93), mentions her expectation
and failure of finding this drama in one of the annual editions
of *The Winter's Wreath.*
　　　Two sections are Shelley's work: the Hymn of Apollo (pp. 51-
53) and the Hymn of Pan (pp. 53-55), both published first in
Posthumous Poems.
　　　For reviews, see IIC104-C106. For Koszul's Introduction, see
A237.
　　　Facsimile reprint: Folcroft, Pa.: Folcroft Library Editions,
1974.

D STORIES

a) A Tale of the Passions

D1a   "A Tale of the Passions, or, the Death of Despina," *The Liberal*,
No. 1 (1822), 289-325.
     Anonymous. Atrributed by William H. Marshall [IIA269] and
Charles W. Dilke [B63].

*D2a   "A Tale of the Passions, or the Death of Despina," *The Weekly
Entertainer, and West of England Miscellany*, 7 (1823), 57-60, 65-
68, 81-83, 137-140, 148-151.
     Source: IIA269.

D3a   "A Tale of the Passions, or the Death of Despina." In *The Romanti-
cist, and Novelist's Library: The Best Works of the Best Authors*.
London: J. Clements, 1839, Vol. I, pp. 14-16.
     By Mrs. Shelley.

D4a   "A Tale of the Passions; or, The Death of Despina." In Mary Wollstonecraft Shelley. *Tales and Stories*. Richard Garnett, ed.
London: William Paterson, 1891, pp. 112-147.

b) The Bride of Modern Italy

D1b   "The Bride of Modern Italy," *The London Magazine*, 9 (April 1824),
351-363.
     Anonymous. MS identified as author in IIA50.

c) The Sisters of Albano

D1c   "The Sisters of Albano." In *The Keepsake for MDCCCXXIX*. Frederic
Mansel Reynolds, ed. London: Published for the Proprietor, by
Hurst, Chance, and Co., and R. Jennings [1828], pp. 80-100.
     By the Author of Frankenstein.

D2c   "The Sisters of Albano." In Mary Wollstonecraft Shelley. *Tales
and Stories*. Richard Garnett, ed. London: William Paterson, 1891,
pp. 1-19.

d) Ferdinando Eboli

D1d   "Ferdinando Eboli. A Tale." In *The Keepsake for MDCCCXXIX*. Frederic Mansel Reynolds, ed. London: Published for the Proprietor, by Hurst, Chance, and Co., and R. Jennings [1828], pp. 195-218.
     By the Author of Frankenstein.

D2d   "Ferdinando Eboli." In Mary Wollstonecraft Shelley. *Tales and Stories*. Richard Garnett, ed. London: William Paterson, 1891, pp. 20-41.

e) The Mourner

D1e   "The Mourner." In *The Keepsake for MDCCCXXX*. Frederic Mansel Reynolds, ed. London: Published for the Proprietor, by Hurst, Chance, and Co., and R. Jennings [1829], pp. 71-97.
     By the Author of "Frankenstein."
     See also IIB9.

D2e   "The Mourner." In Mary Wollstonecraft Shelley. *Tales and Stories*. Richard Garnett, ed. London: William Paterson, 1891, pp. 83-107.
     P. 87, between $\P^1$ and $\P^2$, lacks $\P^2$ and half of $\P^3$ of D1e (p. 75).

f) The Evil Eye

D1f   "The Evil Eye. A Tale." In *The Keepsake for MDCCCXXX*. Frederic Mansel Reynolds, ed. London: Published for the Proprietor, by Hurst, Chance, and Co., and R. Jennings [1829], pp. 150-175.
     By the Author of "Frankenstein."
     See also IIB9.

D2f   "The Evil Eye." In Mary Wollstonecraft Shelley. *Tales and Stories*. Richard Garnett, ed. London: William Paterson, 1891, pp. 42-65.

g) The False Rhyme

D1g   "The False Rhyme." In *The Keepsake for MDCCCXXX*. Frederic Mansel Reynolds, ed. London: Published for the Proprietor, by Hurst, Chance, and Co., and R. Jennings [1829], pp. 265-268.
     By the Author of "Frankenstein."
     See also IIB9.

D2g   "The False Rhyme," *The Athenæum*, No. 107 (November 11, 1829), 702-703.
     By the Author of "Frankenstein." Printed in full from *The Keepsake* [D1g], as part of a review.

*D3g   "The False Rhyme," *The Polar Star*, 2 (1829), 171-172.
        Source: IIE1 (p..674, Item 166).

D4g   "The False Rhyme." In Mary Wollstonecraft Shelley. *Tales and
      Stories. Richard Garnett, ed. London: William Paterson, 1891,
      pp. 108-111.

*D5g   "The False Rhyme," *Golden Book Magazine*, 13 (March 1931), 68.
        Source: *Readers Guide to Periodical Literature*.

      h) Transformation

D1h   "Transformation." In *The Keepsake for MDCCCXXXI*. Frederic Mansel
      Reynolds, ed. London: Published for the Proprietor, by Hurst,
      Chance, and Co., and Jennings and Chaplin [1830], pp. 18-39.
        By the Author of "Frankenstein."

*D2h   "Transformation." In *The Tale Book*. 2nd Series. Paris: Baudry,
      1835, pp. 32-51.
        Source: IIE1 (p. 674, Item 168).

*D3h   "Transformation," *International Magazine* (N.Y.), 3 (1851), p. 70.
        Source: *Poole's Index to Periodical Literature*.

D4h   "Transformation." In Mary Wollstonecraft Shelley. *Tales and
      Stories. Richard Garnett, ed. London: William Paterson, 1891,
      pp. 165-185.
        P. 169, ¶[1], last line omits "and an insolent display of satis-
      fied vanity" from end of sentence in D1h; p. 184, ¶[2], sentence 1,
      reads "return" for "returned" in D1h.

D5h   "Transformation." In Peter Haining, ed. *The Gentlewomen of Evil:
      An Anthology of Rare Supernatural Stories from the Pens of Victo-
      rian Ladies*. London: Robert Hale, 1967, pp. 15-31.
        Text follows D4h.

D6h   "The Transformation." In Alden H. Norton, ed. *Masters of Horror*.
      N.Y.: Berkley Publishing Corporation, 1968, pp. 70-87.
        Text follows D4h.
        See also IIA297.

      i) The Swiss Peasant

D1i   "The Swiss Peasant." In *The Keepsake for MDCCCXXXI*. Frederic
      Mansel Reynolds, ed. London: Published for the Proprietor, by
      Hurst, Chance, and Co., and Jennings and Chaplin [1830], pp. 121-
      146.
        By the Author of "Frankenstein."

*D2i   "The Swiss Peasant." In *The Tale Book*. 1st Series. Paris: Baudry, 1834, pp. 416-438.
       Source: IIE1 (p. 674, Item 170).

*D3i   "The Swiss Peasant." In C. A. Bowles, J. S. Knowles, and M. W. Shelley. *The Tale Book*. Königsberg: J. H. Bon, 1859, pp. 55-74.
       Source: IIE1 (p. 674, Item 171) and the catalogue of the Bibliothéque Nationale.

D4i   "The Swiss Peasant." In Mary Wollstonecraft Shelley. *Tales and Stories*. Richard Garnett, ed. London: William Paterson, 1891, pp. 186-209.
       P. 186, ¶1, last sentence omits lines 11-13 from Dli; p. 202, between ¶4 and ¶5, lacks ¶ beginning "'Mais'" from Dli; p. 205, ¶1 omits at end of last sentence "—at his mercy" from Dli.

   j) The Dream

D1j   "The Dream, A Tale." In *The Keepsake for MDCCCXXXII*. Frederic Mansel Reynolds, ed. London: Published by Longman, Rees, Orme, Brown, and Green [1831], pp. 22-38.
       By the Author of Frankenstein.

D2j   "The Dream." In Mary Wollstonecraft Shelley. *Tales and Stories*. Richard Garnett, ed. London: William Paterson, 1891, pp. 66-82.
       P. 69, ¶6 lacks at the beginning "'Palestine!' said Constance;" from D1j.

D3j   "The Dream." In Peter Haining, ed. *Great British Tales of Terror. Gothic Stories of Horror and Romance 1765-1840*. London: Victor Gollancz, 1972, pp. 288-300.
       Text follows D2j.
       See also IIA181.
       Reprinted, Harmondsworth, Middlesex: Penguin Books, 1973 (pp. 327-342).

   ?k) The Pole

D1k   "The Pole," *The Court Magazine and Belle Assemblée*, 1 (August 1832), 64-71.
       By the Author of "Frankenstein." Part 1 of the story; see D2k for continuation.
       Attributed to Claire Clairmont by Bradford Allen Booth [IIA66, B33].

D2k   "The Pole," *The Court Magazine and Belle Assemblée*, 1 (September 1832), 129-136.
       By the Author of "Frankenstein." Part 2 of the story; continuation of D1k.

D3k   "The Pole." In Mary Wollstonecraft Shelley. *Tales and Stories*. Richard Garnett, ed. London: William Paterson, 1891, pp. 274-310.

D4k   "The Pole." In Bradford Allen Booth, ed. *A Cabinet of Gems. Short·Stories from the English Annuals*. Berkeley: University of California Press/London: Cambridge University Press, 1938, pp. 161-197.
     By Claire Clairmont.
     See also IIA66.

l)   The Brother and Sister

Dll   "The Brother and Sister, An Italian Story." In *The Keepsake for MDCCCXXXIII*. Frederic Mansel Reynolds, ed. London: Published by Longman, Rees, Orme, Brown, Green, and Longman/Paris: Rittner and Goupill/Frankfurt: Charles Jügill [1832], pp. 105-141.
     By the Author of Frankenstein.

*D2l   "Le Frère et la Sœur." In *Le Salmigondis. Contes de toutes les couleurs*. Paris: H. Fournier Jne., 1832, tome III, pp. 159-219.
     French translation. Source: de Palacio [IIEl, p. 675, Item 174] and Nitchie [A12, p. 207].
     Copy at the Bibliothéque Nationale.

D3l   "The Brother and Sister." In Mary Wollstonecraft Shelley. *Tales and Stories*. Richard Garnett, ed. London: William Paterson, 1891, pp. 227-261.

m)   The Invisible Girl

Dlm   "The Invisible Girl." In *The Keepsake for MDCCCXXXIII*. Frederic Mansel Reynolds, ed. London: Published by Longman, Rees, Orme, Brown, Green, and Longman/Paris: Rittner and Goupill/Frankfurt: Charles Jügill [1832], pp. 210-227.
     By the Author of Frankenstein.

D2m   "The Invisible Girl." In Mary Wollstonecraft Shelley. *Tales and Stories*. Richard Garnett, ed. London: William Paterson, 1891, pp. 210-226.

n)   The Mortal Immortal

Dln   "The Mortal Immortal." In *The Keepsake for MDCCCXXXIV*. Frederic Mansel Reynolds, ed. London: Published by Longman, Rees, Orme, Brown, Green, and Longman/Paris: Rittner and Goupill/Berlin: A. Asher [1833], pp. 71-87.
     By the Author of Frankenstein.
     See also IIBll.

*D2n   "The Mortal Immortal." In Charles Gibbons, ed. *The Casquet of
         Literature: Being a Selection in Poetry and Prose from the Works
         of the most admired Authors*. London: Blackie and Son, 1873,
         Vol. 3, pp. 353-359.
             Source: IIE1 (p. 675, Item 177 & 177 *bis*).
             Not at the Library of Congress or Bodleian.
             See also IIA164.

D3n   "The Mortal Immortal." In Mary Wollstonecraft Shelley. *Tales and
         Stories*. Richard Garnett, ed. London: William Paterson, 1891,
         pp 148-164.

D4n   *The Mortal Immortal*. [N.Y.?:] Mossant, Vallon & Co. [1900?].
             Copies at Boston Public Library, New York Public Library, and
         Princeton.

         o) The Elder Son

Dlo   "The Elder Son." In *Heath's Book of Beauty. 1835*. Countess of
         Blessington, ed. London: Longman, Rees, Orme, Brown, Green, and
         Longman/Paris: Rittner and Goupil/Berlin: A. Asher [1834], pp. 83-
         123.
             By Mrs. Shelley.

D2o   "The Elder Son." In Mary Wollstonecraft Shelley. *Tales and
         Stories*. Richard Garnett, ed. London: William Paterson, 1891,
         pp. 328-358.
             P. 347, ¶3 lacks the first sentence from Dlo.

         p) The Trial of Love

Dlp   "The Trial of Love." In *The Keepsake for MDCCCXXXV*. Frederic
         Mansel Reynolds, ed. London: Published for Longman, Rees, Orme,
         Brown, Green, and Longman/Paris: Rittner and Goupil/Berlin: A.
         Asher [1834], pp. 70-86.
             By the Author of Frankenstein.

D2p   "The Trial of Love." In Bradford Allen Booth, ed. *A Cabinet of
         Gems. Short Stories from the English Annuals*. Berkeley: Univer-
         sity of California Press/London: Cambridge University Press, 1938,
         pp. 141-158.

         q) The Parvenue

Dlq   "The Parvenue." In *The Keepsake for MDCCCXXXVII*. The Lady Emmeline
         Stuart Wortley, ed. London: Published for Longman, Rees, Orme,
         Green, and Longman/Paris: Delloy and Co. [1836], pp. 209-221.
             By Mrs. Shelley.
             See also IIB11, B146.

D2q   "The Parvenue." In Mary Wollstonecraft Shelley. *Tales and Stories*.
      Richard Garnett, ed. London: William Paterson, 1891, pp. 262-273.

D3q   "The Parvenue." In Reginald Hargreaves and Lewis Melville [pseud.
      of Lewis S. Benjamin], eds. *Great English Short Stories*. N.Y.:
      Viking Press, 1930, pp. 221-228.

      r)   The Pilgrims

D1r   "The Pilgrims." In *The Keepsake for MDCCCXXXVIII*. London: Pub-
      lished by Longman, Orme, Brown, Green, and Longmans/Paris: Delloy
      and Co. [1837], pp. 128-155.
      Anonymous.

D2r   "The Pilgrims." In Mary Wollstonecraft Shelley. *Tales and Stories*.
      Richard Garnett, ed. London: William Paterson, 1891, pp. 359-386.

      s)   Euphrasia

D1s   "Euphrasia, A Tale of Greece." In *The Keepsake for MDCCCXXXIX*.
      Frederic Mansel Reynolds, ed. London: Published for Longman,
      Orme, Brown, Green, and Longmans/Paris: Delloy and Co. [1838],
      pp. 135-152.
      By Mrs. Shelley.

D2s   "Euphrasia. A Tale of Greece." In Mary Wollstonecraft Shelley.
      Tales and Stories. Richard Garnett, ed. London: William Paterson,
      1891, pp. 311-327.
      As Sylva Norman notes [IIA310, p. 84], the snowdrift "frame"
      is omitted from D1s.

      t)   The Heir of Mondolpho

D1t   "The Heir of Mondolpho," *Appleton's Journal: A Monthly Miscellany
      of Popular Literature* (N.Y.), n.s. 2 (January 1877), 12-23.
      See also IIB13, B80, B83.

D2t   "The Heir of Mondolfo." In Robert Donald Spector, ed. *Seven
      Masterpieces of Gothic Horror*. N.Y.: Bantam Books, 1963, pp. 333-
      361.
      Included with Horace Walpole, *The Castle of Otranto*; Clara
      Reeve, *The Old English Baron*; Matthew Gregory Lewis, *Mistrust or
      Blanche and Osbright*, Nathaniel Hawthorne, "The White Old Maid";
      Edgar Allan Poe, "The Fall of the House of Usher"; and Sheridan
      Le Fanu, *Carmilla*.

u) *Collected Stories*

Dlu   *Tales and Stories*. Richard Garnett, ed. London: William Paterson, 1891.
The Treasure House of Tales by Great Authors. The second page of advertisements at the conclusion of the text identify the collection as No. 2 in the series, the first the tales of Leigh Hunt, the third those of Douglas Jerrold, and the fourth those of Disraeli as "Lord Beaconsfield." The page also notes that the frontispiece of MS is by Ad. Lalauze, "from an unpublished Portrait by Lady Shelley"—the Easton miniature now in the Bodleian permanent exhibit. Notice of a limited edition is also included: "An impression of 55 copies printed on the best Dutch Handmade Paper has been prepared with the Portraits printed on Japanese Paper, each copy numbered."
Contents: Introduction by Richard Garnett [cf. IIA157]; "The Sisters of Albano"; "Ferdinando Eboli"; "The Evil Eye"; "The Dream"; "The Mourner"; "The False Rhyme"; "A Tale of the Passions; or, The Death of Despina"; "The Mortal Immortal"; "Transformation"; "The Swiss Peasant"; "The Invisible Girl"; "The Brother and Sister"; "The Parvenue"; "The Pole"; "Euphrasia"; "The Elder Son"; and "The Pilgrims." For collations, see D2e, D4h, D4i, D2j, D20, D2s.
Facsimile reprint supposedly by Folcroft, Pa: Folcroft Press, n.d., but actually only re-binding of 1891 ed.
For reviews, see IIc107-C108.

E POEMS

E1   "Absence; 'Ah! he is gone—and I alone!—.'" In *The Keepsake for MDCCCXXXI*. Frederic Mansel Reynolds, ed. London: Published for the Proprietor, by Hurst, Chance, and Co., and Jennings and Chaplin [1830], p. 39.
        By the Author of "Frankenstein."
        Reprinted, with facsimile of manuscript, in IIA445, pp. 22-23, as one of three copies (special binding) of IE11; and in IIA6, p. 302.

E2   "A Dirge; 'This morn, thy gallant bark, love.'" In *The Keepsake for MDCCCXXXI*. Frederic Mansel Reynolds, ed. London: Published for the Proprietor, by Hurst, Chance, and Co., and Jennings and Chaplin [1830], p. 85.
        By the Author of "Frankenstein."
        Reprinted in IE11, p. 14 n. 2; IIA6, p. 304; and as IE3.

E3   ["A Dirge";] 'This morn thy gallant bark.' In her "Note on Poems Written in 1822." In *The Poetical Works of Percy Bysshe Shelley*. Mrs. Shelley, ed. 4 vols. London: Edward Moxon, 1839, Vol. IV, pp. 225-236 [225].
        Revised version of E2.

E4   "A Night Scene; 'I see thee not, my gentlest Isabel.'" In *The Keepsake for MDCCCXXXI*. Frederic Mansel Reynolds, ed. London: Published for the Proprietor, by Hurst, Chance, and Co., and Jennings and Chaplin [1830], pp. 147-148.
        By Mary S.
        Attributed by Elizabeth Nitchie [IIA12, p. 210], with reservations; by Jean de Palacio [E1, p. 687, Item 260]; by Paula Feldman, of the University of South Carolina; and by the present author.

?E5   "Song; 'When I'm no more, this harp that rings.'" In *The Keepsake for MDCCCXXXI*. Frederic Mansel Reynolds, ed. London: Published for the Proprietor, by Hurst, Chance, and Co., and Jennings and Chaplin [1830], p. 157.
        By Mrs. Godwin.
        Attributed by Paula Feldman, of the University of South Carolina, and by the present author.

E6   "Ode to Ignorance; 'Hail, Ignorance! majestic queen!'" *The Metropolitan Magazine*, 9 (January 1834), 29-31.
        Signed M. W. S.

*?E7   "Fame." In *The Drawing-Room Scrap-Book*. 1835 [1834].
       Attributed by Elizabeth Nitchie [IIA12, pp. 157, 210], who notes
       that the poem is included only in "advance copies" of the annual—
       which I have not located.
       See also IIB144.

E8   "Stanzas; 'How like a star you rose upon my life.'" In *The Keepsake
       for MDCCCXXXIX*. Frederic Mansel Reynolds, ed. London: Published
       for Longman, Orme, Brown, Green, and Longmans/Paris: Delloy and Co.
       [1838], p. 179.
       By the Author of Frankenstein.
       Reprinted in IIA310, p. 87.

E9   "Stanzas; 'O come to me in dreams, my love!'" In *The Keepsake for
       MDCCCXXXIX*. Frederic Mansel Reynolds, ed. London: Published for
       Longman, Orme, Brown, Green, and Longmans/Paris: Delloy and Co.
       [1838], p. 201.
       By the Author of Frankenstein.
       Reprinted in IIA310, p. 87.
       See also E14.

E10   *"Oh Listen While I Sing to Thee," Canzonet, With Accompaniment for
       the Harp or Piano Forte, Composed and Inscribed to his Friend Berry
       King, Esqr. by Henry Hugh Pearson, Professor of Music in the Uni-
       versity of Edinburgh*. London: D'Almaine & Co. [ca. 1842].
       Lyrics by MS, music by Pearson.
       Copy at the British Library.
       Reprinted (lyrics only) in IA7 (Vol. II, p. 532 n. 1 [to p.
       531]), and in IIA12 (pp. 234-235).

E11   *The Choice. A Poem on Shelley's Death by Mary Wollstonecraft
       Shelley*. H[arry] Buxton Forman, ed. London: Printed for the
       Editor for Private Distribution, 1876.
       Prefatory Note and Notes to the poem by H. Buxton Forman
       [cf. IIA146].
       Reprinted in IIA6, pp. 297-301.
       For descriptive bibliography of this edition, see IIA445.
       Facsimile reprint of Forman's edition: Folcroft, Pa.: Fol-
       croft Library Editions, 1972.

E12   "On Reading Wordsworth's Lines on Peel [sic] Castle; 'It is with
       me, as erst with you.'" In R[osalie] Glynn Grylls. *Mary Shelley.
       A Biography*. London, N.Y.: Oxford University Press, 1938, pp. 302-
       303.
       Dated December 8th 1825.

E13   "Fragment; (To Jane with the Last [Man]) 'Tribute for thee, dear
       solace of my life.'" In R[osalie] Glynn Grylls. *Mary Shelley. A
       Biography*. London, N.Y.: Oxford University Press, 1938, p. 303.

E14 "To the Dead; 'O, Come to me in dreams, my Love,'" *Keats-Shelley Memorial Bulletin*, No. 4 (1952), 52-54.
Variation of E9, from the manuscript; described by R. Glynn Grylls [cf. IIB112].

E15 *"Tempo e' piu di Morire/Io ho tardato piu ch' i' non vorrei;* 'Sadly borne across the waves.'" In Elizabeth Nitchie. *Mary Shelley, Author of Frankenstein.* New Brunswick, N.J.: Rutgers University Press, 1953, pp. 231-233.

E16 *"La Vida es sueño;* 'The tide of Time was at my feet.'" In Elizabeth Nitchie. *Mary Shelley, Author of Frankenstein.* New Brunswick, N.J.: Rutgers University Press, 1953, pp. 233-234.

E17 [Fragment] "Alas I weep my life away." In Elizabeth Nitchie. *Mary Shelley, Author of Frankenstein.* New Brunswick, N.J.: Rutgers University Press, 1953, p. 235.
Entry in MS journal for September 14, 1831.

E18 [Fragment] "Struggle no more, my Soul with the sad chains." In Elizabeth Nitchie. *Mary Shelley, Author of Frankenstein.* New Brunswick, N.J.: Rutgers University Press, 1953, p. 235.
Entry in MS journal for September 16, 1831.

F TRAVEL WORKS

a) *History of a Six Weeks' Tour*

F1a [with Percy Bysshe Shelley.] *History of a Six Weeks' Tour through a Part of France, Switzerland, Germany, and Holland: with Letters Descriptive of a Sail round the Lake of Geneva, and of the Glaciers of Chamouni.* London: T. Hookham, Jun.; and C. and J. Ollier, 1817.
Two letters and majority of journal by MS.
Copies at the Library of Congress, British Library, Bodleian, Bibliothéque Nationale, Cleveland Public Library, Harvard, New York Public Library, and UCLA.
For descriptive bibliography, see IIA445. See also A177.
For review, see IIC109.

*F2a [with Percy Bysshe Shelley]. *History of a Six Weeks' Tour through a Part of France, Switzerland, Germany, and Holland: with Letters Descriptive of a Sail round the Lake of Geneva, and of the Glaciers of Chamouni.* London: J. Brooks, 1829.
Copy at the University of Texas.

F3a "Journal of a Six Weeks' Tour"; "Letters Descriptive of a Sail Round the Lake of Geneva, and of the Glaciers of Chamouni." In *Essays, Letters from Abroad, Translations and Fragments, By Percy Bysshe Shelley.* Mrs. Shelley, ed. 2 vols. London: Edward Moxon, 1840 [1839], Vol. II, pp. 1-46; 47-95.
Reprinted in most editions of Shelley's prose.

b) *Rambles in Germany and Italy*

F1b *Rambles in Germany and Italy, in 1840, 1842, and 1843.* 2 vols.
London: Edward Moxon, 1844.
Copies at the Library of Congress, British Library, Bodleian, Harvard, and Yale.
For descriptive bibliography, see IIA445.
For reviews, see IIC110-C127.
For excerpt, see F2b.

F2b "The Villa Serbelloni," *The Mirror of Literature, Amusement, and Instruction,* n.s. 2 [44] (August 17, 1844), 121-122.
Excerpt from F1b.

G BIOGRAPHIES

a) *Lives of the most Eminent Literary and Scientific Men of Italy, Spain, and Portugal*

G1a [with James Montgomery.] *Lives of the most Eminent Literary and Scientific Men of Italy, Spain, and Portugal.* Vol. I. Vol. 86 of The Cabinet of Biography, Conducted by the Rev. Dionysius Lardner (Lardner's Cabinet Cyclopedia). London: Printed for Longman, Orme, Brown, Green, & Longman; and John Taylor, 1835.

Contents: lives of Dante, Petrarch, Boccaccio, Lorenzo de' Medici, Marsiglio Ficino, Giovanni Pico della Mirandello, Angelo Poliziano, Bernardo Pulci, Luca Pulci, Luigi Pulci, Cieco da Ferrara, Burchiello, [Matteo Maria] Bojardo, [Francesco] Berni, Ariosto, and Machiavelli. Of these, MS certainly wrote the lives of Petrarch, Boccaccio, and Machiavelli; and Montgomery that of Dante; but the others, including the short essays on the Pulcis, Ferrara, and Burchiello, are of doubtful authorship. See also IA7 (Vol. II, pp. 106 n. 1, 108); IIA22, p. 127.

Copies at the Library of Congress, British Library, Bodleian, Huntington Library, New York Public Library, and University of Michigan.

For reviews, see IIC128-C132.

G2a [with James Montgomery and Sir David Brewster.] *Lives of the most Eminent Literary and Scientific Men of Italy, Spain, and Portugal.* Vol. II. Vol. 87 of The Cabinet of Biography, Conducted by the Rev. Dionysius Lardner (Lardner's Cabinet Cyclopedia). London: Printed for Longman, Orme, Brown, Green, & Longman; and John Taylor, 1835.

Contents: lives of Galileo, [Francesco] Guicciardini, Vittoria Colonna, [Battista] Guarini, Tasso, [Gabriello] Chiabrera, [Alessandro] Tassoni, [Giambattista] Marini, [Vincenzo da] Filicaja, [Pietro] Metastasio, [Carlo] Goldoni, [Vittorio] Alfieri, [Vincenzo] Monti, and Ugo Foscolo. Of these, MS wrote the lives of Metastasio, Goldoni, Alfieri, Monti, and Foscolo; Brewster that of Galileo; Montgomery that of Tasso; the others are doubtful. See also annotation in G1a.

Copies at the Library of Congress, British Library, Bodleian, Huntington Library, New York Public Library, and University of Michigan.

For reviews, see IIC133-C135. See also B198.

G3a   [with others?] *Lives of the most Eminent Literary and Scientific Men of Italy, Spain, and Portugal.* Vol. III. Vol. 88 of The Cabinet of Biography, Conducted by the Rev. Dionysius Lardner (Lardner's Cabinet Cyclopedia). London: Printed for Longman, Orme, Brown, Green, & Longman; and John Taylor, 1837.

     Contents: Introduction; lives of [Mosen Juan Boscan Almogaver] Boscan, Garcilaso de la Vega, Diego Hurtado de Mondoza, Luis de Leon, [Fernando] Herrera, Saa de Miranda, Jorge de Montemayor, and [Cristova] Castillejo; The Early Dramatists; lives of [Don Alonso de] Ercilla, Cervantes, Lope de Vega, Vicente Espinel—Esteban de Villegas, [Don Luis del Gongora [y Argote], [Don Francisco Gomez de] Quevedo [Villegas], and Calderón; Early Poets of Portugal (Ribeyra, Gil Vecente, Saa de Miranda, and [Antonio] Ferreira); and the life of [Luis de] Camoens. MS possibly the author of all the essays; Walling [IIA22, p. 128] notes only the essay on Ercilla as by another hand.

     Copies at the Library of Congress, British Library, Bodleian, Huntington Library, New York Public Library, and University of Michigan.

     For review, see IIc136.

*G4a *Lives of Eminent Literary and Scientific Men of Italy.* 2 vols. Philadelphia: Lea and Blanchard, 1841.

     By Mrs. Shelley, Sir D. Brewster, James Montgomery, and others.

     Copies at Brown University and Free Library of Philadelphia.

   b)   *Lives of the most Eminent Literary and Scientific Men of France*

G1b   *Lives of the most Eminent Literary and Scientific Men of France.* Vol. I. Vol. 102 of The Cabinet of Biography, Conducted by the Rev. Dionysius Lardner (Lardner's Cabinet Cyclopedia). London: Printed for Longman, Orme, Brown, Green, & Longmans; and John Taylor, 1838.

     Contents: lives of Montaigne, Rabelais, Corneille, Rouchefoucauld, Molière, La Fontaine, Pascal, [Madame de] Sévigné, [Nicholas] Boileau, Racine, and [François de Salignac de la Mothe] Fénélon.

     Copies at the Library of Congress, British Library, Bodleian, Boston Public Library, John Crear Library (Chicago), Free Library of Philadelphia, Haversford College, Midwest Inter-Library Center (Chicago), and University of Chicago.

     For reviews, see IIc137-C138. See also A186.

G2b   *Lives of the most Eminent Literary and Scientific Men of France.* Vol. II. Vol. 103 of The Cabinet of Biography, Conducted by the Rev. Dionysius Lardner (Lardner's Cabinet Cyclopedia). London: Printed for Longman, Orme, Brown, Green, & Longmans; and John Taylor, 1839.

     Contents: lives of Voltaire, Rousseau, [Marie Jean Antoine de Canitat, marquis of] Condorcet, Mirabeau, Madame Roland, and Madame

de Staël.
Copies at the Library of Congress, British Library, Bodleian, and Boston Public Library.

G3b   *Lives of the Most Eminent French Writers.* 2 vols.   Philadelphia: Lea and Blanchard, 1840.
By Mrs. Shelley and others.
Copies at Detroit Public Library, New York Public Library, Oberlin College, and Ohio Wesleyan University, and in the present author's collection.
For review, see IIc139.

*G4b   *Lives of Eminent French Authors.* 2 vols.   London: Longmans, 1851.
Listed in *The English Catalogue of Books.*

c)   *Biographical fragments*

G1c   Unfinished life of Percy Bysshe Shelley.   In Thomas Jefferson Hogg. *Life of Percy Bysshe Shelley.* 2 vols.   London: Edward Moxon, 1858, Vol. I, pp. v-vii, viii-ix, 22, 31, 33-34, 40-41, 117-118.
MS notes for a contemplated biography of Shelley, incorporated by Hogg and occasionally amended, without credit to MS.   MS passages are collated from the manuscript with Hogg's printed versions by Elizabeth Nitchie in IIB249.

G2c   Unfinished life of William Godwin.   In C[harles] Kegan Paul. *William Godwin: His Friends and Contemporaries.* 2 vols.   London: Henry S. King, 1876, Vol. I, pp. 25-26, 36-37, 47, 64, 73-74, 76, 78-79, 79-80, 81-83, 120-125, 128-135, 161-162, 231-232, 238-239, 332-333.
MS notes for a contemplated biography of Godwin, credited by Paul to MS, who transcribed them from manuscripts then in the possession of Sir Percy Florence Shelley.

H ARTICLES AND REVIEWS

H1 "Madame D'Houtetôt," The Liberal, No. 2 (1823), 67-83.
Attributed by William H. Marshall [IIA269] and Charles W.
Dilke [B63].

H2 "Giovanni Villani," The Liberal, No. 2 (1823), 281-297 [printed
"197"].
Attributed by William H. Marshall [IIA269], Charles W. Dilke
[B63], and Jean de Palacio [E1, p. 682, Item 228].

H3 "Narrative of a Tour round the Lake of Geneva, and of an Excursion
through the Valley of Chamouni," La Belle Assemblée, or Court and
Fashionable Magazine, n.s. 28 (July 1823), 14-19.
Noticed by Stephen Robert Van Luchene [IID19] and Jean de
Palacio [E1, p. 682, Item 229].

H4 "Recollections of Italy," The London Magazine, 9 (January 1824),
21-26.
Attributed by Jean de Palacio [IIE1, p. 682, Item 230].

H5 "On Ghosts," The London Magazine, 9 (March 1824), 253-256.
Signed Σζ.
Attributed by Frederick L. Jones [IA7, Vol. I, p. 272 n. 8]
and Elizabeth Nitchie [IIA12, p. 208].

H6 "Defense of Velluti," The Examiner, No. 958 (June 11, 1826), 372-
373.
Letter, signed Anglo-Italicus. Attributed by Frederick L.
Jones [IA7, Vol. I, p. 344 n. 1]. For the second part, see H18.
For response, see IIB344.

H7 "The English in Italy," Westminster Review, 6 (October 1826), 325-
341.
Review of The English in Italy, Continental Adventures. A
Novel, and Diary of an Ennuyée. Attributed by Frederick L. Jones
[IA7, Vol. I, pp. 122-123 n. 2, 346 n. 1], who also prints a portion
of the review.

H8 "Illyrian Poems—Feudal Scenes," Westminster Review, 10 (January
1829), 71-81.
Review of [Prosper Mérimée's] La Guzla, ou Choir de Poesies
Illyriques recueillies dans la Dalmatie, la Croatie et l'Herzego-
wine; and La Jaquerie; Feudal Scenes, followed by the Family of
Carvajal, a Drama. Elizabeth Nitchie [IIA12, p. 209] mistakenly

notes the review of Mérimée in the October 1829 issue.
Reprinted as "Appendix B, Mary Shelley's article on Mérimée,"
in A. W. Raitt. *Prosper Mérimée*. N.Y.: Charles Scribner's Sons/
London: Eyre and Spottiswoode, 1970, pp. 375-382. (See also
IIA346.)

H9   "Modern Italy," *Westminster Review*, 11 (July 1829), 127-140.
Review of *Italy as it is*; and J. Simond. *A Tour in Italy and
Sicily*. Attributed by Frederick L. Jones [IA7, Vol. II, p. 11
n. 2].

H10   Review of *The Loves of the Poets*, *Westminster Review*, 11 (October
1829), 472-477.
Author of the work reviewed also author of *Diary of an Ennuyée*
in H7. Attributed by Frederick L. Jones [IA7, Vol. II, p. 19 n. 1].

H11   "Recollections of the Lake of Geneva," *The Spirit and Manners of
the Age*, 2 (December 1829), 913-920.
Signed M. W. S.

H12   Review of *Cloudesley; a Tale*, *Blackwood's Edinburgh Magazine*, 27
(May 1830), 711-716.
Review of Godwin's novel attributed by Burton R. Pollin, in
Godwin Criticism. A Synoptic Bibliography ([Toronto:] University
of Toronto Press, 1967), p. 33; Walter E. Houghton, in his ed.
Wellesley Index to Victorian Periodicals, 1824-1900 ([Toronto:]
University of Toronto Press/London: Routledge & Kegan Paul, 1966),
Vol. I, p. 34, No. 832; and, with reservations, by Jean de Palacio,
in IIE1 (pp. 683-684, Item 240).

?H13 Review of *1572 Chronique du Temps de Charles IX—Par l'Auteur du
Theatre de Clara Gazul*, *Westminster Review*, 13 (October 1830), 495-
502.
Noticed by Jean de Palacio [IIE1, p. 683, Item 239].

H14   "Memoirs of William Godwin." In William Godwin. *Caleb Williams*.
London: Colburn and Bentley, 1831, pp. iii-xiii.
Burton R. Pollin, in *Godwin Criticism. A Synoptic Bibliography* ([Toronto:] University of Toronto Press), Item 1698, notes
that the memoirs, uncredited in this third edition of the novel,
their first appearance, are signed by MS in a Paris 1832 edition,
which was verified in a letter from the New York Public Library
to the present author. Also contained in the present edition is
"Criticism on the Novels of.Godwin," pp. xiv-xviii, and dated 1816
at the bottom of p. xviii, which does not appear to be by MS.

?H15 Review of Thomas Moore. *The Life and Death of Lord Edward Fitz-
gerald*, *Westminster Review*, 16 (January 1831), 110-121.
Attributed by Elizabeth Nitchie [IIA12, p. 209], and disputed
by Jean de Palacio [E1, p. 684, Item 241].

?H16　"Living Literary Characters, No. II. *The Honourable Mrs. Norton*,"
　　　New Monthly Magazine and Literary Journal, 1 (February? 1831),
　　　180-183.
　　　　　Frederick L. Jones [IA7, Vol. II, p. 39 n. 3] speculates that
　　　either this article or H17 may be by MS.
　　　　　Note: date is approximate; Library of Congress bound volume
　　　of this periodical lacks precise dates.

?H17　"Living Literary Characters, No. IV. *James Fenimore Cooper*," *New
　　　Monthly Magazine and Literary Journal*, 1 (April? 1831), 356-362.
　　　　　See annotation and note in H16.

H18　"Appendix III, Mary Shelley's Second Defense of Velluti." In
　　　Frederick L[afayette] Jones, ed. *The Letters of Mary W. Shelley*.
　　　2 vols. Norman, Okla.: University of Oklahoma Press, 1944,
　　　Vol. II, pp. 354-356.
　　　　　Second part of H6, intended for publication as a letter in
　　　The Examiner.

I EDITED WORKS

I1   Percy Bysshe Shelley. *Posthumous Poems Of Percy Bysshe Shelley*.
       London: Printed for John and Henry L. Hunt, 1824.
       Preface by MS, pp. iii-viii.
       For descriptive bibliography, see IIA445.
       Copies at the Library of Congress, British Library, and
       Bodleian.

I2   [Edward John Trelawny.] *Adventures of a Younger Son*. London:
       Colburn and Bentley, 1831.
       Editorial help attributed by Elizabeth Nitchie [IIA12, p. 209].
       Also published, N.Y.: J. & J. Harper, 1832; London: Richard
       Bentley, 1835 [and 1846]; London: T. F. Unwin, 1890; Nardon, N.Y.;
       Oxford: Humphrey Milford, Oxford University Press [1925?]; Oxford:
       Oxford University Press, 1974. Translated into French, Paris:
       Michel Lévy frères, 1860; into Gaelic, 1936.

I3   William Godwin, Jun. *Transfusion; or, The Orphan of Unwalden*.
       London: Macrone, 1835.
       Editorial help attributed by Elizabeth Nitchie [IIA12, pp.
       106, 209].
       Also published, N.Y.: G. Dearburn & Co., 1837.

I4   Percy Bysshe Shelley. *The Poetical Works of Percy Bysshe Shelley*.
       Mrs. Shelley, ed. 4 vols. London: Edward Moxon, 1839.
       The following are MS contributions:
       Vol. I: "Preface by the Editor" (pp. vii-xvi); "Note on Queen
       Mab" (96-106); "Note on Alastor" (139-142); "Note on The Revolt of
       Islam" (374-380).
       Vol. II: "Note on The Prometheus Unbound" (129-144); "Note on
       The Cenci" (272-280); "Note on Hellas" (343-347).
       Vol. III: "Note on The Early Poems" (15-17); "Note on Poems
       of 1816" (35-36); "Note on Poems of 1817" (68-72); "Note on Poems
       Written in 1818" (159-164); "Note on Poems of 1819" (205-210).
       Vol. IV: "Note on Poems Written in 1820" (49-54); "Note on
       Poems of 1821" (149-154); "Note on Poems Written in 1822" (225-
       236); reprinting of "Preface to the Volume of Posthumous Poems,
       Published in 1824" (237-240).
       For descriptive bibliography, see IIA445.
       Also published, 1840, 1847, 1855, 1882, [1884?], 1889, 1890.
       See also I5, I6, I9.
       Copies at the Library of Congress, British Library, and Bodleian.

I5   Percy Bysshe Shelley. *The Poetical Works of Percy Bysshe Shelley*.
Mrs. Shelley, ed. London: Edward Moxon, 1840 [1839].
One-volume edition of I4, with added "Postscript" by MS.
For descriptive bibliography, see IIA445.

I6   Percy Bysshe Shelley. *Poetical Works*. Thomas Hutchinson, ed.
London, N.Y., Toronto: Oxford University Press, 1967.
The most current edition of Shelley's poetry containing MS
notes.
First published, 1905. Reprinted, 1907, 1908, 1909, 1911,
1912, 1914, 1917, 1919 (twice), 1921, 1923, 1926, 1927 (twice),
1929, 1932, 1935, 1940, 1943. Reset, 1943. Reprinted, 1945,
1947, 1949, 1952, 1956, 1960 (twice), 1961, 1965.

I7   Percy Bysshe Shelley. *Essays, Letters from Abroad, Translations
and Fragments, By Percy Bysshe Shelley*. Mrs. Shelley, ed. 2 vols.
London: Edward Moxon, 1840 [1839].
Vol. I contains "Preface by the Editor" (pp. v-xxviii). Vol.
II contains "Journal of a Six Weeks' Tour (pp. 1-46) and "Letters
Descriptive of a Sail Round the Lake of Geneva, and of the Glaciers
of Chamouni" (47-95) [see F3a]. Also in Vol. II are Shelley
letters to MS (134-140, 283-286, 299-324, 344-345, 358-360).
Copies at the Library of Congress, British Library, and
Bodleian.
For descriptive bibliography, see IIA445.
For reprinting, see I8.

I8   Second edition of I7, 1841.
Copies at British Library and Bodleian.

I9   Percy Bysshe Shelley. *The Poetical Works of Percy Bysshe Shelley.
With His Tragedies and Lyrical Dramas. To which are added His
Essays and Fragments, History of a Six Weeks' Tour Through France,
Switzerland, Germany, and Holland; Letters from Abroad &c., &c.*
Mary Wollstonecraft Shelley, ed. London, N.Y., Melbourne: Ward,
Lock and Co., 1889.
One-volume edition of I1, I4, and I7, containing all MS notes.

PART II

WORKS ABOUT MARY SHELLEY

II WORKS ABOUT MARY SHELLEY

A BOOKS

1. Entire Books

A1   Bigland, Eileen. *Mary Shelley*. N.Y.: Appleton-Century-Crofts, 1959.
Chiefly biographical, except for brief mention of *Frankenstein*,
pp. 95-96. Lack of references (including dates for letters quoted)
and novel-like format. Typical insight: "The arrival of Mrs. Clairmont was little Mary Godwin's first introduction to the harsh realities
of the world." Brief bibliography.

A2   Church, Richard. *Mary Shelley*. London: Gerald Howe, 1928.
Anecdotal, occasionally unreliable biography. Quotes not attributed, and last 28 years of MS life condensed into one chapter. Little
criticism: pp. 52-57 cover *Frankenstein* ("an adolescent's version of
the eternal story of Man's attempt to create life"); pp. 75, 84 offer
brief comments on *Valperga* and *The Last Man*.
Reprinted as A96. Also published, N.Y.: Viking Press, 1928. Facsimile reprints of N.Y. ed.: Folcroft, Pa.: Folcroft Press, 1972;
Freeport, N.Y.: Books for Libraries, 1972.

A3   Gerson, Noel Bertram. *Daughter of Earth and Water: A Biography of
Mary Wollstonecraft Shelley*. N.Y.: William Morrow, 1973.
Superficial biography, concentrating on the "tragic, poignant"
MS-Shelley relationship. Rare comments on the novels: Victor Frank-
enstein erroneously termed "a German nobleman"; "the scholar does not
classify [*Frankenstein*] as literature." Shows little familiarity with
any of MS works. Brief bibliography.
For review, see B89.

A4   Glut, Donald F. *The Frankenstein Legend: A Tribute to Mary Shelley
and Boris Karloff*. Metuchen, N.J.: Scarecrow Press, 1973.
Examination of the Frankenstein theme in all media, including later
fiction, the theater, film, radio, and comic-books. Many facts, but
lacking in insightful comment. Section on MS contains numerous errors.

A5   Godwin, William. *The Elopement of Percy Bysshe Shelley and Mary Woll-
stonecraft Shelley as Narrated by William Godwin*. H[arry] Buxton
Forman, ed. [Boston:] The Bibliophile Society; Privately Printed for
W[illiam] K. Bixby, 1911.
In a letter to John Taylor (Aug. 27, 1814), Godwin accuses Shelley

of seducing MS, and MS of deceiving him and his family.
Facsimile reprint: Folcroft, Pa.: Folcroft Press, 1969.

A6   Grylls, R[osalie] Glynn [Lady Mander]. *Mary Shelley. A Biography.*
London, N.Y.: Oxford University Press, 1938.
Extensive use of previously unpublished MS letters and portions
of MS journal form the basis of this well-documented biography. Brief
criticism of *Frankenstein* on pp. 319-322, announcing that such criticism also applies "in general to [MS] other works." Nevertheless, a
valuable biography of MS until Shelley's death. Description of A16
in Appendix A, Bibliography.
Reprinted, 1941. Facsimile reprints: N.Y.: Haskell House, 1969;
Havertown, Pa.: Richard West, 1973; Folcroft, Pa.: Folcroft Press,
1973.

A7   Leighton, Margaret [Carver]. *Shelley's Mary: A Life of Mary Godwin
Shelley.* N.Y.: Farrar, Straus, and Giroux, 1973.
Superficial biography, written for junior high school audience.

Mander, Lady. *See* Grylls, R[osalie] Glynn, A6.

A8   Marshall, Mrs. Julian [Florence A. Marshall]. *The Life and Letters
of Mary Wollstonecraft Shelley.* 2 vols. London: Richard Bentley and
Son, 1889.
Primarily a chronological collection of MS letters and journal,
used judiciously, with editorial comments interspersed. Many incidents, such as MS role in the elopement with Shelley and the origin
of *Frankenstein*, are treated lightly or ignored.
Facsimile reprint: N.Y.: Haskell House, 1970.
See also A122.

A9   Massey, Irving. *Posthumous Poems of Shelley. Mary Shelley's Fair
Copy Book. Bodleian MS. Shelley Adds. d. 9 Collated with the Holo-
graphs and the Printed Texts.* Montreal: McGill-Queen's University
Press, 1969.
MS as editor of Shelley's poems; she "drew an intimate pleasure
from working with his notebooks."

A10   Moore, Helen. *Mary Wollstonecraft Shelley.* Philadelphia: J. B.
Lippincott, 1886.
First full-length biography of MS, consisting mainly of extracts
from her letters and journal. (Chapter VI, for example, is eighty
per cent extracts). Point of view: "While it is true that Mrs.
Shelley's place among eminent women does not rest upon the circum-
stance that she was Shelley's wife, it is in every sense due to the
fact that she was his companion." Psychological criticism of *Frankenstein*, and brief consideration of biographical elements in the
novels.

A11   Nicholson, E. W. B. *The Shelley Collection Conditions proposed by
Lady Shelley and accepted by the Bodleian Curators on June 11, 1892.*
n.p. [ca. 1892], unpaginated.
Bodley's Librarian lists, in three pages, the contents of two

volumes of A16, and the conditions of acceptance, including lack of access for readers until July 9, 1922.

A12   Nitchie, Elizabeth. *Mary Shelley, Author of Frankenstein*. New Brunswick, N.J.: Rutgers University Press, 1953.
    Essentially critical; tries to find, "chiefly in her writings," "what she was really like" and "how successful and how good a writer she was." Generally positive and intelligent criticism of the novels, although it is admitted that MS fiction "reveals little originality and invention in plotting"—"except for *Frankenstein*." Appendix VI contains a helpful list of "Persons Real and Fictitious Referred to in the book"; detailed list of MS works, but with minor errors and incomplete references.
    Appendix III is a reprinting, with revised footnotes, of B246; Appendix IV of B250.
    Also published, Toronto: Smithers and Bonellie, 1953. Facsimile reprint of N.J. ed.: Westport, Conn.: Greenwood Press, 1970.

A13   Rossetti, Lucy Madox [Brown]. *Mrs. Shelley*. Eminent Women Series. London: W. H. Allen, 1890.
    Although MS works are supposed to be "the *raison d'être* for this biography," there is scant criticism: *Frankenstein* is merely summarized, *The Last Man* termed "stilted writing" (although it has "powerful ideas"). Biographical sections are not particularly valuable, and are occasionally hysterical in tone.
    Facsimile reprint: Folcroft, Pa.: Folcroft Press, 1969.

A14   [Sanborn, F(ranklin) B(enjamin), ed.] *The Romance of Mary W. Shelley, John Howard Payne and Washington Irving*. Boston: The Bibliophile Society; Printed for Members Only, 1907.
    Letters previously unpublished, editorial remarks between each series. (The text of the letters is occasionally difficult to distinguish from the remarks, since the same type-face is used for both.) Sanborn's conclusion: "It seems clear that, had Payne been a little more pressing in his suit, or more fortunate in his affairs, Mrs. Shelley would have married him,—failing her dream of friendship or love with Washington Irving."
    Facsimile reprint: Folcroft, Pa.: Folcroft Press, 1972.
    See also A190.

A15   Scott, Walter Sidney, ed. *Harriet and Mary, Being the Relations between Percy Bysshe Shelley, Harriet Shelley, Mary Shelley, and Thomas Jefferson Hogg, as shown in Letters between them*. [London:] The Golden Cockerel Press, 1944.
    Extensive annotations of all letters, including the MS-Hogg series (pp. 42-65). Limited to 500 copies.
    Also published, with A376, in A385, with less annotation. See also A86, A222.

A16   [Shelley, Lady Jane Gibson, and Sir Percy Florence Shelley, eds.] *Shelley and Mary*. 4 vols. [also 3 vols.] For Private Circulation Only [1882].
    The prefatory note by Sir Percy states that in the 1243 pages of

the volumes are contained all letters and documents "of a biographical character at present in the hands of Shelley's representatives." Dispute has ranged over this since initial publication. Arrangement of volumes is chronological: Vol. I covers July 28, 1814-1817; Vol. II, Jan. 1, 1818-1819; Vol. III, Jan. 1, 1820-1822; Vol. IV, Jan. 11, 1823-Feb. 1857. MS journal the main content, interrupted by letters and editorial comments by Lady Shelley.

One of the Bodleian copies (Shelley adds. d. 2, 3, 4, 5) contains handwritten notes by Lady Shelley on pp. 39, 90, 91, 198, 208, 267, 274, 277, 610, 663, 678, 1222, with the normal excisions on pp. 611, 969, 1221.

Only 12 copies were allegedly printed, two of which are in the Bodleian, two in the Carl H. Pforzheimer Library, one in the Huntington Library, one in Yale, one in UCLA, the remaining five possibly in the hands of private collectors. (The present author was recently offered a copy by a London bookseller, for £650; to my query concerning previou ownership, he replied that he could only state that the volumes were no from Lord Abinger's collection. Lord Abinger is reputed to have two copies.)

See also IA1; IIA6, A8, A10, A11, A223, B18, B30, B31, B32, B224.

A17   Shelley, Percy Bysshe. *The Letters of Percy Bysshe Shelley.* 2 vols. Frederick L[afayette] Jones, ed. Oxford: The Clarendon Press/N.Y.: Oxford University Press, 1964.

33 letters from Shelley to MS; references to MS in other letters thoroughly indexed (in four columns).

A18   Small, Christopher. *Ariel Like a Harpy: Shelley, Mary and Frankenstein.* London: Victor Gollancz, 1972.

Examination of *Frankenstein* on all levels, as a separate entity and in connection with Shelley's *Prometheus Unbound.* "When some of [*Frankenstein*'s] personal connections are assembled and studied . . . its impersonal life as a work of art can be more fully understood." Partial conclusion: "it is because the Monster is not loved . . . that he becomes wicked." Author disclaims "scholarly" pretensions in his Preface.

Also published as *Mary Shelley's Frankenstein: Tracing the Myth.* [Pittsburgh:] University of Pittsburgh Press, 1973.

A19   Smith, Robert Metcalf, in collaboration with T[heodore] G[eorge] Ehrsam and L. A. Waters. *The Shelley Legend.* N.Y.: Charles Scribner' Sons, 1945.

Definition of the Shelley legend: the "fallacious views about the life of Shelley and his writings . . . under the careful supervision first of MS and after her death . . . of Lady Shelley." Treatment of MS occasionally inaccurate and misleading; for detailed rebuttals, see A87 [and B43], A226 [and B141], A437 [and B349].

Reprinted, Port Washington, N.Y.: The Kennikat Press, 1967.

A20   Spark, Muriel. *Child of Light: A Reassessment of Mary Wollstonecraft Shelley.* Hadleigh, Essex: Tower Bridge, 1951.

First part biographical, covering little new ground; second critical, with all approaches to *Frankenstein*, and occasional biographical

criticism of the other novels. Noteworthy is the discussion of MS affinities with Poe, pp. 187-189. Appendix contains an abridged version of *The Last Man*, with editorial comments throughout. Bibliography.
For an assessment of Spark's attitude towards MS, see D10.

A21   Taylor, Charles H[enry], Jr. *The Early Collected Editions of Shelley's Poems: A Study in the History and Transmission of the Printed Text*. New Haven, Conn.: Yale University Press, 1958.
Examines the reliability of MS as editor of Shelley's poems, especially detailed in Chapters 3, 4, and 5. (For a brief but thorough review, see that of K[enneth] N[eill] C[ameron], *Philological Quarterly*, 38 [April 1959], 164-165.)
Originally dissertation; see D18. Also published, London: Oxford University Press, 1959.
See also B334.

A22   Walling, William A. *Mary Shelley*. Twayne's English Authors Series, No. 128. N.Y.: Twayne Publishers, 1972.
Intelligent, multi-level criticism of all MS works (directed to the undergraduate), but particularly detailed on *Frankenstein*, *The Last Man*, and *Valperga*. Annotated bibliography contains minor errors.

2. *Portions of Books*

A23   Adelman, Joseph [Ferdinand Gottlieb]. *Famous Women. An Outline of Feminine Achievement Through the Ages with Life Stories of Five Hundred Noted Women*. N.Y.: Ellis M. Lonow, 1926, pp. 136-137.
Biographical sketch, and brief comments on *Frankenstein*: the Monster becomes "an outcast whose sole resource is self-immolation."
Also published anonymously as "Shelley, Mary Wollstonecraft." In *The Encyclopædia Britannica*. Chicago, London, Toronto, Geneva: Encyclopædia Britannica, 1963, Vol. 20, p. 494.

Adkinson, Robert. *See* Eyles, Allen, A139.

A24   Aldiss, Brian W. "Chapter 1, The Origins of the Species: Mary Shelley." In his *The Billion Year Spree. The True History of Science Fiction*. Garden City, N.Y.: Doubleday, 1973, pp. 7-39; and 82, 83, 144, 199, 286, 316-317.
Reprinting of B3, with additional mention of the themes of *Frankenstein* and *The Last Man* in later works.
Reprinted, N.Y.: Schocken Books, 1974 (same pagination).

A25   Allsop, Thomas, ed. *Letters, Conversations and Recollections of S. T. Coleridge*. 2 vols. London: Edward Moxon, 1836, Vol. I, pp. 223-225.
Allsop was favorably impressed when he met MS—likens her to "a picture by Titian in the Louvre."
Also published, N.Y.: Harper & Brothers, 1836. Second edition: London: Groombridge & Sons, 1858.

A26   Altick, Richard D[aniel]. *The Scholar Adventurers*. N.Y.: Macmillan
       Company, 1951, pp. 104, 162-163, 164, 165-167, 168.
       MS mentioned in connection with the Elena Adelaide affair and the
       forger Major Byron.

A27   Amis, Kingsley. *New Maps of Hell. A Survey of Science Fiction*.
       N.Y.: Harcourt, Brace, 1960, pp. 32-33.
       Brief glancing comments: "Frankenstein, in the popular mind, is
       easily the most outstanding representative of the generic mad scien-
       tist who plagued bad early-modern science fiction"; "the scientific
       character descend[ing] from [*Frankenstein*] is that of the morally ir-
       responsible researcher indifferent to the damage he may cause or
       render possible."
       Also published as *New Maps of Hell*. N.Y.: Ballantine Books, 1960
       (pp. 26-27).

A28   Amis, Kingsley. "Starting Points." In Dick Allen, ed. *Science
       Fiction: The Future*. N.Y.: Harcourt Brace Jovanovich, 1971, pp.
       245-262 [255-256].
       Brief examination of *Frankenstein* as precursor of the science
       fiction novel, the one "Gothic novel" that does serve in this way:
       "Frankenstein . . . far from being possessed of supernatural powers .
       . . is a physiologist with academic training . . . a feature he has
       retained in his modern incarnations, while altogether losing the sen-
       timental Shelleyan quality that marked his original appearance."

A29   Angeli, Helen R[ossetti]. *Shelley and His Friends in Italy*. London:
       Methuen, 1911, pp. 3-8, 13-15, 17, 19-21, 23-25, 27, 34-39, 49, 51-
       55, 65-68, 71-73, 79 n. 1, 80, 87, 90-91, 93, 95-99, 102-104, 107,
       115, 116-117, 119, 122, 127-133, 142-143, 145-147, 157-158, 161, 162-
       163, 165-167, 169, 174-178, 181, 189, 191-193, 195, 214-215, 216,
       217-220, 227, 231, 238, 244-245, 248-249, 251, 253-254, 267, 269,
       270-272, 275-276, 281-282, 285, 288, 294, 295, 297-298, 304, 313-315.
       Detailed examination of MS in Italy, with original comparisons of
       her with Mary Wollstonecraft and Claire Clairmont. Occasionally, a
       condescending attitude: "If Mary Shelley had died with her husband,
       she would have remained as a luminous figure. . . . But she survived
       him thirty years."
       Facsimile reprint: N.Y.: Haskell House, 1973.

A30   Anobile, Richard J. "Introduction" to his ed. [*James Whale's*]
       Frankenstein. The Film Classics Library. N.Y.: Universe Books; A
       Darien House Book, 1974, pp. 5-7 [5, 6].
       Brief comparison of the novel and the 1931 film version (the
       filmscript of which is here reproduced): "[Mary] Shelley's articu-
       late creature was converted into a grunting monstrosity"; "Universal
       [Film Studios] originally felt that the Shelley novel was not hor-
       rible enough for the type of film they had in mind."

A31   Antal, Fredrick. *Fuseli Studies*. London: Routledge & Kegan Paul,
       1956, pp. 149, 151 n. 5.
       Note on [Theodor?] von Holst, early illustrator of *Frankenstein*,
       "a novel of terror on a rather high literary level."

A32   Armstrong, Margaret. *Trelawny. A Man's Life*. N.Y.: Macmillan
      Company, 1940, pp. 188, 191-192, 199-200, 203-204, 207, 208, 210,
      217, 219, 220, 225-244 *passim*, 248-252 *passim*, 257-261, 265, 266,
      268, 272, 275-282 *passim*, 288, 303, 314-321 *passim*, 326, 330-332,
      333, 337-338, 339-340, 345, 350-359 *passim*, 367.
      Generally unsympathetic remarks about MS, many in passing,
      stressing her dependence on Trelawny after Shelley's death.

A33   Armytage, W. H. G. *Yesterday's Tomorrows. A Historical Survey of
      Future Societies*. Toronto: University of Toronto Press/London:
      Routledge & Kegan Paul, 1968, pp. 43-45.
      MS is representative of the Gothic novelists, who juggled with
      time. *The Last Man* summarized, with little comment: "The wheel
      comes full circle when, as the last man, Verney finds himself in
      Rome—robber and shepherd like its first founder."

A34   Arnold, Matthew. "Shelley." In his *Essays in Criticism*. Second
      Edition. London, N.Y.: Macmillan and Co., 1889, pp. 205-252 [205-
      206, 207].
      Arnold recalls an anecdote, in which MS states that she would not
      have her son Percy "think for himself."
      See also A256, B183.

A35   Ash, Russell. "*The Vampyre* and Its Author Doctor John William
      Polidori 1795-1821." In John William Polidori. *The Vampyre. A
      Tale. With an introductory note about the tale and its author by
      Russell Ash together with the background history on which the super-
      stition is based*. Tring, Hertfordshire: The Gubblecote Press, 1974,
      pp. 1-9 [3, 4].
      Brief mention that Polidori taught MS Italian in 1816, and
      "probably spoke further to her about paranormal phenomena."

A36   Asimov, Isaac. "Introduction" to his *Eight Stories from The Rest of
      the Robots*. N.Y.: Pyramid Books, 1966, pp. 7-11 [7-9, 11].
      Brief description of the experiments of Galvani, Volta, and Davy
      that might have influenced *Frankenstein*; and superficial comments on
      the MS novel: "Frankenstein was another Faust, seeking knowledge not
      meant for man, and he had created his Mephistophelean nemesis." Also
      suggests that *Frankenstein* influenced his story, "Robot AL-76 Goes
      Astray."
      See also A182.
      Reprinted, 1966, 1974. Originally published as *The Rest of the
      Robots*. N.Y.: Doubleday, 1964.

A37   Atwood, Margaret [Eleanor]. "Speeches for Dr Frankenstein." In her
      The Animals in That Country. Boston: Little, Brown, 1968, pp. 42-47.
      Poem in ten sections which demonstrates sensitive reading of
      Frankenstein.
      Poem also published separately in a limited edition with woodcuts
      by Charles Pachter.
      See also B97.

A38   Aylesworth, Thomas G. "Man-Made Monsters." In his *Monsters from the Movies*. The Weird and Horrible Library. Philadelphia, N.Y.: J. B. Lippincott, 1972, pp. 22-45 [22-27, 29, 34].
        Sketches the possible influence of alchemical experiments and the Golem legend on *Frankenstein*.

A39   Bailey, J[ames] O[sler]. *Pilgrims through Space and Time: Trends and Patterns in Scientific and Utopian Fiction*. N.Y.: Argus Books, 1947, pp. 28-29, 32, 34-35, 62, 100, 158, 183, 196, 216, 255, 271, 281.
        Connections are noted between *Frankenstein* and three other works— *Erehwon*, Clyde C. Campbell's "The Avatar," and H. G. Wells' *The Island of Dr. Moreau*. *The Last Man* is mentioned: "as anticipation of a recurrent pattern in scientific fiction, [it] is a more important book than *Frankenstein*."
        Originally dissertation; see D2. Facsimile reprint: Westport, Conn.: Greenwood Press, 1972.

A40   Baker, Carlos. "The Necessity of Love: *Alastor* and the Epipsyche." In George M. Ridenour, ed. *Shelley. A Collection of Critical Essays*. Twentieth Century Views. Englewood Cliffs, N.J.: Prentice-Hall, 1965, pp. 51-68 [62-63].
        Excerpt from A41, concerned with MS as one of Shelley's "pleasing delusions."

A41   Baker, Carlos. *Shelley's Major Poetry: The Fabric of a Vision*. Princeton, N.J.: Princeton University Press, 1948, pp. 14, 42, 50, 52, 54-55, 64, 68, 79 n. 32, 93, 121 n. 2, 122-123, 143 & n. 45, 160 n. 8, 168, 173, 176 n. 35, 181-182, 213, 231, 269, 278, 287-291.
        Examines MS effect on Shelley's poetry. In Appendix IV, "The Date of Mary's Despondency" (pp. 287-291), denies that an estrangement occurred between MS and Shelley in late 1818.
        Excerpt printed as A40.

A42   Baker, Ernest A. *A Guide to Historical Fiction*. N.Y.: Macmillan Company [1914], pp. 36, 333.
        Brief comments on *Perkin Warbeck* ("Mrs. Shelley firmly believed that Warbeck was the lost Duke of York"), and *Valperga* ("The love-romance is worked out on idealistic lines").

A43   Baker, Ernest A. *The Novel of Sentiment and Gothic Romance*. Vol. V of *A History of the English Novel*. London: H. F. & G. Witherby, 1934, p. 219.
        MS later works are "painstaking, not incorrect, but devoid of historical imagination, too often grandiloquent, and generally dull."

A44   Ball, Patricia M. *The Central Self. A Study in Romantic and Victorian Imagination*. London: The Athlone Press, University of London, 1968, p. 132.
        MS "knew Shelley must write his ideal, Promethean poems, but she wished for more of *The Cenci*'s 'sad realities' of flesh and blood to stimulate his imaginative life."†
        Also published, N.Y., Toronto: Oxford University Press, 1968.

A45   Barber, Dulan. "Frankenstein." In his *Monsters Who's Who*. N.Y.:
       Crescent Books, 1974, pp. 34-40.
          Superficial consideration of the novel: "[MS] was more concerned
       to write an allegory about man's responsibility than to provide
       suspense and chills." The novel has never been successfully trans-
       lated to film because of the difficulty in presenting her central
       argument.

A46   Barnard, Ellsworth. *Shelley's Religion*. Minneapolis: The University
       of Minnesota Press, 1936, pp. 98 n. 1, 146-147 n. 60.
          MS was unable to understand Shelley; it was "hard for her to be
       married to a man who would perversely see only pettiness, banality,
       and smug mediocrity in that fashionable society where she aspired to
       shine."

A47   Baugh, Albert C. *A Literary History of England*. N.Y.: Appleton-
       Century-Crofts, 1967, p. 1196 and supplementary paragraph 1196 (on
       later un-numbered page).
          "*Frankenstein* (1817) [*sic*] [is] the only novel of terror that is
       still famous." Brief bibliography.

A48   Beach, Joseph Warren. *The Concept of Nature in Nineteenth-Century
       English Poetry*. N.Y.: Macmillan Company, 1936, p. 255.
          "Some light may be thrown on Shelley's symbolism by Mary Shelley's
       account in *Valperga* [II, 99-102] of the cave of the human mind."
       Facsimile reprint: N.Y.: Pageant Book Company, 1956.

A49   Beachcroft, J. O. *The Modest Art. A Survey of the Short Story in
       English*. London, N.Y., Toronto: Oxford University Press, 1968, pp.
       94-95.
          "Even such a distinguished name as Mary Shelley cannot raise
       [silly romantic stories] very high."†

       Beale, Kenneth. *See* Bojarski, Richard, A65.

A50   Beddoes, Thomas Lovell. *The Letters of Thomas Lovell Beddoes*. [Sir]
       Edmund Gosse, ed. London: Elkin Mathews & John Lane/N.Y.: Macmillan
       and Co., 1894, pp. 2, 22, 23-24, 32, 35, 66, 104, 106, 149.
          First-hand knowledge of MS reflected in the letters. Identifies
       MS as author of "On Ghosts" (pp. 23-24) and "The Bride of Modern
       Italy"; and briefly discusses *The Last Man*.

       Belcher, Susan. *See* Manley, Seon, A266.

       Bell, Eric Temple. *See* Taine, John, A410.

A51   Benét, William Rose. "Frankenstein." In his ed. *The Reader's
       Encyclopedia*. N.Y.: Thomas Y. Crowell, 1969, p. 404.
          The creature "is only animal life, a parody on the creature man,
       bent on evil." Also quotes from an 1866 speech by Lord Avebury, who
       uses *Frankenstein* "incorrectly" to refer to the Monster.

Benson, Baroness Dorothea Mary Ruby. *See* Charnwood, Lady, A92.

A52   Bergonzi, Bernard. *The Early H. G. Wells. A Study of the Scientific Romances.* Manchester: The University Press, 1969, pp. 34, 46, 102, 106, 109, 117, 120, 167-168.
       Griffin of Wells' *The Invisible Man* and Moreau of *The Island of Dr. Moreau* are romantic scientists influenced by *Frankenstein*.
       First published, 1961.

A53   Biagi, Guido. *The Last Days of Percy Bysshe Shelley. New Details from Unpublished Documents.* London: T. Fisher Unwin, 1090, pp. 2 3, 6, 8-9, 21, 25-26, 28-30, 32-34, 38, 41, 44, 45-46, 55-68, 70-73.
       The documents bear only on Shelley's death and the disposition of his body, but some new information is revealed about MS, despite the idealistic prose: MS was "the poet's gentle companion . . . who loved and comforted him, confident and trusting as an indulgent mother, superior to all feminine distrust."
       First published as E3. Facsimile reprint of London ed.: Havertown, Pa.: Richard West, 1973.

A54   Binder, Eando [Otto O. Binder]. "Chapter 2, *Frankenstein!*" In his *Adam Link—Robot.* N.Y.: Paperback Library, 1965, pp. 12-17 [16].
       In this novelized version of B23, Adam Link only discovers the novel *Frankenstein*, then realizes the mob pursuing him believes a parallel exists between it and him.
       See also A55, A234, B36.

A55   Binder, Eando [Otto O. Binder]. "I, Robot." In Sam Moskowitz, ed. *The Coming of the Robots.* N.Y.: Collier Books/London: Collier-Macmillan, 1966, pp. 23-45 [44].
       Reprinting of B23; first published in this edition, 1963.
       See also A54, A234, B36.

A56   Birkhead, Edith. "Later Developments of the Tale of Terror." In her *The Tale of Terror. A Study of the Gothic Romance.* N.Y.: E. P. Dutton/London: Constable, 1921, pp. 157-184 [158-169].
       Study of the horrific elements in *Frankenstein, The Last Man, Valperga,* and MS short stories, the last revealing "a stronger sense of proportion than her novels, [and] written in a more graceful, fluent style."
       Also published, London: Hodder and Stoughton, n.d. Facsimile reprint of 1921 ed.: N.Y.: Russell and Russell, 1963.

A57   Black, Frank Gees. *The Epistolary Novel in the Late Eighteenth Century. A Descriptive and Bibliographical Study.* Eugene, Ore.: University of Oregon Press, 1940, pp. 110, 148.
       Frankenstein listed as an epistolary novel.
       Also published as B24.

A58   Blackstone, Bernard. *The Lost Travellers. A Romantic Theme with Variations.* London: Longmans, Green and Co., 1962, p. 7.
       "Revenge plus a Faustus-motif is the mainspring for Mary Shelley's *Frankenstein.*"†

A59   Block, Andrew. *The English Novel, 1740-1850*. London: Dawsons of
       Pall Mall, 1961, p. 213.
       Identifies copies of MS novels in libraries and private col-
       lections.
       Also published, Dobbs Ferry, N.Y.: Oceana Pubs., 1962.

A60   Bloom, Harold. "Afterword" to Mary Shelley. *Frankenstein Or, The
       Modern Prometheus*. N.Y.: The New American Library; A Signet Classic,
       1965, pp. 212-223.
       Reprinting of B26.
       See also A61.

A61   Bloom, Harold. "Chapter 8, Frankenstein: or the New Prometheus."
       In his *The Ringers in the Tower. Studies in Romantic Tradition*.
       Chicago, London: University of Chicago Press, 1971, pp. 119-129.
       Reprinting of B26.
       See also A6o.

A62   Blunden, Edmund [Charles]. *Shelley. A Life Story*. London: Collins,
       1946, pp. 112-113, 114-115, 146, 152-159, 168-171, 183-184, 203, 232,
       235, 243, 255, 271, 273-274, 282-283, 288-289, 295, 296; (references
       to MS works) 38, 39-40, 115, 135-136, 169, 171, 183-184, 240.
       This interpretive biography of Shelley has little to recommend it
       for shedding new light on MS, but the prose style is eminently
       readable, making it a good source for a summarization of the MS-
       Shelley relationship.
       Also published, N.Y.: Viking Press, 1947.

A63   Blunden, Edmund [Charles], ed. *Shelley and Keats as They Struck
       Their Contemporaries. Notes partly from manuscript sources*. London:
       C. W. Beaumont, 1925, pp. 55-57, 58.
       Section of a Jane Williams letter to Leigh Hunt (April 28, 1823)
       discussing "coldness" of MS; Hunt letter to MS (Aug. 17, 1822).
       Facsimile reprints: Folcroft, Pa.: Folcroft Library Editions,
       1970; N.Y.: Haskell House, 1971.

A64   Boas, Louise Schutz. *Harriet Shelley. Five Long Years*. London:
       Oxford University Press, 1962, pp. 106, 108-109, 150-151, 152, 154,
       156-158, 162, 163, 166, 172, 175-177, 180, 191, 199, 201, 208, 211,
       214, 215, 223 n. 3.
       Reflections on MS from Harriet's point of view, and a brief
       comment (p. 223 n. 3) on Shelley's influence on *Frankenstein*.

A65   Bojarski, Richard, and Kenneth Beale. "The Bride of Frankenstein."
       In their *The Films of Boris Karloff*. Secaucus, N.J.: The Citadel
       Press, 1974, pp. 100-108 [102].
       Concerning editor's cuts in the film *Bride of Frankenstein*:
       "The prologue containing references to the scandalous behavior of
       the three writers (Lord Byron, Percy and Mary Shelley) and its
       deletion made the remaining dialogue at times curiously uneven."†

A66   Booth, Bradford Allen. "Introduction"; Prefatory Notes to Mary
       Shelley. "The Trial of Love" [and] Claire Clairmont. "The Pole."
       In his ed. *A Cabinet of Gems. Short Stories from the English
       Annuals.* Berkeley: University of California Press/London: Cambridge
       University Press, 1938, pp. 16-17; 140; 160.
           The trouble in MS stories is not in the development but in the
       plot: they read "like summarized novels." "The Trial of Love" is
       "sustained by the saving grace of a few good touches of character-
       ization and description." "The Pole" attributed to Claire.

A67   Boyle, Andrew. *The Authors (1820 1850).* Vol. I of *An Index to the
       Annuals.* Worcester: Andrew Boyle (Booksellers), 1967, pp. 260-261.
       (Only Vol. I published.)
           20 items are listed as MS contributions to three annuals.

       Boynton, Henry Walcott. *See* Higginson, Thomas Wentworth, A202.

A68   Brailsford, Henry Noel. *Shelley, Godwin, and their Circle.* London:
       Williams and Norgate/N.Y.: Henry Holt [1913], pp. 143-144, 180.
           Godwin's *Caleb Williams* "was a hereditary nightmare, and with a
       less pedestrian imagination, his daughter, Mary Shelley, used the
       same theme of a remorseless pursuit in *Frankenstein*"; "It was an un-
       lucky timidity which caused Mrs. Shelley to suppress her father's
       religious essays when the manuscript was bequeathed to her for publi-
       cation on his death."†
           Translated into Spanish by Margarita Villegas de Robles as
       Shelley, Godwin y su círculo. Mexico City: Fondo de Cultura
       Económica, 1942. Also published, Hamden, Conn.: Archon Books, 1969.
       Facsimile reprint of 1913 ed.: Havertown, Pa.: Richard West, 1973.

A69   Brand, C[harles] P[eter]. *Italy and the English Romantics. The
       Italian Fashion in Early Nineteenth-Century England.* Cambridge at
       the University Press, 1957, pp. 187, 193.
           Valperga, along with Shelley's *The Cenci* and Byron's *Marino
       Faliero,* is listed as one of the "imaginative works" that were
       "inspired by episodes in the history of Italy," and in which the
       authors "paid close attention to the historical sources of their
       productions."

A70   Brew, Claude C. *Shelley and Mary in 1817. A Critical Study of the
       Text and Poetical Evolution of the "Dedication" of "The Revolt of
       Islam," based on a new examination of the manuscripts and including
       hitherto unpublished material.* London: Keats-Shelley Memorial
       Association, 1971, pp. 17, 19, 20, 23, 24, 25-26, 27, 29.
           The significance of Shelley's references to MS in the "Dedica-
       tion."

A71   [Brewer, Ebenezer Cobham.] "Frankenstein." In his *Brewer's Dictio-
       nary of Phrase and Fable.* Eighth (revised) edition. N.Y.; Evanston,
       Ill.: Harper and Row, 1963, p. 375.
           Frankenstein "made a soulless monster out of corpses."†
           First published, 1870; many reprintings.

A72   Brewer, E[benezer] Cobham. "Frankenstein." In his *Reader's Handbook of Famous Names in Fiction, Allusions, References, Proverbs, Plots, Stories, and Poems*. Revised edition. 2 vols. Philadelphia: J. B. Lippincott, 1889, Vol. I, pp. 392-393.
       Incorrectly dates *Frankenstein* 1817, and mentions that "The monster hides himself from the eye of man in the Ultima Thule of the habitable globe and slays Frankenstein on his way home [*sic*]."
       Facsimile reprint: Detroit: Gale Research Company, 1966.

A73   Brooks, Van Wyck. *Fenellosa and His Circle, with Other Essays in Biography*. N.Y.: E. P. Dutton/Toronto: Clarke, Irwin & Co., 1962, pp. 92-93.
       Brief mention of MS relationship with Fanny Wright and Robert Dale Owen. MS termed "gentle and womanly."

A74   Brown, Ford K[eeler]. "Chapter 12, Part III, Frankenstein; or, The Modern Prometheus." In his *Fathers of the Victorians. The Age of Wilberforce*. Cambridge at the University Press, 1961, pp. 487-533 [520].
       Title of chapter has little to do with its content; *Frankenstein* is referred to as "not much read nowadays, but often referred to by its title," as the author does herein.

A75   Brown, Ford K[eeler]. "Chapter XXV, Mary Wollstonecraft Godwin— Francis Place Concluded"; "Chapter XXVI, The New Shelleys—Social Life in Skinner Street." In his *The Life of William Godwin*. London, Toronto: J. M. Dent & Sons/N.Y.: E. P. Dutton, 1926, pp. 284-296; 297-310.
       The MS-Shelley elopement and subsequent return to London are discussed from Godwin's biased point of view.

A76   Browning, Robert, and Elizabeth Barrett Browning. *The Letters of Robert Browning and Elizabeth Barrett Browning 1845-1846*. 2 vols. N.Y., London: Harper & Brothers, 1898, Vol. I, pp. 185, 196, 226, 286.
       Casual observations by Robert Browning upon MS: "[she] surely was something better once upon a time."
       Reprinted, [1899], [1926], [1935]. Also published, 2 vols. Elvan Kintner, ed. Cambridge, Mass.: The Belknap Press of Harvard University Press, 1969 (Vol. I, pp. 179ff, 189ff, 219, 278).

A77   Burr, Aaron. *The Private Journal of Aaron Burr, during his residence of four years in Europe; with selections from his correspondence*. 2 vols. Matthew L. Davis, ed. N.Y.: Harper & Brothers, 1838, Vol. II, pp. 249, 251, 268, 307, 318, 321, 328, 337, 353, 365.
       Burr's impressions, in his journal, of MS as a young girl during his visits to the Godwins' house, of Dec. 21, 1811; Jan. 22, 1812; Feb. 24, 1812; Feb. 28, 1812; March 5, 1812; and March 26, 1812.
       Reprinted, Saddle River, N.J.: Literature House, 1970.

A78   Burrows, Victor [pseud. of Laurence Victor Thompson]. *The Blue
        Plaque Guide to Historic London Houses and the Lives of Their Famous
        Residents*. London: Newman Neame, 1953, p. 87.
            Identifies No. 26, Nelson Square, Southwark, as lodging of MS,
        Shelley, and Claire from 1814 to 1815.

A79   Burton, Anthony, and John Murdoch. *Byron. An exhibition to commemo-
        rate the 150th anniversary of his death in the Greek War of Liberation,
        19 April 1824. 30 May-25 August 1974. (Victoria and Albert Museum)*.
        London: Her Majesty's Stationery Office, 1974, pp. 78-79, 84, 85, 106,
        100, 122 [Items K10, K11, K12, K24, K29, O8, P1, P2, R9].
            Biographical sketch of MS, and brief comments on *Frankenstein*
        (the Monster's psychology "is that of the Byronic hero"); 1st edition
        of *Frankenstein*; MS letters to Byron; MS fair copy of *Don Juan*; MS
        letters to John Hanson.
            Bound enclosure, *Byron. Additions and Corrections to the Cata-
        logue of the Exhibition 30 May-25 August 1974*, p. [8], contains an
        "Index of Lenders": Lord Abinger (P1), National Portrait Gallery,
        London (K10), Victoria and Albert Museum (K11, K12), Private Collec-
        tions (K24, K29, O8, P2, R9).

A80   Bush, Douglas. *Mythology and the Romantic Tradition in English
        Poetry*. Cambridge, Mass.: Harvard University Press, 1969, pp. 133-
        134 n. 9, 171-172.
            Brief comments on MS two dramas: *Midas* has "the usual fanciful
        and descriptive elaboration"; "In *Proserpine* Mrs. Shelley expresses
        her own spontaneous pleasure in the beauties of nature and myth, and,
        while she cannot take wing like her husband, she does at moments
        catch something of the pure Shelleyan limpidity."
            First published, 1937.

A81   Butler, Ivan. *Horror in the Cinema*. London: A. Zwemmer/N.Y.: A. S.
        Barnes, 1970, pp. 36, 46, 50.
            Notes that the moral in *Frankenstein* does not carry on to the
        film versions, and describes Hamilton Deane's performance as the
        Monster in Peggy Webling's stage version.
            First published as *The Horror Film*. 1967.

A82   Buxton, John. *Byron and Shelley: The History of a Friendship*.
        London: Macmillan, 1968, pp. 10, 13-16, 34-37, 51, 55, 101-102, 103-
        104, 107, 122-123, 168, 193-194, 199-200, 204, 246-259, 267, 269-
        270 n. 4, 271 n. 10.
            Usually detailed biographical and critical references, including
        Byron and Keats' observations of MS.
            First published, Middletown, Conn.: Center for Advanced Studies,
        Wesleyan University, 1967. Also published, N.Y.: Harcourt, Brace &
        World, 1968.

A83   Byron, George Gordon Noël, Baron. *Letters and Journals.* 6 vols.
       In *The Works of Lord Byron.* Rowland E. Prothero, ed. London: John
       Murray, 1898-1900, Vol. II, pp. 74 n. 1, 370 n. 1.

       _____. Vol. III, pp. 332 n. 2, 336 n. 1, 347 n. 1, 427, 446.

       _____. Vol. IV, pp. 83 n. 1, 123-124 n. 1, 258-259 n. 1, 286-
       287 n. 1, 482, 483.

       _____. Vol. V, pp. 14 n. 1, 74 n. 1, 263 n. 2, 266-267, 269,
       307 n. 1, 390 n. 1.

       _____. Vol. VI, pp. 93 n. 1, 103-105 n. 1, 119-120, 148, 158,
       165, 408, 420.
       First-hand impressions of MS.
       Facsimile reprint: N.Y.: Octagon Books, 1966.

A84   *The Cambridge Bibliography of English Literature.* 4 vols. Frederick
       Bateson, ed. Cambridge at the University Press, 1966, Vol. III, cols.
       761-764.
       Lists one bibliography, one collection, 28 primary works, and 57
       secondary works, in the usual abbreviated and incomplete form. Two
       of the secondary works refer not to MS, but to Mary Wollstonecraft:
       "Harper, G. M. Mary Shelley's residence with Thomas Taylor the
       platonist. N & Q Dec 1962"; and "Peter, M. A portrait of Mary W.
       Godwin by John Opie in the Tate Gallery. Keats-Shelley Memorial Bull
       14 1963."

A85   Cameron, Kenneth Neill. "Chapter 7, Shelley and Mary." In his
       Shelley. The Golden Years. Cambridge, Mass.: Harvard University
       Press, 1974, pp. 252-310.
       The significance of Shelley's references to MS in *Rosalind and
       Helen, Julian and Maddalo, Lines . . . Euganean Hills, Letter to
       Maria Gisborne, The Witch of Atlas, Epipsychidion, The Sensitive
       Plant, Fragments of an Unfinished Drama, Lyrics,* and *Translations.*

A86   [Cameron, Kenneth Neill.] Comments on Mary Shelley letters to Thomas
       Jefferson Hogg. In his ed. *Shelley and his Circle 1773-1822.*
       6 vols. Cambridge, Mass.: Harvard University Press, 1970, Vol. III,
       pp. 434-473 *passim.*
       Comments and glosses after each letter.

A87   Cameron, Kenneth N[eill]. "A New Shelley Legend." In Newman I[vey]
       White, Frederick L[afayette] Jones, and Kenneth N[eill] Cameron. *An
       Examination of "The Shelley Legend."* Philadelphia: University of
       Pennsylvania Press, 1958, pp. 94-114.
       Reprint of B43.

A88   Cameron, Kenneth N[eill]. *The Young Shelley: Genesis of a Radical.*
       N.Y.: Macmillan Company, 1950, p. 396 n. 69.
       MS repeats a footnote phrase from Holbach's *Le Système de la
       Nature* in *The Last Man* [III, 192].
       Facsimile reprint: N.Y.: Octagon Books, 1973.

A89   Campbell, Olwen Ward. *Shelley and the Unromantics*. Second, revised edition. London: Methuen & Co., 1924, pp. 16, 52, 66, 116 n. 1, 121, 128-129, 130-136, 143, 144, 148, 150-151, 158, 165, 167-168, 172, 231 n. 1.
       Treats MS relationships with Trelawny and Shelley, and stresses Godwin's influence on her: "we find his stamp on everything she wrote and nearly everything she did."
       Reprinted, N.Y.: Russell and Russell, 1966. Facsimile reprint: N.Y.: Haskell House, 1966.

A90   Canby, Henry Seidel. *The Short Story in English* N.Y.: Henry Holt, 1909, p. 214.
       In her stories, MS "deals mainly in pathos."

A91   Carne, John. *John Carne Letters 1813-1837*. Privately Printed by T. & A. Constable, Edinburgh University Press, 1885, pp. 150-153.
       MS reactions to Shelley's cremation.
       For a response to Carne, see B61.

A92   Charnwood, Lady [Baroness Dorothea Mary Ruby Thorpe Benson]. *Call Back Yesterday. A book of old letters chosen from her collection with some memories of her own*. Second edition. London: Eyre and Spottiswoode, 1938, pp. 201-205.
       Two MS letters to Leigh and Marianne Hunt.
       First edition (1937) does not contain the letters.

A93   Chesser, Eustace. *Shelley & Zastrozzi: self-revelation of a neurotic*. London: Gregg Press and The Archive Press, 1965, pp. 39-40.
       MS was more compatible with Shelley than was Harriet: she was a more apt pupil of Shelley's, and "there was a masculine quality in her intellect to which Shelley's bisexuality responded."

A94   Chew, Samuel C[laggett]. *Byron in England. His fame and after-fame*. London: John Murray, 1924, pp. 149-151.
       MS portrayal of Byron in *The Last Man* and *Lodore* is briefly noted.
       Facsimile reprints: N.Y.: Russell and Russell, 1965; St. Clair Shores, Mich.: Scholarly Press, 1970.

A95   Child, Harold. "Chapter XI, Lesser Novelists." In *The Nineteenth Century*. Vol. XII of *The Cambridge History of English Literature*. Sir A. W. Ward and A. R. Waller, eds. N.Y.: G. P. Putnam's Sons, 1916, pp. 272-279 [274-275].
       Disputes Richard Garnett's claim that Shelley influenced MS in *Frankenstein*, and notes that Catherine Crowe's *The Night Side of Nature* (1848) "went further than [*Frankenstein*]" in giving "some rational basis to the terror."
       Latest reprinting, Cambridge at the University Press, 1961.

A96   Church, Richard. "Mary Shelley." In his *Six Women of the World*. London: Gerald Howe, 1930, pp. 9-92 [last chapter].
       Reprint of A2.

A97　Clairmont, Claire [Mary Jane Clairmont]. *The Journals of Claire Clairmont*. Marion Kingston Stocking, ed., with the assistance of David MacKenzie Stocking. Cambridge, Mass.: Harvard University Press, 1968, pp. 23-63, 79-92, 98-163, 167-289, 305-397, 401-411.

The above pages refer to the journals themselves, *passim* understood, since the observations on and opinions concerning MS are numerous. Early ones are generally friendly, later ones often hostile. Valuable for first-hand information, if used in conjunction with MS journal.

A98　Clarke, Charles Cowden, and Mary Cowden Clarke. *Recollections of Writers*. N.Y.: Charles Scribner's Sons, 1878, pp. 37-39, 40, 41-42, 218-219, 219-220.

First-hand observations of MS, MS letter to Mary Cowden Clarke's father, and Leigh Hunt letter mentioning MS.

First published, 1876. Facsimile reprint of 1878 ed.: Fontwell, Sussex: Centaur Press, 1969. Portions originally appeared in *Gentleman's Magazine*, but none concerning MS.

A99　Clarke, I[gnatius] F[rederick]. "The Tale of the Future: Its origins and development." In his *The Tale of the Future. From the Beginning to the Present Day. An Annotated Bibliography of those satires, ideal states, imaginary wars and invasions, political warnings and forecasts, interplanetary voyages and scientific romances—all located in an imaginary future period—that have been published in the United Kingdom between 1644 and 1970*. Second edition. London: The Library Association, 1972, pp. 1-6 [4].

The Last Man is "the best of the early utopias of the future," with a "laboured introduction" and "no lack of confidence in describing the future of mankind."

A100　Clarke, I[gnatius] F[rederick]. *Voices Prophesying War 1763-1984*. London: Oxford University Press, 1966, pp. 184, 201.

Samuel Butler, in "Darwin among the Machines" (1863), "was able to state clearly what had merely been hinted at by Mary Shelley [in *Frankenstein*, of man's fear of machines]." *Frankenstein* is also briefly paralleled with John Wyndham's *The Day of the Triffids* (1951).

A101　Clarke, Isabel C[onstance]. *Shelley and Byron. A Tragic Friendship*. London: Hutchinson, 1934, pp. 22-37 *passim*, 38-48 *passim*, 64-67 *passim*, 71-78 *passim*, 79ff.

MS in connection with Shelley and Byron (her life "a hard struggle"), with glancing remarks on her works (*Frankenstein* "still a living book").

Clarke, Mary Cowden. *See* Clarke, Charles Cowden, A98.

A102   Cline, C[larence] L[ee]. *Byron, Shelley, and Their Pisan Circle*.
        London: John Murray, 1952, pp. 1-2, 4, 6-7, 8, 10-11, 14, 25, 26,
        32-33, 36, 44, 53, 54, 56, 59, 60, 70, 71, 73, 77, 93, 97-99, 102-
        105, 110, 114, 122, 123, 124, 130, 150, 153, 157, 159, 162-163, 181-
        182, 183, 185, 186, 187, 191, 196-197, 199, 223 nn. 4 & 10, 241-242,
        248 n. 7.
            Devoted entirely to the Pisan period, with most of the new infor-
        mation on Byron, some in connection with MS relationship with Byron.
        Sympathetic treatment; after 1831, "she lived much in the past."
            Reprinted, N.Y.: Russell & Russell, 1969.

A103   Cohen, John. *Human Robots in Myth and Science*. London: George Allen
        & Unwin, 1966, pp. 7, 41, 61, 111, 127.
            The Golem legend as an inspiration for *Frankenstein*.

A104   Colby, Robert A[lan]. *Fiction With a Purpose. Major and Minor
        Nineteenth-Century Novels*. Bloomington, Ind.: Indiana University
        Press, 1967, pp. 156, 322 n. 23.
            T. H. Lister felt that "Jane Austen was being unduly neglected in
        favor of more lurid novelists like Mrs. Shelley."

A105   Cone, Helen Gray. "Mary W. Godwin (Shelley)." In her and Jeanette
        L. Gilder, eds. *Pen-Portraits of Literary Women. By Themselves and
        Others*. 2 vols. Boston: Educational Publishing Company, 1887,
        Vol. I, pp. 109-128 [109-112].
            Superficial biographical sketch, justified by MS-Shelley relation-
        ship: "Immeasurably greater as he was, we may yet claim for his wife
        that she influenced his genius in one respect [in *The Cenci*]." Rest
        of chapter contains excerpts from other works and from MS writings.

A106   Conklin, Groff. "Introduction" to his ed. *Science-Fiction Thinking
        Machines: Robots, Androids, Computers*. N.Y.: The Vanguard Press,
        1954, pp. ix-xiii [x]; and 102.
            Frankenstein, an "ineffably dull and moralistic epic," is listed
        along with the mechanical chess players of Poe and Ambrose Bierce,
        and Karel Capek's *R.U.R.*, in the series of automata that have "fasci-
        nated writers of imagination." Also notes that with *R.U.R.* "the word
        'Frankenstein' went out of fashion and the word 'robot' took over."
            Also published, Toronto: Copp Clark, 1954.

A107   Courtney, William Prideaux. *The Secrets of Our National Literature*.
        London: Archibald Constable, 1908, pp. 59-60, 89.
            Brief mention of MS novels, "the success of [which] carried . . .
        a strange and severe penalty" (not clarified); and notice of MS role
        in publication of Trelawny's *Adventures of a Younger Son*.

A108   Cowling, George. "Chapter I, The Adolescent; Part IV, Mary." In his
        Shelley and Other Essays. Freeport, N.Y.: Books for Libraries, 1967,
        pp. 37-51 [41-46, 47-48, 51].
            MS was a "benign influence" upon Shelley, under whom it became
        clear that he had poetic genius.
            First published, 1936, publisher unknown.

A109   Crompton, Margaret. "Part Three, The Godwin Daughters"; "Part Four,
        Mary Shelley"; "Part Five, Last Attachments." In her *Shelley's Dream
        Women*. London: Cassell, 1967, pp. 81-139; 141-186; 187-249.
            MS discussed as Shelley's third "dream woman," one of "those im-
        possible beings conjured up in a world of fantasy." Sympathetic
        treatment; lacking in depth.
            Also published, N.Y.: A. S. Barnes, 1967.

A110   Cross, Wilbur L. *The Development of the English Novel*. N.Y.:
        Macmillan Company/London: Macmillan & Co., 1917, pp. 108, 158.
            "Mrs. Shelley created a monster on pseudo-scientific principles";
        "The inability to rival Mrs. Mary Shelley was one of the woes of Lord
        Byron."
            First published, 1899.

A111   Cross, Wilbur L. "Frankenstein." In *The Encyclopedia Americana*.
        N.Y.: Americana Corporation, 1957, Vol. XII, p. 5.
            MS "also lived to know that she had added a new word to the
        English language"—as Frankenstein has now come to mean a being
        "having no trace of the moral sense whatever."

A112   Davenport, Basil. *Inquiry into Science Fiction*. N.Y., London,
        Toronto: Longmans, Green and Co., 1955, pp. 19-20, 52.
            MS, "almost against her will . . . evoked [sympathy] for the
        monster she had set out to make purely horrible." Brief mention of
        the Monster as "literary ancestor" of the android-robots in Karel
        Capek's *R.U.R.*

A113   de Beer, [Sir] Gavin. Comments on Claire Clairmont's Journal. In
        Kenneth Neill Cameron, ed. *Shelley and his Circle 1773-1822*. 6 vols.
        Cambridge, Mass.: Harvard University Press, 1970, Vol. III, pp. 342-
        375 *passim*.
            Passing references to MS as viewed by Claire.

A114   De Camp, L[yon] Sprague. *Science Fiction Handbook*. *The Writing of
        Imaginative Fiction*. N.Y.: Hermitage House, 1953, pp. 41-42.
            Mention of *Frankenstein*'s impact "upon the whole field of imagi-
        native fiction."

A115   deF[ord], M[iriam] A[llen]. "Shelley, Mary Wollstonecraft Godwin."
        In Stanley J[asspon] Kunitz and Howard Haycraft, eds. *British Authors
        of the Nineteenth Century*. N.Y.: The H. W. Wilson Company, 1936, pp.
        555-556.
            Superficial comments: "There was too much of her father in Mary
        Shelley to make her completely a sympathetic character"; "there is a
        certain reminiscent strength in *Lodore*."

A116   Devonshire, M[arian] G[ladys]. *The English Novel in France 1830-1870*.
        London: University of London Press, 1929, p. 121.
            Mention of the 1821 French translation of *Frankenstein*: "Though
        of powerful conception, its publication had left no sign or trace in
        France at this period."†
            Facsimile reprint: N.Y.: Octagon Books, 1967.

A117 Dillard, R. H. W. "Even a Man Who Is Pure at Heart: Poetry and
      Danger in the Horror Film." In W. R. Robinson, ed. *Man and the
      Movies*. Baltimore: Penguin Books, 1969, pp. 60-96 [83-85].
         All the film versions of *Frankenstein*, especially *Bride of
      Frankenstein*, follow the novel to some degree, "but they have changed
      her rational and argumentative monster substantially and succeeded in
      transmuting a minor philosophical novel into a cinematic myth."
         First published, Baton Rouge: Louisiana State University Press,
      1967.

A118 Dillon, Arthur. "Shelley's Philosophy of Love." In *The Shelley
      Society's Papers*. 1st series, Part II. London: Published for The
      Shelley Society by Reeves and Turner, 1891, pp. 262-268 [265].
         Shelley's occasional complaints that "full sympathy was lacking in
      Mary Shelley" are not very manly, or just to her, and "smack hardly of
      love, perhaps more of the wish to be loved."

A119 Dobrée, Bonamy. "Introduction" to Ann Radcliffe. *The Mysteries of
      Udolpho. A Romance. Interspersed with some pieces of poetry*.
      London, Oxford, N.Y.: Oxford University Press, 1966, pp. vii-xvi
      [xiv-xv].
         Briefly notes that Radcliffe influenced *Frankenstein*.
         Reprinted, 1970.

A120 Dodson, Charles B. "Introduction" to Thomas Love Peacock. *Nightmare
      Abbey. The Misfortunes of Elphin. Crotchet Castle*. N.Y.: Holt,
      Rinehart and Winston, 1971, pp. vii-xxviii [xxiv].
         "Although Stella (Celinda Toobad) [in *Nightmare Abbey*] does
      provide Scythrop the kind of intellectual companionship that Shelley
      found in Mary Godwin, for whom he left his wife, Peacock gives her a
      physical appearance and mercurial temperament very different from
      Mary's."†
         See also F9.

A121 Donner, H[enry] W[olfgang]. *The Browning Box; or, The Life and Works
      of Thomas Lovell Beddoes as reflected in letters by his friends and
      admirers*. London: Oxford University Press, Humphrey Milford, 1935,
      pp. lxi-lxii, 18-19, 143, 144, 175.
         Two MS letters, one to Bryan Waller Procter, the other to Thomas
      Forbes Kelsall—both described on the later pages.

A122 Donner, H[enry] W[olfgang]. *Thomas Lovell Beddoes. The Making of a
      Poet*. Oxford: Basil Blackwell, 1935, pp. 65, 138.
         Pronounces Beddoes' *Leopold* "a not unworthy successor to *Franken-
      stein*," and states that an MS letter in A8 [II, 122] does *not* refer to
      Beddoes.

A123 Donohue, Joseph W., Jr. *Dramatic Character in the English Romantic
      Age*. Princeton, N.J.: Princeton University Press, 1970, pp. 166, 168.
         MS note to *The Cenci* about actress Eliza O'Neill did not state
      clearly enough that her acting "influenced the composition of the
      play."

A124   Dorland, W[illiam] A[lexander] Newman. *The Sum of Feminine Achieve-*
        ment. A Critical and Analytical Study of Woman's Contribution to the
        Intellectual Progress of the World. Boston: The Stratford Company,
        1917, pp. 45, 193-194, 225.
        Both *Frankenstein* and *Valperga* are "remarkable." A clinical chart
        (p. 225) lists MS "Duration of Mental Activity" as 34 years, and both
        her "Age at Beginning of Activity" and "Age at Acme of Ability" as 20.

A125   Douglas, Drake [pseud.]. "The Monster." In his *Horror!* N.Y.: Collier
        Books, 1969, pp. 77-129; and 5, 37.
        Combined retelling of the novel and film versions of *Frankenstein*,
        concentrating on the 1931 James Whale film. Interesting, but often
        confusing.
        First published, N.Y.: Macmillan Company/Toronto: Collier-Macmillan
        Canada, 1966.

        Dowden, Edward. *See Letters about Shelley*, A245.

A126   Dowden, Edward. *The Life of Percy Bysshe Shelley.* 2 vols. London:
        Kegan Paul, Trench & Co., 1886, Vol. I, pp. 306-534 *passim*.

        _____. Vol. II, pp. 6, 25, 33-538 *passim*; (on *Frankenstein*)
        35-36, 111, 115.
        Usually objective treatment of MS, always in connection with
        Shelley. Dowden's use of MS letters and journal was under the same
        restriction of Lady Shelley as that imposed upon Marshall [A8] and
        Moore [A10].
        See also A127.

A127   Dowden, Edward. *The Life of Percy Bysshe Shelley.* N.Y.: Barnes &
        Noble, 1966, pp. 157, 229-477 *passim*, 485, 497, 511-583 *passim*.
        Condensed one-volume edition of A126, with much deleted on MS.
        First published, London: Kegan Paul, Trench, Trübner and Co.,
        1896; reprinted, 1909.

A128   Dowse, Robert E., and D. J. Palmer. "Introduction" to Mary W.
        Shelley. *Frankenstein.* Everyman's Library, No. 616. London: J. M.
        Dent & Sons/N.Y.: Dutton, 1973, pp. v-xiii.
        Examination of Faust theme, Gothic "trappings," and "superficial
        didacticism" in the novel. "The strength of her story lies in its
        imaginative vision, not in the overt didacticism with which she over-
        lays it."
        Introduction first included in the 1965 edition.

A129   Duerksen, Roland A. *Shelleyan Ideas in Victorian Literature.* London,
        The Hague, Paris: Mouton & Co., 1966, pp. 20, 22, 138, 145.
        Random notes on MS: her note on evil in Shelley's *Prometheus
        Unbound* "an oversimplification"; she followed Peacock's lead (in his
        Nightmare Abbey) in presenting Shelley as a character in her novels;
        mention of Rossetti's praise of her in his sonnet, "Mary Shelley,
        1851"; she intended to publish Shelley's *Philosophical View of Reform*
        when she made a transcript of it.

A130   Ehrsam, Theodore G[eorge]. *Major Byron: The Incredible Career of a Literary Forger.* N.Y.: Charles S. Boesen/London: John Murray, 1951, pp. 19-32; 43; 49; 52 n. 61; 54; 55 & n. 13; 56-58; 62 n. 9; 75 & nn. 2, 5, & 6; 78 & n. 12; 79; 80 & n. 30; 82; 97; 98; 99 & n. 107; 116 & n. 2; 117; 118 & n. 15; 119; 120 & n. 21; 121-125; 133-136; 141; 169; 170; 173; 179; 180; 181 n. 15; 182; 187-189; 205-211.

Contends that MS bought forgeries of Shelley letters to her from "Major Byron" [Major George Gordon de Luna Byron]. Bibliography (pp. 193-201) includes locations of letters; pp. 205-211 list the forgeries chronologically.

A131   Eigner, Edwin M. *Robert Louis Stevenson and Romantic Tradition.* Princeton, N.J.: Princeton University Press, 1966, pp. 143-144, 161-164, 187.

Likens parts of *Frankenstein* to Conrad's Marlow and Stevenson's *Strange Case of Dr. Jekyll and Mr. Hyde.*

A132   Ellis, S[tewart] M[arsh]. *William Harrison Ainsworth and His Friends.* 2 vols. London: John Laine/N.Y.: John Laine Company, 1911, Vol. I, p. 122.

Ainsworth letter (March 25, 1825): "I met Mrs. Shelley at [Charles Lamb's] house the other evening. She is very handsome; I am going to the theatre with her some evening."†

A133   Elton, Charles I. "Chapter 2, Tour of 1814: France"; "Chapter 3, Tour of 1814: Switzerland and the Rhine"; "Chapter 4, Tour of 1816: The Lake of Geneva"; "Chapter 5, Tour of 1816: Chamouni." In his *An Account of Shelley's Visit to France, Switzerland and Savoy, in the years 1814 and 1816.* London: Bliss, Sands, & Foster, 1894, pp. 15-32; 33-44; 45-67; 68-104.

Although primarily geographical descriptions, noting the effects upon Shelley's imagination, much of this also refers to MS imagination, especially as reflected in *Frankenstein.* Especially valuable are pp. 37, 39, 47-48, 74-75, 85-87, 92, 95.

Limited to 50 copies; one at the Bodleian, one in the present author's collection.

A134   Elton, Oliver. *A Survey of English Literature 1780-1830.* 2 vols. N.Y.: Macmillan Company, 1924, Vol. I, pp. 216-217, 332.

In *Frankenstein,* "Mrs. Shelley's force of imagination is shown, and also strained to breaking point." Excerpt from and comment upon C9.

A135   English, Thomas H. "Shelley, Mary Wollstonecraft." In *Collier's Encyclopedia.* [N.Y.:] Crowell-Collier Educational Corporation, 1972, Vol. 20, p. 663.

Brief biographical sketch, noting that "the social philosophy of William Godwin pervades the tale [of *Frankenstein*]."

A136   *English Literary Manuscripts in the Boston Public Library: A Checklist.* Boston: Boston Public Library, 1966, p. 21.

Identifies two MS letters in the Boston Public Library.

A137 Evans, I[drisyn] O[liver]. Prefatory Note to Mary Shelley. "The Recalcitrant Robot." In his ed. *Science Fiction Through the Ages I*. London: Panther Books, 1966, p. 104.

The note to this excerpt from *Frankenstein* classifies it and *The Last Man* as science fiction.

A138 Ewbank, Inga-Stina. "Frankenstein." In *The Encyclopedia Americana*. International Edition. N.Y.: The Americana Corporation, 1974, Vol. 12, pp. 4-5.

MS novel is rarely read and is "absurd and technically crude." The philosophy of education and evil, however, is "a forerunner of modern science fiction."

A139 Eyles, Allen, Robert Adkinson, and Nicholas Fry, eds. *The House of Horror. The Story of Hammer Films*. London: Lorrimer Publishing, 1973, pp. 14, 20, 29-30.

Remarks by director Terence Fisher and actor Peter Cushing concerning their approaches to film versions of *Frankenstein*. For *Curse of Frankenstein* (1957), Jimmy Sangster based his screenplay on the MS novel.

A140 Fairclough, Peter. Notes to Mary Shelley. *Frankenstein*. In his ed. *Three Gothic Novels*. Harmondsworth, Middlesex: Penguin Books, 1968, pp. 502-505.

Identifies literary allusions in the novel.

Reprinted, 1970, 1972, 1973.

A141 Flexner, Eleanor. *Mary Wollstonecraft. A Biography*. N.Y.: Coward, McCann & Geoghagen, 1972, pp. 251-252, 257-259, 260-262, 283.

Notes the influence of her mother upon MS, and compares the two: unlike Mary Wollstonecraft, MS "was extremely ambivalent regarding 'equal rights' for women."

A142 Florescu, Radu, and Raymond T. McNally. "Dracula in Literature—From Hero to Vampire." In their *Dracula. A Biography of Vlad the Impaler 1431-1476*. N.Y.: Hawthorn Books/Scarborough, Ontario: Prentice-Hall of Canada, 1973, pp. 137-161 [153].

"Mary Shelley wrote [*Frankenstein*] to show in a sympathetic way the failure of a would-be scientific savior of mankind. . . . [But] the public turned it all upside down."†

Floss, Robert. *See* Kaplan, Morton, A229.

A143 Forman, H[arry] Buxton. "Introduction" to Percy Bysshe Shelley. *The Mask of Anarchy, Written on the Occasion at Manchester. Fac-simile of the Holograph Manuscript*. Shelley Society Publications, Extra Series, No. 4. London: Published for The Shelley Society by Reeves and Turner, 1887, pp. 1-48 [36-43].

The biographical significance of the characters in *The Last Man*. See also A147.

A144 Forman, H[arry] Buxton, ed. *Note Books of Percy Bysshe Shelley. From the originals in the library of W. K. Bixby.* 3 vols. The Bibliophile Society. St. Louis, Mo.: Privately Printed for William K. Bixby, 1911, Vol. I, pp. 87, 89-91, 108-109, 119-120, 122-124, 128, 159, 173-175, 176, 191, 192.

_____. Vol. II, pp. 4, 5, 6, 7, 8, 10, 13, 14, 17-18, 27-28, 35, 39, 49, 51, 52, 53, 56, 58-60, 64-65, 68, 69-71, 75, 78, 79, 84, 103-105, 123, 181-183.

_____ Vol. III, pp. 22-23, 25-26, 30, 32, 35-36, 46, 48, 50, 53-62, 67-70, 73-74, 96, 99, 130, 133-135.
        Though generally favorable in his comments upon MS, Forman supposes her to have made many critical errors—human ones—in her editing of Shelley's works. Corrections are made of her mistakes.

A145 Forman, H[arry] Buxton. Notes to Percy Bysshe Shelley. *The Works of Percy Bysshe Shelley, in verse and prose.* 8 vols. London: Reeves and Turner, 1880, Vol. I, pp. xlii, cxvi.
        MS notes to Shelley's works are "of the highest value, and form."

_____. Vol. II, p. 432 n. 1.
        Significance of MS letter to Emilia Viviani.

_____. Vol. IV, p. 34 n. 1.
        Shelley wrote the hymns in *Midas* at the request of Edward Williams.

_____. Vol. VI, p. 116.
        Bibliographical description of *History of a Six Weeks' Tour*, excerpts from which are printed, pp. 117-204.

A146 Forman, H[arry] Buxton. Prefatory Note and Notes to Mary Wollstone-craft Shelley. *The Choice. A Poem on Shelley's Death by Mary Woll-stonecraft Shelley.* London: Printed for the editor for private distribution, 1876, pp. 5, 7, 8, 9-10, 13, 14.
        Explains the origin of the poem, found "among the Shelley poems of Leigh Hunt." Biographical references noted.
        Limited to 150 copies.
        Facsimile reprint: Folcroft, Pa.: Folcroft Library Editions, 1972.

A147 Forman, H[arry] Buxton. "Shelley, 'Peterloo,' and The Mask of Anarchy." In *The Shelley Society's Papers.* 1st series, Part I. London: Published for The Shelley Society by Reeves and Turner, 1889, pp. 81-101 [84, 87-88, 89-98].
        Corrections of MS editing of the works, the biographical signifi-cance of the characters in *The Last Man*, and the connection between Perdita and the holograph *Mask of Anarchy*.
        Uses material from A143.

A148 Forman, H[arry] Buxton. *The Shelley Library: An Essay in Bibliog-raphy.* London: Reeves and Turner, 1886, pp. 44-45, 70-71, 109.
        Annotated listings of MS copy of Shelley's *Queen Mab* and *History of a Six Weeks' Tour*, and printing of MS letter to publisher Ollier

concerning publication of Shelley's *Posthumous Poems*.
Facsimile reprint: N.Y.: Haskell House, 1971.

A149 Forman, H[arry] Buxton. "The Vicissitudes of Queen Mab, A Chapter in
the History of Reform." In *The Shelley Society's Papers*. 1st series,
Part I. London: Published for The Shelley Society by Reeves and
Turner, 1889, pp. 19-35 [23].
Shelley "was as powerless to check [*Queen Mab*'s] vitality as his
wife's imaginary Frankenstein was to unmake the monster he had made."†

A150 "The Frankenstein Story." In Forrest J. Ackerman, ed. *The Best from
Famous Monsters of Filmland*. N.Y.: Paperback Library, 1964, pp. 46-
63.
Reprinting of B88.
First published in this form, June 1964; reprinted, June and
July 1964.

A151 Freye, Walter. *The Influence of "Gothic" Literature on Sir Walter
Scott*. Rostock: H. Winterberg's Buchdruckerei, 1902, p. 12.
Frankenstein is termed "another of these more ghastly produc-
tions," but no influence upon Scott is mentioned.

A152 Friederich, Werner P[aul]. *Dante's Fame Abroad 1350-1850. The
Influence of Dante Alighieri on the Poets and Scholars of Spain,
France, England, Germany, Switzerland, and the United States. A
Survey of the Present State of Scholsrship*. Rome: Storia e Littera-
tura/Chapel Hill, N.C.: University of North Carolina Press, 1950,
p. 277.
Notes a Dantean reference in *Frankenstein*, and MS mention of
reading *Purgatorio* and *Paradiso* in her *Rambles*.

Fry, Nicholas. *See* Eyles, Allen, A139.

A153 Fuller, Jean Overton. *Shelley: A Biography*. London: Jonathan Cape,
1968, pp. 125, 143-145, 148-149, 153-156, 159, 162-163, 166, 168, 169,
171, 172, 173-178, 179, 180, 183-186, 192-193, 195-196, 197, 202-207,
209, 214, 219, 227-234, 240, 246-251, 253, 255-256, 259-260, 263-264,
267, 268, 272, 274, 277, 279-280, 281-288, 290-291, 297-299, 305, 311-
314; (references to MS works) 183, 306, 320 & n. 4, 329.
Occasionally new slants on MS life, and worthwhile but scarce
criticism of the novels: section of *Perkin Warbeck* is paralleled with
Shelley's proposal to MS at Mary Wollstonecraft's grave (p. 320 n. 4).

A154 *The Future. Science Fiction Book Exhibit. Presented by Houston Public
Library in connection with Houston Arts Festival October 1968*. n.p.
[ca. 1968], unpaginated.
Category of "Man and Machines" contains the 1818 *Frankenstein* as
Item 1: "Entwined throughout the story are the themes of scientific
curiosity and the loneliness of those who are different."

Garnett, R. S. *See Letters about Shelley*, A245.

A155 Garnett, Richard, and [Sir] Edmund Gosse. *From the Age of Johnson to the Age of Tennyson*. Vol. II of their *English Literature. An Illustrated Record in Four Volumes*. N.Y.: Grosset & Dunlap, 1904, pp. 126-127, 181, 182-183.
      Frankenstein is termed (probably by Garnett) "a ghastly romance." Brief bibliography on MS.

A156 Garnett, Richard. "Introduction" to Thomas Love Peacock. *Headlong Hall and Nightmare Abbey*. London, Toronto: J. M. Dent & Sons/N.Y.: E. P. Dutton, 1929, pp. 7-42 [19].
      The problem in resolving Shelley's conduct when he forsook Harriet for MS is "exceedingly simple": if he had transferred his affections elsewhere before seeing MS, he cannot be blamed.

A157 Garnett, Richard. "Introduction" to Mary Wollstonecraft Shelley. *Tales and Stories*. London: William Paterson, 1891, pp. v-xiii.
      Brief discussion of *Frankenstein* and *The Last Man*, and the stories (pp. ix-xiii), in which "the theme is always interesting, and the sequence of events natural."
      Facsimile reprint supposedly by Folcroft, Pa.: Folcroft Press, n.d., but actually only re-binding of 1891 ed.

A158 Garnett, Richard. "Introduction" to Edward Ellerker Williams. *Journal of Edward Ellerker Williams. Companion of Shelley and Byron in 1821 and 1822*. London: Elkin Mathews, 1902, pp. 1-12 [4-5].
      The diary was originally given to MS by Jane Williams, and MS "copied a considerable portion, probably for use in a [contemplated] biography of Shelley."
      Facsimile reprints: Folcroft, Pa.: Folcroft Press, 1970; Havertown, Pa.: Richard West, 1973.
      See also A441.

      Garnett, Richard. *See Letters about Shelley*, A245.

A159 Garnett, Richard, ed. *Relics of Shelley*. London: Edward Moxon, 1862, pp. 109-111, 114-144, 191.
      MS letters to Leigh and Marianne Hunt, and her postscript to a Shelley letter to Hunt.

A160 G[arnett], R[ichard]. "Shelley, Mary Wollstonecraft." In Sir Leslie Stephen and Sir Sidney Lee, eds. *The Dictionary of National Biography*. Oxford University Press, 1921-1922, Vol. XVIII, pp. 29-31.
      Undistinguished biographical sketch, including an oft-quoted sentence: "Nothing but an absolute magetizing of her brain by Shelley's can account for her having risen so far above her usual self as in 'Frankenstein.'"

A161 Gerald, Gregory Fitz, and Jack C. Wolf. "Introduction" to their eds. *Past, Present, and Future Perfect. A Text Anthology of Speculative and Science Fiction*. A Fawcett Premier Book. Greenwich, Conn.: Fawcett Publications, 1973, pp. 14-19 [15, 16].
      Brief comments on *Frankenstein* and *The Last Man*: the former, although often labeled Gothic literature, "is solid science fiction.

And the number of stories derivative from it is growing daily." Nevil
Shute's *On the Beach* (1957) is "a direct descendant of *The Last Man*."

A162 Gerould, Gordon Hall. *The Patterns of English and American Fiction.*
A History. N.Y.: Russell & Russell, 1966, pp. 188-189.
Frankenstein is MS only achievement. Victor Frankenstein fails
not because of "egoistic pride but [because of] the hope of benefiting
mankind," and the Monster "is a compound modeled after the villains of
Brockden Brown."
First published, Boston: Little, Brown, 1942.

A163 Gettman, Royal A[lfred]. *A Victorian Publisher. A Study of the*
Bentley Papers. Cambridge at the University Press, 1966, pp. 232,
234.
"[An agreement] with Mary Shelley for *Perkin Warbeck* called for
three volumes with '320 pages at least' in each"; "Mary Shelley's
Frankenstein, published in 1818, numbers only 67,150 words."†

*A164 Gibbon, Charles, ed. *The Casquet of Literature: Being a Selection in*
Poetry and Prose from the Works of the most admired Authors. London:
Blackie and Son, 1873, Vol. 3, pp. 353-359.
Comment on reprinting of "The Mortal Immortal."
de Palacio [El, p. 675, Item 177 *bis*] quotes Gibbon presenting the
story as "a specimen of Mrs. Shelley's eerie powers of imagination."
Not in the Library of Congress or the Bodleian.

A165 Gibson, Strickland. "Chapter XV, Bibliographica." In Frederick S.
Boas, ed. *The Year's Work in English Studies. 1948*. London: Oxford
University Press, 1950, Vol. XXIX, pp. 272-283 [280-281].
Description of 23 MS letters from the collection of Major R. J.
Jefferson Hogg, recently sold at auction.

A166 Gifford, Denis. "The Monster." In his *Movie Monsters*. London:
Studio Vista, 1969, pp. 9-37.
Description of selected plays and films based on *Frankenstein*.

A167 Gifford, Denis. *A Pictorial History of Horror Movies*. London: The
Hamlyn Publishing Group, 1973, p. 114.
Description of characters in the prologue to the film *Bride of*
Frankenstein: "Lord Byron ([played by] Gavin Gordon) muses over
Mary's morality of the Modern Prometheus: 'I relish each separate
horror . . . I roll them over on my tongue.'"

A168 Gilfillan, George. "Mrs. Shelley." In his *Second Gallery of Literary*
Portraits. Edinburgh: James Hogg, 1850, pp. 194-203.
Reprint of B95.
Also published, London: R. Groombridge & Sons, 1852.
See also B93, B94.

A169 Godwin, William. Letter. In his *Memoirs of Mary Wollstonecraft*.
London: Constable/N.Y.: Greenberg, 1927, pp. 333-334.
Letter to publisher Ollier (April 3, 1835) concerning *Lodore*.

A170 Gordon, Armistead C[hurchill]. *Allegra. The Story of Byron and Miss Clairmont.* N.Y.: Minton, Balch & company, 1926, pp. 101-103, 106, 109, 110, 143-145, 191-192, 194-195.

Generally unsympathetic remarks on MS, noting that she had offered Claire an excuse for her conduct with Byron in her own relations with Shelley, and that she never really liked Claire.

Facsimile reprint: N.Y.: Haskell House, 1973.

Gosse, [Sir] Edmund. *See* Garnett, Richard, A155.

A171 Gosse, [Sir] Edmund. "Memoir" [or "Introduction"] In his ed. Thomas Lovell Beddoes. *The Poetical Works of Thomas Lovell Beddoes.* 2 vols. Temple Library. London: J. M. Dent & Co., 1890, Vol. I, p. xxxvii.

"For many years in and out of season, Beddoes, who had pledged his whole soul to the finishing of ["Death's Jest-Book"], assailed it with all the instruments of his art, and at last produced a huge dramatic Frankenstein, which, by adroit editing, could be forced into the likeness of a tragedy."†

For review, see B276.

A172 Gosse, [Sir] Edmund. "Shelley's Widow." In his *Silhouettes.* N.Y.: Charles Scribner's Sons [1925], pp. 229-238.

Uncomplimentary remarks on MS, with superficial comments on the biographical elements in *The Last Man.*

A173 Gotlieb, Howard B. *William Beckford of Fonthill: Writer, Traveller, Collector, Caliph, 1760-1844: A Brief Narrative and Catalogue of an Exhibition to Mark the Two Hundredth Anniversary of Beckford's Birth.* New Haven, Conn.: Yale University Library, 1960, pp. 60-61.

"Beckford had written a note on the flyleaf [of his copy of *Frankenstein*] stating that 'This is, perhaps, the foulest toadstool that has yet sprung up from the reeking dunghill of the present times.'"

A174 Goulianos, Joan. "Mary Shelley." In her ed. *by a woman writt. Literature from Six Centuries By and About Women.* Baltimore: Penguin Books, 1974, pp. 165-197 [165].

Biographical sketch. The selections from MS journal (pp. 165-188) show how MS "felt isolated and helpless without [Shelley]"; the excerpt from *The Last Man* (pp. 188-197) testifies that "as if she believed a woman's loneliness was not an important enough subject for fiction—she chose as her main character a man." Occasional notes.

First published, Indianapolis: Bobbs-Merrill, 1973.

A175 Grabo, Carl [Henry]. *The Magic Plant. The Growth of Shelley's Thought.* Chapel Hill, N.C.: The University of North Carolina Press, 1936, pp. 58, 96, 129, 131-132, 134, 143, 148, 171, 184, 189, 192, 202-203, 206, 214, 228, 232, 234-235, 237, 267-268, 271, 273, 275, 277, 285, 292, 295, 324, 327, 329, 330, 333, 337, 341-346, 351-352, 365, 373-378, 380-381, 395, 397-399, 403, 412, 415-416, 419.

MS in connection with Shelley and his poetry. Unfortunately, "she had but a hazy notion of [his ideas]."

A176 Graham, William. *Last Links with Byron, Shelley, and Keats*.
London: Leonard Smithers & Co., 1898, pp. 1-63 *passim*.
Reprinting of B106. White [A436, II, 570] notes that this
book is "regarded by most Shelleyans as untrustworthy, or worse."
Facsimile reprint: Folcroft, Pa.: Folcroft Press, 1969.

A177 Graniss, Ruth S. *A Descriptive Catalogue of the First Editions in
Book Form of the Writings of Percy Bysshe Shelley*. Based on a
*memorial exhibition held at the Grolier Club from April 20 to May 20,
1922*. N.Y.: Grolier Club, 1923, pp. 44-45, 56, 81, 105-106, 110-111,
117-119.
Descriptions of *History of a Six Weeks' Tour*, Forman's copy of
The Cenci with a list of errata in MS handwriting, MS and Shelley
notebook, MS and Shelley letters to Claire Clairmont, other MS
letters, and eight leaves of *Valperga* manuscript.

A178 Gribble, Francis Henry. *Romantic Life of Shelley and the Sequel*.
N.Y.: G. P. Putnam's Sons, 1911, pp. 185, 207, 209-215, 221-223, 224-
255, 268-275, 279-280, 282-283, 285-286, 287, 288-290, 294, 297-298,
300-304, 309, 311-312, 315-316, 320-328, 329-331, 333, 335, 337-348,
350-354, 359-384.
A popular account of MS-Shelley relationship, with most attention
paid to potentially sordid affairs. "The Choice" is "as formal as
one can expect a confession in verse to be."

A179 Grylls, R[osalie] Glynn [Lady Mander]. *Claire Clairmont. Mother
of Byron's Allegra*. London: John Murray, 1939, pp. 254-256, 281-284.
Reflections on MS-Claire relationship; MS letter to Alexander
Burry.

A180 Grylls, R[osalie] Glynn [Lady Mander]. *Trelawny*. London: Constable,
1950, pp. 26, 33 n. 1, 72-76, 82, 92, 96, 98, 100, 101, 103-104, 114,
115, 121, 129, 137, 140, 143, 146, 149, 151, 153, 154-156, 160-163,
166, 173-175, 176, 194-195, 196-197, 201-202, 208, 212, 228, 229,
243.
MS-Trelawny relationship, including consideration of his change
of attitude towards MS in his *Records* [A419]. More detailed on this
relationship than in A6.

A181 Haining, Peter. "Introduction" to Mary Wollstonecraft Shelley.
"The Dream." In his ed. *Great British Tales of Terror. Gothic
Stories of Horror and Romance 1765-1840*. London: Victor Gollancz,
1972, pp. 287-288.
MS is at home with the short story: *Frankenstein* is laborious
in parts, probably as a result of the expansion of the shorter draft
at Shelley's urging; but "The Dream" is "a fine example of the
Gothic romance story dating from the hey-day of the genre."
Reprinted, Harmondsworth, Middlesex: Penguin Books, 1973 (pp.
327-328).

A182   Haining, Peter. Prefatory Notes to Mary Shelley. "The Monster
        Lives!"; Wallace West. "The Incubator Man"; Isaac Asimov. "Robot
        AL-76 Goes Astray"; and Carol Emshwiller. "Baby." In his ed. *The
        Monster Makers*. London: Victor Gollancz, 1974, pp. 17-18; 138-139
        [139]; 252-253; 270-271.
            The selection from Chapter V of *Frankenstein* is, as MS originally
        thought, complete in itself; the links between West's story and
        Frankenstein "are very clear"; Asimov's inspiration for his story
        was *Frankenstein* [cf. A36]; Emshwiller's story employs "Miss
        Shelley's [sic] original concept of the being created hopefully to
        serve, and extended to its logical—or perhaps illogical—conclusion."
            For younger readers.

A183   Halleck, Reuben Post. *Halleck's New English Literature*. N.Y.:
        American Book Company, 1913, p. 442.
            "Mrs. Shelley put some of her most sacred mementos of the poet
        [Shelley] between the leaves of *Adonais*, which spoke to her of his
        own immortality and omnipresence."†

A184   *Hand-List of Manuscripts, Letters, Printed Books and Personal Relics
        of Percy Bysshe Shelley and His Circle. Exhibited in the Guildhall
        Library, London. (By Permission of the Library Committee). July 11-
        29, 1893*. London: Blades, East and Blades, 1893, pp. 3, 4, 5, 6, 7,
        8, 10, 13, 16, 25.
            Bibliographical descriptions of MS works and editions of
        Shelley's poetry; descriptions of six MS letters, one from Peacock
        to MS, and one of Jane Williams on MS death.
            Limited to 50 copies; one in the Bodleian.

A185   Harding, D. W. "The Character of Literature from Blake to Byron."
        In Boris Ford, ed. *From Blake to Byron*. Vol. 5 of *The Pelican
        Guide to English Literature*. 7 vols. Harmondsworth, Middlesex:
        Penguin Books, 1957, pp. 45-46.
            Frankenstein illustrates the characteristics of early 19th-
        century literature in its use of typically Romantic scenery and the
        ideal family of cottagers.

A186   Harding, Walter. *Emerson's Library*. Charlottesville, Va.: Univer-
        sity Press of Virginia, 1967, pp. 247-248.
            Identifies Vol. I of the Philadelphia edition of MS French
        Lives in Emerson's collection.

A187   H[ardy], B. "Shelley, Mary Wollstonecraft." In S. H. Steinberg,
        ed. *Cassell's Encyclopedia of World Literature*. 2 vols. N.Y.:
        Funk & Wagnalls, 1954, Vol. II, pp. 1476-1477.
            Frankenstein is "an extraordinary cross between the novel of
        terror and a Godwinian tract."

A188   Harper, Henry H[oward]. "Introduction" to *Letters of Mary W.
        Shelley (Mostly Unpublished)*. Boston: Printed only for Members of
        the Bibliophile Society [Norwood, Mass.: The Plimpton Press], 1918,
        pp. 7-28.
            Glowing comments on MS, noting that her correspondence "shows

her to have been a keen observer, of unusual perceptive faculties,
a critic of art, literature, the drama, and especially the opera."
Justifies printing the letters because they shed new light on other
"luminaries."
Limited to 448 copies. Facsimile reprint: Folcroft, Pa.:
Folcroft Library Editions, 1972.
See also A189.

A189   Harper, Henry Howard. "Mary Wollstonecraft Shelley." In his
*Literary Essays about Books, Bibliographies, Writers and Kindred
Subjects*. Boston: Printed only for Private Distribution, 1924,
pp. 39-57.
Revised version of A188, new material touching on MS influence
on Shelley (pp. 41-42), "Mary's daring exploit [the elopement] with
Shelley" (p. 53), and Payne's courting of MS (p. 56).
Facsimile reprint: Folcroft, Pa.: Folcroft Press, 1972.

A190   H[arper], H[enry] H[oward]. "Prefatory" to [Franklin Benjamin
Sanborn, ed.] *The Romance of Mary W. Shelley, John Howard Payne and
Washington Irving*. Boston: The Bibliophile Society; Printed for
Members Only, 1907, pp. 9-12.
Explains the origin of the letters.

A191   Hart, Frances Russell. "The Experience of Character in the English
Gothic Novel." In Roy Harvey Pearce, ed. *Experience in the Novel.
Selected Papers from the English Institute*. N.Y., London: Columbia
University Press, 1968, pp. 84-105 [92, 95, 96-97].
Briefly compares *Frankenstein* and Maturin's *Melmoth the Wanderer*,
pronouncing the former a novel of "ambiguous demonology." Many
questions, few answers.

A192   Harvey, Alexander. *Shelley's Elopement. A Study of the Most
Romantic Episode in Literary History*. N.Y.: Alfred A. Knopf, 1918,
pp. 269-271.
Biographical sketch influenced by Trelawny's hostile reflections
[in A419]. (Rest of book, in novel-like format, treats MS as the
villain in the elopement.)

A193   Harvey, Sir Paul. "Frankenstein." In his ed. *The Oxford Companion
to English Literature*. Dorothy Eagle, rev. Fourth edition. Oxford,
N.Y.: Oxford University Press, 1967, p. 312.
The novel is termed "a tale of terror."

A194   Häusermann, H[ans] W[alter]. *The Genevese Background. Studies of
Shelley, Francis Danby, Maria Edgeworth, Ruskin, Meredith, and Joseph
Conrad in Geneva (with hitherto unpublished letters)*. London:
Routledge and Kegan Paul, 1952, p. 6.
Identifies MS description of the Villa Diodati in *Frankenstein*.

A195 Haweis, the Rev. H[ugh] R[eginald]. "Introduction" to Mrs. Shelley.
Frankenstein or the Modern Prometheus. Routledge's World Library.
London: George Routledge and Sons, 1886, pp. 5-8.
        Although the subject of the novel is revolting, the treatment
hideous, the execution unequal, and the construction and plot weak,
the *mise en scene* is admirable and the natural descriptions very
imaginative. Admits to issuing the novel "with some degree of hesi-
tation."

A196 Hayward, Abraham. *A Selection from the Correspondence of Abraham
Hayward, Q. C., from 1934 to 1984. With an Account of His Early
Life.* Henry E. Carlisle, ed. 2 vols. London: John Murray, 1886,
Vol. I, pp. 82-84.
        MS letter to Hayward (Nov. 1840).

A197 Heilbrun, Carolyn G. *The Garnett Family.* N.Y.: Macmillan Company,
1961, pp. 52-57.
        Recounts Richard Garnett's role in the preparation of A382, and
mentions a notebook, "which had been kept by Mary in a casket with
Shelley's heart and the hair of the two children they had lost, [and
which Garnett] gave to his friend Violet Kneale." (Notebook now in
the Library of Congress.)

A198 Herford, C[harles] H[arold]. *The Age of Wordsworth.* Handbooks of
English Literature. London: George Bell and Sons, 1897, pp. 97-98.
        Frankenstein belongs more to Godwin's *St. Leon* than to the
school of M. G. Lewis, and *The Last Man* shadows MS "own tragic
loneliness."
        Reprinted, 1901. Facsimile reprint of 1897 ed.: Freeport,
N.Y.: Books for Libraries, 1971.

A199 Herford, C[harles] H[arold]. "Chapter III, Shelley." In Sir A. W.
Ward and A. R. Waller, eds. *The Nineteenth Century.* Vol. XII of
The Cambridge History of English Literature. Cambridge at the
University Press, 1961, pp. 63-86 [69].
        In Shelley's *Rosalind and Helen*, "Helen's lover fades and dies
as Shelley and Mary believed was soon to be his own destiny."

A200 Herford, C[harles] H[arold]. "Chapter XI, The Nineteenth Century
and After. Poets. Part I. Shelley." In Sir Sidney Lee and
F[rederick] S. Boas, eds. *The Year's Work in English Studies. 1922.*
London: Humphrey Milford, Oxford University Press, 1923, pp. 164-207
[178].
        "Shelley also supervised [MS] work [in *Proserpine* and *Midas*],
and the present writer suspects in at least one passage his actual
hand."

A201 Hewlett, Maurice [Henry]. "The Children Who Ran Away." In his
Wiltshire Essays. Oxford: Oxford University Press, Humphrey Milford,
1923, pp. 198-209.
        Extremely emotional account of the MS-Shelley elopement, the
point of which, apparently, is that MS was badly treated by Shelley.

A202   Higginson, Thomas Wentworth, and Henry Walcott Boynton. *A Reader's History of American Literature*. Boston, N.Y., Chicago: Houghton, Mifflin, 1903, pp. 71-72.
"Mrs. Shelley, in her novel of *The Last Man* founds her whole description of an epidemic, which nearly destroys the human race, on 'the masterly delineations of the author of *Arthur Mervyn*.'"

A203   Hill, R[eginald] H[arrison]. *The Shelley Correspondence in the Bodleian Library. Letters of Percy Bysshe Shelley and others, mainly unpublished, from the collection presented to the Library by Lady Shelley in 1892*. Oxford: Printed for the Bodleian Library by J. Johnson, 1926, pp. vii-xv, 10, 11-12, 15-20, 41-42, 44-45.
Chronological table of Shelley letters to MS, and MS letters to Shelley, Maria Gisborne, and John Parke.

A204   Hoffman, Harold Leroy. *An Odyssey of the Soul. Shelley's Alastor*. N.Y.: Columbia University Press, 1933, pp. 3-4, 62.
Brief discussion of MS in Shelley's poems; *History of a Six Weeks' Tour* is a record mainly of MS impressions, not Shelley's.
Originally dissertation; see D9.

A205   Hogg, Thomas Jefferson. *The Life of Shelley*. In *The Life of Percy Bysshe Shelley. As Comprised in* The Life of Shelley *by Thomas Jefferson Hogg.* The Recollections of Shelley and Byron *by Edward John Trelawny.* Memoirs of Shelley *by Thomas Love Peacock.* 2 vols. London, Toronto: J. M. Dent and Sons/N.Y.: E. P. Dutton, 1933, Vol. II, p. 148.
Hogg's first view of MS: "A very young female, fair and fair-haired, pale indeed, and with a piercing look." Hogg states that he will "have much to say hereafter" of MS, but he never wrote his intended sequel, ending his present account before the MS-Shelley elopement.
First published as *The Life of Percy Bysshe Shelley*. 2 vols. London: Edward Moxon, 1858. Some early issues have "In Four Volumes" on the title-pages, but only two volumes were published. Also published, Edward Dowden, ed. London: George Routledge & Sons/N.Y.: E. P. Dutton, 1906; N.Y.: Scholarly Press, 1971; Havertown, Pa.: Richard West, 1973; Folcroft, Pa.: Folcroft Press, 1973.

A206   Horne, R[ichard] H[enry]. "Mrs. Shelley." In his ed. *A New Spirit of the Age*. N.Y.: Harper & Brothers, 1844, pp. 407-414.
Frankenstein is contrasted with "the delightful fiction of Peter Schlemihl" and William Howitt's stories in *Pantika*. Brief remarks on *Valperga* and *Falkner*: "Mrs. Shelley's plots are always of deep interest."
Also published, London: H. Frowde, Oxford University Press, 1907. For review, see B320.

A207   Houston, Percy Hazen. *Main Currents of English Literature. A Brief Literary History of the English People*. Revised edition. N.Y.: F. S. Crofts, 1934, pp. 253, 294.
Frankenstein is "the most fantastic and grewsome [of all the

Gothic Romances]." Also brief biographical sketch.
Revised edition first published, 1926.

A208   Howard, Leon. *Herman Melville. A Biography.* Berkeley, Los
Angeles: University of California Press, 1951, p. 223.
"As an author, [Melville] had created such Frankenstein monsters
as Captain Ahab and Pierre, who had seriously damaged his reputation
even though they had not slain him as the architect Bannadonna [in
"The Bell-Tower"] had been slain by his mechanical creature who
seemed alive."†
Also published, London: Cambridge Press, 1951. California Press
ed. reprinted, 1958 (same pagination as above). Also published,
Minneapolis: University of Minnesota Press, 1961.

A209   [Hubbard, Elbert.] "Mary W. Shelley." In his *Little Journeys to the
Homes of Famous Women.* N.Y., London: G. P. Putnam's Sons, 1897, pp.
395-429 [398, 401-402, 408, 415-417, 418-429].
Overdramatized account of MS and Shelley until the latter's
death: "Their eyes met, and they smiled just a little" while at the
grave of Mary Wollstonecraft. *Frankenstein* was written "under the
immediate spell of Shelley's presence."
Originally issued in monthly parts, of which this was No. 12.
Also published, East Aurora, N.Y.: The Roycrofters, 1908.

A210   Hunt, [James Henry] Leigh. *The Autobiography of Leigh Hunt, with
Reminiscences of Friends and Contemporaries.* J. E. Morpurgo, ed.
London: The Cresset Press, 1949, pp. 266, 349, 368.
MS mentioned only in passing, marrying Shelley and returning to
England in 1823.
First published, 2 vols. London: Smith, Elder & Co., 1850; re-
printed, 1872, 1891. Also published, 2 vols. N.Y.: Harper &
Brothers, 1850; Roger Ingpen, ed. Westminster: A. Constable, 1903;
London: Humphrey Milford, Oxford University Press, 1928. Facsimile
reprint of Thornton Hunt's 1859 revised ed.: N.Y.: AMS Press, 1969.

A211   Hunt, [James Henry] Leigh. *The Correspondence of Leigh Hunt.*
Thornton Hunt, ed. 2 vols. London: Smith, Elder & Co., 1862, Vol.
I.
MS letters to Hunt: pp. 112-113, 142-144, 160, 176-177, 238-
244, 252-253.
Hunt letters to MS: pp. 119-130, 132-136, 145-149, 154-155,
163-167, 171-176, 181-182, 184-185.
References to MS in other Hunt letters: pp. 119 (on *Franken-
stein*), 130, 131, 142, 153, 157, 162, 169, 179, 180, 182, 184, 187,
195, 196-197, 208, 211.
MS often referred to as "Marina"; after Shelley's death, as
"Mrs. Shelley."

A212   Hunt, [James Henry] Leigh. *Lord Byron and Some of his Contempora-
ries; with Recollections of the Author's Life, and of His Visit to
Italy.* London: Henry Colburn, 1828, pp. 61, 176-177, 186, 190 n.,
193, 238-239, 242.
MS mentioned in passing.
Facsimile reprint: N.Y.: AMS Press, 1966.

A213 Huss, Roy. "Almost Eve: The Creation Scene in *The Bride of Frank-*
enstein." In his and T. J. Ross, eds. *Focus on the Horror Film.*
A Spectrum Book. Englewood Cliffs, N.J.: Prentice-Hall, 1972, pp.
74-82 [75-76].
Similarities are pointed out between the creation scenes in MS
novel and James Whale's 1935 film: "it seems as if Whale were
trying, in spite of his satiric undertone, to bring his sequel [to
the 1931 film] closer than his first film to the spirit of its
literary inspiration."

A214 Hutton, Laurence. "Percy Bysshe Shelley." In his *Literary Land-*
marks of London. Boston: Ticknor and Company, 1888, pp. 271-272.
Notes addresses of Shelley and MS, and of St. Pancras Graveyard.
First published, Boston: J. R. Osgood and Company, 1885. Also
published, N.Y.: Harper & Brothers, 1892.

A215 Ingpen, Roger. *Shelley in England. New Facts and Letters from the*
Shelley-Whitton Papers. London: Kegan Paul, Trench, Trübner & Co.,
1917, pp. 56, 376, 398, 433-434, 436-437, 438, 444, 445-446, 454,
455, 462, 466-467, 469, 473-474, 484, 487, 488-490, 498, 501, 505-
506, 517-518, 519, 521-522, 523-526, 528, 529, 533, 534-536, 540,
542, 543, 546, 560, 562-569, 571, 572-576, 579, 580, 583, 585-586,
591-598, 601-602, 604, 606, 608-609, 613-614, 615-616, 618-622, 623-
624, 652.
New slants and some new facts on MS, especially in the "Alle-
gation of P. B. Shelley and Wm. Godwin" concerning MS marriage
(p. 652).
Facsimile reprint: Havertown, Pa.: Richard West, 1973.

A216 "Introduction" to Mary W. Shelley. *Frankenstein, or the Modern*
Prometheus. Everyman's Library, No. 616. London, Toronto: J. M.
Dent & Sons/N.Y.: E. P. Dutton, 1912, pp. vii-xii [vii, xii].
Brief superficial comments before excerpt from MS 1831 Intro-
duction, mentioning *Valperga, The Last Man,* and *Lodore;* bibliography
after.
Possible author of Introduction is Ernest Rhys, general editor
of the Everyman series.
Everyman ed. with this Introduction reprinted, 1922, 1927, 1930,
1933, 1945, 1949, 1951. Introduction also published (without ac-
knowledgement) in Mary W. Shelley. *Frankenstein or, The Modern*
Prometheus. Illustrated with scenes from the Universal Photoplay.
N.Y.: Grosset & Dunlap [ca. 1932]; Mary Shelley. *Frankenstein* [and]
Bram Stoker. *Dracula. The Horror Omnibus. Containing Two Complete*
Novels. N.Y.: Grosset & Dunlap, n.d. Also published (without ac-
knowledgement) in Mary Shelley. *Frankenstein.* N.Y.: Pyramid Books,
1957; reprinted, 1959, 1964, 1965.

A217 Jack, Ian [Robert James]. *English Literature, 1815-1832.* Oxford
History of English Literature Series. Oxford: Clarendon Press,
1963, pp. 96, 104, 243-245.
MS is the basis for Cynthia in Shelley's *The Revolt of Islam,*
understood the truth about Shelley more clearly than anyone, and
wrote a "philosophical romance" in *Frankenstein.*

A218   Jeaffreson, John Cordy. *The Real Shelley. New Views of the Poet's Life*. 2 vols. London: Hurst and Blackett, 1885, Vol. I, pp. 430-431.
       MS intimacy with Hogg discussed.

       _____. Vol. II, pp. 53-55, 58-59, 60, 63, 65-66, 68, 69, 71-72, 74-75, 76, 131, 132-133, 142, 191-192, 210-212, 215, 217-218, 220, 222, 223, 224-230, 231, 233, 234-249, 251, 252-253, 254, 256, 260, 261-265, 272-274, 275, 276-280, 281, 285, 287, 288-290, 294-296, 297, 301-303, 318-319, 323, 327, 362-363, 365, 366, 367, 368-370, 371, 373-374, 375-376, 377, 379-304, 305, 306, 307-309, 396-405 *passim*, 416, 420, 422, 425, 426, 427-435, 437, 439, 441, 445, 447, 453-457, 462-463, 465-466, 468, 471, 476.
       Digressive and unreliable, though attempting to "correct" previous Shelley biographers. Disputes influence of parents on MS, who was a "naughty girl" in the elopement, and who had "a lack of housewifely knowingness and capacity."

A219   Jensen, Paul. "*Frankenstein*." In Arthur Lennig, ed. *The Sound Film: An Introduction*. Troy, N.Y.: Printed for Walter Snyder, 1969, pp. 225-243 [232, 239-240].
       Brief comparison of MS novel and 1931 film version, in both of which MS desire to "make the reader dread to look round" [her 1831 Introduction] becomes "a means of supporting theme and characterization."
       See also B127.

A220   Johnson, R[eginald] Brimley, ed. *Shelley-Leigh Hunt. How Friendship Made History. And Extended the Bounds of Human Freedom and Thought. Being Reviews and Leaders from* The Examiner, *etc.; with intimate Letters between the Shelleys and Leigh Hunt, partly from unpublished manuscripts*. London: Ingpen and Grant, 1928, pp. 335-336, 338-342.
       Previously unpublished MS letters to Byron and Hunt.
       Facsimile reprint: N.Y.: Haskell House, 1972.

A221   Johnson, Reginald Brimley. *The Women Novelists*. London, Glasgow: Collins, 1918, pp. 143-145.
       Frankenstein is "eminently characteristic of an age which hankered after the byways of science, imagined unlimited possibilities from the extension of knowledge, and was never tired of speculation."
       Also published, N.Y.: Charles Scribner's Sons, 1919.

A222   Jones, Frederick L[afayette]. "Mary Godwin to T. J. Hogg: The 1815 Letters." In Kenneth Neill Cameron, ed. *Shelley and his Circle 1773-1822*. 6 vols. Cambridge, Mass.: Harvard University Press, 1970, Vol. III, pp. 423-434.
       History of the letters and examination of the "affair" as seen by other biographers. Even though there was an affair, MS is exonerated because she was only following Shelley's wishes. (Letters on pp. 434-473.)
       Reprinted in Kenneth Neill Cameron, ed. *Romantic Rebels. Essays*

on *Shelley and his Circle*. Cambridge, Mass.: Harvard University Press, 1973, pp. 84-120.

A223 Jones, Frederick L[afayette]. "Preface" to his ed. *Mary Shelley's Journal*. Norman, Okla.: University of Oklahoma Press, 1947, pp. vii-xvii.

Explains the source of the journal (MLA rotograph of Edward Dowden's copy of A16), and justifies its printing as "the most important single document in Shelley biography."

See also IA1.

A224 Jones, Frederick L[afayette]. "Preface"; "Editor's Introduction" to his ed. *The Letters of Mary W. Shelley*. 2 vols. Norman, Okla.: University of Oklahoma Press, 1944, Vol. I, pp. v-vii; xxix-xxxii.

Sources of letters explained. Letters are supposedly complete, and are published not because of their general quality or because MS was an important letter-writer, but because "as the wife of Shelley . . . she excites our interest."

_____. "Appendix II, Mary Shelley, John Howard Payne and Washington Irving." Vol. II, pp. 347-353.

Superficial sketch of the relationship, as shown in the letters between the three correspondents.

Reprinted, 1946.

See also IA7; IIA14, B105.

A225 J[ones], F[rederick] L[afayette]. "Shelley, Mary Wollstonecraft." In *Encyclopædia Britannica*. N.Y.: The Britannica Company, 1972, Vol. 20, pp. 370-371.

The style of *Frankenstein* is immature, "but the basic idea is fascinating," although *The Last Man* "ranks as her best book."

A226 Jones, Frederick L[afayette]. "The Shelley Legend." In Newman I[vey] White, Frederick L[afayette] Jones, and Kenneth N[eill] Cameron. *An Examination of "The Shelley Legend."* Philadelphia: University of Pennsylvania Press, 1958, pp. 31-93.

Reprint of B141.

A227 Joseph, M[ichael] K[ennedy]. "Introduction"; "Note on the Text"; "A Chronology of Mary Shelley"; "Appendix A, The Composition of *Frankenstein*"; "Appendix B, Shaftesbury on Prometheus"; "Appendix C, Chamonix, July 1816"; "Textual Notes"; "Explanatory Notes." In his ed. *Mary W. Shelley. Frankenstein or the Modern Prometheus*. Oxford English Novels Series. London, Oxford, N.Y.: Oxford University Press, 1969, pp. vii-xv; xvii; xx-xxii; 224-227; 228-229; 230-232; 233-234; 235-241.

All themes in the novel touched upon, as well as influences. Textual notes attempting to collate 1818 and 1831 editions are very selective. (See A356 for another collation.)

Reprinted, 1971.

A228   Kagarlitski, Julius. "Realism and Fantasy." In Thomas D. Clareson,
        ed. *SF: The Other Side of Realism. Essays on Modern Fantasy and
        Science Fiction.* Bowling Green, Ohio: Bowling Green University
        Popular Press, 1971, pp. 29-52 [43-44].
            On Scott's opinion of *Frankenstein* [cf. C9]: "By no means can
        it be said that Walter Scott understood the artistic principles of
        Mary Shelley . . . very deeply."

A229   Kaplan, Morton, and Robert Floss. "Fantasy of Paternity and the
        Doppelgänger: Mary Shelley's *Frankenstein*." In their *The Unspoken
        Motive. A Guide to Psychoanalytic Literary Criticism.* N.Y.: The
        Free Press, 1973, pp. 119-145; and 5, 36, 39.
            Frankenstein creates the Monster because of an infantile fantasy,
        showing his unfulfilled sexuality and paternal obsession, and rejects
        it when "fantasy becomes fact." The *doppelgänger* motif is best
        illustrated in the series of murders. Two errors: "the early movie
        version which starred (who could forget?) Bela Lugosi, Basil Rath-
        bone, and Boris Karloff" had only the last actor, unless *Son of
        Frankenstein* (1939) is meant (p. 121); after Elizabeth's death, the
        world does *not* believe Frankenstein's story of the Monster (p. 144).

A230   Karloff, Boris [William Henry Pratt]. "Introduction" to his ed.
        The Boris Karloff Horror Anthology. London: Souvenir Press, 1965,
        pp. 9-10.
            In *Frankenstein*, Bram Stoker's *Dracula*, and the stories in the
        anthology, "the most important factor is not the reader's location,
        but the ability of story and author to entrance one's conscious from
        the here and now, from the mundane, to those other worlds of fear,
        terror, and black magic."

A231   Keel, John A. *Jadoo.* N.Y.: Julian Messner, 1957, p. 34 n. 1.
            Concerning the "Frankenstein Monster" legend of the 13th-century
        Rhine area: "When Mary Shelley . . . heard the story centuries
        later she used it as the basis of her classic novel of man's inhu-
        manity to monsters." Cites no proof, however. (For the legend, see
        F. J. Kiefer. "Frankenstein. George of Frankenstein." In his *The
        Legends of the Rhine from Basle to Rotterdam.* L. W. Garnham, trans.
        New Edition. Mayence: David Kapp [1868], pp. 72-75.) (Appendix III.)

A232   Kiely, Robert. "Frankenstein. Mary Wollstonecraft Shelley. 1818."
        In his *The Romantic Novel in England.* Cambridge, Mass.: Harvard
        University Press, 1972, pp. 155-173; and 141, 252, 267-268.
            Intelligent, detailed examination of the novel, with special
        attention to the "two dominant themes": "that man discovers and
        fulfills himself through others and destroys himself alone," and
        "that the genius, even in his failures, is unique, noble, and iso-
        lated from other men by divine right."

A233   King-Hele, Desmond. *Shelley. His Thought and Work.* London:
        Macmillan & Co./N.Y.: St. Martin's Press, 1960, pp. 51-52, 53, 65-
        66, 67-68, 72-73, 77-78, 99, 100-101, 118-119, 212, 246-247, 270-
        271, 315, 347-349.
            Mostly biographical references, with occasional comments on MS
        novels: "*Frankenstein* stands to-day in a unique position halfway

between the Gothic novel and the Wellsian scientific romance."
Also published as *Shelley. The Man and the Poet*. N.Y.: Thomas
Yoseloff, 1961. Second, revised ed.: Rutherford, N.J.: Fairleigh
Dickinson University Press, 1972.

A234   Knight, Damon [Francis]. *In Search of Wonder. Essays on Modern
Science Fiction.* Second, revised edition. Chaicago: Advent Publishers, 1967, p. 133.
     Eando Binder's "I, Robot" [cf. A55, B23] "is nothing more or
less than a clumsy pastiche of *Frankenstein*."
     First published, 1956.

A235   Knight, G[eorge] Wilson. *Neglected Powers. Essays in Nineteenth
and Twentieth Century Literature.* London: Routledge and Kegan Paul,
1971, pp. 62, 449.
     The work of Jules Verne and H. G. Wells was forecast by *Frank-
enstein*. Concerning Francis Berry's *The Iron Christ*: "Within
[Christ's] very 'stillness' there yet 'lurks a typhoon power' re-
sembling 'Frankenstein's incipient robot stalk.'"

A236   Knight, Grant C[ochran]. *The Novel in English*. N.Y.: Richard R.
Smith, 1931, p. 85.
     Frankenstein is "a creditable production for a girl of nineteen"
and "perhaps one of the best and perhaps the most intelligent of the
Gothic romances."
     Also published, N.Y.: Farrar and Rinehart, 1935.

A237   Koszul, A[ndré] [Henri]. "Prefatory Note"; "Introductory" to Mary
Shelley. *Proserpine & Midas. Two Unpublished Mythological Dramas
by Mary Shelley*. London: Humphrey Milford, 1922, pp. iii-iv; v-xxi.
     Little criticism of the two dramas, which Koszul believes he is
presenting for the first time. [Cf. Norman, A310, p. 91.] They
"bridge the gap" between *Frankenstein* and MS other novels and tales,
and reflect Shelley's "guidance and supervision."
     Facsimile reprint: Folcroft, Pa.: Folcroft Library Editions,
1974.

A238   Kurtz, Benjamin P. *The Pursuit of Death. A Study of Shelley's
Poetry.* N.Y.: Oxford University Press, 1933, pp. 117-118.
     The "Love of Shelley and Mary" as reflected in *The Revolt of
Islam*.
     Facsimile reprint: N.Y.: Octagon Books, 1970.

A239   Lamb, Charles. *The Letters of Charles Lamb, to which are added
those of his sister Mary Lamb.* E. V. Lucas, ed. 3 vols. New
Haven, Conn.: Yale University Press, 1935, Vol. II, p. 407.
     Letter to MS, inviting her to tea.

     _____. Vol. III, pp. 109-111, 142-143, 239-240.
     Letters to MS (one doubtful), mostly chatty.

A240 Lea, F[rank] A[lfred]. *Shelley and the Romantic Revolution*. London: Routledge, 1945, pp. 51-52, 53-54, 56, 57-58, 60, 62-63, 65, 174-175, 177, 178, 179-203, 216, 240.

MS did not understand Shelley's poetry, yet "apart from her sympathy and her talk of her mother, Mary Godwin came closer to embodying Shelley's ideal of what his wife should be than any woman he had met."

Facsimile reprint: N.Y.: Haskell House, 1971.

A241 Leathers, Victor. *British Entertainers in France*. Toronto: University of Toronto Press, 1959, pp. 55-57.

Concerning the popularity of T. P. Cooke's Parisian appearances in *Le Monstre et le magicien*, the French adaptation of *Presumption, or the Fate of Frankenstein*.

A242 Legouis, Émile [Hyacinthe]. *A Short History of English Literature*. V. F. Boyson and J. Coulson, trans. Oxford: The Clarendon Press, 1934, p. 297.

In *Frankenstein*, MS "imagined the creation by human science of a monstrous being devoid of all feeling."

First published as E29. First translated as Emile Legouis and Louis Cazamian. *A History of English Literature*. 2 vols. London, Toronto: J. M. Dent & Sons, 1926-1927. Also published, N.Y.: Macmillan Company, 1926-1927. Oxford *Short* ed. reprinted, 1961.

A243 Lennig, Arthur. *The Count. The Life and Films of Bela "Dracula" Lugosi*. N.Y.: G. P. Putnam's Sons, 1974, p. 247.

In the film *Ghost of Frankenstein*, "some of Mary Shelley's original concepts, though sentimentalized in the child [in the film], still remain."

A244 Leopold, Richard William. *Robert Dale Owen*. Cambridge, Mass.: Harvard University Press, 1940, pp. 51, 52.

As part of MS-Owen-Fanny Wright connection, MS letter to Owen (Nov. 9, 1827) is printed.

Also published, London: Humphrey Milford, Oxford University Press, 1940. Facsimile reprint of Harvard ed.: N.Y.: Octagon Books, 1965.

A245 *Letters about Shelley, interchanged by three friends—Edward Dowden, Richard Garnett, and Wm. Michael Rossetti*. R. S. Garnett, ed. London, N.Y., Toronto: Hodder and Stoughton, 1917, pp. 27, 28, 32, 43, 49, 61, 63, 80, 84, 93, 108, 117, 118, 119, 125, 126, 131, 134, 135, 138, 139, 140, 148, 152, 155, 178, 188, 210, 236, 237, 248, 251, 252, 253, 255, 258.

The letters, from 1869 to 1906, lend perspective to the three writers' attitudes towards MS.

A246 *Letters of English Authors from the Collection of Robert H. Taylor: A Catalogue of an Exhibition in the Princeton University Library May 13 to September 30, 1960*. Princeton, N.J.: Princeton University, 1960, p. 19.

Excerpt from MS letter to Shelley (Jan. 17, 1817), previously

unpublished according to William S. Dit in the Introduction, and not in Jones' collection [IIA14].
See also B161.

Lewis, Gogo. *See* Manley, Seon, A267.

A247 *The Library of Jerome Kern.* N.Y.: The Anderson Galleries, January 21-24, 1929, Part II, pp. 344-346.
Items 1062-1072 are MS and MS-related, including an 1818 *Frankenstein* containing a Shelley letter to the publishers (partially printed herein), 17 pages of the manuscript of *Valperga* (with a brief note on differences between them and printed version), 1st edition of *The Last Man* with an autograph receipt by Peacock for MS account, MS scrapbook, and MS letter to Payne (Jan. 28, 1826).

A248 Liptzin, Solomon. *Shelley in Germany.* Columbia University Germanic Studies. N.Y.: Columbia University Press, 1924, pp. 75-87.
MS meeting with Wilhelm Hamm in 1846 mentioned, and discussion of MS and Shelley as depicted in German novels about their lives [not included in "Mary Shelley in Fiction" section of this bibliography].

A249 Locke, George. "Introduction" to *The Land of the Unseen. Lost Supernatural Stories 1828-1902.* Ferret Ephemera 2. London: Ferret Fantasy, 1973, pp. 6-8 [8].
Notes resemblance between Kate Dodd's story, "Where Angels Fear to Tread" (1885; reprinted here, pp. 62-77) and *Frankenstein.*
Limited to 500 copies; one in the present author's collection.

A250 Lovecraft, Howard Phillips. *Supernatural Horror in Literature.* N.Y.: Dover Publications, 1973, pp. 38-39.
Frankenstein is "somewhat tinged but scarcely marred by moral didacticism," and "has the true touch of cosmic fear, no matter how much the movement may lag in places."
Present text a corrected version of that published, N.Y.: Ben Abramson, 1945. Also published, Toronto: General Publishing Company, 1973; London: Constable, 1973. The complicated history of Lovecraft's text is covered by E. F. Bleiler in his Introduction, pp. iii-viii.

A251 Lovell, Ernest J[ames]. *Captain Medwin. Friend of Byron and Shelley.* Austin, Tex.: University of Texas Press, 1962, pp. 3, 59, 79, 106-108, 139, 146, 162, 167-170, 199-201, 220, 236-238, 253, 284, 313-317.
Excerpts from previously unpublished MS letters and letters to MS, and brief comments on her connection with Medwin: "Her evidence against [him] must be heavily discarded."
Reprinted, London: Macdonald, 1963 (same pagination).

A252 Lowell, James Russell. "Memoir of Shelley." In Percy Bysshe Shelley. *The Poetical Works of Percy Bysshe Shelley, edited by Mrs. Shelley.* 2 vols. Boston: Little, Brown and company; Shepard, Clark and Brown, 1857, Vol. I, pp. 13-31 [13].
MS ommitted details of Shelley's life "either from a natural reserve or a very pardonable delicacy."

A253 Luke, Hugh J., Jr. "Introduction"; "Mary Shelley: A Brief Chronology"; "A Note on the Text." In his ed. Mary Shelley. *The Last Man*. Lincoln, Neb.: University of Nebraska Press, 1965, pp. vii-xviii; xix-xx; xxi.

Biographical criticism, and examination of the theme of social progress and the myth of the solitary figure, noting Wordsworthian elements. Also briefly traces the history of the text.

Introduction an expanded version of B173.

*A254 Lundwall, Sam. *Science Fiction—What It's All About*. N.Y.: Ace Books [1974?].

Reprinting of E30.

In the publisher's catalogue of September 1974, but, as they have informed me, currently out of print.

A255 Lupoff, Richard A. *Edgar Rice Burroughs: Master of Adventure*. Revised, enlarged edition. N.Y.: Ace Books, 1968, pp. 137, 287.

Notes the Frankenstein motif in Burroughs' *The Master Mind of Mars* (1928) and *The Monster Men* (1929).

First published, N.Y.: Canaveral Press, 1965 (pp. 106, 256).

A256 Lyster, Gertrude, ed. *A Family Chronicle. Derived from Notes and Letters Selected by Barbarina, The Hon. Lady Grey*. London: John Murray, 1908, p. 333.

Fanny Kemble relates a talk with MS in which the latter commented upon the education of her son Percy. Mention is made of Arnold's version of the anecdote [cf. A34] without crediting Mrs. Kemble.

See also B183.

A257 McAleer, Edward C. *The Sensitive Plant: A Life of Lady Mount Cashell*. Chapel Hill, N.C.: North Carolina University Press, 1950, pp. 131-142, 147, 150, 166-167, 170-174, 175-176, 177-180, 181-182, 185, 188, 190, 193, 201-202.

MS relationship with "Mrs. Mason," including previously unpublished letters to MS. Manuscript sources listed, pp. 232-235.

Also published, N.Y.: Oxford University Press, 1950.

A258 McCarthy, B[ridget] G. *The Later Women Novelists*. Oxford: B. H. Blackwell, Cork University Press, 1947, pp. 182-183.

"The most glaring fault" in *Frankenstein* is the addition of the four prefatory chapters to the initial draft. Also, "There are queer echoes of Godwin and Mary Wollstonecraft in the protracted account of [the Monster's] education, and in the evil effects upon him of humanitarian doctrines."

A259 McCloskey, Frank H. "Mary Shelley's Frankenstein." In Charles Angoff, ed. *The Humanities in the Age of Science. In Honor of Peter Sammartino*. Rutherford, Madison, Teaneck, N.J.: Fairleigh Dickinson University Press, 1968, pp. 116-138.

Attention to the influence of Godwin and Mary Wollstonecraft on *Frankenstein*: "[MS] novel, from one point of view, may be considered almost a continuous preachment of her parents' revolutionary doctrines." Still, the novel "failed as revolutionary document."

A260 McConnell, Frank. "Rough Beasts Slouching: A Note on Horror
      Movies." In Roy Huss and T. J. Ross, eds. *Focus on the Horror
      Film*. A Spectrum Book. Englewood Cliffs, N.J.: Prentice-Hall,
      1972, pp. 24-35 [28].
      Reprint of B178.

A261 MacFarlane, Charles. *Reminiscences of a Literary Life*. London:
      John Murray, 1917, p. 9.
      "That evening, I saw [Shelley's] second wife. . . . She was, at
      that period [1820], a very delicate, elegant, charming person; and
      there seemed to be great affection and an entire confidence between
      them."†

      McNally, Raymond T. *See* Florescu, Radu, A142.

A262 Macqueen-Pope, W[alter] [James], and D. L. Murray. *Gaiety: Theatre
      of Entertainment*. London: W. H. Allen, 1949, pp. 260-262, 264, 265-
      266, 305.
      Description of the 1887 stage version of *Frankenstein*.

A263 Mabbott, Thomas Ollive, and Frank Lester Pleadwell. *The Life and
      Works of Edward Coote Pinkney*. N.Y.: Macmillan Company, 1926,
      p. 192.
      Pinkney's burlesque [cf. A335, B274] "cannot be praised very
      highly from a literary point of view."

A264 Madariaga, Salvador de. "Shelley and Calderón." In his *Shelley
      and Calderón, and other essays in English and Spanish Poetry*. Port
      Washington, N.Y.: Kennikat Press, 1965, pp. 3-47 [17-18, 25-26, 44].
      MS did not really understand Shelley, and her note on evil in
      his *Prometheus Unbound* is "naive."
      First published, 1920, publisher unknown.

A265 Magnus, Laurie. *English Literature in the Nineteenth Century. An
      Essay in Criticism*. London: Andrew Melrose, 1909, p. 129.
      MS is "the clever author of *Frankenstein*."

      Mander, Lady. *See* Grylls, R[osalie] Glynn, A179 & A180.

A266 Manley, Seon, and Susan Belcher. "Chapter 2, Frankenstein's Mother.
      Mary Shelley." In their *O, Those Extraordinary Women! or the joys
      of literary lib*. Philadelphia: Chilton Book Company/Ontario: Thomas
      Nelson & Sons, 1972, pp. 31-56; and 81.
      Dramatized account of MS life, with special attention to *Frank-
      enstein* with a vaguely feminist slant.

A267 Manley, Seon, and Gogo Lewis. Introductory Note to Mary Shelley.
      "The Making of a Monster." In their eds. *Ladies of Horror. Two
      Centuries of Supernatural Stories by the Gentle Sex*. N.Y.: Lothrop,
      Lee & Shepard, 1971, pp. 11-13.
      Brief sketch of MS; *Frankenstein* "remarkable."

A268   Marchand, Leslie A[lexis]. *Byron. A Biography.* 3 vols. N.Y.:
        Alfred A. Knopf, 1957, Vol. II, pp. 623, 628, 629, 643, 646, 655,
        680, 731-732, 754, 757, 762, 876, 921, 924, 925-926 n.

        _____. Vol. III, pp. 944, 945, 947-948, 949, 950 n., 957,
        959, 961, 964, 965, 966, 974, 976, 980, 982, 984, 986, 989, 995,
        997, 1003, 1005, 1016, 1017-1018, 1025 n., 1036, 1037, 1042, 1043,
        1050, 1051, 1053, 1054, 1069, 1076, 1079-1080, 1081, 1082-1083,
        1085, 1130, 1153, 1245, 1257, 1260-1261.
        Detailed, even examination of MS-Byron relationship; speculates
        that MS wished "he might have been to her something more than a
        friend."
        Also published, 3 vols. London: John Murray, 1958. Condensed
        one-volume edition published as *Byron. A Portrait.* London: John
        Murray, 1971.

A269   Marshall, William H[arvey]. *Byron, Shelley, Hunt and The Liberal.*
        Philadelphia: University of Pennsylvania Press, 1960, pp. 76; 135;
        143 & n. 56; 148 & nn. 83, 84; 159-160; 174 & n. 44; 178 & n. 68;
        191 & n. 36; 238-239.
        Identifies MS contributions to *The Liberal.*

A270   "Mary Shelley." In Mary W. Shelley. *Frankenstein.* Adapted by Ruth
        A. Roche. Classics Illustrated, No. 26. N.Y.: Classics Illustrated,
        Gilberton Company, December 1945, unpaginated.
        Brief biographical sketch following text; "Perhaps much of the
        sorrow of Mary's life would have been avoided had her liberally-
        minded and strong-willed mother survived."
        Re-issued, Spring 1971.

A271   "Mary Wollstonecraft Godwin Shelley." In Frank N[orthen] Magill, ed.
        Cyclopedia of World Authors. N.Y.: Harper & Brothers, 1958, pp. 969-
        970.
        "Authorship of *Frankenstein* was not the only claim to distinc-
        tion possessed by [MS]." Other distinctions, however, not detailed.
        Brief bibliography.

A272   "Mary Wollstonecraft Shelley." In [Robert Chambers, original com-
        piler.] David Patrick, ed. *Chambers's Cyclopædia of English Liter-
        ature. Vol. III: 19th-20th Century.* Revised and expanded by J.
        Liddell Geddie and J. C. Smith. Philadelphia, N.Y.: J. B. Lippin-
        cott, 1938, pp. 519-520.
        Frankenstein is "on the model of [Godwin's] *St. Leon.* On the
        story: "after revolting experiments, [Frankenstein] constructs a
        gigantic figure eight feet high, and, a veritable Demiurgus, breathes
        into its nostrils the breath of life."

A273   "Mary Wollstonecraft Shelley." In Charles Wells Moulton, ed. *The
        Library of Literary Criticism of English and American Authors. Vol.
        V: 1825-1854.* Buffalo, N.Y.: The Moulton Publishing Company, 1902,
        pp. 700-704.
        Brief biographical sketch and bibliography, and quotations from
        19 other works.

A274 "Mary Wollstonecraft Shelley 1797-1851." In Mary W. Shelley.
      Frankenstein. The World's Popular Classics. N.Y., Boston: Books,
      Inc., n.d., pp. 219-225.
      Thoroughly unreliable biographical sketch, more on Shelley than
      MS, riddled with errors and oversimplifications.

A275 Massingham, H[arold] J[ohn]. "Chapter IV, The Poet's Wife";
      "Appendix I, Shelley's Heart." In his *The Friend of Shelley. A
      Memoir of Edward John Trelawny*. N.Y.: D. Appleton, 1930, pp. 186-
      230; 339-341.
      The relationship between MS and Trelawny, "between the sentimen-
      talist and this man of fire and follies . . . between a cold-blooded
      woman and a hot-blooded man." Trelawny was truthful in his revised
      portrait of MS [cf. A419], and acted honorably in the affair of
      Shelley's heart.
      Also published, London: Cobden-Sanderson, 1930.

A276 Maurois, André. *Ariel. The Life of Shelley*. Ella D'Arcy, trans.
      N.Y.: D. Appleton, 1926, pp. 114, 147-155, 159-165, 166-169, 170-
      176, 177-179, 182-185, 185-188, 194-195, 197, 200, 202-203, 205,
      206, 207-209, 215, 216-218, 224-229, 232, 238-240, 241, 245-249,
      250, 252, 254-255, 256-257, 259, 260-261, 267-268, 270-272, 274-
      282, 283, 285-286, 287, 290, 297, 298-299, 302-304, 305-306, 308-
      310, 315, 323-326, 328, 329, 333-334.
      MS described only when she enters Shelley's life; no material
      concerning her after his death except Trelawny and Hogg's proposals.
      Generally sympathetic; told in narrative form.
      First published as E32. First published in England, London:
      John Lane, The Bodley Head, 1924; reprinted, 1924, 1925; illustrated
      ed., 1925.

A277 Mayer, Gertrude Townshend. "Mary Wollstonecraft Shelley." In her
      Women of Letters. 2 vols. London: Richard Bentley & Son, 1894,
      Vol. 2, pp. 207-260.
      Reprinting of B200.
      See also B199.

A278 Mays, Milton A. "*Frankenstein*, Mary Shelley's Black Theodicy." In
      Thomas D. Clareson, ed. *SF: The Other Side of Realism. Essays on
      Modern Fantasy and Science Fiction*. Bowling Green, Ohio: Bowling
      Green University Popular Press, 1971, pp. 171-180.
      Reprinting of B202.

A279 Mazlish, Bruce. "The Fourth Discontinuity." In Melvin Kranzberg
      and W. H. Davenport, eds. *Technology and Culture*. N.Y.: Schocken,
      1972, pp. 216-232 [223, 227-229, 230].
      Reprinting of B203.

A280 Medwin, Thomas. *Conversations of Lord Byron: noted during a resi-
      dence with his lordship at Pisa, in the years 1821 and 1822*.
      London: Henry Colburn, 1824, pp. 120-121.
      Supposedly in Byron's own words: MS "sketched on that occasion
      [the 1816 summer in Geneva] the outline of her Pygmalion story, 'The

Modern Prometheus,' the making of a man, (which a lady who had read it afterwards asked Sir Humphry Davy, to his great astonishment, if he could do)."†

Also published, N.Y.: Wilder & Campbell/Philadelphia: E. Littell, 1824; Ernest J. Lovell, ed. Princeton, N.J.: Princeton University Press, 1966. See Lovell, A251, pp. 170-171, for other editions.

A281 Medwin, Thomas. *The Life of Percy Bysshe Shelley*. 2 vols. London: Thomas Cautley Newby, 1847, Vol. I, pp. iii-iv, vi, 44, 50, 91, 96 [incorrectly marked 69], 100, 107, 136, 164, 211, 219, 240-241, 247, 280-281, 311, 319, 329-330, 332 n., 337-338, 348-349, 350, 351-352; (references to *Frankenstein*) 258-260, 264 n.

Casual references to MS involvement with Shelley, usually "respectfully" treated. Cites Paracelsus as a partial source for *Frankenstein*, which is a "wild and wonderful romance."

_____. Vol. II, pp. 2-3, 24, 30-31, 39, 45, 47, 48, 50, 52, 58, 59-60, 65, 77, 80-81, 86, 121, 133-134, 136, 139, 150, 166, 200, 235, 241-242, 243, 268-269, 271-273, 274, 282, 284, 292, 304, 309-310, 339, 350; (references to MS novels) 59-60, 241-242.

Casual references, and the note that "Valpurga" [*sic*] is a "talented work, full of eloquence and beauty and poetry, lost on the world of readers of fiction."

Facsimile reprint: N.Y.: Scholarly Press, 1971.

See also A282.

A282 Medwin, Thomas. *The Life of Percy Bysshe Shelley*. *A New Edition printed from a copy copiously amended and extended by the Author and left unpublished at his death*. H[arry] Buxton Forman, ed. Oxford: Humphrey Milford, Oxford University Press, 1913, pp. xviii-xx, xxvii, 1, 63, 81, 97, 129, 189, 190, 193-194, 220-221, 222, 234, 250, 252-253, 254-255, 262, 265, 276, 290, 294, 304, 313, 319, 320, 322, 323, 325, 326, 333, 343, 362, 364, 374, 375, 386, 387-388, 389, 390, 393, 395, 398, 399, 404, 407, 410, 411, 430, 433, 456-458, 458-462, 463, 464, 468, 469, 471, 491, 492, 501, 504.

New material concerning MS on pp. 386, 468, 469.

A283 Medwin, Thomas. *The Shelley Papers*. *Memoir of Percy Bysshe Shelley*. London: Whittaker, Treacher, & Co., 1833, pp. 63-64, 78-79, 84-85, 192.

Reprinting of B204, B205, B206, B207.

A284 Metzdorf, Robert F., compiler. *The Tinker Library: A Bibliographical Catalogue of the Books and Manuscripts Collected of Chauncey Brewster Tinker*. New Haven, Conn.: Yale University Library, 1959, p. 381.

Descriptions of 1st and 2nd English editions of *Frankenstein*.

A285 Middleton, Charles S. *Shelley and His Writings.* 2 vols. London:
Thomas Cautley Newby, 1858, Vol. I, pp. 282, 285-292, 297-299, 303,
317-322.

_____. Vol. II, pp. 53-54, 87-88, 91, 141, 220-221, 232,
309, 317, 320, 330.
Glancing comments on MS, who was "a highly sensitive and
accomplished girl."
Facsimile reprint: Folcroft, Pa.: Folcroft Press, 1972.

A286 Miller, Barnette. *Leigh Hunt's Relations with Byron, Shelley, and
Keats.* N.Y.: Columbia University Press, 1910, pp. 69, 73, 75 n. 51,
112.
MS-Marianne Hunt relationship; MS financial contributions to
Leigh Hunt; MS literary contributions to *The Liberal* ("all rather
stilted and dreary").
Facsimile reprint: Folcroft, Pa.: Folcroft Press, 1969.

A287 Miyoshi, Masao. *The Divided Self: A Perspective on the Literature
of the Victorians.* N.Y.: New York University Press/London: University of London Press, 1969, pp. 25, 49, 79-89, 130, 312.
Psychological criticism of *Frankenstein*, with notice of the
Faustian theme. "*Frankenstein* could hardly avoid reflecting a great
many serious concerns of the Romantics: the dualism of poetry and
science, of the individual and society, and of faith and humanistic
rationalism."

A288 Moore, Doris Langley[-Levy]. *The Late Lord Byron. Posthumous
Dramas.* Philadelphia, N.Y.: J. B. Lippincott, 1961, pp. 402-413,
417-422, 426-428.
Focuses on MS portrayal of Byron in *The Last Man* ("a fantasy on
a theme totally beyond her powers"), noting that "her feelings for
[him] were strongly emotional and tinged with eroticism."

A289 Moore, Patrick. *Science and Fiction.* London: George G. Harrap,
1957, p. 124.
MS idea in *The Last Man* was used ingeniously by J. J. Connington
in *Nordenholt's Million.*

A290 Moore, Thomas. *The Journal of Thomas Moore 1818-1841.* Peter
Quennell, ed. London: B. T. Batsford, 1964, pp. 106, 151, 152,
154, 173, 180, 189, 191, 239.
Edited version of the Journal in A294; passing references to MS.

A291 Moore, Thomas. *Letters and Journals of Lord Byron: With Notices of
his Life.* 2 vols. N.Y.: Harper & Brothers, 1855, Vol. II, pp. 17,
20, 23, 145, 146, 314 n., 315-316, 389, 428.
Glancing references to MS; one on p. 389 to Mrs. ——— is doubtful.
First published, 2 vols. London: John Murray, 1830; reprinted,
1833. Also published, London: Chatto and Windus, 1875.
See also A293.

A292   Moore, Thomas. *The Letters of Thomas Moore*. Wilfrid S. Dowden, ed.
        2 vols. Oxford: The Clarendon Press, 1964, Vol. II, pp. 569-570,
        571-572, 573-576, 578-579, 580-581, 583, 586, 592, 600-601, 603-
        604, 606, 608-609, 609-610, 612-613, 617-618, 619-620, 626-627, 638,
        639-640, 643, 645, 646, 648, 651, 652-653, 654, 658-659, 660, 663-
        664, 673-676, 681-682, 685, 687, 689-690, 692, 694, 718-719, 725,
        734, 742-743, 752-753, 768, 783, 789-790, 793-794, 796-797, 803-
        804, 824, 834, 838-839, 846-847, 854, 866, 893, 894, 899, 909.
        89 letters from Moore to MS.

A293   Moore, Thomas. *The Life, Letters and Journals of Lord Byron*.
        London: John Murray, 1901, pp. 319, 574-575.
        Brief comment on *Frankenstein* ("one of those original concep-
        tions that take hold of the public mind at once, and for ever");
        undated Byron letter to MS.
        First published as A291.

A294   Moore, Thomas. *Memoirs, Journal, and Correspondence of Thomas
        Moore*. Lord John Russell, ed. 8 vols. London: Longman, Brown,
        Green, and Longmans, 1853, Vol. IV, pp. 20, 221.
        Passing references to MS; covers Sept. 1822-Oct. 1825.

        _____. 1853, Vol. V, pp. 173, 178, 186, 189, 194, 196, 271,
        277, 321.
        Notes MS promise to help him with his life of Byron [cf. A291,
        A293], as references change from "Mrs. Shelley" to "Mary." Covers
        Nov. 1, 1825-Nov. 1828.

        _____. 1854, Vol. VI, pp. 15, 84-85, 112, 115, 160, 225-
        226.
        Covers 1829-Oct. 1833.

        _____. 1856, Vol. VII, pp. 45, 251-252, 259.
        Casual references to MS, one (p. 259) to "Mrs. S." Covers
        Nov. 1, 1833-Dec. 1844.
        Also published, Boston: Little, Brown, 1853-1856. Edited
        version published as A290.

A295   Moskowitz, Sam. "Fritz Leiber." In his *Seekers of Tomorrow.
        Masters of Modern Science Fiction*. N.Y.: Ballantine Books, 1967,
        pp. 283-301 [299-300].
        "It is debatable if today's practitioners [of the world-doom
        story] have added much that was not in *The Last Man* by Mary Woll-
        stonecraft Shelley in 1826 or in *Deluge* by S. Fowler Wright over a
        century later (1929)."†

A296   Moskowitz, Sam. "Introduction" to his ed. *The Coming of the
        Robots*. N.Y.: Collier Books, 1963, pp. 9-19 [11].
        Suggests the Golem legend as "the prototype for the monster of
        Mary Wollstonecraft Shelley's *Frankenstein*, a work whose importance
        to the literary history of the mechanical man lies in its plot inno-
        vation, the concept of an artificial man turning on its creator."
        Reprinted, 1966.

A297 Moskowitz, Sam. Introductory Note to Mary Wollstonecraft Shelley. "The Transformation." In Alden H. Norton, ed. *Masters of Horror*. N.Y.: Berkley Publishing Corporation, 1968, pp. 68-70.
      Perhaps because MS knew that if Shelley had lived he would have discarded her, she "strove to stress morality" in the story.

A298 Moskowitz, Sam. "The Sons of Frankenstein." In his *Explorers of the Infinite. Shapers of Science Fiction*. Cleveland: World Publishing Company, 1963, pp. 33-45.
      Reprinting of B233.

A299 Moss, Robert F. *Karloff and Company: The Horror Film*. A Pyramid Illustrated History of the Movies. N.Y.: Pyramid Communications, 1973, p. 26.
      Brief contrast of *Frankenstein* and the 1931 film version: "In the novel the creation of the monster is a far more medieval, incantatory business than the famous scientific-laboratory birth of the film."

Murdoch, John. *See* Burton, Anthony, A79.

Murray, D. L. *See* Macqueen-Pope, A262.

A300 Neumann, Robert. "Chapter 1, Mr. P. B. Shelley is confronted with the Seriousness of Life." In his *Passion: Six Literary Marriages*. Brian W. Downs, trans. N.Y.: Harcourt, Brace and Company, 1932, pp. 3-25 [13-14, 16].
      MS was "tense, sensible and pure, [with] a self-discipline and charm, [and] became the celebrated Shelley's fate." The flowery prose (of Neumann or Downs?) contains many factual errors. Translation of E35.

A301 Newton, A[lfred] Edward. *The Amenities of Book-Collecting and Kindred Affections*. Boston: Atlantic Monthly Press, 1918, p. 108.
      Brief description of Shelley's inscribed copy of *Queen Mab* to MS, and its history in auctions. Reprinted, 1920, 1922.

A302 Newton, Alfred Edward. "Skinner Street News." In his *The Greatest Book in the World, and other papers*. Boston: Little, Brown, 1925, pp. 343-407 [364, 365-369, 376-382, 387-401].
      Pompous description of MS: "A pretty girl with a strong mind and a high voice, singularly bold and persevering; insufficiently educated, but fond of reading." Claims that Shelley was in love with Claire.

A303 Nicoll, Allardyce. *A History of Early Nineteenth-Century Drama*. 2 vols. Cambridge: The University Press, 1930, Vol. I, p. 96 & n. 2. Notes stage versions of *Frankenstein* in 1823 and 1849.

A304 Nicoll, W[illiam] Robinson, and Thomas J[ames] Wise. *Literary*
      Anecdotes of the Nineteenth Century: Contributions Towards a
      Literary History of the Period. 2 vols. London: Hodder & Stoughton,
      1895-1896, Vol. I, pp. 333-335, 338, 343.
          MS letter to Marianne Hunt, and sections of Shelley letters con-
      cerning MS.

      _____. Vol. II, pp. 459-461.
          Disputes William Graham's claim [cf. A176, B106] that MS and
      Shelley were aware on the journey to Geneva of Claire's relations
      with Byron.

A305 Nitchie, Elizabeth. "Preface"; "Introduction"; Notes to Mary Woll-
      stonecraft Shelley. *Mathilda*. Chapel Hill, N.C.: University of
      North Carolina Press [1959], pp. iii-iv; vii-xv; 81-89, 103-104.
          Concentrates on the biographical significance of the novella and
      its rough draft, *The Fields of Fancy*: "she poured out on the pages
      of *Mathilda* the suffering and the loneliness, the bitterness and the
      self-recrimination of the past months [of 1818]." Notes to *Mathilda*
      consider "the most significant revisions" made from the rough draft.
          Also published as B247.

A306 Nitchie, Elizabeth. *The Reverend Colonel Finch*. N.Y.: Columbia
      University Press, 1940, p. 6 & n. 6.
          Glosses references in MS letter to Maria Gisborne (April 16,
      1819).

A307 Nolan, William F. "Editor's Preface" to his ed. *The Pseudo-People*.
      Androids in Science Fiction. Los Angeles: Sherbourne Press, 1965,
      pp. xi-xii [xii].
          "Frankenstein's monster, strictly speaking, does not classify
      as an android."†

A308 Norman, Sylva, ed. *After Shelley. The Letters of Thomas Jefferson*
      Hogg to Jane Williams. London: Oxford University Press, Humphrey
      Milford, 1934, pp. xii, xviii, xx, xxii, xxiii, xxv, xxvi, xxvii-
      xxviii, xliii, 4, 10-11, 16, 17-18, 27, 28, 29 n. 1, 34, 46, 61.
          MS relationships with Hogg and Jane Williams, and glancing
      remarks concerning MS in Hogg letters.

A309 Norman, Sylva. *Flight of the Skylark: The Development of Shelley's*
      Reputation. Norman, Okla.: University of Oklahoma Press, 1954, pp.
      viii, 3, 8, 27, 28, 29-30, 37, 40-43 *passim*, 50-51, 53, 54-55, 56-
      57, 64, 66, 70-81 *passim*, 107-109, 111, 112, 114, 116, 117, 118,
      123, 125, 132, 140, 143-145, 156-171 *passim*, 176, 181-184, 192, 200,
      223, 249, 279, 285; (references to MS works) 21, 32, 36, 37, 42, 44-
      45, 53, 61, 62, 67, 121, 126, 131-132, 140, 161, 171, 279.
          Closely follows MS after Shelley's death, "in her unique posi-
      tion of widow, mother, editor, and society lover." Balanced, criti-
      cal perspective on MS in later years.

A310 Norman, Sylva. "Mary Shelley: Novelist and Dramatist." In *On Shelley*. Oxford: Oxford University Press, 1938, pp. 55-99.

Examination of all MS novels except *Frankenstein* (but mainly plot synopses), stories, poetry, and dramas, the last of which "do not really call for analytical and comparative study."

Facsimile reprint: Folcroft, Pa.: Folcroft Press, 1970.

A311 Norman, Sylva. "Mary Wollstonecraft Shelley." In Kenneth Neill Cameron, ed. *Shelley and his Circle 1773-1822*. 6 vols. Cambridge, Mass.: Harvard University Press, 1970, Vol. III, pp. 397-422.

Mainly biographical re-examination of MS, with some comment on *Frankenstein* as the creator of the science fiction genre. "Mary was safest as a writer when the theme constrained her—either by historical claims or through responsibility to a challenging postulate."

Reprinted in Kenneth Neill Cameron, ed. *Romantic Rebels. Essays on Shelley and his Circle*. Cambridge, Mass.: Harvard University Press, 1973, pp. 59-83.

A312 *The Note-Book of the Shelley Society*. First Series, No. 2. London: Published for The Shelley Society by Reeves and Turner, 1888, pp. 152-153.

MS letter to J. Bowring (Feb. 25, 1826).

A313 Oliphant, Mrs. [Margaret Wilson]. *Literary History of England. Vol. III: XVIII-XIX Century*. London: Macmillan and Co., 1882, pp. 51-54, 58, 69, 70.

Description of MS (a "fair small girl, with her big forehead and her sedate aspect"), and of *Frankenstein* ("one of the most extraordinary accidents in literature").

Reprinted, 1889. Facsimile reprint of 1882 ed.: N.Y.: AMS Press, 1970.

A314 Origo, Iris. "Allegra." In her *A Measure of Love*. N.Y.: Pantheon Books, 1957, pp. 15-87 [20, 21, 24, 25, 26, 35, 37-38, 39, 42, 44, 49, 60, 61, 69-70, 71, 75, 77, 83, 85, 86].

Occasionally a new slant on the complex MS-Byron-Claire-Allegra relationship.

First published as *Allegra*. London: Leonard and Virginia Woolf at the Hogarth Press, 1935.

A315 Origo, Iris. *The Last Attachment. The Story of Byron and Teresa Guiccioli as told in their unpublished letters and other family papers*. N.Y.: Charles Scribner's Sons [1949], pp. 9, 12, 14, 19, 294-295, 318, 327-328, 330-332, 336, 346, 347, 396, 409, 479, 480, 499 n. 35.

Previously unpublished MS letters to Teresa Guiccioli, and excerpts from Guiccioli's letters concerning MS.

A316 Owen, Robert Dale. "Paper X, Frances Wright, General Lafayette, and Mary Wollstonecraft Shelley." In his *Threading My Way. Twenty-Seven Years of Autobiography*. N.Y.: G. W. Carleton, 1874, pp. 301-330 [321-325].

Reprinting of B258.

Reprinted, N.Y.: A. M. Kelley, 1967.

A317   *The Oxford English Dictionary. Supplement and Bibliography.* 1961,
        p. 393 col. 1.
        Three examples of "incorrect" use of the word "Frankenstein"
        are included in its definition.
        See also A408.

        Palmer, D. J. *See* Dowse, Robert E., A128.

A318   Panshin, Alexei, and Cory Panshin. "Science Fiction: New Trends
        and Old." In Reginald Brentnor, ed. *Science Fiction, Today and
        Tomorrow.* N.Y.. Harper & Row, 1974, pp. 217-233 [230].
        Glancing comments on *Frankenstein*: "There is a dimension in
        Faust that cannot be duplicated in the symbols available in *Frank-
        enstein.*"

A319   *Parke-Bernet Catalog.* No. 1503. March 23-24, 1954, pp. 127, 129.
        Description and facsimile of Shelley's letter to publishing
        form of Lackington, Hughes concerning *Frankenstein.*

A320   Parks, Edd Winfield. *William Simms as Literary Critic.* University
        of Georgia Monographs, No. 7. Athens, Ga.: University of Georgia,
        1961, p. 22.
        Discusses Simms' criticism of *Frankenstein* [cf. B320], noting
        that unlike MS, "he was careful that his own Gothic effects were
        rationally explainable."

A321   Partington, [Sir] Wilfred [George]. *Sir Walter's Post-Bag. More
        Stories and Sidelights from his unpublished letter-books.* London:
        John Murray, 1932, p. 271.
        MS letter to Sir Walter Scott asking for his help with *Perkin
        Warbeck.*

A322   Paston, George [pseud. of Emily Morse Symonds]. *At John Murray's.
        Records of a Literary Circle. 1843-1892.* London: John Murray,
        1932, pp. 68-69.
        MS letter to Abraham Hayward (1835 or 1836).

A323   Paul, C[harles] Kegan. *William Godwin: His Friends and Contempo-
        raries.* 2 vols. London: Henry S. King, 1876, Vol. I, pp. 273,
        289-290.
        Circumstances of birth and early childhood of MS.

A324   Peacock, Thomas Love. "Memoirs of Shelley" [Part II]; "Percy
        Bysshe Shelley. Supplementary Notice." In Thomas Love Peacock.
        Memoirs of Shelley and Other Essays and Reviews. Howard Mills, ed.
        London: Rupert Hart-Davis, 1970, pp. 49-82 [51, 55, 57, 61, 63, 64,
        71, 72, 77, 80, 81]; 83-89 [84, 85, 86-87, 88].
        Reprinting of B265, B266.
        Also published in *The Life of Percy Bysshe Shelley. As Comprised
        in* The Life of Shelley *by Thomas Jefferson Hogg.* The Recollections
        of Shelley and Byron *by Edward John Trelawny.* Memoirs of Shelley *by
        Thomas Love Peacock.* 2 vols. London, Toronto: J. M. Dent and Sons/
        N.Y.: E. P. Dutton, 1933, Vol. II.

A325   Peacock, Thomas Love. *The Works of Thomas Love Peacock. Vol. 8: Essays, Memoirs, Letters, & Unfinished Novels.* 8 vols. London: Constable/N.Y.: Gabriel Wells, 1934, pp. 478-479.
        MS letter to Peacock, undated and first published here.
        Facsimile reprint: N.Y.: AMS Press, 1967.

A326   Pearlman, Gilbert. *Young Frankenstein.* N.Y.: Ballantine Books, 1974, pp. 16, 48, 49, 50, 53.
        In this novelization of Mel Brooks' 1974 film (of the same title) are interwoven sections from MS 1831 Introduction to *Frankenstein* and parts of the novel, the latter as "How I Did It, by Victor Frankenstein."

A327   Pearson, Edmund Lester. "Introduction" to Mary Wollstonecraft Shelley. *Frankenstein or The Modern Prometheus.* N.Y.: The Heritage Press, 1953, pp. v-xv.
        Superficial discussion of MS creation of the novel, with mention of stage adaptations and other works influenced by the novel.
        Re-issued, ca. 1962. Also published, N.Y.: The Limited Editions Club, 1934 (same pagination).
        Also included with the Heritage edition is *The Heritage Club Sandglass,* No. IR:38 [pp. 4], signed "The Directors," with a biographical sketch of MS and production details of this edition.

A328   Peck, Walter Edwin. *Shelley. His Life and Work.* 2 vols. Boston, N.Y.: Houghton Mifflin, 1927, Vol. I, pp. 26-27, 55, 162, 167, 216 n. 106, 302 n. 77, 309, 362, 363, 364-368, 369-394, 395-397, 399-406, 414-419, 435-436, 445, 446-450, 453-455, 464-476, 493 n. 20, 494, 503-504, 509, 519-520, 524, 525-526, 531; (references to MS works) 26, 55, 167, 283, 365 n., 371, 374, 375, 376, 380, 382-384, 385, 386, 390, 391, 392, 393, 397, 415-419, 435, 436, 446-448, 453, 454, 465, 466, 468, 469, 476, 524, 525, 526.
        Covers 1792-1817.

        _____. Vol. II, pp. 53-58, 67-68, 73-74, 78-79, 81, 83-84, 91-94, 96, 97-98, 108-109, 111-114, 117, 121, 152, 165, 179, 181, 184, 185-186, 187-188, 189, 191, 192-195, 217, 232, 234-237, 238, 249, 254, 256, 264-265, 271, 273-274, 282, 287-294, 411, 435, 440-443; (references to MS works) 57, 67, 94, 97, 98, 108, 109, 121, 236.
        Covers 1817-1822. Balanced, though subordinate, treatment of MS, from meeting with Shelley until his death. Facts and evaluation of both Shelley and MS are often disputed by later biographers.
        Also published, N.Y.: B. Franklin, 1969. Facsimile reprint of 1927 ed.: Havertown, Pa.: Richard West, 1973.

A329   Penzoldt, Peter. *The Supernatural in Fiction.* London: Peter Nevill, 1952, p. 50.
        In the Gothic novel, "the astrologer and the alchemist represent a link between modern science and medieval superstition. . . . [But] *Frankenstein* is an exception."

A330 "Percy Bysshe Shelley, Esq." In Newman Ivey White, ed. *The Unextinguished Hearth. Shelley and His Contemporary Critics*. Durham, N.C.: Duke University Press, 1938, pp. 329-330.
Reprinting of B273.

A331 "Percy Bysshe Shelley, Esq." In Newman Ivey White, ed. *The Unextinguished Hearth. Shelley and His Contemporary Critics*. Durham, N.C.: Duke University Press, 1938, pp. 331-335 [332].
Reprinting of B272.

A332 Perkins, Jane Gray. *The Life of Mrs. Norton*. London: John Murray, 1909, pp. 89-91, 95-96, 133-139, 141-145, 177, 184.
Letters from Caroline (Sheridan) Norton to MS.
Also published as *The Life of the Honourable Mrs. Norton*. N.Y.: Henry Holt, 1909.

A333 Philmus, Robert M. "*Frankenstein*; or, Faust's Rebellion Against Nature." In his *Into the Unknown: The Evolution of Science Fiction from Francis Godwin to H. G. Wells*. Berkeley, Los Angeles: University of California Press, 1970, pp. 82-90; and 22, 24, 41, 99, 102.
Psychological discussion of the Faustian myth: "The clue to the Faustian nature of the conflict between Frankenstein and the monster lies in their being necessarily dependent on one another in their relationship as creator-and-destroyer and in their seesawing role as master-and-slave, pursuer-and-pursued."
Originally dissertation; see D14.

A334 Pierce, Edward L[illie]. *Memoirs and Letters of Charles Sumner*. 4 vols. N.Y.: Arno Press and The New York Times, 1969, Vol. 2, pp. 19-23, 42-47.
MS letters to George S. Hilliard (Dec. 4, 1838 and Jan. 23, 1839).
First published, 4 vols. London, 1877-1893. Also published, 4 vols. Boston: Roberts brothers, 1877-1893; 2 vols. Boston: Roberts bros., 1881. Facsimile reprint of 1881 ed.: Miami, Fla.: Mnemosyne Pub. Co., 1969. My reference above is a facsimile reprint of Vols. 1 and 2 of the Boston 1877-1893 ed., and Vols. 3 and 4 of an "1894" ed.

A335 Pinkney, Edward Coote. "The New Frankenstein." In Thomas Ollive Mabbott and Frank Lester Pleadwell. *The Life and Works of Edward Coote Pinkney*. N.Y.: Macmillan Company, 1926, pp. 192-197.
Pinkney calls his brief story "a harmless parody," and claims that MS was not the author of *Frankenstein*: "on collating the novels supposed to be hers, with the poems of her husband, it becomes apparent that they are the offspring of one brain [Shelley's]."
First published as B274.
See also A263.

A336 Pirie, David. "Chapter 4, Approaches to Frankenstein: Fisher,
      Francis and Sangster." In his *A Heritage of Horror*. *The English
      Gothic Cinema 1946-1972*. London: Gordon Fraser, 1973, pp. 66-81.
      Discussion of the British film versions of *Frankenstein* from
      Hammer Studios. The novel cannot be faithfully adapted to the
      screen without becoming ludicrous, although it is surprising that
      the novel's descriptive set pieces have not been used. In *Curse of
      Frankenstein*, the Monster is close to that in the novel, but Victor
      Frankenstein resembles Baudelaire's "Dandy" more than the MS charac-
      ter.

      Pleadwell, Frank Lester. *See* Mabbott, Thomas Ollive, A263.

A337 Polidori, John William. *The Diary of John William Polidori,
      relating to Byron, Shelley, etc*. William Michael Rossetti, ed.
      London: E. Mathews, 1911, pp. 99, 100-101, 102, 106, 107-108, 110,
      113, 115, 116, 118, 123, 124, 125-126, 127-129, 132, 133, 134, 135,
      219, 220-221.
      Passing references to MS. Rossetti remarks that his father
      liked MS fairly well, but thought she "was ugly," and speculates
      that Gaetano Polidori may have supplied her with information for the
      biography of Alfieri (in Vol. II of the Italian *Lives*).

A338 Pollin, Burton R. "Introduction" to William Godwin. *Italian
      Letters Or, The History of the Last St. Julian*. Lincoln, Neb.:
      University of Nebraska Press, 1965, pp. vii-xxxvi [xxxv-xxxvi].
      MS was severe towards Godwin's *Letters* in her unfinished bio-
      graphical sketch of Godwin, attributing its weaknesses to hasty
      writing.

A339 Pollin, Burton R. "The Role of Byron and Mary Shelley in Poe's
      'Masque.'" In his *Discoveries in Poe*. Notre Dame, London: Univer-
      sity of Notre Dame Press, 1970, pp. 75-90 [75-76, 79-90].
      The Last Man "could easily have directed Poe's mind to the sub-
      ject [of 'The Masque of the Red Death']." Possible MS link also
      with "Fall of the House of Usher."

      Pratt, William Henry. *See* Karloff, Boris, A230.

A340 Praz, Mario. "Introductory Essay" to Peter Fairclough, ed. *Three
      Gothic Novels*. Harmondsworth, Middlesex: Penguin Books, 1968, pp.
      7-34 [7-8, 18, 25-32].
      Although *Frankenstein* surpasses Walpole's *Castle of Otranto* and
      Beckford's *Vathek* "in its capacity of stirring our sense of horror,
      [it has] a fundamental weakness which seriously hampers the suspense
      of disbelief": it is "pseudo-scientific." The attempts to make an
      artificial man by François Quesnay, H. Jean-Baptiste Bertin, and
      Claude-Nicolas Le Cat are mentioned as possible sources for the idea
      in *Frankenstein*.
      Reprinted, 1970, 1972, 1973.

A341 Praz, Mario. *The Romantic Agony*. Angus Davidson, trans. Meridian
      Books. Cleveland, N.Y.: The World Publishing Company, 1967, pp. 76,
      113-114, 130.
          The similarity in names between de Sade's *Justine* and Justine in
      Frankenstein: "the innocent woman . . . is called—by an odd coinci-
      dence—Justine, like Sade's unhappy virtuous heroine."
          First published in this edition, 1956. First published in U.S.,
      N.Y.: Oxford University Press, 1933; reprinted, 1951.

A342 "Preface to the Present American Edition." In Mrs. Mary W. Shelley.
      Frankenstein; or, the Modern Prometheus. New Library of Standard
      Novels, No. 1. N.Y.: Henry G. Daggers, 1845, pp. v-x [v, vi].
          Concerning the early Philadelphia edition of *Frankenstein*:
      "[the novel] was as much read and admired, as the exorbitant price
      then asked [the present edition sold for 25¢] for the most poorly
      printed novel permitted." Notes that *Frankenstein* has "long been a
      scarce book, and is now obtainable by purchase in the United States."

A343 Price, Vincent. "Introduction" to Peter Haining, ed. *The Ghouls*.
      N.Y.: Stein and Day, 1971, pp. 13-15 [14].
          "[Frankenstein's Monster] was made up of human parts, and there
      was some humanity left over—so it was with the Golem. These are
      not monsters as such, for the trace of man that was left with them
      was their tragedy, it was outweighed by their inhumanity."†

A344 Pulos, C. E. *The Deep Truth. A Study of Shelley's Skepticism*.
      Lincoln, Neb.: University of Nebraska Press, 1962, pp. 37-38.
          Examines MS statement (p. 25 of this edition) about Shelley as
      a disciple of Berkeley; she was really suggesting the influence of
      Hume, since her "appreciation of Berkeley does not appear to have
      been in advance of her age," which "little heeded the positive side
      of Berkeley's thought."

A345 Railo, Eino. *The Haunted Castle: A Study of the Elements of
      English Romanticism*. London: George Routledge & Sons/N.Y.: E. P.
      Dutton, 1927, pp. 117, 157, 309, 311-312.
          Brief comments on *Frankenstein*'s influences on "terror-romanti-
      cism" ("by making its mysterious centre . . . the laboratory of a
      cabbalistic seeker after knowledge"), and Godwinian influences on
      the novel.

A346 Raitt, A. W. *Prosper Mérimée*. N.Y.: Charles Scribner's Sons/
      London: Eyre and Spottiswoode, 1970, pp. 43 n. 43, 69-71, 84, 375.
          The MS-Mérimée relationship, with speculation concerning its
      possible continuation and brief comments on her review of Mérimée
      ("enthusiastic and well informed"; reprinted, with notes, on pp.
      375-382).

A347 Read, [Sir] Herbert [Edward]. *A Coat of Many Colours. Occasional
      Essays*. London: George Routledge & Sons, 1945, pp. 119, 123-124.
          MS as Shelley's editor: "[she] did nothing but sentimentalize
      him in death."
          Second, revised ed., 1956. Also published (without subtitle),
      N.Y.: Horizon Press, 1956.

A348   Redding, Cyrus. *Fifty Years' Recollections, Literary and Personal, with Observations on Men and Things.* 3 vols. London: Charles J. Skeet, 1858, Vol. 2, pp. 363-366.
Favorable impression of MS when he met her: she "possessed a very superior mind." Also two MS letters to Redding.
Revised ed., 1858.

A349   Reiman, Donald H. Introductory Notes to his ed. *Part C: Shelley, Keats, and London Periodical Writers.* "Analytical Review—General Weekly Register." Vol. I of *The Romantics Reviewed. Contemporary Reviews of British Romantic Writers.* N.Y., London: Garland Publishing, 1972, pp. 42, 73.
Brief descriptive notes preceeding two reviews of *Frankenstein* [cf. Cl, C9].

_____. "Gentleman's Magazine—Theological Inquirer." Vol. II, pp. 742, 764, 819.
Brief descriptive notes preceeding two reviews of *Frankenstein* [cf. C3, C4] and one of *The Last Man* [cf. C42].

A350   Reiman, Donald H., ed. *Shelley and his Circle 1773-1822.* 6 vols. Cambridge, Mass.: Harvard University Press, 1973, Vol. V, pp. 7, 8, 15 n. 11, 16, 22, 31, 32, 33, 34 & n. 4, 35, 82, 83, 84, 87-88, 89, 100, 110, 115, 127, 129 n. 28, 133, 196, 197, 198, 214-215, 225-231, 242, 256-258, 263, 264, 267, 272, 273, 274, 291-292, 292 n. 1, 292-293, 298-299, 301, 315-316, 316 n. 4, 317, 327, 330, 331, 332-337, 338, 339, 340, 341-342, 346-347, 359, 360-361, 363, 364, 371, 372, 381, 382, 384, 385 & n. 3, 387-388, 389, 390-392, 393-394, 395-398, 437, 445, 450, 467, 468, 472-473, 477, 483 n. 22, 484, 502, 503, 505-508, 511, 512-513.
MS letters in the Carl H. Pforzheimer Library (many previously unpublished in entirety, although all included in above citations), references to MS in other letters, and extended editorial comments on the letters, ranging from glosses on the publication of *Frankenstein* to identifications of MS handwriting.
See also A351.

A351   Reiman, Donald H., ed. *Shelley and his Circle 1773-1822.* 6 vols. Cambridge, Mass.: Harvard University Press, 1973, Vol. VI, pp. 523-530, 543-546, 547-548, 553, 555, 556, 557, 559, 574, 575, 577, 597-600, 603, 604, 605-618, 627, 628, 635 n. (on line 12), 639-641, 642, 644, 646-647, 654 n. 5, 655, 656, 657, 660, 661 n. 14, 666, 668, 672-680, 689, 690, 691 n. 3, 692, 693 n. 2, 707-708, 739-745, 765-766, 768, 778, 779, 780, 781, 782 n. 1, 784 n. 7, 790-798, 806, 808, 838, 839-840, 841, 842, 844, 845-850, 852, 853, 855, 857-865, 873, 874, 877, 879-892, 893-894, 897-898, 899, 900, 904-916, 953, 955-956, 961, 963-1066 *passim* (notes to line references), 1080, 1083, 1090, 1091, 1092, 1094, 1095, 1096, 1101.
As with A350, MS letters, references to MS in other letters, and extended editorial comments, including notation of errors in Jones' edition of MS journal (p. 691 n. 3; cf. IA1).
Both Vols. V and VI are indexed in Vol. VI; these citations are intended to supplement that index.

A352   Reiman, Donald H., ed. *Shelley's The Triumph of Life: A Critical Study. Based on a Text Newly Edited from the Bodleian Manuscript.* Illinois Studies in Language and Literature, 55. Urbana, Ill.: University of Illinois Press, 1965, pp. 119-121, 242.
       MS role in the development of the text of Shelley's poem, also mentioned in notes to the poem (pp. 136-225). Parallel between the poem and *Mathilda* noted on p. 242.

A353   [Rennie, Eliza.] *Traits of Character. Being Twenty-Five Years' Literary and Personal Recollections.* 2 vols. London: Hurst and Blackett, 1860, Vol. I, pp. 101-110.
       First-hand impressions Of MS in her later years: "a partial solution for the circumscribed fame of Mrs. Shelley as a writer may be traced to her own shrinking and sensitive retiringness of nature."

       _____. Vol. II, pp. 202-203, 206-209.
       MS mentioned in passing.

A354   "Review: Frankenstein." In Jonathan D. Culler, ed. *Harvard Advocate Centennial Anthology.* Cambridge, Mass.: Schenkman, 1966, p. 10.
       Reprinting of C12.

A355   Ricci, Seymour de, compiler. *A Bibliography of Shelley's Letters, Published and Unpublished.* Paris: Privately Printed, 1927, pp. 234-247.
       Shelley letters to MS.

A356   Rieger, James. "Introduction" ('Mary Shelley's Life and the Composition of "Frankenstein"'; '"Frankenstein" as Novel and Myth'); "Note on the Text"; "Appendix B, Collation of the Texts of 1818 and 1831." In his ed. Mary Wollstonecraft Shelley. *Frankenstein or The Modern Prometheus.* The Library of Literature. Indianapolis, N.Y.: Bobbs-Merrill, 1974, pp. xi-xxxvii (xi-xxiv; xxiv-xxxvii); xliii-xlv; 230-259.
       Disputes MS version of the origin of the novel, as detailed in her 1831 Introduction, and considers the myth of the novel as developed by stage and film versions. Thorough collation of the two texts.

A357   Rieger, James. *The Mutiny Within. The Heresies of Percy Bysshe Shelley.* N.Y.: George Braziller, 1967, pp. 29, 44-45, 46, 53, 56, 81-89, 95, 121-125, 127-128, 200-203, 237-247.
       Note on the "ghastly" humor of "The Mortal Immortal," comparison of *Frankenstein* with Godwin's *Caleb Williams* and *St. Leon*, the two Beatrices of *Valperga* and Shelley's *The Cenci*, and MS as reflected in Shelley's *Epipsychidion*.
       Chapters 1, 3, and 4, and part of 5, originally appeared in his dissertation [cf. D16]; pp. 121-125, 127-128 as B298; Appendix, "Dr. Polidori and the Genesis of *Frankenstein*" (pp. 237-247) as B297.

A358   Robinson, Henry Crabb. *The Correspondence of Henry Crabb Robinson with the Wordsworth Circle (1808-1866) the greater part now for the first time printed from the originals in Dr. Williams's Library, London.* Edith J[ulia] Morley, ed. 2 vols. Oxford: The Clarendon Press, 1927, Vol. II, pp. 603-604.

MS mentioned in Robinson letter to his brother Thomas (July 2, 1845): "I breakfasted at Sam: [sic] Rogers's (our oldest poet) with Mrs. Shelley, the *worthy* descendant of Godwin and Mrs. Woolstonecraft [sic] and the consort of a man [of] poetic genius."†

A359   Robinson, Henry Crabb. *Henry Crabb Robinson on Books and Their Writers.* Edith J[ulia] Morley, ed. 3 vols. London: J. M. Dent and Sons, 1938, Vol. I, pp. 199, 203, 204, 211, 212, 223, 235-236, 274, 299, 316, 412-413, 418-419, 446.

Personal reflections upon MS, including unfavorable comments on *Frankenstein.*

_____. Vol. II, pp. 464, 552, 569, 574, 648, 654, 777.
More personal reflections, including comments on *Lodore.*

_____. Vol. III, pp. 943-944.
Five MS-related letters indexed in volumes of Robinson's correspondence in Dr. Williams's Library.

A360   Rodway, Allan. *The Romantic Conflict.* London: Chatto & Windus/ Toronto: Clarke, Irwin & Co., 1963, pp. 59-61.

Frankenstein "enacts the romantic conflict" "with greater control than most horror novels." "[Although] it is the first psychological novel, as well as the first *serious* horror novel, its psychology and style are both exceedingly crude."

A361   Roe, Ivan. *Shelley: The Last Phase.* London: Hutchinson, 1953, pp. 18-19, 31-32, 46, 76, 114, 115, 121, 128-156, 163-165, 166-167, 171-172, 178, 180-181, 190, 213, 228-230, 240, 241.

As part of the "biographical mysteries involving Mary," argues that the MS-Hogg letters reveal an affair between them in April-May 1815, with the birth of William Shelley the result. Further argues that "the maniac" and "scornful lady" in Shelley's *Julian and Maddalo* reflect a quarrel between Shelley and MS in the fall of 1818 when she told him of the child's paternity.

A362   Rolleston, Maud. *Talks with Lady Shelley.* The King's Treasury of Literary Masterpieces. London: George G. Harrap, 1925, pp. 25-32, 33-45, 67, 71-72, 75-76, 90-95, 112, 122-124, 126-127, 128, 135-137.

Unreliable, sentimental account of Lady Jane Shelley's reminiscences of MS, with brief mention of MS after Shelley's death.

A363   Rosenberg, Samuel. "Frankenstein, or Daddy's Little Monster." In his *The Come As You Are Masquerade Party.* Englewood Cliffs, N.J.: Prentice-Hall, 1970, pp. 27-66.

Considerably revised version of B301; more humorous material, but also more evidence to support his thesis of biographical

significance in *Frankenstein*.
Also published in his *Confessions of a Trivialist*. Baltimore: Penguin Books, 1972, pp. 29-74.
See also B300.
This series is mentioned by Ellen Moers in her reply to letters concerning her articles [cf. B219, B220] in *The New York Review of Books*, 21 (May 30, 1974), 45.

A364   Rosenberg, Samuel. *Naked Is the Best Disguise. The Death and Resurrection of Sherlock Holmes*. N.Y.: Bobbs-Merrill, 1974, pp. 23-25, 52-55, 61-62, 100-101.
Parallels between *Frankenstein* and Conan Doyle's "Uncle Bernac" and some of the Holmes stories. The thesis that Doyle copied from MS work is proved fairly well, but its significance is not always commented upon.

A365   R[oss], A[ngus]. "Shelley, Mary Wollstonecraft (Godwin) (1797-1851)." In David Daiches, ed. *The Penguin Companion to Literature. I. Britain and the Commonwealth*. Harmondsworth, Middlesex: Penguin Books, 1971, pp. 472-473.
Frankenstein is "a judicious blend of sentimental humanitarianism and 'scientific' notions," *Lodore* and *Falkner* are "defences of Shelley," and her edition of Shelley's poems is "idiosyncratic."

A366   Ross, T. J. "Introduction" to his and Roy Huss, eds. *Focus on the Horror Film*. A Spectrum Book. Englewood Cliffs, N.J.: Prentice-Hall, 1972, pp. 1-10 [3-4].
Brief mention of MS "explicit" meaning in *Frankenstein*.

Rossetti, William Michael. *See Letters about Shelley*, A245.

A367   Rossetti, William Michael. *Memoir of Shelley*. London: Published for The Shelley Society by R. Clay & Sons, 1886, pp. vi, 48-49, 50, 51-52, 53-56, 58, 62, 63, 64-65, 68, 70-72, 80, 86-88, 90-91, 92, 114, 117, 121, 123, 130, 150.
Idealistic portrayal of MS in connection with Shelley: "Shelley and [she] perfectly at one in regarding mutual love"—although it is admitted that she was depressed in later years.
Enlarged version of his "Memoir of Shelley" in his ed. *The Poetical Works of Percy Bysshe Shelley*. London: Edward Moxon, 1870, pp. xxix-clxxix [lxii-lxiii, lxxv-lxxvii, lxxviii-lxxx, lxxxii, lxxxiii, lxxxvii, lxxxix, xcv-xcvi, c, cxiv, cxvi-cxvii, cxxx, cxlvii, cliii]. Also published, N.Y.: Ward, Luck & Co., 1879. Facsimile reprint of 1886 ed.: · N.Y.: AMS Press, 1971.

A368   Russell, Bertrand. *A History of Western Philosophy*. 14th edition. N.Y.: Simon and Schuster, 1964, pp. 680-681.
Frankenstein is "an allegorical prophetic history of the development of romanticism."
First published, 1945. Paperback reprint of 14th ed., A Touchstone Book. N.Y.: Simon and Schuster [ca. 1974] (same pagination).

A369   Sargent, Pamela. "Introduction: Women and Science Fiction." In
       her ed. *Women of Wonder. Science Fiction Stories By Women About
       Women*. N.Y.: Vintage Books, 1975, pp. xiii-lxiv [xvi-xvii].
           Besides quoting from A24 and B220, mentions that "It is inter-
       esting to note the absence of important female characters in
       [*Frankenstein*], which introduced a new literary form and set the
       mold for later science-fiction works."

A370   Scarborough, Dorothy. *The Supernatural in Modern English Fiction*.
       N.Y.: G. P. Putnam's Sons, 1917, pp. 14, 17, 34-35.
           Psychological evaluation of *Frankenstein* and mention of its
       "supernatural biology."
           Facsimile reprint: N.Y.: Octagon Books, 1967.

A371   Scott, Clement [William]. *The Drama of Yesterday and To-Day*. 2
       vols. London, N.Y.: Macmillan and co., 1899, Vol. 2, p. 153.
           Biographical information on Thomas Potter Cooke, who played
       the Monster in a stage version of *Frankenstein* and also in "The
       Vampyre" "365 times."

A372   Scott, Sir Walter. *The Journal of Sir Walter Scott 1825-1832*.
       Popular Edition. N.Y.: Harper & Brothers, 1891, pp. 112 n. 1,
       174 n. 1.
           Quotes from James Ballantyne and Scott concerning *Frankenstein*.
       Also published, N.Y.: Harper & Brothers, 1890; Edinburgh:
       Published for the Editor [J. G. Tait] by Oliver Boyd, 1939.

A373   Scott, Sir Walter. *The Letters of Sir Walter Scott*. H. J. C.
       Grierson, ed. London: Constable, 1933, Vol. V, p. 109 & n. 1.
           Scott intended his notice of *Frankenstein* [cf. C9] for John
       Murray. Also, MS letter to Scott (June 14, 1818).
           Facsimile reprint: N.Y.: AMS Press, 1971.

A374   Scott, Sir Walter. *The Private Letter-Books of Sir Walter Scott*.
       Wilfred Partington, ed. London: Hodder and Stoughton, 1930, pp.
       186-187.
           Letter from J. B. S. Morritt to Scott (Jan. 8, 1818) concerning
       the latter's recommendation of *Frankenstein*.

A375   Scott, Sir Walter. *Sir Walter Scott on Novelists and Fiction*.
       Ioan Williams, ed. London: Routledge & Kegan Paul/N.Y.: Barnes &
       Noble, 1968, pp. 11, 190, 482 n. 6.
           Brief remarks on *Frankenstein*.

A376   Scott, W[alter] S[idney], ed. *Shelley at Oxford. The Early Corres-
       pondence of Shelley with T. J. Hogg, together with letters of Mary
       Shelley and T. L. Peacock and a hitherto unpublished prose fragment
       by Shelley*. [London:] The Golden Cockerel Press, 1944, pp. 67-76.
           MS letters, with extensive annotations.
           Also published, with A15, in A385, with less annotation.

A377   Sealts, Merton M., Jr. *Melville's Reading. A Check-List of Books
        Owned and Borrowed.* Madison, Wisc.: University of Wisconsin Press,
        1966, p. 94.
            Entries 466-469 are A382, 1849 ed. of *Frankenstein*, MS ed. of
        Shelley's *Essays* (1852), and MS ed. of *The Poetical Works* (Boston,
        1857 [cf. A252]).

A378   Sharp, R[obert] Farquharson. "Shelley (Mrs. Mary Wollstonecraft),
        1797-1851." In his *A Dictionary of English Authors*. Boston: Milford
        House, 1972, p. 254.
            Brief biographical sketch and list of MS works
            First published, London: G. Rodway, 1897. Also published,
        London: Kegan Paul, Trench, Trübner & co., 1904.

A379   Sharp, William. *The Life and Letters of Joseph Severn.* N.Y.:
        Charles Scribner's Sons, 1892, pp. 203-204.
            MS letter to Severn (Dec. 15, 1843).
            First published, London: Sampson Low, Marston, 1892. Facsimile
        reprint of N.Y. ed.: N.Y.: AMS Press, 1973.

A380   Sharp, William. *Life of Percy Bysshe Shelley.* London: W. Scott,
        1887, pp. 97-98, 101-110, 117-118, 119-124, 131-132, 135-140, 144,
        152, 154, 156, 157-166, 170-171, 181, 186, 187-188.
            Favorable remarks upon MS as Shelley's wife, and reserved com-
        ments upon her as an individual ("fair to look upon rather than
        lovely, of an intellectual type"); *Frankenstein* "an extraordinary
        romance."
            Facsimile reprints: Port Washington, N.Y.: Kennikat Press,
        1972; Folcroft, Pa.: Folcroft Press, 1973.

A381   Shaw, George Bernard. "Shaming the Devil about Shelley." In his
        Pen Portraits and Reviews. London: Constable, 1931, pp. 236-246
        [239-240].
            Reprinting of B313.

A382   Shelley, Lady [Jane Gibson], ed. *Shelley Memorials: From Authentic
        Sources. To Which Is Added An Essay on Christianity, By Percy
        Shelley: Now First Printed.* London: Smith, Elder and Co., 1859,
        pp. v, 52-53, 67-68, 72-73, 74, 78, 88, 93, 95, 97, 98-108, 109,
        112-114, 115, 127-130, 132, 133, 134-135, 140-142, 143-145, 158 n.,
        161-164, 174-175, 178-179, 180-181, 181-182, 185, 189, 195, 199,
        200, 205-229, 230-251.
            Selective account of MS, with favorable extracts from her
        journal, and the earliest printing of many of her letters—all used
        by Lady Shelley with extreme care.
            Lady Shelley's copy (Bodleian, 2796 e. 1050) contains hand-
        written notes by her on pp. 43 and 78, and a "Preface to Second
        Edition" written on the back of the "Contents" page, in which she
        defends the selective publication of Shelley materials: "in acting
        as they do, the family of Shelley feel their conduct to be such as
        Shelley himself would have desired." Scholars have not always seen

fit to agree with Lady Shelley.
Also published, Boston: Ticknor and Fields, 1859; reprinted,
1875. Facsimile reprint of Boston 1859 ed.: St. Clair Shores,
Mich.: Scholarly Press, 1970.
See also A197. For review, see B317.

A383 Shelley, Percy Bysshe. *The Complete Works of Percy Bysshe Shelley.*
10 vols. "Julian Edition." Roger Ingpen and Walter E[dwin] Peck,
eds. London: Ernest Benn/N.Y.: Charles Scribner's Sons, 1926, Vol.
VIII, pp. LVII-LIX.

_____. Vol. IX, pp. 97-109, 110, 215-218, 247-250, 322-330,
331-332.

_____. Vol. X, pp. 195-197, 206, 293-305, 308-316, 383-384,
412-413.
Shelley letters to MS.
Facsimile reprint: N.Y.: Gordian Press/London: Ernest Benn,
1965.

A384 Shelley, Percy Bysshe. "Journal." In Mrs. [Mary Wollstonecraft]
Shelley, ed. *Essays, Letters from Abroad, Translations and Frag-
ments, By Percy Bysshe Shelley.* 2 vols. London: Edward Moxon,
1840 [1839], pp. 96-106.
Shelley's account of the ghost stories told at Geneva in the
summer of 1816.
Also published in H[arry] Buxton Forman, ed. *The Works of
Percy Bysshe Shelley, in verse and prose.* 8 vols. London: Reeves
and Turner, 1880, Vol. VI, pp. 207-215; and most collections of
Shelley's prose.

A385 [Shelley, Percy Bysshe.] *New Shelley Letters.* W[alter] S[idney]
Scott, ed. London: The Bodley Head, 1948, pp. 80-89, 138-152,
167-170.
MS letters to Hogg.
Condensed version of A15, A376, and *The Athenians* (the last con-
taining material not directly related to MS).

A386 Shelley, Percy Bysshe. "On 'Frankenstein.'" In T[homas] Medwin.
The Shelley Papers. Memoir of Percy Bysshe Shelley. London:
Whittaker, Treacher & Co., 1833, pp. 165-170.
First appearance in book form of B314.
Reprinted in A383 (Vol. VI, pp. 263-265); David Lee Clark, ed.
Shelley's Prose or The Trumpet of a Prophecy. Albuquerque, N.M.:
University of New Mexico Press, 1954, pp. 307-308; Bruce R. McElder-
berry, ed. *Shelley's Critical Prose.* Regents Critics Series. A
Bison Book. Lincoln, Neb.: University of Nebraska Press, 1967, pp.
106-108; and most collections of Shelley's prose.

A387 "Shelley, Mary Wollstonecraft." In *The Encyclopædia Britannica.*
N.Y.: The Encyclopædia Britannica Company, 1911, Vol. XXIV, p. 827.
Frankenstein is "a remarkable performance for so young and in-
experienced a writer." Brief notes on other MS novels.

A388   "Shelley, Mary Wollstonecraft." In *The New Encyclopædia Britannica*. 15th edition. *Micropædia*. Chicago: The Encyclopædia Britannica Educational Corporation, 1974, Vol. IX, pp. 129-130.

Brief critical overview of MS novels: *Frankenstein* immature but fascinating, *Valperga* her best work for style, and *The Last Man* "in popular esteem her best novel."

A389   Smiles, Samuel. *A Publisher and His Friends. Memoirs and Correspondence of the Late John Murray*. 2 vols. London: John Murray, 1891, Vol. II, pp. 290, 309-311, 318-319, 328-329.

MS letters to Murray, and mention of her in others. Also published, 2 vols. N.Y.: Charles Scribner's Sons, 1891.

A390   Smith, Dick. "Chapter 11, Advanced Make-ups. New Frankenstein Monster." In his *Monster Make-Up Hand Book. Famous Monsters of Filmland* special issue. N.Y.: Warren Publishing Company, 1965, pp. 94-98, inside back cover.

Attempt by a professional make-up artist to follow MS description of the Monster.

A391   Smith, George Barnett. *Shelley: A Critical Biography*. Edinburgh: D. Douglas, 1877, pp. 38-40, 46-48, 52-54, 109, 122, 145, 149-151, 162-163, 164, 209-210.

Extremely complimentary treatment of MS, almost more so than of Shelley: "The strength of her character, and the acuteness of her intellect, made her an inestimable companion for her erratic husband, whose love for her appears to have amounted almost to idolatry."

A392   Smith, Harry B[ache]. *A Sentimental Library. Comprising Books Formerly Owned by Famous Writers, Presentation Copies, Manuscripts, and Drawings*. N.Y.: Privately Printed [by the De Vinne Press], 1914, pp. 173-174, 175-176, 177, 179, 182, 183-184, 191, 194.

Annotations of MS and MS-related letters, and copies of her works.

A393   Smith, Horace. Letter. In Arthur Henry Beavan. *James and Horace Smith. A Family Narrative Based upon hitherto unpublished Private Diaries, Letters, and Other Documents*. London: Hurst and Blackett, 1899, pp. 168-177 [168-169].

"[Shelley] was now united to his second wife, whose talents justified her illustrious descent as the daughter of Godwin and Mary Wollstonecraft, while her virtues and her amiability, blessing their union with a domestic happiness which suffered no intermission up to the moment of her husband's death, infused a reconciling sweetness into the grievously bitter cup of his life."† [Letter not dated.]

A394   Snow, Royall Henderson. *Thomas Lovell Beddoes, Eccentric and Poet*. N.Y.: Covici-Friede, 1928, pp. 30-31, 34.

Beddoes sought out MS because of his "unlimited enthusiasm" for Shelley.

A395   Solve, Levin T[heodor]. "Shelley and the Novels of Brown." In
       Fred Newton Scott Anniversary Papers. Chicago: University of
       Chicago Press/Cambridge: The University Press, 1929, pp. 141-156
       [141-143, 148].
          Either MS or Shelley disapproved of Charles Brockden Brown's
       Jane Talbot, probably because "Jane Talbot had no power of reason,
       no will of her own."

A396   Southey, Robert. *New Letters of Robert Southey*. Kenneth Curry,
       ed. 2 vols. N.Y., London: Columbia University Press, 1965, Vol. 2,
       p. 240.
          Brief mention of MS in Southey letter to Bernard Barton (Nov.
       26, 1822).

A397   Spark, Muriel. "Editor's Foreword" to her ed. Mary Shelley. *The
       Last Man. A Novel in Three Books by Mary Shelley. Author of
       'Frankenstein.'* London: The Falcon Press [1954], pp. v-xiii.
          Unbeknownst to MS, both *The Last Man* and *Frankenstein* satirize
       Godwin's progressive ideals. *Frankenstein* centers round the indi-
       vidual; *The Last Man* treats "her theme of disintegration on a uni-
       versal scale."
          A handwritten note by A. Muirhead in the Bodleian copy (256 e.
       16843) states that a half-dozen proof copies of this book were in
       existence when the Falcon Press ceased publication; this copy, bound
       at the Bodleian, is one of these.

A398   Spark, Muriel, and Derek Stanford. "Introduction" to their eds.
       My Best Mary. The Selected Letters of Mary Wollstonecraft Shelley.
       London: Allan Wingate, 1953, pp. 7-17.
          Significance of the MS letters in what they reveal of her re-
       lationship with Shelley, Hogg, Mérimée, and others; and what they
       do not reveal of MS the author.

A399   Spector, Robert Donald. "Introduction: Mary's Monster." In Mary
       Shelley. *Frankenstein or The Modern Prometheus*. N.Y.: Bantam
       Books, 1967, pp. v-ix.
          Brief and superficial examination of terror and the literary
       merits of the novel.

A400   Spector, Robert Donald. "Introduction"; "Mary Shelley (1797-1851)."
       In his ed. *Seven Masterpieces of Gothic Horror*. N.Y.: Bantam
       Books, 1963, pp. 1-11 [2, 10, 11]; 332.
          Frankenstein "was a warning against man's domination by the
       machines he was creating"; the story "The Heir of Mondolfo" "makes
       good use of the Gothic tradition."

       Stanford, Derek. *See* Spark, Muriel, A398.

A401   Steiger, Brad. "Man Made Monsters & Monstrous Men." In his
       Monsters, Maidens & Mayhem. Merit Books. Chicago: Camerarts
       Publishing Co., 1965, pp. 15-33 [15-16, 16-17].
          Very brief mention of "Mary Wollstone Shelley" [sic], her
       creation of *Frankenstein*, and the portrayal of her in the film
       Bride of Frankenstein.

A402   Stevenson, Lionel. *The English Novel. A Panorama*. Boston: Hough-
       ton, Mifflin, 1960, pp. 205-206.
          Frankenstein echoes Godwin's "humanitarian themes and the
       Rousseauistic idea of the noble savaqe."

A403   Stoddard, Richard Henry, ed. *Anecdote Biography of Percy Bysshe
       Shelley*. Sans-Souci Series. N.Y.: Scribner, Armstrong & Co., 1877,
       pp. 191, 192, 205-206.
          Superficial comments on MS, mentioning that her family con-
       sidered her a child at 15, and that she and Shelley knew nothing of
       Claire's passion for Byron. (Extracts from other works not cited
       here.)
          See also A451.

A404   Stokoe, F[rank] W[oodyer]. *German Influence in the English Romantic
       Period, 1788-1818; with Special Reference to Scott, Coleridge,
       Shelley, and Byron*. N.Y.: Russell & Russell, 1963, pp. 163-164.
          The influence of the *Fantasmagoriana* stories upon *Frankenstein*.
       First published, Cambridge: Cambridge University Press, 1926.

A405   Stowell, H[elen] E[lizabeth]. *An Introduction to English Literature*.
       London: Longman Group Limited, 1966, p. 110.
          Frankenstein "may be read today as a parable of man and his
       miraculous machine."
          Second impression, 1970.

A406   Stuart, James. *Reminiscences by James Stuart*. London: Printed for
       private circulation at the Chiswick Press, 1911, pp. 10-11, 52, 60,
       61, 66, 84, 96, 102.
          MS relationship with Robert Baxter and Mary Limeburner MacKnight
       (Stuart's grandmother).

A407   Summers, Montague. *A Gothic Bibliography*. London: The Fortune
       Press [ca. 1941], pp. 330-331.
          List of editions of *Frankenstein*, 1818-1940, and stage versions,
       1823-1887. Also erroneously lists "Frankenstein's Wife" as a film—
       actually *Bride of Frankenstein*.

A408   *A Supplement to the Oxford English Dictionary*. R. W. Burchfield, ed.
       Vol. I: A-G. 1972, p. 1151 col. 2.
          Five uses of "Frankenstein" in print, in addition to those in
       A317.

       Symonds, Emily Morse. *See* Paston, George, A322.

A409   Symonds, John Addington. *Shelley*. English Men of Letters. London: Macmillan and Co., 1878, pp. 79-80.

"With her freedom from prejudice, her tense and high-wrought sensibility, her acute intellect, enthusiasm for ideas, and vivid imagination, Mary Godwin was naturally a fitter companion for Shelley than the good Harriet, however beautiful."†

A410   Taine, John [pseud. of Eric Temple Bell]. *The Greatest Adventure*. N.Y.: E. P. Dutton, 1929, pp. 184-186.

This novel of an attempt to find the origin of life in a land where "evolution has run wild" contains a discussion of *Frankenstein* in which the central character, Dr. Eric Laine, explains the novel's influence upon his life's work.

Also published in *Three Science Fiction Novels by John Taine*. N.Y.: Dover Publications, 1964, pp. 187-342 [298-299]; N.Y.: Ace Books, n.d. (pp. 183-184).

A411   Taylor, Gordon Rattray. *The Biological Time Bomb*. Cleveland: The World Publishing Company, 1968, p. 186.

The novel *Frankenstein* is used as the starting point for a discussion of the possibility of artificial creation of life.

First published, London: Thames & Hudson, 1968. Also published, A Signet Book. N.Y.: The New American Library, 1969 (p. 187).

A412   Taylor, Una [Ashworth]. *Guests and Memories. Annals of a Seaside Villa*. London, N.Y.: Humphrey Milford, Oxford University Press, 1924, pp. 28, 46-47, 336-337.

Passing biographical references to MS, including one in a letter from George Taylor.

Thompson, Laurence Victor. *See* Burroughs, Victor, A78.

A413   Thorslev, Peter L., Jr. "The Wild Man's Revenge." In Edward Dudley and Maximillian E. Novak, eds. *The Wild Man Within. An Image in Western Thought from the Renaissance to Romanticism*. [Pittsburgh:] University of Pittsburgh Press, 1972, pp. 281-307 [303-305].

Frankenstein has had "a prodigious progeny" in the "last development of the wild man as the savage yet pathetic monster." And "the theme is still not dead . . . even for first-rate works of literature."

A414   Threapleton, Mary M. "Introduction" to Mary Shelley. *Frankenstein [or, The Modern Prometheus]*. N.Y.: Airmont Books, 1963, pp. 1-4.

Discussion of the frames used in the novel as a necessary device, and their faults.

A415   Tomory, Peter. *The Life and Art of Henry Fuseli*. N.Y.; Washington, D.C.: Praeger Publishers, 1972, pp. 204-205.

Parallels Fuseli's *The Rosicrucian Cavern* (1804), a story of Rosicrucius' Sepulchre in the *Spectator*, and MS description of the Monster in *Frankenstein*.

A416 Toynbee, Paget. "Mary Wollstonecraft Shelley (1797-1851)." In his
Dante in English Literature. From Chaucer to Cary (c. 1380-1844).
2 vols. London: Methuen [1909], Vol. II, pp. 280-286.
Collection of MS references to Dante in *Frankenstein* and her
letters and journal, briefly annotated.

A417 Trelawny, Edward J[ohn]. *The Letters of Edward J. Trelawny.*
H[arry] Buxton Forman, ed. London: Henry Frowde, Oxford University
Press, 1910, pp. 26-27, 32-34, 48-49, 53-55, 67-68, 81-86, 90, 101-
112, 114, 116-118, 133-136, 139-145, 156-168, 170-171, 176-178, 191-
192, 203-205; 19, 25, 55, 59, 61, 62, 67, 68, 88, 102, 108, 127,
137, 159, 162, 163, 171-172, 177, 194, 197, 198, 201, 209, 215, 225,
229, 232, 234, 240, 259, 260, 263, 265.
First group of citations, Trelawny letters to MS; second,
references to her in his other letters. Forman, on pp. xiii-xiv,
mentions that MS did *not* help Trelawny to write *Adventures of a
Younger Son.*

A418 Trelawny, Edward John. *The Recollections of Shelley and Byron.* In
The Life of Percy Bysshe Shelley. As Comprised in The Life of
Shelley *by Thomas Jefferson Hogg.* The Recollections of Shelley and
Byron *by Edward John Trelawny.* Memoirs of Shelley *by Thomas Love
Peacock.* London, Toronto: J. M. Dent and Sons/N.Y.: E. P. Dutton,
1933, Vol. II, pp. 172-173, 188, 190, 191, 194-195, 196, 209, 214-
215, 218, 226, 227, 230, 232, 236-237, 240, 241.
Mainly favorable comments upon MS, usually in passing.
First published as E. J. Trelawny. *Recollections of the Last
Days of Shelley and Byron.* London: Edward Moxon, 1858. Also pub-
lished, Boston: Ticknor and Fields, 1858; London: Humphrey Milford,
1931.
See also A419, A420.

A419 Trelawny, Edward John. *Records of Shelley, Byron, and the Author.*
2 vols. London: Basil Montague Pickering, 1878, Vol. I, pp. xii,
32, 33, 35, 46, 58-59, 77-79, 92, 93, 110, 120, 121, 122, 154, 163,
164.

_____. Vol. II, pp. 8, 10-14, 24, 33, 42-44, 63-64, 229-
232, 242.
Revised version of A418, extending chapters by "dialogue"
sections, in which MS often appears nagging and reproachful towards
Shelley. Vicious attack on MS in Appendix I (pp. 229-232).
Also published, N.Y.: E. P. Dutton, 1905; N.Y., London: Ben-
jamin Blom, 1968.
See also A180, A192, A420, B90.

A420 Trelawny, Edward John. *Records of Shelley, Byron, and the Author.*
David Wright, ed. The Penguin English Library. Harmondsworth,
Middlesex: Penguin Books, 1973, pp. 50, 68-69, 74-76, 82, 88, 89,
99-100, 103, 107, 108, 112, 114, 116, 118-119, 123-124, 138, 141,
146, 153, 156, 157, 161, 178, 180, 182-183, 188, 189, 194, 196, 199-
200, 203, 211, 215-216, 299-300, 306, 311 n. 29, 316 n. 53.
Unlike those in A419, citations here are in full, incorporating

those in A418, since the text contains both versions of Trelawny's narrative, and since the present text is the most widely available of the editions.
See also A180, A192, B90.

A421 Tuck, Donald H[emy]. *A Handbook of Science Fiction and Fantasy. Part 2: Main Text, M-Z and Appendices.* A collection of material acting as a bibliographic survey to the fields of science fiction and fantasy (including weird), covering the magazines, books, pocket books, personalities, etc., of these fields up to December 1957. Second edition. Hobart, Tasmania, n.p., 1959, pp. 256-257.
Entry on MS states that "Frankenstein mechanically creates a man-monster" and that she has "poor imagination of the future" in *The Last Man*.

A422 Underwood, Peter. *Karloff. The Life of Boris Karloff.* N.Y.: Drake Publishers, 1972, pp. 56-60.
Superficial comments on *Frankenstein*; *The Last Man* "a subject fit to range with [it], but . . . only half-realized."
First published as *Horror Man. The Life of Boris Karloff*. London: Frewin, 1972.

A423 Varma, Devendra P. *The Gothic Flame. Being a History of the Gothic Novel in England, its origins, efflorescence, disintegration, and residuary influences.* N.Y.: Russell & Russell, 1966, pp. 38, 131-132, 154-158, 206, 212.
Minimal comments on *Frankenstein*: "another Gothic novel which falls within the orbit of the Schauer-Romantik, not so much for the treatment of horror, as for the individuality of theme."
Also published, London: Arthur Baker, 1957.

A424 Vincent, E[ric] R[eginald] [Pearce]. *Gabriele Rossetti in England.* Oxford: The Clarendon Press, 1936, p. 51.
MS asked Rossetti's advice concerning her Italian *Lives*.
Facsimile reprint: Folcroft, Pa.: Folcroft Press, 1972.

A425 Wagenknecht, Edward. *Cavalcade of the English Novel. From Elizabeth to George VI.* N.Y.: Henry Holt, 1943, pp. 125-126, 126 n. 14.
Frankenstein is "a 'thriller' with an idea behind it," *Falkner* "a complicated mystery story," and *The Last Man* "the most remarkable of the group."

A426 Walsh, William S[hepard]. "Frankenstein"; "Frankenstein's Man Monster." In his *Heroes and Heroines of Fiction. Modern Prose and Poetry. Famous Characters and Famous Names in Novels, Romances, Poems and Dramas, Classified, Analyzed and Criticised, with Supplementary Citations from the Best Authorities.* Philadelphia, London: J. B. Lippincott, 1914, p. 160.
Mechanistic plot synopsis of the novel, and the brief comment that "The story of this creature who can find no fellowship among men, is either consciously or unconsciously an allegorical portrayal of the charcater [sic] of Percy Bysshe Shelley."

A427   Wardle, Ralph M. *Mary Wollstonecraft. A Critical Biography*. Bison
        Books. Lincoln, Neb.: University of Nebraska Press, 1966, pp. 310,
        331-338.
            MS as an infant, and compared with her mother.
            First published, Topeka, Kans.: University of Kansas Press,
        1951.

A428   Ware, Malcolm. *Sublimity in the Novels of Ann Radcliffe. A Study
        of the Influence upon her Craft of Edmund Burke's Enquiry into the
        Origin of our Ideas of the Sublime and Beautiful.* Upsala University
        Institute: Essays and Studies in English Language and Literature.
        Upsala, Sweden: A.-B. Lundequistka Bokhandeln/Copenhagen: Ejnar
        Munksgaard, 1963, pp. 57-60.
            MS "highly developed and conventional taste for the sublime in
        nature" is reflected in passages of *Frankenstein*.

A429   Waterlow, Syndney. *Shelley*. Port Washington, N.Y.; London:
        Kennikat Press, 1970, pp. 24-25.
            "Frankenstein [*sic*] [was] composed when she had Shelley to fire
        her imagination; but her other novels are competent, and her letters
        are the work of a vigorous intellect."
            First published, London: T. C. & E. J. Jack, 1913, of which the
        present edition may be a facsimile reprint. Another facsimile re-
        print: Folcroft, Pa.: Folcroft Press, 1973.

A430   W[atts], A[laric] A[lexander]. "Preface" to his ed. *The Literary
        Souvenir; or, Cabinet of Poetry and Romance*. London: Longman, Rees,
        Orme, Brown, & Green; and John Andrews, 1827, pp. v-xvi [xvi].
            Regrets that a contribution from the author of *Frankenstein*
        reached him too late for inclusion in the present volume.

A431   *Webster's Third New International Dictionary*. 1971, p. 903a.
            Seven uses of "Frankenstein" in print included in the word's
        definition.

A432   Wedd, A[nnie] F., ed. *The Love Letters of Mary Hays (1779-1780),
        edited by her great-great-niece, A. F. Wedd*. London: Methuen,
        1925, pp. 6, 247-248.
            MS returned Hays' letter to Godwin in 1836. Also, MS letter to
        Hays (April 20, 1836).

A433   Wheeler, William A[dolphus]. "Frankenstein." In his *An Explanatory
        and Pronouncing Dictionary of the Noted Names of Fiction; including
        also familiar pseudonyms, surnames bestowed on eminent men, and
        analogous popular appellations often referred to in literature and
        conversation*. Boston: Ticknor and Fields, 1865, pp. 138-139.
            The Monster is "endued, apparently through the agency of
        galvanism, with a sort of spectral and convulsive life." Also
        quotes from Charles Sumner, using "Frankenstein" in regard to the
        Southern Confederacy.

A434   White, John J. *Mythology in the Modern Novel: A Study of Pre-figurative Techniques.* Princeton, N.J.: Princeton University Press, 1971, p. 15.
"The Titanic gods are often espoused by the Romantics (even, for example, in the mythological Gothic of Mrs. Shelley's *Frankenstein; or, The Modern Prometheus.*)"†

A435   White, Newman Ivey. *Portrait of Shelley.* N.Y.: Alfred A. Knopf/ Toronto: Random House of Canada, 1945, pp. 116, 153ff.
Condensed version of A436, footnotes and appendices deleted, for the "general reader."
Reprinted, 1959, 1968.

A436   White, Newman Ivey. *Shelley.* 2 vols. London: Secker & Warburg, 1940, Vol. I, pp. 260, 335, 336, 338-340, 342-352, 353, 355-356, 359-360, 361, 365, 366, 368, 370, 371, 374, 378, 379, 380-383, 384, 385, 387, 388, 389, 390, 391-393, 400-402, 403, 404, 406, 407, 408-409, 418, 420, 426, 432, 438, 439, 440-441, 443, 444, 451, 453, 457, 458-459, 462, 463, 466, 469, 472, 473, 478, 487, 488-489, 498, 499, 501, 505-507, 509, 510, 515, 518, 520, 527, 533, 534, 535, 536, 537-539, 540-541, 542-543, 544-547, 555, 556, 563, 570, 571, 576-596 *passim,* 651-672 *passim,* 678, 679, 680, 681, 682, 683, 689, 690, 694, 698, 705, 710, 711, 712, 720, 724, 734, 735, 736-737, 740; (references to MS works) 188, 215, 281, 299, 327, 328, 361-362, 443-444, 457, 473, 506, 520, 527, 679 n. 35, 680-682, 711 n. 11, 735 n. 80, 736 n. 2.

_____. Vol. II, pp. 3, 6, 7, 15, 17-18, 19, 20, 22, 26, 27, 29, 31, 36, 37, 39-40, 41, 45, 46, 47-48, 49, 54-55, 66, 69-70, 71, 73, 74, 75, 76, 77, 78, 82, 88-89, 92, 93, 94-95, 96, 97, 98-99, 100, 101, 108, 123, 127, 128, 132, 138, 154, 162, 163, 168-169, 173, 182, 184, 185, 188-190, 191, 200, 201-202, 204, 205, 206, 215, 216, 219, 225, 232, 238, 242-243, 244-245, 248-249, 251, 252-253, 256, 257-258, 262-264, 266, 281, 282, 298, 299, 306, 307, 308-309, 309-310, 310-313, 314-315, 316, 319, 324-325, 327, 328, 334, 336, 337, 338-339, 341-342, 354, 361-362, 367-368, 374, 375, 379-380, 381, 384, 385-387, 396, 397, 400-401, 426-427, 446, 467, 468, 469-471, 472-479, 480-481, 484, 505, 508-517, 518, 521, 555, 558, 560-562, 564, 568, 569, 574, 578-588 *passim,* 590-591, 603-619 *passim,* 632, 635 ff; (references to MS works) 41, 55-56, 101, 249, 319, 555 n. 65, 564 n. 53, 605.
Valuable, detailed work on Shelley, and on MS until his death. Thorough use of seminal sources. Criticism of MS not quite as detailed.
Also published, 2 vols. N.Y.: Alfred A. Knopf, 1947. Facsimile reprint of London ed.: N.Y.: Octagon Books, 1972.
See also A435.

A437   White, Newman I[vey]. "*The Shelley Legend* Examined." In Newman I[vey] White, Frederick L[afayette] Jones, and Kenneth N[eill] Cameron. *An Examination of "The Shelley Legend."* Philadelphia: University of Pennsylvania Press, 1958, pp. 1-30.
Reprinting of B349.

A438   Whiteford, Robert Naylor. *Motives in English Fiction*. N.Y.,
       London: G. P. Putnam's Sons, The Knickerbocker Press, 1918, pp.
       198, 231-232, 233, 282-285.
           Frankenstein is a link between Godwin's *St. Leon* and Maturin's
       Melmoth the Wanderer; mention of biographical elements in *The Last
       Man* and *Lodore*.

A439   Whitmore, Clara H[elen]. "Chapter XII, Lady Caroline Lamb (1785-
       1828)—Mary Shelley (1797-1851)." In her *Woman's Work in English
       Fiction. From the Restoration to the Mid-Victorian Periods*. N.Y.,
       London: G. P. Putnam's Sons, The Knickerbocker Press, 1910, pp.
       200-215 [204-215].
           The Monster in *Frankenstein* "is closely related to our own
       human nature"; synopsis of *Valperga*; biographical elements in *The
       Last Man* and *Lodore*.

A440   Wiley, Lulu Rumsey. *The Sources and Influence of the Novels of
       Charles Brockden Brown*. N.Y.: Vantage Press, 1950, pp. 56-57, 188,
       273, 274, 281, 283-287.
           The influence of *Wieland* on *Frankenstein*, and *Arthur Mervyn* on
       The Last Man.

A441   Williams, Edward Ellerker. *Journal of Edward Ellerker Williams,
       Companion of Shelley and Byron in 1821 and 1822*. Richard Garnett,
       ed. London: Elkin Mathews, 1902, pp. 16, 19, 20, 22, 23, 26, 27,
       29, 32, 33, 35, 36, 39, 40, 41, 42, 43, 46, 48, 49, 50, 54, 55, 62,
       65.
           First-hand record of MS from Oct. 21, 1821 to July 4, 1822.
       Typical entry: "Jan. 3rd. Pass the evening with Mary."
           Facsimile reprints: Folcroft, Pa.: Folcroft Press, 1970;
       Havertown, Pa.: Richard West, 1973.
           See also A158.

A442   Williams, George G., with the assistance of Marian and Geoffrey
       Williams. *Guide to Literary London*. N.Y.: Hastings House, 1973,
       pp. 51, 99, 105-106, 131, 192, 243, 266, 297, 332-333, 359, 384.
           Identifies 11 dwellings and meeting-places of MS (not all of
       which, for the novice traveler in London, are quite as easy to find
       as the author allows).

A443   Williams, Stanley T[homas]. *The Life of Washington Irving*. N.Y.:
       Oxford University Press/London: Humphrey Milford, 1935, Vol. I, pp.
       251, 259, 263, 286-288, 463 nn. 62-80.
           The MS-Payne-Irving affair; detailed on Irving's role.

A444   Wilson, Milton. "Hymns of Pan and Apollo." In his *Shelley's Later
       Poetry: A Study of his Prophetic Imagination*. N.Y.: Columbia Uni-
       versity Press, 1959, pp. 30-37 [30].
           Consideration of the hymns as written for the opening scene of
       MS drama *Midas*, and summary of this scene.
           Also published in George M. Ridenour, ed. *Shelley. A Collec-
       tion of Critical Essays*. Twentieth Century Views. Englewood
       Cliffs, N.J.: Prentice-Hall, 1965, pp. 153-158 [153-154].

Wise, Thomas J[ames]. *See* Nicoll, W[illiam] Robertson, A304.

A445   Wise, Thomas J[ames]. *A Shelley Library. A Catalogue of Printed Books, Manuscripts and Autograph Letters by Percy Bysshe Shelley, Harriet Shelley, and Mary Wollstonecraft Shelley.* London: Printed for private circulation only, 1924, pp. 6-7, 8-25, 70-73, 87-88.

Descriptive bibliographies of first editions of *Frankenstein, Valperga, The Last Man, Perkin Warbeck, Lodore, Falkner, Rambles, The Choice, Proserpine & Midas,* Shelley's *Posthumous Poems,* Shelley's *Essays,* and first and second edition of Shelley's *Poetical Works;* MS letters.

Facsimile reprint: N.Y.: Haskell House, 1971.

Wolf, Barbara H. *See* Wolf, Jack C., A446.

Wolf, Jack C. *See* Gerald, Gregory Fitz, A161.

A446   Wolf, Jack C., and Barbara H. Wolf. "Introduction" to "Part Four, Human Monsters." In their ed. *Ghosts, Castles, and Victims: Studies in Gothic Terror.* A Fawcett Crest Book. Greenwich, Conn.: Fawcett Publications, 1974, pp. 268-270 [269-270].

Both Frankenstein and the Monster begin with good intentions and end "victims of their own needs and desires." Brief, superficial.

A447   Wolf, Leonard. "Frankenstein." In his *Monsters. Twenty Terrible and Wonderful Beasts from the Classic Dragon and Colossal Minotaur to King Kong and the Great Godzilla.* San Francisco: Straight Arrow Books, 1974, pp. 92-97.

Superficial comments on the novel, and brief comparison with the 1931 film ("a much starker, much simpler affair").

*A448 Wood, Clement. *Shelley and the Women He Loved.* Girard, Kans.: Haldeman-Julius Company, 1924.

Item not seen, but assume it discusses MS in some detail. Not in the British Library, Bodleian, or Yale; item in the card catalogue at the Library of Congress, but a year's search has failed to uncover it, so assume it is lost.

A449   Woodberry, George Edward. "Notes on a Manuscript of Shelley's Poems." In *The Shelley Notebook in the Harvard Library. Reproduced with Notes and a Postscript by George Edward Woodberry.* Cambridge, Mass.: John Barnard Associates (Harvard University Press)/London: Humphrey Milford, 1929, pp. 7-18.

Identifies MS and Shelley handwriting in the notebook.

Facsimile reprint: Folcroft, Pa.: Folcroft Press, 1969.

A450   Woskey, Leah. "The Monster of Frankenstein"; "Bride of Frankenstein." In her *Monster Gallery.* San Francisco: Troubadour Press, 1973, unpaginated.

Brief summary of the novel, for children, and very brief comparison of novel and film *Bride of Frankenstein.*

A451   Wotton, Mabel E. "Mary Wollstonecraft Shelley." In her *Word
       Portraits of Famous Writers*. London: Richard Bentley & Son, 1887,
       pp. 275-277.
           Excerpts from A98, A403.

A452   Wright, Andrew. "Introduction" to his ed. Horace Walpole. *The
       Castle of Otranto*. Ann Radcliffe. *The Mysteries of Udolpho
       (Abridged)*. Jane Austen. *Northanger Abbey*. N.Y.: Holt, Rinehart
       and Winston, 1963, pp. vii-xxi [viii].
           "Mary Shelley's justly maliqned *Frankenstein* also appeared in
       1818."†

A453   Wright, David. "Introduction" to his ed. Edward John Trelawny.
       Records of Shelley, Byron, and the Author. The Penguin English
       Library. Harmondsworth, Middlesex: Penguin Books, 1973, pp. 7-34
       [19-21].
           Examines Trelawny's attack on MS [cf. A419, A420], but gives
       no reasons for its ferocity.

A454   Wright, Raymond. "Biographical Notes." In his ed. *Prose of the
       Romantic Period 1780-1830*. Vol. IV of Kenneth Alcott, ed. *The
       Pelican Book of English Prose*. Harmondsworth, Middlesex: Penguin
       Books, 1956, pp. 275-285 [284].
           Frankenstein "is basically a terror novel, but its speculative
       and scientific curiosity is [MS] own invention."

A455   Wright, Walter Francis. *Sensibility in English Prose Fiction 1760-
       1840. A Reinterpretation*. Urbana, Ill.: University of Illinois
       Press, 1937, p. 124.
           In the novels of MS and others, "the reader for the moment
       identifies himself with the evil doer and experiences with [the
       pathetic victim] the horror of his act."
           Facsimile reprint: Folcroft, Pa.: Folcroft Press, 1970.

A456   Wyatt, Sibyl White. *The English Romantic Novel and Austrian
       Reaction. A Study in Hapsburg-Metternich Censorship*. An Exposition-
       University Book. N.Y.: Exposition Press, 1967, pp. 30, 134-138, 142,
       146, 148, 150.
           The Last Man was censored by the Austrian Empire because of its
       political and religious statements.

B1   Adams, Richard P. "Hawthorne: The Old Manse," *Tulane Studies in English*, 8 (1958), 115-151 [132 n. 23].
      "A probable source for 'The Birthmark' is Mary Shelley's *Frankenstein* (1818). Frankenstein, like Aylmer, is an eighteenth-century scientist who is also a disciple of Cornelius Agrippa, Paracelsus, and Albertus Magnus; he is challenged by the secret of creation, which he discovers and uses; and his greatest triumph ends in a fatal disaster."†

B2   *The Age* (London), April 2, 1837, p. 106 col. 2.
      "Mrs. Shelley's New Work.—The new work which Mrs. Shelley has just published, entitled 'Falkner,' it is quite sufficient to say, is worthy of the author of 'Frankenstein.' There is a tone in all Mrs. Shelley's productions which bespeaks a mind of deep and accurate reflection. The work before us is eminently one of intellect and feeling. It contains scenes which rivet the attention, and which cannot fail of leaving a lasting impression on the reader. We have heard it designated as her best production; and probably few of the numcrous [*sic*] admirers of her works will be disposed to dissent from that opinion."†

B3   Aldiss, Brian W. "The Billion Year Spree. I. Origin of the Species," *Extrapolation*, 14 (May 1973), 167-191.
      Examination of the scientific themes in *Frankenstein* and *The Last Man*, with a brief notice of the *doppelgänger* in "The Transformation."
      Also published in A24.

B4   Aldiss, Brian. "The Gothic Imagination," *Queen* (London), 434 (December 10-January 6, 1969), 70-71.
      Light treatment of the themes in *Frankenstein*, mentioning that MS was "under the influence of the poet Ossian."

B5   Allen, Edmund. "A Home for Mr. Holmes," *In Britain*, 29 (1974), 16-19 [16].
      MS "created the Frankenstein monster from paramythical bric-a-brac and odds and ends of physiological knowledge. She breathed life into the thing and then stepped quietly into literary oblivion. The monster continued to live." The parallels with Conan Doyle's creation, Sherlock Holmes, serve to introduce the latter topic.†
      See also B6.

B6   Allen, Edmund. "A Home for Mr. Holmes," Washington *Post*, October
      27, 1974, pp. M7, M10 [M7].
          Reprinting of B5.

B7   "Amelioration of the Condition of the Slave Population in the West
      Indies (House of Lords)," [Hansard's] *Parliamentary Debates*, n.s.
      10 (March 16, 1824), cols. 1046-1198 [1103].
          Although not mentioned by name, the Monster in *Frankenstein* is
      compared to the Negro slaves, as part of an argument against
      freeing them: "To turn [the Negro] loose in the manhood of his
      physical strength, in the maturity of his physical passions, but
      in the infancy of his uninstructed reason, would be to raise up a
      creature resembling the splendid fiction of a recent romance; the
      hero of which constructs a human form, with all the corporeal
      capabilities of man, and with the thews and sinews of a giant;
      but being unable to impart to the work of his hands a perception
      of right and wrong, he finds too late that he has only created a
      more than mortal power of doing mischief, and himself recoils from
      the monster which he has made."

B8   Anderson, (Mrs.) G. A. Letter, "A Šhelley Letter," *Times Literary
      Supplement*, February 6, 1919, p. 70.
          Suggests that the "young friend of great intellectual promise"
      mentioned by Shelley in a letter to M. G. Lewis (Jan. 2, 1818) was
      really MS, since Shelley does not mention the sex of the friend,
      and since both MS and Shelley were acquainted with Lewis.

      Butterworth, S. Letter, "A Shelley Letter," *Times Literary Supple-
      ment*, March 20, 1919, p. 153.
          Agrees with Anderson, citing supporting evidence in the notice
      of intended publication of *Frankenstein* in *The Observer* [cf. B255],
      and in Dowden's biography of Shelley [cf. A126].

B9   "The Annuals. (An interview between the Editor and his Friends),"
      The Spirit and Manners of the Age, n.s. 2 (December 1829), 881-888
      [883].
          Concerning the stories in the 1830 *Keepsake*, MS "The Mourner"
      among them, the editor states that "the literary contents . . .
      are far from what they might be, and ought to be."

B10   "The Annuals for 1832," *New Monthly Magazine*, 32 (November 1831),
      455-461 [458, 460].
          Proserpine, MS contribution to the 1832 *Winter's Wreath*, is
      not mentioned directly, but the annual's pages "give the idea of
      cultivated mind and refined taste, rather than talent." "The
      Dream," in the 1832 *Keepsake*, "is a very original idea."

B11   "The Annuals for 1837," *The Athenæum*, No. 471 (November 5, 1836),
      782-784 [783].
          Concerning "The Parvenue" in the 1837 *Keepsake*: "Mrs. Shelley
      has contributed a striking but painful story."†

B12   [Anster, J. H.] "Life and Writings of Percy Bysshe Shelley,"
        North British Review, 8 (November 1847), 218-257 [218, 242].
            In a review of five works by and about Shelley, including MS
        edition of his *Poetical Works* and A281, MS is termed "a woman of
        great genius . . . who regarded Shelley with almost idolatrous
        veneration," and is complimented on producing an "exceedingly
        beautiful edition of [Shelley's] poetical works."

B13   *Appleton's Journal: A Monthly Miscellany of Popular Literature*
        (N.Y.), n.s. 2 (January 1877), 12 n.
            "This posthumous story by Mrs. Shelley ['The Heir of Mondolfo']
        has not before appeared in print. It was found among the unpub-
        lished papers of Leigh Hunt and is authenticated by S. R. Town-
        shend Mayer, Esq., Editor of *St. James Magazine*, London."†
            Also printed in full in A6 (p. 323 n. 1).

B14   Armitt, Annie. "The Story of Mary Shelley," *Scottish Review*
        (Paisley, Scotland), 20 (October 1892), 254-275.
            Sentimental account of MS as sad, lonely, troubled, and
        suffering.

B15   Arnold, Donna. "Frankenstein's Monster: Paragon or Paranoiac?"
        Trace, 54 (Autumn 1964), 285-287.
            Confusing paraphrasing of the novel, possibly satirical: the
        Monster is "a decent sort as monsters go."

B16   Awad, Louis. "The Alchemist in English Literature. I.—Franken-
        stein," *Bulletin of Faculty of Arts* (Fuad I University, Cairo,
        Egypt), 13 (May 1951), 33-82 [39, 44, 45, 52, 62-82].
            Shelley as reflected in *Frankenstein*, primarily using Hogg's
        Life [cf. A205] as the source for Shelley's scientific experiments;
        parallels between *Frankenstein* and Shelley's *St. Irvyne*; Victor
        Frankenstein as the chemist of the modern world, a renovation of
        the Promethean alchemist.

B17   "Back Numbers—LXXXV," *Saturday Review* (London), 146 (August 11,
        1928), 181.
            Excerpt from B317, and the comment that *Frankenstein* "is
        proverbial, but how many of those who like it have given any
        thought to its author in her capacity as Shelley's wife?"

B18   Baker, Carlos. "Rounding Out the Shelley Record," *The New York
        Times Book Review*, October 5, 1947, p. 3.
            Review of IA1, noting the history of MS journal.

B19   Barber, Giles. "Galignani's and the Publication of English Books
        in France from 1800 to 1852," *The Library*, Fifth Series, 16
        (December 1961), 267-286 [273, 278].
            Cyrus Redding as a go-between for MS with the Galignanis; note
        on the Flemish printing of *Lodore*.

B20   Bebbington, W. G. "Shelley's Cottage," *Notes and Queries*, 18
        (May 1971), 163-165.
            Discovery of the cottage in Bishopsgate, and mention of its
        possible connection with "Perdita's cottage" in *The Last Man.*

B21   *La Belle Assemblée, or Court and Fashionable Magazine*, n.s. 3
        (April 1826), 176.
            Brief mention that *The Last Man* "is well calculated to rank
        with its predecessors."

B22   *Bell's Weekly Messenger*, May 23, 1830, p. 165 col. 3.
            "Mrs. Shelley's new novel, 'The Fortunes of Perkin Warbeck,'
        exhibits a stirring picture of the deeply interesting adventures
        of that mysterious claimnant of the British throne."†

        Benton, Robert. *See* Newman, David, B239.

        Besterman, Theodore. *See* Norman, Sylva, B251.

B23   Binder, Eando [Otto O. Binder]. "I, Robot," *Amazing Stories*,
        13 (January 1939), 8-18.
            In this short story, the robot Adam Link discovers the novel
        Frankenstein: "But it is the most stupid premise ever made: that
        a created man must turn against his creator, against humanity,
        lacking a soul. The book is all wrong.
            "Or is it?"
            Reprinted as A55; revised as A54.
            See also A234, B36.

B24   Black, Frank Gees. *The Epistolary Novel in the Late Eighteenth
        Century. A Descriptive and Bibliographical Study.* University of
        Oregon Monograph series, *Studies in Literature and Philology*,
        No. 2 (April 1940), pp. 110, 148.
            Simultaneous publication of A57.

B25   *Blackwood's Edinburgh Magazine*, 19 (January 1826), 91.
            "A Romance to be entitled 'The Last Man,' from the pen of Mrs.
        Shelley, is in a state of considerable forwardness."†

B26   Bloom, Harold. "Frankenstein, or The New Prometheus," *Partisan
        Review*, 32 (Fall 1965), 611-619.
            Psychological evaluation of antitheses, the mythology of the
        self, and paradoxes in the novel.
            See also A60, A61.

B27   Bloom, Harold. "A Letter of Consolation to Mary Shelley," *The
        Yale University Library Gazette*, 33 (July 1958), 35-40.
            Letter from Charles Clairmont to MS (Sept. 18, 1822), con-
        soling her after Shelley's death.

B28   Blunden, Edmund [Charles]. "Mary Shelley's Romances," *English
       Studies in Japan: Essays and Studies presented to Dr. Y. Yamato
       in Honor of His Sixtieth Birthday*, special issue of *Bulletin of
       the English Literary Society of the Nihon Univ., Tokyo* (1958),
       1-4.
            Besides *Frankenstein*, *The Last Man* is the most readable work
       of MS, in which she has few scientific predictions, but has "a
       longing for the gigantesque, the terrific contrast, the rhetorical
       immensity, the huge ambition and mighty wreck of human story."

B29   Boas, Louise Schutz. Letter, "Dowden's Life of Shelley," *Times
       Literary Supplement*, August 2, 1957, p. 471.

       Ehrsam, Theodore G[eorge]. Letter, "Dowden's Life of Shelley,"
       Times Literary Supplement, September 6, 1957, p. 533.
            Both Garnett and Dowden [cf. A126] were victims of their "Vic-
       torian morality" in their attempts to exonerate Shelley in his
       role in the elopement.

B30   Boas, Louise Schutz. Letter, "Shelley and Mary," *Times Literary
       Supplement*, November 14, 1963, p. 927.

       Michell, Anne Lee. Letter, "Shelley and Mary," *Times Literary
       Supplement*, December 12, 1963, p. 1038.

       Boas, Louise Schutz. Letter, "Shelley and Mary," *Times Literary
       Supplement*, February 20, 1964, p. 153.

       Michell, Anne Lee. Letter, "Shelley and Mary," *Times Literary
       Supplement*, March 12, 1964, p. 220.

       Boas, Louise Schutz. Letter, "Shelley and Mary," *Times Literary
       Supplement*, July 10, 1964, p. 631.
            A complaint about the difficulty of access to the volumes of
       Shelley and Mary [cf. A16] leads to a discussion of Lady Shelley's
       excisions, with Boas mentioning (in the last letter) an additional
       excision previously unnoticed on p. 969 of the copy in the Beinecke
       Library at Yale University.

B31   Boas, Louise Schutz. "A Letter About *Shelley and Mary*," *Huntington
       Library Quarterly*, 28 (May 1965), 283-285.
            Letter from Frances Power Cobbe to Frederick R. Halsey giving
       the requested information about the volumes [cf. A16].

B32   Booth, Bradford A. Letter, "Shelley and Mary," *Times Literary
       Supplement*, April 30, 1938, p. 304.
            In response to Grylls attempt to locate copies of A16 [cf. A6],
       notes the locations of two others.

B33   Booth, Bradford A. "*The Pole*: A Story by Claire Clairmont,"
       Journal of English Literary History, 5 (March 1938), 67-70.
            Partly on the basis of internal evidence, claims the story was
       written not by MS but by Claire. MS may have revised it, and it

was published as "by the author of 'Frankenstein'" because "Mary thought that the revision was of such nature that she was entitled to put her name to it."

B34   Boyce, George K. "Modern Literary Manuscripts in the Morgan Library," *PMLA*, 67 (February 1952), 3-36 [21].
       Lists, under MS, "*Valperga* (scattered leaves), 17 pp.; marginalia in a copy of her *Frankenstein* (1818); letters (6), 1832 and undated"; under Percy B. Shelley, "'The Aziola' (autograph of Mary Shelley), 2 pp," in the Pierpont Morgan Library.†

B35   Brack, O M, Jr. "Lord Byron, Leigh Hunt and *The Liberal*: Some New Evidence," *Books at Iowa*, No. 4 (April 1966), 36-38.
       Letter from Byron to MS (Oct. 14, 1822) concerning John Murray's reluctance to turn over manuscripts to John Hunt.

B36   Brazier, Donn. Letter, "In Support of the Observatory," *Amazing Stories*, 13 (March 1939), 130-131 [131].
       Response to B23: "'I, Robot,' by Binder, though clearly patterned after *Frankenstein*, was the best of last issue. However, I wonder if Binder read the book, or saw the movie; for the premise that a created man must turn against humanity was not made in the book as Binder says."†

B37   Bright, Henry A. Note, under "Miss Clairmont," *The Athenæum*, No. 2684 (April 5, 1879), 438.
       MS letter to Claire (Feb. 20, ?), "was given by [the latter] to a relative of mine in the March of 1822 at Pisa . . . [and] was evidently written in some moment of great excitement."

B38   Brown, T. J. "Some Shelley Forgeries by 'Major Byron,'" *Keats-Shelley Memorial Bulletin*, No. 14 (1963), 47-54 [51-54].
       Lists 15 forgeries of Shelley letters to MS.

B39   Buchanan, Robert. "Thomas Love Peacock: A Personal Reminiscence," *New Quarterly Magazine*, 4 (April 1875), 238-255 [248-249].
       Brief remarks on Peacock's bad opinion of MS: "I fancy [he] never really liked her. . . . he certainly preferred Harriet."

B40   Burr, Jeff. Letter, "Monsters should be ugly," *TV Guide*, 23 (January 25, 1975), A-6.
       Response to B55, quoting MS description of the Monster to prove lack of physical resemblance to actor Michael Sarrazin in the 1974 television production, *Frankenstein: The True Story*.

Butterworth, S. *See* Anderson, (Mrs.) G. A., B8.

B41   Buyers, Geoffrey. "The Influence of Schiller's Drama and Fiction upon English Literature in the Period 1780-1830," *Englische Studien*, 48 (1915), 349-393 [383-384].
       Possible influence of "The Criminal" upon *Frankenstein*.

B42   Callahan, Patrick J. "*Frankenstein*, Bacon, and the 'Two Truths,'"
       Extrapolation, 14 (December 1972), 39-48.
         Details alchemical references in the novel, presenting Victor
       Frankenstein as an empirical scientist.

B43   Cameron, Kenneth N[eill]. "A New Shelley Legend," *Journal of
       English and Germanic Philology*, 45 (October 1946), 369-379.
         Partial rebuttal of points made in A19, many concerning MS.
       Also published as A87.
         See also B141 [and A226], B349 [and A437].

B44   Cameron, Kenneth Neill. "The Planet-Tempest Passage in *Epipyschi-
       dion*," *PMLA*, 63 (September 1948), 950-972.
         MS coldness towards Shelley in 1817 accounts for the references
       to her in the poem as "the cold, chaste moon."

B45   Mrs. Carey. "Impromptu. On hearing some ill-natured remarks on
       Mrs. Shelley's Last Man," *The Country Literary Chronicle and Weekly
       Review*, No. 361 (April 15, 1826), 237.
         "Take courage, fair Shelley! though cynics contemn,
           And dull prosers find faults where they can;
         The ladies will read, since there's not one of them
           But must wish to behold the *Last Man*."†

B46   Carter, John Stewart. "Poetry and the Hucksters," *Tri-Quarterly*,
       1 (Winter 1965), 55-60 [57-58].
         "Mrs. Shelley devoted her life to selling her husband, dis-
       torting his meaning to meet the rising Victorianism, suppressing
       his letters and notes, making him acceptable to the reactionaries
       he bitterly loathed."

B47   Clarke, I[gnatius] F[rederick]. "Science Fiction: Past and
       Present," *The Quarterly Review*, 295 (July 1957), 260-270 [261].
         Brief mention of *The Last Man*: "as in most of her early
       stories, her future world is not essentially modified by the
       impact of science upon society: steam-driven balloons and vast
       canals exist in a world of old-fashioned infantry tactics and
       Godwinian economics."

B48   Cline, C[larence] L[ee]. "Two Mary Shelley Letters," *Notes and
       Queries*, 195 (October 28, 1950), 475-476.
         One to Disraeli (between Nov. 15 and Dec. 7, 1837), the other
       to Aubrey Beauclerk ("shortly after" March 14, 1838).

B49   Cocks, Jay. "Monster Mash," *Time*, 104 (December 30, 1974), 2.
         Notes, in this review of the film *Young Frankenstein*, that the
       film "is a satirical exhumation of the Mary Shelley classic. The
       Shelley story ought to have been turned wormy by this time from
       virtually constant exposure. It is, however, still a powerful
       myth."

B50   [Coleridge, John Taylor.] Review of Leigh Hunt, *Foliage*, *The
       Quarterly Review*, 18 (January 1818), 324-335 [327 n.]
         Contemplating a review of *Frankenstein* (not mentioned by

name), reviewer wonders whether it "would be morally right" to "lend notoriety" to it with a review, even though it possesses "some beauty."

B51   Cooper, Arthur. "Mel Brooks: Chasing Rabbits," *Newsweek*, 83 (April 22, 1974), 98, 103-103A.
        Brooks, planning a film, "Young Frankenstein," claims to have read the MS novel 52 times. "For him the message is Freudian. 'She was writing about womb envy. . . . Why else would a man be literally creating a child?'"

B52   *The Courier* (London), April 13, 1835, p. 4 col. 5.
        "We recollect no period when we have noticed so many works of great merit as have recently issued from the press. We allude particularly to Mrs. Shelley's new romance entitled 'Lodore,' a story which will raise still higher the fame of this popular author. . . . Works like these will go far to raise the standard by which productions in this class of literature have of late years been judged."†

B53   *The Court Journal*, No. 364 (April 16, 1836), 245.
        Obituary of Godwin. "He leaves a daughter, the widow of the poet Shelley, who inherits much of her father's genius."† (Credit given to the *Daily Paper*.)

B54   Crafts, Stephen. "*Frankenstein*: Camp Curiosity or Premonition?" *Catalyst* (State University of New York at Buffalo), 3 (Summer 1967), 96-103.
        Marcusian application of "one-dimensionality" to the novel: "Mary Shelley explores metaphorically the usurpation of sensibility by intellect and the concomittant human relationships the perversion produces." Also, brief examination of Frankenstein as Faust figure, the Monster as Noble Savage.

B55   Crist, Judith. "This Week's Movies," *TV Guide*, 22 (December 28, 1974), A-7.
        The television production *Frankenstein: The True Story* "offers us the most faithful adaptation of the Mary Shelley work so far."
        For reader's response, see B40.

B56   Crosse, Mrs. Andrew. "Alexander Knox and His Friends," *Temple Bar*, 94 (April 1892), 495-517 [495-498].
        Knox in connection with MS and her son Percy's tour that resulted in her *Rambles*.

B57   Cude, Wilfred. "Mary Shelley's Modern Prometheus: A Study in the Ethics of Scientific Creativity," *Dalhousie Review*, 52 (Summer 1972), 212-225.
        Opposes past attempts to classify the novel as a ghost story, tale of terror, or Gothic romance; instead, it is "the most original (and certainly the most bizarre) of [the Romantic] adaptations of the Prometheus legend."

B58   Dalby, J[ohn] W[atson]. "Sonnet. Written after Reading 'Valperga,'
       a Tale, by Mary Wollstonecraft Shelley," *The Pocket Magazine of
       Classic and Polite Literature*, n.s. 4 (1826), 360.
           "Exquisite lessons for the human heart
             Are these, and much of nature's mystery
           Is here laid open with that delicate art
             Which beautifies the things it bids us see.
           That poison of the soul—that rank disease—
             Ambition—glory—call it what you will,—
           Deprived of all but its deformities,
             Stands here, depicted with consummate skill.
           Turning from warrior-guilt and callousness,
             Sweet Beatrice! thy form comes to me,
           Thou wild and weak, but glorious prophetess!
             Ne'er may thy love and fate forgotten be!
           And Euthanasia! *thy* firm placidness
             And worth, in all life's better things I see."
       November 2nd, 1825.†
       (Preceeding the sonnet are the six lines from Shelley's "On Muta-
       bility" included in Chapter X of *Frankenstein*.)

       Darbishire, Helen. *See* Kessel, Marcel, B148.

B59   Darbishire, Helen. Review of *The Shelley Note-Book in the Harvard
       College Library* [A449], *Review of English Studies*, 8 (July 1932),
       352-354.
           Distinguishes MS and Shelley's handwriting.

B60   Davies, Rosemary Reeves. "Charles Brockden Brown's *Ormond*: A
       Possible Influence Upon Shelley's Conduct," *Philological Quarterly*,
       43 (January 1964), 133-137.
           Shelley's passion for MS and their elopement may have been
       partially caused by their reading of the similar situation in
       Brown's novel.

B61   de Beer, [Sir] Gavin. "Byron on the Burning of Shelley," *Keats-
       Shelley Memorial Bulletin*, No. 13 (1962), 8-11.
           Reprints John Carne letter from A91, with notice of its errors
       and omissions.

B62   de Beer, [Sir] Gavin. "Some Blunders on Shelley's Elopement in
       1814," *Keats-Shelley Memorial Bulletin*, No. 18 (1967), 36-38.
           Refutes the contentions made in E51 concerning the elopement.

B63   Dilke, Charles W. "'The Liberal,'" *Notes and Queries*, Series 8,
       4 (July 1, 1893), 10.
           Mentions the contributions of MS to *The Liberal*, identified
       from C. A. Brown's copy: "A Tale of the Passions," "Madame
       d'Houtetôt," and "Giovanni Villani."

B64   "Documentary Melodrama of Poet's Life," London *Times*, October 19,
       1965, p. 16.
           Review of Ann Jellicoe's drama of Shelley's life: "Francis

Cuka's Mary [Shelley] has one speech, blaming Italian exile for the death of her children, that has the true voice of feeling."

Dowse, Robert E. *See* Palmer, D. J., B262.

B65   "Dramatic Necrology for 1822," *The Drama, or Theatrical Pocket Magazine*, 3 (December 1822), 380-393 [388].
MS, "springing from such a philosophical source [as Godwin and Mary Wollstonecraft], has received an education and turn of mind, which rendered her, in every respect, a congenial companion for Mr. Shelley. She has acquired great literary celebrity by her 'Frankenstein,' and other works, which evince the power and depth of her imagination, and has now in the press a work around which recent circumstances will throw an intense and extraordinary interest."†
See also B272.

B66   Dunleavy, Gareth W.   "Two Mary Shelley Letters and the 'Irish' Chapters of *Perkin Warbeck*," *Keats-Shelley Journal*, 31 (Winter 1964), 6-10.
Two "unpublished" MS letters to Thomas Crofton Croker (previously published in B328), and discussion of Croker's help in the completion of the novel.

B67   "The Early Years of Frankenstein," *Castle of Frankenstein*, No. 2 (1962), 19-28 [20].
"A primary defect of the Karloff [1931] *Frankenstein* [film], although the best to date, was the limited boundaries of the monster's travels. The original novel screamed for color and vast backgrounds of ice and snow. Yet, within its budget, *Frankenstein* remained fairly close to the original book, and remains a true film classic. *Bride of Frankenstein* took another careful look at the book and drew forth much that had been bypassed the first time around."†

B68   Ebsworth, Raymond.   "Frankenstein's Children," *The Listener*, 68 (August 23, 1962), 272.
Brief editorial comments on the novel, briefly mentioning the publication of B262: "[the novel's] power resides in the strength of the author's original vision more than in its horrific trappings."

B69   Edwards, Roy.   "A Tribute to James Whale," *Sight and Sound*, 27 (Autumn 1957), 95-98 [95-97].
The fertile image of the created Monster was brought to film by James Whale in 1931, then caricatured by him in the 1935 sequel, *Bride of Frankenstein*.

B70   Egeria [pseud.].   "Character and Writing of Shelley," *The Literary Journal and Weekly Register of Science and the Arts* (Providence, R.I.), 1 (January 11, 1834), 252-253.
Passing remarks on MS: "In her were united with great kindness of heart and gentleness of disposition, all that power of intellect which she inherited as a birthright from her celebrated parents."

B71   Ehrsam, Theodore G[eorge]. Letter, "Shelley's Letter to Mary
       Godwin," *Times Literary Supplement*, September 30, 1949, p. 633.

       Norman, Sylva. Letter, "Shelley's Letter to Mary Godwin," *Times
       Literary Supplement*, October 7, 1949, p. 649.

       Ehrsam, Theodore G[eorge]. Letter, "Shelley's Letter to Mary
       Godwin," *Times Literary Supplement*, November 4, 1949, p. 715.

       Norman, Sylva. Letter, "Shelley's Letter to Mary Godwin," *Times
       Literary Supplement*, November 11, 1949, p. 733.
       Wishing to clear up the mystery surrounding the December 16,
       1816 letter, Ehrsam states that two different manuscripts exist,
       one a forgery. Norman then notes that this is in opposition to
       his published view in A19, and he replies that he had access only
       to photostats when he made that claim. Norman then congratulates
       him on "dissassociating himself from a tendentious view."

       Ehrsam, Theodore G[eorge]. *See* Boas, Louise Schutz, B29.

B72   Ehrsam, Theodore G[eorge]. "Mary Shelley in Her Letters," *Modern
       Language Quarterly*, 7 (September 1946), 297-302.
       Corrections and additions to MS letters as published in IA7.

B73   Ellis, F. S. Letter, *The Athenæum*, No. 3091 (January 22, 1887),
       129.
       Quotes from MS letter to Sir John Bowring.

B74   *The Examiner*, No. 505 (August 31, 1817), 552.
       Response to B225: "second, that the Lady with whom [Shelley]
       lives, and who inherits an intellect equally striking and prema-
       ture, is not his wife." Disputing this statement, goes on to
       emphasize that "the Lady *is* his wife."
       Reprinted in Kenneth Neill Cameron, ed. *Shelley and his
       Circle*. 6 vols. Cambridge, Mass.: Harvard University Press,
       1973, Vol. V, p. 274.

B75   *The Examiner*, No. 510 (October 5, 1817), 626 n.
       An excerpt from a MS letter concerning "Cobbett's No. 23 to
       the Borough-Mongers" is introduced, probably by Leigh Hunt, as
       follows: "A lady of what is called a masculine understanding,
       that is to say, of great natural abilities not obstructed by a
       bad education, writes thus in a letter to her husband."

B76   *The Examiner*, No. 545 (June 7, 1818), 361.
       "A Literary Notice next week on the excellent Works of Charles
       Lamb. . . . The succeeding Notice will be on Frankenstein."† The
       notice was never published.

B77   *The Examiner*, No. 826 (November 30, 1823), 775.
       "No one who reads this work (says the *Scotsman*) can ever
       forget its power and eloquence. Like *Caleb Williams*—written by
       the father—*Valperga*, the work of the daughter, clings to the

memory. Like the other works of the same school, also, it gives the history of the growth of passion—we should say of two passions—love and ambition—which, in so far as the latter is concerned, is conducted with great skill, and displays talent of the highest order."†

B78 "Extract of a Letter from Geneva," *New Monthly Magazine*, 11 (April 1, 1819), 193-195.
A version of the ghost-story contest at Geneva in the summer of 1816, concentrating on the hysterical reaction of Shelley to Byron's reading of *Christabel*; with an editorial note stating that the outline of Miss Godwin's story, already published as *Frankenstein*, is in his possession.
John William Polidori possibly the author.

B79 Fairweather, David. "The Film World," *Theatre World*, 17 (March 1932), 144.
Review of the 1931 film *Frankenstein*: "With the object of piling horror upon horror, the adapters of Mary Shelley's novel have entirely disregarded the pathos of the man-made monster's striving after human affection."†

B80 Fitz. "'The Heir of Mondolfo,' by Mrs. Shelley," *Notes and Queries*, 5th series, 5 (February 12, 1876), 129.
"Can any one acquainted with the works of Mrs. Shelley inform me where and when this story was published?"†
For response, see B83. See also B13.

B81 Fleck, P. D. "Mary Shelley's Notes to Shelley's Poems and *Frankenstein*," *Studies in Romanticism*, 6 (Summer 1967), 226-254.
On the basis of passages in the novel, her notes to the poems, and two journal entries, "there is every reason to suppose that *Frankenstein* . . . represent[s] Mary's view of the danger of the Romantic idealism her hero and Shelley's fall prey to."

B82 Ford, George H. "Shelley or Schiller? A Note on D. H. Lawrence at Work," *Texas Studies in Literature and Language*, 4 (Summer 1962), 154-156 [155].
A passage in *Women in Love* (versions A, B, and C), "to see . . . Shelley's first glance at Mary Godwin," shows the taste of Lawrence's character for 19th-century Romantics.

B83 Forman, H[arry] Buxton. "'The Heir of Mondolfo,'" *Notes and Queries*, 5th series, 7 (May 5, 1877), 357.
Response to B80: "If Fitz is still anxious to know where this story of Mrs. Shelley's may be seen in print, he will find it on looking into *Appleton's Journal* (New York) for January last. Whether it has ever appeared before I cannot say; but I never saw it mentioned anywhere till his question was asked."†
See also B13.

B84   Forman, H[arry] Buxton. "Shelley's Life Near Spezzia, His Death
      and Burials," *Macmillan's Magazine*, 42 (May 1880), 43-58 [46-52,
      54-56].
         MS letters to Maria Gisborne and Claire Clairmont.

B85   Forrest, Mark. "Films," *Saturday Review* (London), 153 (January
      30, 1932), 124.
         Review of the 1931 film *Frankenstein*: "The scenarist of the
      screen version has destroyed the whole meaning and purpose of the
      original by making man triumph over his creation."

B86   "Frankenstein, 1973. the version made for tv," *Famous Monsters of
      Filmland*, No. 104 (January 1974), 18-21.
         Brief discussion of plot differences between the MS novel and
      the 1973 ABC-television version.

B87   "'Frankenstein' is Banned," The New York *Times*, September 5, 1955,
      Section 9, p. 4.
         The novel is banned from South Africa as "indecent, objection-
      able, or obscene," under a "fine of £1,000 or up to five years in
      prison."

B88   "The Frankenstein Story," *Famous Monsters of Filmland*, No. 1
      (1958), 24-35.
         Summary of film versions, and the discovery that "the author
      of FRANKENSTEIN was not only a girl, but a *teenager!!!*"
         Reprinted as A150.
         Forrest J. Ackerman possibly the author.

B89   Fredman, Alice Green. Review of Jean de Palacio. *Mary Shelley
      dans son œuvre. Contributions aux études shelleyennes* [E1];
      William A. Walling. *Mary Shelley* [A22]; Christopher Small.
      Ariel Like a Harpy: Shelley, Mary, and "Frankenstein" [A18]; and
      Noel B. Gerson. *Daughter of Earth and Water: A Biography of
      Mary Wollstonecraft Shelley* [A3], *Keats-Shelley Journal*, 22
      (1974), 129-138.
         Valuable critical descriptions, favorable on E1, A22, and A18;
      selective regarding the numerous errors in A3 ("Shelley, Mary.
      Works. London, 1894. 20 vols.," in Gerson's bibliography).

B90   Garnett, Richard. "Shelley's Last Days," *Fortnightly Review*,
      n.s. 23 [29] (June 1878), 850-866 [855-857, 861, 866].
         Review of A419: attacks Trelawny's changed portrait of MS;
      "he liked her better living than dead."

B91   Gaylin, Willard. "The Frankenstein myth becomes a reality—We
      Have the Awful Knowledge to Make Exact Copies of Human Beings,"
      The New York Times Sunday Magazine, March 5, 1972, pp. 12-13, 41,
      43-44, 48-49 [12, 49].
         Uses the novel *Frankenstein* as a starting point for a discus-
      sion of cloning, concluding that "The tragic irony is that Mary
      Shelley's 'fantasy' once again has a relevance. . . . we no longer
      identify with Dr. Frankenstein but with his monster."

B92   "Gets a Shelley Relic. Bodleian Library Obtains lock of Hair of
       Poet's Wife," The New York *Times*, December 27, 1931, Section 3,
       p. 4 col. 2.
           The lock of hair was attached to a gold locklet, and was given
       originally by MS to Mrs. T. W. Rolleston.

B93   Gilfillan, George. "Female Authors.—No. III.—Mrs. Shelley,"
       Eclectic Magazine of Foreign Literature (N.Y.), 13 (February
       1848), 167-173.
           Reprinting of B94.
           See also A168, B95.

B94   Gilfillan, George. "Female Authors.—No. III.—Mrs. Shelley,"
       Tait's Edinburgh Magazine, 14 (December 1847), 850-854.
           MS is similar in genius to her husband, but not his equal.
       Frankenstein is favorably considered, with a superficial exami-
       nation of isolated episodes.
           See also A168, B93, B95.

B95   Gilfillan, George. "Mrs. Shelley," *Littell's Living Age*, 16
       (March 1848), 446-450.
           Reprinting of B94.
           See also A168, B93, B94.

B96   Girdansky, Michael. "Science and Science Fiction: Who Borrows
       What?" *Worlds of Tomorrow*, 1 (December 1963), 59-65 [62].
           "Frank L. Baum's *Oz* books used many themes since recurrant
       [*sic*] in S-F of later days: Tin Woodman (universal prothesis),
       Scarecrow (Golem-Frankenstein), even—stretching a point—Cowardly
       Lion (intelligent animal a la Eric Frank Russell's *The Undecided*
       or Wells['] *Island of Dr. Moreau*)."†

B97   Glicksohn, Susan Wood. "The Martian Point of View," *Extrapolation*,
       15 (May 1974), 161-173 [163-164].
           Margaret Atwood's poem "Speeches for Doctor [*sic*] Franken-
       stein" [cf. A37] "exists on many levels, unified by Mary Shelley's
       structure."

B98   *The Globe* (London), May 7, 1830, p. 3 col. 4.
           "Mrs. Shelley, the distinguished Authoress of 'Frankenstein,'
       'The Last Man,' &c. has just ready for publication an historical
       romance under the above title ['The Fortunes of Perkin Warbeck'],
       on which she has been engaged for a considerable time. Another
       work under the same title having however been just published by
       Mr. Newman, the public should be careful in giving their orders,
       to prevent mistakes."†
           Reprinted as B230. According to de Palacio [El, pp. 666-667,
       Item 109], also reprinted in *The Standard*, May 7, 1830 (no page
       given) and *The Morning Journal*, May 6, 1830 (no page given), both
       items which I have not seen, and which are not in the Library of
       Congress or the Bodleian, or, according to my correspondence, in
       the British Library.

B99   *The Globe* (London), May 26, 1830, p. 3 col. 4.
      Notice of the publication of *Perkin Warbeck*, giving a brief
      history of Warbeck and noting that the development of his adven-
      tures "could scarcely have fallen into better hands."
      Reprinted as B231.

B100 *The Globe* (London), April 13, 1835, p. 4 col. 5.
      Lodore is "A story which will raise still higher the fame of
      this popular novelist."†
      See also B101, B52.

B101 *The Globe* (London), June 3, 1835, p. 3 col. 5.
      Paraphrasing of B100: *Lodore* is "A work which will raise still
      higher the reputation of this successful novelist."

B102 Goldberg, M. A. "Moral and Myth in Mrs. Shelley's *Frankenstein*,"
      Keats-Shelley Journal, 8 (Winter 1959), 27-38.
      All three of the central characters in the novel are isolated
      from society: Walton and Frankenstein sin against the moral and
      social order, their pursuit of knowledge leading them from a com-
      passionate society; the Monster is similarly estranged, though *by*
      society. Parallel themes noted in Godwin, Paine, Milton, Byron,
      and Shelley.

B103 Goshko, John M. "Frankenstein's castle is no horror show," Boston
      Globe, November 19, 1972, p. B-38.
      Reprinting of B104.

B104 Goshko, John M. "Frankenstein's Facelift," Washington *Post*,
      October 29, 1972, pp. G1, G4.
      MS may have visited the area near "Castle Frankenstein" in
      Darmstadt, West Germany, and heard about "baron" Johann Konrad
      Dippel (1673-1734).
      See also B103.

B105 Grabo, Carl. Review of Frederick L[afayette] Jones, ed. *The
      Letters of Mary W. Shelley*, *Modern Language Notes*, 60 (December
      1945), 572-573.
      Review of IA7. MS "had little sympathy with liberal ideas
      and without being wholly mercenary or socially ambitious she was
      forever occupied with trivial material things. She spent much of
      her time and strength in writing fiction and compiling hack biog-
      raphies, but seldom is there revealed in her later letters a gleam
      of intellectual curiosity."

B106 Graham, William. "Chats with Jane Clairmont," *The Nineteenth
      Century*, 34 (November 1893), 753-769 [760, 761, 764].
      MS approved of Jane's [Claire's] affair with Byron: "Mary
      docilely followed [Shelley's] lead in these things."
      Reprinted as A176.
      See also A304 (Vol. II).

B107   Gribble, Francis [Henry]. "Mary Shelley's Suitors," *Fortnightly
        Review*, 90 [mistakenly printed "CX"] (October 2, 1911), 652-663.
            Dismissal of the idea that Trelawny proposed marriage to MS,
        then a superficial examination of the MS-Payne letters.

B108   Griffith, Ben W., Jr. "Mary Shelley's Inscribed Copy of 'Queen
        Mab,'" *Notes and Queries*, 200 (September 1955), 408.
            Asks for whereabouts of the copy.
            See B164 for response.

B109   Grigson, Geoffrey. "Lovers Who Meet in Churches (Suggested by
        Mary Godwin's Letter to Shelley, October 25th, 1814)," *Times
        Literary Supplement*, June 11, 1964, p. 512.
            A poem.

B110   Grylls, R[osalie] Glynn [Lady Mander]. "Former Coronations,"
        London *Times*, March 1, 1937, p. 10 col. 4.
            Quotes an "unpublished entry" from MS journal concerning the
        coronation of William IV. (Misprint in the *Times Index* has
        "George IV.")

B111   Grylls, R[osalie] Glynn [Lady Mander]. Letter, "Mrs. Shelley's
        Novels," *Times Literary Supplement*, April 11, 1935, p. 244.
            Suggests a re-reading of *The Last Man*: "in her creation of
        an atmosphere charged with panic, fear and the sense of over-
        whelming desolation . . . Mary Shelley succeeds in rendering a
        terror beyond that of 'Frankenstein.'"

B112   Grylls, R[osalie] Glynn [Lady Mander]. "To the Dead," *Keats-
        Shelley Memorial Bulletin*, No. 4 (1952), 52-54.
            Description of the MS poem (published in the 1839 *Keepsake* as
        "Stanzas, O, Come to me in dreams, my Love") and circumstances
        surrounding its composition.

B113   H., R. W. "Gift of Shelley Manuscripts," *Bodleian Library Record*,
        2 (July 1946), 144-145.
            Recent gift by Sir John Shelley-Rolls included "5 volumes
        containing transcriptions of poems and of prose works by Mary
        Shelley," a box containing MS works, and 119 MS letters (1823-
        1850).

B114   Harrison, Harry. "At Last, The True Story of Frankenstein,"
        Science Fantasy, 24 (September 1965), 42-48.
            Short story in which Victor Frankenstein's son explains to a
        reporter that MS misused his father's story for her own ends.

B115   Häusermann, H[ans] W[alter]. "Shelley's House in Geneva," *English
        Miscellany*, 1 (1950), 183-189.
            Attempts to identify the two houses in Geneva where MS and
        Shelley lived, 1816-1817.

B116 Haydock, Ron. "Frankenstein's Castle," *The Monster Times*, 1
(April 1973), 19.
The Frankenstein Castle near Niederbeerbach has "no relation"
to MS novel. On the derivation of "Victor Frankenstein": "Victor"
implies conquest, "Franken-" from Benjamin Franklin, and "-stein"
from a medical doctor named Eisenstein.

B117 Healy, Dennis M. "Mary Shelley and Prosper Mérimée," *Modern
Language Review*, 36 (July 1941), 394-396.
Two MS letters, one to Victor Jacquemont, the other possibly to
Mérimée.

B118 Herford, C[harles] H[arold]. "Mary Wollstonecraft Shelley," *Lippincott's Magazine*, 45 (April 1890), 596-607.
Review of A8, and capsule biography of MS. "Her intellectual
faculty, though distinguished, and capable, under casual impulses,
of remarkable achievements, was not of the stuff from which lasting
relationships spring. Quickened to its utmost vigor by Shelley's
companionship, it steadily flagged and faded when that was with-
drawn."

B119 H[ill], R[eginald] H[arrison]. Introductory Note to "The Letters
of Mary Shelley in the Bodleian Collection," *The Bodleian Quarterly
Record*, 6 (3rd Quarter 1929), 51-59 [51-52].
Description of the collection of MS letters, mostly to Maria
Gisborne [cf. IA3, A4, A5, A6].

B120 Hillegas, Mark R. "A Draft of the Science-Fiction Canon to be
proposed at the 1961 MLA Conference on Science Fiction," *Extrapolation*, 3 (December 1961), 26-30 [30].
No. 99 is *Frankenstein*.

B121 Hirsch, E. D., Jr. "Further Comment on 'Music, When Soft Voices
Die,'" *Journal of English and Germanic Philology*, 60 (April 1961),
296-298.
Response to B192: "We should ruthlessly relegate Mrs. Shelley's
unauthorized version to a footnote."

B122 "Hood's Whims and Oddities," *Blackwood's Edinburgh Magazine*, 21
(January 1827), 45-60 [54].
Review of Thomas Hood's *Whims and Oddities* (London: Lupton
Relfe, 1826), with a satirical reference to MS *The Last Man* as
her "abortion."

B123 Hume, Robert D. "Gothic versus Romantic: A Revaluation of the
Gothic Novel," *PMLA*, 84 (March 1969), 282-290 [285-286, 287].
Frankenstein as a Gothic novel, "a skillfully constructed
book and one of real psychological insight," its theme of "Pro-
methean overreaching" compared to that in *Melmoth the Wanderer*
and *Moby Dick*.

B124 [Hunt, Thornton.] "Shelley. By One Who Knew Him," *Atlantic Monthly*, 11 (February 1863), 184-204 [187, 188, 189, 190, 191, 193, 194, 195, 196, 198, 199, 201, 202].

MS was "a woman of extraordinary power, of heart as well as head," in whose writings are "the best materials for forming an estimate of [Shelley's] character."

Reprinted in A63 (pp. 11-53).

B125 Huscher, Herbert. "Alexander Mavrocordato, Friend of the Shelleys," *Keats-Shelley Memorial Bulletin*, No. 16 (1965), 29-38 [31-32].

MS letter to Mavrocordato (Feb. 22, 1825?), in French.

B126 Jackson, Joseph F. A. "An Old Time Literary Romance Diclosed," The New York *Times*, March 13, 1904, Part 2, p. 11.

Discovery of the MS-Payne-Irving letters, publishing two from Payne to MS, one from MS to Payne.

B127 Jensen, Paul. "Film Favorites. Paul Jensen on Frankenstein," *Film Comment*, 6 (Fall 1970), 42-46.

In an elaborate, skillful synopsis of the 1931 film, changes are noted between film and MS novel.

Revised version of A219. Also intended to appear in his and Arthur Lennig's "Karloff and Lugosi: Titans of Terror," which, to my knowledge, was never published.

B128 *John Bull*, 6 (January 22, 1826), 30 col. 2.

"Mrs. Shelley's Romance of 'The Last Man' is to make its appearance in a few days. It is not easy to imagine of what description the adventures of so solitary and desolate a creature could possibly be; and yet it is said by those who have seen the manuscript, that the author has invested him and his history with an interest of the most absorbing kind."†

B129 *John Bull*, 6 (February 26, 1826), 70 col. 3.

"Mrs. Shelley's imagination tempts her to the choice of very uncommon subjects. She has already written about the anomalous creation of a monster, and now she gives us the history of the last survivor of the human race! The very title of the book was a riddle; and, as in the wildest fiction there should be some coherence, it was not a little puzzling to imagine how the author could get rid of the solecism committed even in its first announcement. The work would, of course, be an auto-biography; but then for whom could it be supposed to be written, and what readers was it to expect to find? These conundrums have at length been solved by the appearance of the book, in which we are informed that the tale is a prophetic one, and has been collected from the scattered leaves of the cumean Sibyl, by two travellers near Naples, who ventured to explore their way into the secret and awful cave of the inspired damsel, whose prophecies extended even to the time of the dissolution of all things."†

B130 *John Bull*, 6 (March 5, 1826), 75 col. 1.

"Two of the principal characters (Raymond and Adrian) in Mrs. Shelley's Romance, entitled 'The Last Man,' are evidently modelled

from Lord Byron and Mr. Shelley, who as in their actual life are
brought into strict intimacy, notwithstanding the difference
existing between many of their opinions. Few persons [f]or
several years before Lord Byron's death, had a better opportunity
than the author of the above romance, of estimating the strange
mind, temper, and actions of the noble poet."†

B131   *John Bull*, 6 (April 17, 1826), 126 col. 3 [also incorrectly printed
       as April 16].
       Reprinting of B228.

B132   *John Bull*, April 13, 1835, p. 118 col. 3.
       "Mrs. Shelley has published *Lodore*, replete with indications
       of her genius and power."†

B133   Jones, Frederick L[afayette]. Introductory Note to "The Letters
       of Mary W. Shelley in the Bodleian Library (*continued*)," *The
       Bodleian Quarterly Record*, 8 (Spring 1937), 297-310, 360-371 [297].
       Description of the 21 MS letters.
       Continuation of B119. See also ÏA3, A4, A5, A6.

B134   Jones, Frederick L[afayette]. Letter, "A Letter from Claire
       Clairmont," *Times Literary Supplement*, July 10, 1937, p. 512.
       Cites internal evidence to prove that a June 3, 1819 letter
       supposed by Dowden [in A126] and Marshall [in A8] to have been
       written by Amelia Curran for MS was actually written by Claire.

B135   Jones, Frederick L[afayette]. Letter, "Mrs. Shelley's 'Lodore,'"
       Times Literary Supplement, April 4, 1935, p. 228.
       "Mrs. Shelley's mediocre novel 'Lodore' (1835) is of consid-
       erable interest and value because the author put into it much
       that came from her own and Shelley's life."

B136   Jones, Frederick L[afayette]. Letter, "Mary Shelley and *Midas*,"
       Times Literary Supplement, June 25, 1938, pp. 433-434.
       Disputes claim in A145 (Vol. IV) that Edward Ellerker
       Williams wrote *Midas*; cites two unpublished MS letters to prove
       her the author.

B137   Jones, Frederick L[afayette]. "Mary Shelley and Claire Clair-
       mont," *South Atlantic Quarterly*, 42 (October 1943), 406-412.
       Reply to B323. Examines MS-Claire relationship, concentrating
       on the years following Shelley's death, to show how they "loved
       each other sincerely and helped each other as much as they could"—
       although "they could never live together amicably."

B138   Jones, Frederick L[afayette]. "Mary Shelley to Maria Gisborne:
       New Letters, 1818-1822," *Studies in Philology*, 52 (January 1955),
       39-74.
       27 letters, with editorial comments and glosses.

B139   Jones, Frederick L[afayette]. "A Shelley and Mary Letter to
        Claire," *Modern Language Notes*, 65 (February 1950), 121-123.
            The May 11, 1821 letter, published in IA7, IIA126, A383
        (Vol. X), and [Thomas James Wise, ed.] *Letters from P. B. Shelley
        to Jane Clairmont* (London: Privately Printed, 1889), is separated
        into the sections written by MS and Shelley.

B140   Jones, Frederick L[afayette]. "Shelley and Milton," *Studies in
        Philology*, 49 (July 1952), 488-519 [496].
            "It is possible that Shelley read the entire poem [*Paradise
        Lost*] aloud to Mary during these eight days [August 21-23 and
        Nov. 17-21, 1816]."

B141   Jones, Frederick L[afayette]. "'The Shelley Legend,'" *PMLA*, 61
        (September 1946), 848-890.
            Detailed, comprehensive attack on inaccuracies in A19,
        specifically, concerning MS as purveyor of "The Shelley Legend."
            Reprinted as A226.
            See also B54 [and A87], B349 [and A437].

B142   Jones, Frederick L[afayette]. "Shelley's Revised Will," *Modern
        Language Notes*, 59 (December 1944), 542-544.
            From an unpublished letter of John Gisborne to T. J. Hogg
        (Aug. 12, 1822), "we may safely infer that in her letter to
        Peacock [quoted] Mary had mentioned the new will, her vain search
        for it, and probably Hogg's executorship."

B143   Jones, Frederick L[afayette]. "Unpublished Fragments by Shelley
        and Mary," *Studies in Philology*, 45 (July 1948), 472-476 [472,
        473].
            The MS notebook in the Library of Congress contains "Mary's
        incomplete translation of the 'Cupid and Psyche' of Apuleius,"
        "12 pages of Latin vocabulary exercises in Mary's hand," and
        "Shelley's review of *Frankenstein* [cf. A386, B314] (one page is
        missing) in his own hand."

B144   "Judgment of the Annuals. By the Man of Genius," *Fraser's Maga-
        zine for Town and Country*, 10 (November 1834), 610-623 [618-619].
            In a review of the 1835 *Drawing-Room Scrap-Book*, preceeding
        quote from poem, "Fame": "There is much sweetness in the follow-
        ing, from the pen of Mrs. S., a female friend of Edward Lytton
        Bulwer, Esq."
            Then: "The very best advice we ever remember to have been
        given to an exhausted *littérateur*! Of course it will be taken."†
            Poem attributed to MS by Nitchie in A12 (p. 157).

B145   Juel-Jensen, Bent. "Contemporary Collectors XLIII," *Book Collec-
        tor*, 15 (Summer 1966), 152-174 [166-167].
            Notes First Edition and First U.S. Edition of *Frankenstein* in
        his collection.

B146 "The Keepsake," *Tait's Edinburgh Magazine*, 3 (December 1836), 811.
Review of the 1837 *Keepsake*: "[Its] finest things are not
patrician; for they are *Helen*, and the *Parvenue*; the first by one
of the brothers Chorley, the second by Mrs. Shelley."†

B147 Kessel, Marcel. "An Early Review of the Shelleys' 'Six Weeks'
Tour,'" *Modern Language Notes*, 58 (December 1943), 623.
Brief description and analysis of C109.

B148 Kessel, Marcel. Letter, "The Harvard Shelley Notebook," *Times
Literary Supplement*, September 5, 1936, p. 713.
Notes error in A449: MS handwriting mistaken for Shelley's.

Darbishire, Helen. Letter, "The Harvard Shelley Notebook," *Times
Literary Supplement*, September 12, 1936, p. 729.
She made the same identification as Kessel in her B59.

Kessel, Marcel. *See* Norman, Sylva, B251.

B149 Kingston, Marion. "Notes on Three Shelley Letters," *Keats-Shelley
Memorial Bulletin*, No. 6 (1955), 13-17 [14].
Portion of unpublished Claire Clairmont letter to Maria Gis-
borne (Feb. 11, 1820), with two references to MS.

B150 Kmetz, Gail. "Lost Women. Mary Shelley: In the Shadow of
'Frankenstein,'" *Ms.*, 3 (February 1975), 12-16.
The usual background of MS and *Frankenstein*, which "is not a
great novel." "Most of the characters are flat," although "the
monster is an exception." Brief consideration of the other
novels, biographies, and *Rambles*, which, "more than a travel
book . . . tried to convince the English of the cause of Italian
freedom."

B151 *Knight's Quarterly Magazine*, 3 (August-November 1824), 195-199.
Disappointment with *Valperga* leads to a re-examination of
Frankenstein: speculation concerning the possibility of actually
creating such a being, and expression of sympathy with the Monster. MS may have been too aware of the extravagance in her
first novel and tried to be too precise in the next.

B152 Koszul, A[ndré] [Henri]. Letter, "Mary Shelley's 'Proserpine'
and 'Midas,'" *Times Literary Supplement*, December 29, 1927, p.
989.
Apologizes for overlooking another text of *Proserpine* in "an
obscure 'Winter's Wreath' for 1832," when he published A237.

B153 Kotker, Norman. "The Thinking Man's Lake," *Horizon*, 7 (Autumn
1965), 64-79 [72-73].
Brief consideration of the influence of the Lake of Geneva
on MS.

B154 Kriegsman, Alan M. "In the Ranks of Monsterland," Washington
Post, November 17, 1973, p. C6.
Review of the 1973 Thames Television production of *Frankenstein*, which "claims distinction on the basis of its authenticity
and fidelity to the Mary Shelley novel of 1816 [*sic*]."

B155 Kriegsman, Alan M. "The Monster Mish-Mash," Washington *Post*,
December 9, 1973, pp. H1, H5.
Summary of the three 1973 television productions of *Frankenstein*. "Mary Shelley hit an exposed nerve in the human psyche
with [*Frankenstein*] and we're still feeling it tingle today."
Also briefly treats Prometheus, the homunculus, and the Golem as
precedents of the novel.

B156 Lauterbach, Charles E., and Edward S. Lauterbach. "The Nineteenth
Century Three-Volume Novel," *The Papers of the Bibliographical
Society of America*, 51 (Fourth Quarter 1957), 263-302 [277].
The 1818 *Frankenstein* contains 67,150 words of story text, but
is not really of three-volume length.

B157 Le Galliene, Richard. "Old Love-Stories Retold. V. Shelley and
Mary Godwin," *The Cosmopolitan. An Illustrated Monthly Magazine*
(N.Y.), 35 (July 1903), 291-297.
Anecdotal version. "To the dispassionate onlooker Mary
Godwin may lack certain qualities which are popularly supposed to
inspire great passions in men. There was a certain primness about
her. She had been begotten, so to say, on revolutionary princi-
ples, and there was the taint of propaganda about her. Still,
Shelley, assuredly, had no distaste for propaganda, and Mary was
a woman too."

B158 *The Leader* (London), 2 (February 8, 1851), 128.
"The sad news of Mrs. Shelley's death throws the mind back into
that stirring time when her father, Godwin, and her mother, noble
Mary Wolstonecraft [*sic*], were outraging the respectabilities by
earnest utterance of audacities in speculation which now seem in-
capable of alarming even the timid—for the persecuted audacity of
one day becomes the commonplace of to-morrow—and recals [*sic*] her
illustrious husband, the most Christian-hearted man of whom that
epoch gives us any imitation, Percy Bysshe Shelley! To the illustration of parentage, Mrs. Shelley added that of being the author
of *Frankenstein*, *The Last Man*, *Lodore*, &c. *Frankenstein* is one of
those books that become the parent of whole generations of romances."†

B159 Leiber, Fritz. "Monsters and Monster-Lovers," *Fantastic Stories
of Imagination*, 14 (March 1965), 5, 118-126, 130 [5].
Satirically refers to the Frankenstein Monster as a "much
misunderstood humble patchwork of humanity, seeking after truth,
and lover of little children—not knowing his own strength, yet
trying to be gentle."

B160 Leinster, Murray [pseud. of Will F. Jenkins]. "Writing Science Fiction Today," *The Writer*, 81 (May 1968), 16-18 [16].

Frankenstein is "one of the worst-written tales ever put into print."

B161 "Letters of English Authors from the Collection of Robert H. Taylor: A Catalogue of an Exhibition in the Princeton University Library May 13 to September 30, 1960," *The Princeton University Library Chronicle*, 21 (Summer 1960), 200-236 [218].

Reprinting of A246.

B162 Levine, George. "*Frankenstein* and the Tradition of Realism," *Novel. A Forum on Fiction*, 7 (Fall 1973), 14-30.

The novel is non-realistic, but its anti-heroism looks forward to realistic novels, its effects and powers deriving from "its rejection of arbitrariness." Psychological evaluation of the two central characters.

B163 "The Liberal, or 'Verse and Prose from the South,' No. I and II," *The Monthly Censor*, 2 (1823), 454-455.

Possibly referring to MS and Claire Clairmont: "Since the death of Shelly [sic] . . . the *filling up* [of *The Liberal*] is supplied by Leigh Hunt . . . and by some two or three women who having begun their education under philosopher *Godwin*, completed it under Atheist Shelly."

B164 The Librarian. "Shelley's 'Queen Mab,'" *Notes and Queries*, 201 (January 19, 1956), 45.

Reply to B108: "The very interesting copy of *Queen Mab*, inscribed to Mary Wollstonecraft Godwin by P. B. S., is now tucked away safely in the rare-book section of the Henry E. Huntington Library and Art Gallery in San Marino, California."†

B165 *The Literary Magnet or Monthly Journal of the Belles Lettres*, n.s. 1 (January 1826), 56.

"Mrs. Shelley, the authoress of that monstrous literary abortion, Frankenstein or the modern Prometheus, is, we understand, about to produce another Raw-head-and-bloody-bones, called 'The Last Man.'"†

B166 *The London Magazine*, n.s. 4 (March 1826), 422.

"The Last Man is an elaborate piece of gloomy folly—bad enough to read—horrible to write."†

B167 *The London Magazine*, n.s. 4 (April 1826), 527-528.

"24*th* [of March]—The gentle Colburn advertises thus fancifully in the Chronicle of to-day: 'According to the prophecy in Mrs. Shelley's new Romance, or rather Prophetic Tale, [Colburn loves to be particular,] "The Last Man," the world is to be destroyed by a universal plague, in the year 2100; so that posterity will not have three hundred years to figure in.['] This information will be especially useful to architects, who may thus be enabled, without unnecessary waste of material, to build on leases expiring on doomsday. Joking apart, [O ye gods, was that a joke!] there are

many grand things [on the word of a publisher] in 'The Last Man.'
The account of the desolating plague is terrific; and 'this
strange eventful history' concludes with a picture of the solitary
relic of human nature *weltering* amidst the ocean in his tiny bark,
and awaiting his fate in the wilderness of waters!!—Gemini!!!"
(2nd, 4th, and 5th sets of brackets in the original.)
See also B227.

B168   "Lord Byron and his contemporaries, &c., by an intimate Friend of
his Lordship.—No. III," *The Metropolitan Literary Journal of
Literature, Science, The Fine Arts, &c.*, No. 10 (June 11, 1830),
151-154.
The bulk of the essay is a dialogue between the author and MS,
in which she reflects upon Godwin, Leigh Hunt, and Byron. The
dialogue is either fictitious or a blend of fiction and actual
occurrence.
Elizabeth Nitchie, in A12, supposes John H. Hunt the author.

B169   "The Lounger," *The Critic*, 36 (March 1900), 193-212 [201].
Richard Rothwell's portrait of MS just bequeathed by Lady
Shelley to the National Portrait Gallery, London.
See also B235, B236.

B170   Lovell, Ernest J[ames], Jr. "Byron, Mary Shelley, and Madame de
Staël," *Keats-Shelley Journal*, 14 (Winter 1965), 13.
Sources for two anecdotes used by MS in her life of de Staël.

B171   Lovell, Ernest J[ames], Jr. "Byron and Mary Shelley," *Keats-
Shelley Journal*, 2 (1953), 35-49.
Byron's influence on MS as reflected in her novels: he
appeared as "a magnetic and many-sided figure, symbol of one of
her most deeply felt needs, that of a Father-lover, the desired
pillar of masculine power and authority."

B172   Lovell, Ernest J[ames], Jr. "Byron and the Byronic Hero in the
Novels of Mary Shelley," *Texas Studies in English*, 30 (1951),
158-183.
Attempts to show MS attraction to Byron and to identify the
four major Byronic heros in her novels.

B173   Luke, Hugh J., Jr. "The Last Man: Mary Shelley's Myth of the
Solitary," *Prairie Schooner*, 39 (Winter 1965/1966), 316-327.
Shorter version of A253.

B174   Lund, Mary Graham. "Mary Godwin Shelley and the Monster," *University of Kansas City Review*, 28 (Summer 1962), 253-258.
As the result of the influences of Shelley and of other works,
MS "was unconsciously writing the tragedy of the age" in *Frankenstein*, although she little understood it.

B175   Lund, Mary Graham. "Mary Shelley's Father," *Discourse: A Review
of the Liberal Arts*, 12 (Winter 1969), 130-135.
Defense of Godwin using MS opinions of him.

B176 Lund, Mary Graham. "Shelley as Frankenstein. A Poet's Struggle for Self-realization," *Forum* (Houston, Texas), 4 (Fall 1963), 28-31.

Presents Shelley as Victor Frankenstein, using a short-story format. Not without interest.

B177 Lyles, William H. Letter, "Mary Shelley and 'Frankenstein,'" *Times Literary Supplement*, August 2, 1974, pp. 834-835.

Several critics are confused about MS age when making statements concerning *Frankenstein*, ranging from 18 to 21; but she was 31 when she revised the novel and created the superior text.

B178 McConnell, Frank. "Rough Beasts Slouching: A Note on Horror Movies," *Kenyon Review*, 32 (1970), 109-120 [113].

Brief contrast of novel *Frankenstein* and 1931 film version: in the film, the inversion of the Blakean and Shelleyan myth of the integration of self, the movie monster, "is both more ambitious and more omnivorously assimilative than Mrs. Shelley's articulate and anguished creation."

Reprinted as A260.

B179 McKenney, John L. "Nietzsche and the Frankenstein Creature," *Dalhousie Review*, 41 (Spring 1961), 40-48.

Ingenious, if implausible, consideration of parallels between the Frankenstein Monster and Nietzsche's life.

B180 M., E. "French Literature. On the School of the 'Romantiques,'" *The Evening Chronicle* (London), February 3, 1835, p. 3 col. 2.

Brief introduction of *Frankenstein* as an extended simile: "When Frankenstein, eager to emulate the daring deed of Prometheus, resolved to fashion a man, and to 'filch from heaven' the vital spark which should animate his frame, he formed an elegant statue, exquisite in all its proportions, beautifully modeled, beautifully polished—but cold, and without a soul. Such was the literature advocated by the *Classiques* and the *Académiciens*." Author apparently confuses *Frankenstein* with the Pygmalion-Galatea myth.

B181 "M. W. Shelley at Pisa," *Littell's Living Age*, 152 (1882), 374-378.

Reprinting of B182.

B182 "M. W. Shelley at Pisa," *Temple Bar*, 64 (January 1882), 58-65.

Number of letters and portions of letters from MS to Leigh and Marianne Hunt.

See also B181.

B183 Mainwaring, Marion. "Arnold on Shelley," *Modern Language Notes*, 67 (February 1952), 122-123.

Identifies the "lady" in Arnold's anecdote about MS [cf. A34] as Fanny Kemble.

See also A256.

Mander, Lady. *See* Grylls, R[osalie] Glynn, B110, B111, B112.

B184 Marsh, George L.   Review of Frederick L[afayette] Jones, ed. *The
      Letters of Mary W. Shelley* [IA7], *Modern Philology*, 42 (May 1945),
      254-255.
           Notes several errors in Jones' transcriptions of the letters.

B185 "Mary Shelley," *Times Literary Supplement*, February 2, 1951, p. 69.
           Observing the centenary of MS death, appreciating her as
      Shelley's editor ("a discerning critic") and as author of *Frank-
      enstein*.

B186 "Mary Shelley. A Local Reminiscence (From a Correspondent),"
      Dundee *Advertiser* (Dundee, Scotland), September 7, 1897, p. 3.
           The correspondent called on Christy Baxter in 1883, who told
      him anecdotes of her early life with MS, including the mention
      that MS formed the idea for *Frankenstein* while with the Baxters
      in Dundee, 1812-1814.

B187 "Mary Shelley. The Years After the Tragedy," *Times Literary
      Supplement*, January 6, 1945, p. 8.
           Review of IA7, terming the collection of letters the best
      biography of MS, and noting that "Her favourite mark of punctu-
      ation is the dash, which perhaps signifies the principal trait of
      her mind."

B188 "Mary Shelley and G. H. Lewes," *Times Literary Supplement*, January
      12, 1946, p. 24.
           Speculates that Lewes is the author referred to in MS letter
      to Leigh Hunt (undated; ca. Dec. 1839).

B189 "Mary Shelley Goes to Hollywood," *New Statesman*, 3 (January 30,
      1932), 120.
           Brief review of the 1931 film *Frankenstein*: "the novel has
      an artistic interest as an essay in German horrific romanticism";
      it might be interesting if the film were done "by an historically-
      minded German."

B190 Massey, Irving.   "The First Edition of Shelley's *Poetical Works*
      (1839): Some Manuscript Sources," *Keats-Shelley Journal*, 16
      (Winter 1967), 29-38.
           Identifies the main source as MS fair-copy book, in the
      Bodleian Library.

B191 Massey, Irving.   "Mary Shelley, Walter Scott, and 'Maga,'" *Notes
      and Queries*, 9 (November 1962), 420-421.
           Prints the complete version of MS letter to Scott (June 14,
      1818) thanking him for his review of *Frankenstein* [cf. C9], and
      MS letter to *Blackwood's* (March 21, 1831) concerning the publi-
      cation of one of her articles, an article never published in that
      magazine.

B192   Massey, Irving. "Shelley's 'Music, When Soft Voices Die': Text and Meaning," *Journal of English and Germanic Philology*, 59 (July 1960), 430-438.
       MS version of the poem is superior to Shelley's.
       For response, see B121.

B193   Massey, Irving. "Shelley's 'Time': An Unpublished Sequel," *Studies in Romanticism*, 2 (Autumn 1962), 57-60 [58].
       "Mary's editorial method in dealing with 'Time' is strongly reminiscent of the manner in which she approached 'To' ('Music, when soft voices die')."

B194   Mattheisen, Paul F. "Gosse's Candid 'Snapshots,'" *Victorian Studies*, 8 (June 1965), 329-354 [353].
       Extract from Sir Edmund Gosse's unpublished diary, in which MS is mentioned.

B195   Matthews, G. M. "On Shelley's 'The Triumph of Life,'" *Studia Neophilologica*, 34 (1962), 104-134 [128-133].
       The poem gives some insights into the MS-Shelley-Jane Williams relationship: "'The serpent is shut out from Paradise' suggests that . . . he would still have Mary if she had let him."

B196   Matthews, G. M. "Shelley and Jane Williams," *Review of English Studies*, n.s. 12 (February 1961), 40-48.
       Touches on MS in Shelley-Jane Williams relationship to explain passages in Shelley's "Lines written in the Bay of Lerici" and *The Triumph of Life*.

B197   Matthews, G. M. "'The Triumph of Life': A New Text," *Studia Neophilologica*, 32 (1960), 271-309 [271, 272, 273, 275].
       Despite some unreliability, MS work on the poem "is surely one of the most remarkable editorial achievements of her time."

B198   May, Frederick. "A Foscolo Fragment in English," *Modern Language Review*, 51 (January 1964), 41-42 [41 n. 1].
       Mentions MS translation ("part quotation, part paraphrase") of Ugo Foscolo's *Notizia*.

B199   [Mayer, Gertrude Townshend.] "Mary Wollstonecraft Shelley," *The Eclectic Magazine of Foreign Literature* (N.Y.), n.s. 56 (September 1892), 401-413.
       Reprinting of B200.
       See also A277.

B200   [Mayer, Gertrude Townshend.] "Mary Wollstonecraft Shelley," *Temple Bar*, 95 (August 1892), 457-477.
       Superficial comments, based mainly on MS letters: "it is as a loving, suffering, enduring woman; as Shelley's wife, the mother of his son, and the guardian of his fame, that she will live in the hearts of his countrymen and in the history of their literature."
       See also A277, B199.

B201　Mayor, Andreas.　"A Suspected Shelley Letter," *The Library*, Fifth
series, 4 (September 1949), 141-145.
　　　　Discussion of the letter in B71, coming to same conclusions
as Ehrsam.

B202　Mays, Milton A.　"*Frankenstein*, Mary Shelley's Black Theodicy,"
Southern Humanities Review, 3 (Spring 1969), 146-153.
　　　　Examines the Faust myth and *Paradise Lost* in the novel:　MS
"world in *Frankenstein* is a dark one in which fundamental injustice
prevails among men, and, in the allegory of the Monster and his
Creator, between man and God."
　　　　Also published as A278.

B203　Mazlish, Bruce.　"The Fourth Discontinuity," *Technology and Cul-
ture*, 8 (January 1967), 1-15 [9, 11-14, 15].
　　　　Along with *Erehwon*, *Frankenstein* is examined to show the myth
of man's domination by machine:　"the monster, *cum* machine, is
evil, or rather, becomes evil, only because it is spurned by man."
　　　　Also published as A279.

B204　[Medwin, Thomas.]　"Memoir of Shelley," *The Athenæum*, No. 248
(July 28, 1832), 488-489 [488].
　　　　Although not named, MS is involved in Shelley's trip to the
continent in 1814.
　　　　See also A283, B205, B206, B207.

B205　[Medwin, Thomas.]　"Memoir of Shelley," *The Athenæum*, No. 249
(August 4, 1832), 502-504 [502].
　　　　Byron told Medwin that Shelley married MS at Byron's per-
suasion.
　　　　See also A283, B204, B296, B207.

B206　[Medwin, Thomas.]　"Memoir of Shelley," *The Athenæum*, No. 250
(August 11, 1832), 522-524 [522].
　　　　MS present when Medwin hypnotized Shelley.
　　　　See also A283, B204, B205, B207.

B207　[Medwin, Thomas.]　"Memoir of Shelley," *The Athenæum*, No. 251
(August 18, 1832), 535-537.
　　　　MS claiming of Shelley's heart, her miscarriage, and "the
sublime firmness of Mrs. Shelley" when Shelley died.
　　　　Authorship of this and previous installments [cf. B204, B205,
B206] is noted in an editorial footnote to "The Coliseum.　A
Fragment. By Percy Bysshe Shelley," *The Athenæum*, No. 253
(September 1, 1832), 568 n.:　"This is the fragment referred to
by Capt. Medwin in the Memoir."
　　　　See also A283.

B208　Melton, Carrol, Jr.　Letter, "In Defense of Frankestein [*sic*] the
Monster," *Famous Monsters of Filmland*, No. 35 (October 1965), 75.
　　　　Adolescent defense of the Monster's actions, challenging readers
"to find in the book where the monster was at fault."

B209 Metcalf, Carlos. Letter, "The Real and the Unreal," *TV Guide*, 22
      (December 1, 1974), A-9.
      Response to B300: the 1973 television production of *Franken-
      stein: The True Story* has no resemblance to the novel.

      Michell, Anne Lee. *See* Boas, Louise Schutz, B30.

B210 Micklewright, F. H. Amphlett. "The Noble Savage in Mary Shelley's
      'Frankenstein,'" *Notes and Queries*, 191 (July 27, 1946), 41.
      Response to B213: *Frankenstein* is a Gothic novel "and is of
      abiding importance as providing a link between Godwin, the Roman-
      tic Revival, and the Gothic school of novelists, as also do some
      of her other stories."

B211 Millar, A. H. "Mary Godwin in Dundee," *The Bookman* (London), 62
      (July 1922), 161-162.
      Based on the unpublished journal of Christy Baxter, proves
      the date and length of MS visit to Dundee, and that Christy, not
      her sister Isabella, was the intimate friend of MS.

B212 Millar, A. H. "Mary Shelley and Dundee," Dundee *Advertiser*
      (Dundee, Scotland), December 2, 1911, p. 7.
      History of the Baxters, with mention of MS connection.

B213 Millhauser, Milton. "The Noble Savage in Mary Shelley's 'Franken-
      stein,'" *Notes and Queries*, 190 (June 15, 1946), 248-250.
      Although the novel is primarily melodrama, the central theme
      is that of the Noble Savage.
      See B210 for response.

B214 Mimnermus [pseud.]. "Shelley's Mother-In-Law," *The Freethinker*,
      42 (August 13, 1922), 516.
      Brief mention of MS: "[she] had literary gifts of her own
      which merit attention"; *Frankenstein* is "a grim and powerful
      work," and *The Last Man*, *Lodore*, and the *Lives* are "brilliant."

B215 "Mrs. Shelley," *The Athenæum*, No. 1216 (February 15, 1851), 191.
      Obituary notice; mentions that her works all "have a singular
      eloquence of tone—but [also] a pervading melancholy," and "are
      unfairly neglected."

B216 "Mrs. Shelley," *The Literary Gazette and Journal of the Belles
      Lettres, Arts and Sciences*, No. 1779 (February 22, 1851), 149.
      Obituary notice; "It is not, however, even as the authoress of
      'Frankenstein' that she deserves her most enduring and endearing
      title to our affectionate remembrance, but as the faithful and
      devoted wife of Percy Bysshe Shelley."

B217 "Mrs. Shelley," *Saturday Review* (London), 69 (May 3, 1890), 540-
      541.
      Review of A13; wonders why a biography of MS has been pub-
      lished, since "All the lives of her husbands are full of her."
      Also disagrees a bit unenthusiastically with Rossetti's brief

criticism of *Frankenstein*: "It is strange to attack Frankenstein for being 'devoid of all feeling for art' in making his
man, and then to add that the man was 'copied from statues.'
What more could poor Frankenstein do for the interests of art
than copy statues?"

B218   Mobley, Jane. "Towards a Definition of Fantasy Fiction," *Extrapolation*, 15 (May 1974), 117-128 [119].
            "Sometimes [in science fiction] credulity is built by the mere
use of scientific jargon or physical detail, as in *Frankenstein*,
for instance, where surgical and electrical information provides
norms."†

B219   Moers, Ellen. "Female Gothic: Monsters, Goblins, Freaks," *The
New York Review of Books*, 21 (April 4, 1974), 35-39 [35].
            In both Christina Rossetti's *Goblin Market* and MS *Franken-
stein*, "particularly female experiences . . . contributed to the
disturbing eccentricity of the tale."

B220   Moers, Ellen. "Female Gothic: The Monster's Mother," *The New
York Review of Books*, 21 (March 21, 1974), 24-28.
            "*Frankenstein* is a birth myth . . . lodged in the novelist's
imagination . . . by the fact that she was herself a mother."
Biographical information concentrates upon MS pregnancies and
experiences in motherhood, as related to her works. Asserts
that *Frankenstein* is "more than mundane"—in it MS "transform[s]
the standard Romantic matter of incest, infanticide, and patri-
cide into a phantasmagoria of the nursery." A connection between
the MS novel and Stephen Crane's "The Monster" is noted on
p. 28 n. 28.
            See B219 for continuation.

B221   M[offat], W. D. "The Most Horrible Story," *The Mentor*, 10
(April 1922), 36.
            Plot synopsis of *Frankenstein*, with the erroneous statement
that MS wrote "several" introductions to the novel.

B222   *The Monthly Magazine of Politics, Literature, and the Belles
Lettres*, 11 (May 1831), 566.
            In a review of Godwin's *Caleb Williams*, MS is supposed the
author of the memoir.

B223   Moore, Doris Langley[-Levy]. "Byron, Leigh Hunt, and the Shelleys.
New Light on Certain Old Scandals," *Keats-Shelley Memorial Bulletin*, No. 10 (1959), 20-29.
            Defends Byron's "desertion" of MS after Shelley's death.

B224   "More of Mary Shelley," *Times Literary Supplement*, November 1,
1947, p. 560.
            Review of IA1: "Like her father, Mary the diarist excels in
silences or brevities when the striking events of her life occur,"
although occasionally she "wrote some inner thoughts and feelings."

B225 *Morning Chronicle* (London), August 27, 1817, p. 3.
      Concerning the Shelley-Harriet hearings, mentions that Shelley
      "cohabited with a woman [MS] during the life-time of the deceased
      [Harriet]."
      Reprinted in Kenneth Neill Cameron, ed. *Shelley and his
      Circle.* 6 vols. Cambridge, Mass.: Harvard University Press,
      1973, Vol. V, p. 273.
      See also B74.

B226 *Morning Chronicle* (London), March 24, 1826, p. 1 col. 4.
      Trade notice of publication of *The Last Man*, the publisher's
      blurb noting that "If the current of thought ran wild, and full of
      fearful beauty, through the mases [mazes?] of Frankenstein, its
      course is no less distinct from vulgar streams, and no less
      glowing with strong and intellectual powers, in the visionary
      velus of The Last Man."

B227 *Morning Chronicle* (London), March 24, 1826, p. 2 col. 5.
      Publisher's notice of *The Last Man* quoted in B167.

B228 *Morning Chronicle* (London), April 12, 1826, p. 4 col. 1.
      "THE PLAGUE.—It might have been imagined that the accounts of
      the Plagues of Athens, Florence, London, and Philadelphia, as
      given by Thucydides, Boccaccio, De Foe, and the American, Brown,
      would have left nothing to be said on the subject of this fearful
      visitation. Mrs. Shelley, however, whose mind by a strange ten-
      dency for a woman, seems fascinated by ghastly events, has outdone
      all these writers, in her description of the universal world
      wasting pestilences, in her Romance of 'The Last Man.' When once
      the reader is in her thrall, it is not easy to escape from the
      oppressive and startling horrors with which her pages teem."†
      Possibly another publisher's announcement.
      Also incorrectly printed as April 16.
      Reprinted as B131.

B229 *Morning Chronicle* (London), March 26, 1835, p. 3 col. 7.
      "Mrs. Shelley, the distinguished author of 'Frankenstein,'
      has just completed a new romance, which Mr. Bentley will publish
      in a few days. Perhaps no work of fiction has had a greater
      success than 'Frankenstein,' the exciting interest of which, to-
      gether with its power and eloquence, elicited even from Mr.
      Canning, in one of his speeches in the House of Commons, the warm
      eulogy, 'that it was the production of a child of genius.' This
      fair authoress has remained silent for so long a period, that a
      new work from her pen cannot fail to be welcome to the literary
      world. Mrs. Shelley's new romance is to be entitled 'Lodore.'"†

B230 *Morning Post* (London), May 11, 1830, p. 2 col. 3.
      Reprinting of B98.

B231 *Morning Post* (London), May 27, 1830, p. 2 col. 5.
      Reprinting of B99.

B232 Morris, Muriel. "Mary Shelley and John Howard Payne," *The Mercury* (London), 22 (September 1930), 443-450.
    Consideration of the MS-Payne letters: "It is difficult to judge the depth of her feeling for either Payne or Irving; wisps of banter might escape her thorough-going emotional prudence, but not much else."

B233 Moskowitz, Sam. "The Sons of Frankenstein," *Satellite Science Fiction*, 2 (August 1958), 112-121.
    Superficial examination of *Frankenstein* and *The Last Man* as early science fiction novels.
    Also published as A298.

B234 Murray, E. B. Review of Kenneth Neill Cameron, ed. *Shelley and his Circle*. Vols. III-IV, *Keats-Shelley Journal*, 21-22 (1972-73), 236-244 [242].
    Wonders why there is still "so much scholarly hesitancy about allowing the very likely fact that Hogg and Mary did have sex."

B235 "The National Portrait Gallery," *The Magazine of Art* (London), 24 (December 1899), 82.
    Mentions the Rothwell portrait of MS.
    See also B169, B236.

B236 "The National Portrait Gallery," *The Magazine of Art* (London), 24 (January 1900), 130.
    Describes Rothwell's portrait of MS, with a brief biography of Rothwell.
    See also B169, B235.

B237 Neff, Emery. "Mrs. Ariel," *The New York Times Book Review*, January 14, 1945, p. 4.
    Review of IA7, with unflattering remarks on MS: "If anyone ever did see Shelley plain, it was not his second wife."

B238 Nelson, Lowry, Jr. "Night Thoughts on the Gothic Novel," *Yale Review*, 52 (Winter 1963), 236-257 [237, 239, 243-249, 250, 251, 252, 253, 255, 256].
    Investigation of *Frankenstein* as a Gothic novel: "[It] is not a mere tale of terror, but rather a significant fictional model of the mind. For the first time in gothic fiction characters take on the full symbolic resonance of inner psychological reality."

B239 Newman, David, and Robert Benton. "The Basic Library of Trash," *Esquire*, 63 (February 1965), 78-79, 126-127 [79].
    No. 42 is *Frankenstein*: "Much quieter than the movie, much more British. Still, it's that same lovable monster."†

B240 *The News and Sunday Herald* (London), April 9, 1837, p. 153 col. 2.
    Recommends the review of *Falkner* in *The Monthly Repository* [cf. C89].

B241 *The Nic-Nac; or, Oracle of Knowledge*, 1 (April 12, 1823), 159.
Brief quote from *Valperga*, from C27.

B242 Nitchie, Elizabeth. "Byron, Madame de Staël, and Albertine,"
Keats-Shelley Journal, 7 (Winter 1958), 7-8.
Byron as a partial source for MS biography of de Staël.

B243 Nitchie, Elizabeth. "Eight Letters by Mary Wollstonecraft
Shelley," *Keats-Shelley Memorial Bulletin*, No. 3 (1950), 23-32.
Three previously unpublished MS letters: two to Charles
Ollier (Jan. 31, 1833; ca. Nov. 11, 1833), one to Trelawny
(ca. April 10, 1836). Parts of five other letters printed or
described.

B244 Nitchie, Elizabeth. Letter, "Mary Shelley," *Times Literary Supplement*, April 30, 1938, p. 296.
Corrects errors in MS letters from A8, A16, A126, and subse-
quent biographies of MS and Shelley.

B245 Nitchie, Elizabeth. "Mary Shelley, Traveler," *Keats-Shelley
Journal*, 10 (Winter 1961), 29-42.
Evaluates MS records of her travels, primarily in *History of
a Six Weeks' Tour* and *Rambles*, "in order to truly estimate her
quality as a writer."

B246 Nitchie, Elizabeth. "Mary Shelley's *Mathilda*: An Unpublished
Story and Its Biographical Significance," *Studies in Philology*,
40 (July 1943), 447-462.
History of the novelette, and investigation of biographical
and autobiographical elements.
Partially reprinted as Appendix III in A12; some material
also in A305 [and B247].

B247 Nitchie, Elizabeth. "Preface"; "Introduction"; Notes to Mary
Wollstonecraft Shelley. *Mathilda*. *Studies in Philology*, Extra
Series, No. 3 (October 1959), iii-iv; vii-xv; 81-89, 103-104.
Simultaneously published with A305.
See also B246.

B248 Nitchie, Elizabeth. Review of Frederick L[afayette] Jones, ed.
Mary Shelley's Journal [IA1], *Modern Language Notes*, 63 (Decem-
ber 1948), 572-573.
Notes several errors.

B249 Nitchie, Elizabeth. "Shelley at Eton: Mary Shelley vs. Jefferson
Hogg," *Keats-Shelley Memorial Bulletin*, No. 11 (1960), 48-54.
Prints portions of MS notes for an intended biography of
Shelley, and examines Hogg's "irresponsible" use of them.

B250 Nitchie, Elizabeth. "The Stage History of *Frankenstein*," *South
Atlantic Quarterly*, 41 (October 1942), 384-398.
From *Presumption* (1823) to Gladys Hastings-Walton's version

(1933), with passing remarks on film versions of the novel.
Reprinted as Appendix IV in A12.

B251   Norman, Sylva. Letter, *Times Literary Supplement*, March 20, 1937,
p. 222.

Ricci, Seymour de. Letter, *Times Literary Supplement*, March 27,
1937, p. 240.

Norman, Sylva. Letter, *Times Literary Supplement*, April 3, 1937,
p. 256.

Ricci, Seymour de. Letter, *Times Literary Supplement*, April 10,
1937, p. 275.

Pollard, Graham. Letter, *Times Literary Supplement*, April 17,
1937, p. 292.

Ricci, Seymour de. Letter, *Times Literary Supplement*, April 24,
1937, p. 308.

Besterman, Theodore. Letter, *Times Literary Supplement*, April 24,
1937, p. 308.

Pollard, Graham. Letter, *Times Literary Supplement*, May 8, 1937,
p. 364.

Kessel, Marcel. Letter, *Times Literary Supplement*, May 29, 1937,
p. 412.

Norman, Sylva. Letter, *Times Literary Supplement*, June 5, 1937,
p. 428.
    Controversy over the alleged letter of Shelley to MS, December
16, 1816. Norman doubts its authenticity, de Ricci claims it is
genuine, Pollard sums up the controversy, and Besterman wonders if
an examination with scientific apparatus would help. Inconclusive;
see B71 for continuation.

B252   Norman, Sylva. Letter, "Mary Shelley and *Midas*," *Times Literary
Supplement*, July 2, 1938, p. 449.
    Contends that Jones (in B136) still has not proved MS the
author of *Midas*, although "in all probability she was."

Norman, Sylva. *See* Ehrsam, Theodore G[eorge], B71.

B253   Norman, Sylva. "Mary Shelley, 1797-1851," *The Fortnightly*, n.s.
169 [175] (February 1951), 112-117.
    Brief overview of MS importance, skipping about in her life.

B254   Norman, Sylva. "Shelley's Last Residence," *Keats-Shelley Journal*,
2 (January 1953), 1-10.
    Observations culled from a personal visit on the house where
MS and Shelley lived at San Terenzo.

B255 *The Observer* (London), December 28, 1817, p. 1 col. 3.
      Notice of intended publication of *Frankenstein* on the next
      day, "dedicated to William Goodwin [*sic*], a Work of Imagination."

B256 Orange, Ursula. "Elise. Nursemaid to the Shelleys," *Keats-
      Shelley Memorial Bulletin*, No. 6 (1955), 24-34.
      Examines Elise's motives in the "Hoppner Scandal," and con-
      tends that she was the mother of the child, and that MS knew
      this.

B257 Orange, Ursula. "Shuttlecocks of Genius. An Enquiry into the
      Fate of Shelley's Children," *Keats-Shelley Memorial Bulletin*,
      No. 8 (1957), 38-52 [45-52].
      MS felt guilty about the loss of her children, because she
      and Shelley were, as parents, "peculiarly lacking in common
      sense." Wonders if one of the three dead children might have had
      "the spark of genius so conspicuously lacking in the estimable
      Sir Percy."

B258 Owen, Robert Dale. "Frances Wright, General Lafayette, and Mary
      Wollstonecraft Shelley. A Chapter of Autobiography," *Atlantic
      Monthly*, 32 (October 1873), 448-459 [457-459].
      Description of MS and his attraction towards her.
      Reprinted as A316.

B259 Palacio, Jean de. "Mary Shelley and the 'Last Man.' A Minor
      Romantic Theme," *Revue de littérature comparée*, 42 (Janviers-
      Mars 1968), 37-49.
      Investigation of MS indebtedness to sources of *The Last Man*,
      and the novel's success.

B260 Palacio, Jean de. "Mary Shelley's Latin Studies. Her Unpub-
      lished Translation of Apuleius," *Revue de littérature comparée*,
      38 (Octobre-Décembre 1964), 564-571.
      Contrasts MS version with the original and Pater's version.

B261 Palacio, Jean de. "Shelley's Library Catalogue. An unpublished
      document," *Revue de littérature comparée*, 36 (Avril-Juin 1962),
      270-276 [270-272, 276].
      Identifies MS manuscript material in the Shelley collection
      at the Bodleian Library.

B262 Palmer, D. J., and R[obert] E. Dowse. "'Frankenstein': A Moral
      Fable," *The Listener*, 68 (August 23, 1962), 281, 284.
      Concentrates on the creation of the Monster as a myth of the
      origins of evil.
      See also B68.

B263 Panshin, Alexei, and Cory Panshin. "The Resurrection of SF—I,"
      Fantastic Stories, 21 (April 1972), 90-98 [92-93, 94].
      Brief examination of the science in *Frankenstein*, which "made
      the operating power of [the novel] plausible."

B264 Patton, Lewis. "The Shelley-Godwin Collection of Lord Abinger,"
     Library Notes. A Bulletin Issued by the Friends of Duke Univer-
     sity, 27 (April 1953), 11-17.
          Identifies MS material in the microfilm collection now at the
     Duke University Library and the Bodleian, in Reels 4, 5, 6, 8, 9,
     10, 11, 12, 13, 14, 15, and 16.

B265 Peacock, T[homas] L[ove]. "Memoirs of Percy Bysshe Shelley. Part
     II," *Fraser's Magazine for Town and Country*, 61 (January 1860),
     92-109 [93, 94, 95, 96, 97, 98, 99, 100, 103, 104, 106, 109].
          MS mentioned in passing.
          Also published as A324.
          See also B266.

B266 Peacock, T[homas] L[ove]. "Percy Bysshe Shelley. Supplementary
     Notice," *Fraser's Magazine for Town and Country*, 65 (March 1862),
     343-346.
          MS mentioned in passing.
          Also published as A324.
          See also B265.

B267 Peck, Walter Edwin. "The Biographical Element in the Novels of
     Mary Wollstonecraft Shelley," *PMLA*, 38 (March 1923), 196-219.
          Examines *Valperga, The Last Man,* and *Falkner* in detail, with
     extensive quotations from the novels.

B268 Peck, Walter Edwin. "New Shelley Papers," *The Nation & The
     Athenæum*, 28 (March 19, 1921), 876-877.
          Section of Act II of *Proserpine* printed, with Shelley's
     corrections.

B269 Peck, Walter Edwin. "Shelley, Mary Shelley, and *Rinaldo Rinal-
     dini*," *PMLA*, 40 (March 1925), 165-171.
          Possible influence of I. Hinckley's *The Life and Adventures
     of Rinaldo Rinaldini* (1800) upon *The Last Man* and *Frankenstein*.

B270 Peck, Walter Edwin. "Shelley's Reviews Written for the *Examiner*,"
     Modern Language Notes, 39 (February 1924), 118-119.
          Shelley's review of *Frankenstein* [cf. A386, B314] was written
     originally for *The Examiner*.

B271 Pelo, Florence Boylston. "Some Unpublished Letters of Mary
     Shelley," *North American Review*, 204 (November 1916), 727-740.
          Describes and prints 23 MS letters to Leigh and Marianne Hunt.

B272 "Percy Bysshe Shelley, Esq.," *The Drama, or Theatrical Pocket
     Magazine*, 3 (December 1822), 387-393 [388].
          Obituary of Shelley, with passing reference to MS. Incor-
     porated into B65.
          Reprinted as A331.

B273 "Percy Bysshe Shelley, Esq.," *The Gentleman's Magazine*, 92, part 2 (September 1822), 283.

Obituary notice of Shelley, with passing reference to MS: "The wives of Mr. Shelley and Capt. Williams were both at Leghorn overwhelmed with grief." Reprinted as A330.

*B274 Pinkney, Edward Coote. "The New Frankenstein," *The Marylander*, December 5, 1827.

See re-publication, A335, for annotation. The original appearance of this satire is noted by Mabbott and Pleadwell in A263, with only the above information given.

B275 Plank, Robert. "The Golem and the Robot," *Literature and Psychology*, 15 (Winter 1965), 12-27 [19].

Superficial treatment of *Frankenstein*: "like the golem [the Monster] was oversized and therefore naturally malevolent." Published in German as E36.

B276 "The Poetical Works of Thomas Lovell Beddoes," *The Athenæum*, No. 3296 (December 27, 1890), 879-881 [880].

Review of A171: "when [Gosse] goes on to compare 'Death's Jest-Book' with 'Frankenstein' he is surely a little severe upon Mrs. Shelley. Well would it have been for Beddoes if he could have developed a story from a distinct *idée mère* as clearly as Mrs. Shelley has done in that remarkable exercise of fancy, the conception of which—the conception of an ambitious student of nature who, aspiring to vivify a man that he had fashioned out of clay, succeeds in fashioning a monster from which he has to flee—is developed in every sentence of the book."†

Pollard, Graham. *See* Norman, Sylva, B251.

B277 Pollin, Burton R. "Godwin's Account of Shelley's Return in September, 1814: A Letter to John Taylor," *Keats-Shelley Memorial Bulletin*, No. 20 (1970), 21-31.

Textual and biographical discussion of the November 8, 1814 letter, concerning MS and Shelley's return after their elopement.

B278 Pollin, Burton R. "Godwin's *Memoirs* as a Source of Shelley's Phrase 'Intellectual Beauty,'" *Keats-Shelley Journal*, 23 (1974), 14-20 [19].

MS may have inserted the adjective in the phrase "intellectual beauty" used by Shelley in his translation of Plato's *Symposium*.

B279 Pollin, Burton [R.], and Alice Pollin. "In Pursuit of Pearson's Shelley Songs," *Music and Letters*, 46 (October 1965), 322-331 [324, 325, 328-330].

Brief examination of Henry Hugh Pearson's accompaniment of MS, Sir Percy, and Alexander Knox in the tour that resulted in MS *Rambles*.

B280   Pollin, Burton R. "Mary Shelley as the Parvenue," *Review of English Literature*, 8 (July 1967), 9-21.
       Biographical and critical study of "The Parvenue," in which she "clearly was drawing upon her pent-up feelings of inferiority and imposition derived from her years as Shelley's mistress, wife and widow, and as the dutiful daughter of Godwin"; the story itself "an attempt at realism [which] possibly inherits the melancholy memories of other, less serene moments with Shelley as well as the strains of her life after his death."

B281   Pollin, Burton R. "'Ozymandias' and the Dormouse," *Dalhousie Review*, 47 (Autumn 1967), 361-367.
       Glosses "Glirastes" as "lover of the dormouse," yielding a "curious insight" into the MS-Shelley-Hogg relationship.
       See also B284.

B282   Pollin, Burton R. "Philosophical and Literary Sources of *Frankenstein*," *Comparative Literature*, 17 (Spring 1965), 97-108.
       Important study of the influences of Godwin's *Political Justice* and his novels, Mme. de Gerlis' *Pygmalion et Galatée*, Milton's *Paradise Lost*, Ovid's *Metamorphoses*, Locke's *Essay Concerning Human Understanding*, and writings by Condillac and Diderot.

B283   Pollin, Burton R. "'Rappacini's Daughter'—Sources and Names," *Names*, 14 (March 1966), 30-35 [30-32, 35].
       Frankenstein as an influence upon Hawthorne's "Rappacini's Daughter" and novels.

B284   Pottle, Frederick A. "The Meaning of Shelley's 'Glirastes,'" *Keats-Shelley Journal*, 7 (Winter 1958), 6-7.
       Glosses "Glirastes" as "the one who behaves like a dormouse"— Shelley, not MS.
       See also B281.

B285   Prescott, F. C. "*Wieland* and *Frankenstein*," *American Literature*, 2 (May 1930), 172-173.
       Briefly speculates that the inspiration for MS novel may be a passage (quoted) in *Wieland*.

B286   Preu, James A. "The Tale of Terror," *English Journal*, 47 (May 1958), 243-247 [246-247].
       Brief mention of *Frankenstein*, noting that it has been "sadly mangled by the movie-makers."

B287   R., J. E. "Mary Shelley and 'Orpheus,'" *Times Literary Supplement*, March 1, 1923, p. 143.
       Speculates that both MS and Shelley wrote "Orpheus."

B288   Raben, Joseph. "Shelley's 'The Boat on the Serchio': The Evidence of the Manuscript," *Philological Quarterly*, 46 (January 1967), 58-68.
       MS suppressed parts of the poem and dated it incorrectly.

B289 Raben,Joseph. "Shelley's 'Invocation to Misery': An Expanded Text," *Journal of English and Germanic Philology*, 65 (January 1966), 65-74.
MS mangled the poem.

B290 Rao, E. Nageswara. "The Significance of Frankenstein," *Triveni: Journal of Indian Renaissance* (Machilipatnam and Madras), 37 (October 1968), 20-26.
Examination of all themes in the MS novel, concluding that it is a "powerful tragedy," "presented somewhat in the Greek manner."

B291 "Raw Materials for Peers," *Punch in London*, No. 1 (January 14, 1831), 4-5 [5].
One satirical suggestion, demonstrating the popularity of the Frankenstein plays: "Mr. O. Smith, as Lord Frankenstein.—I am induced to create this gentleman a Peer, inasmuch as I do not think it fair that the Marquis of L—— should continue to *play the devil* by himself."†

B292 Raynor, Henry. "Television justice for Mrs. Shelley," London *Times*, November 12, 1968, p. 7.
Review of the 1968 Thames Television production of *Frankenstein*, pronouncing the novel "stiltedly written, hard to read and very important."

B293 [Reeve, H.] "Shelley and Mary," *Edinburgh Review*, 156 (October 1882), 472-507.
Review of A16, applauding the publication of the volumes and quoting extensively.
See also A294.

B294 [Reeve, H.] "Shelley and Mary," *Littell's Living Age*, 155 (November 1882), 387-406.
Reprinting of B293.

B295 Reiman, Donald H. "Shelley's 'The Triumph of Life': The Biographical Problem," *PMLA*, 78 (December 1963), 536-550.
In an intensive investigation, which also summarizes previous approaches, author states that no "affair" developed between Shelley and Jane Williams, and that MS reactions to this and other events were not hostile or unreasonable. Demonstrates very sensitive reading of MS letters.

B296 "Report of the Rome Committee," *Keats-Shelley Journal*, 10 (Winter 1961), 4.
Sylva Norman donated three MS letters to the Keats-Shelley Memorial Library in Rome.

Ricci, Seymour de. *See* Norman, Sylva, B251.

B297 Rieger, James. "Dr. Polidori and the Genesis of *Frankenstein*," *Studies in English Literature 1500-1900*, 3 (Autumn 1963), 461-472.
MS 1831 Introduction is innacurrate; the *Fantasmagoriana* did

not influence the conception of the novel. Also mentions MS fondness for Polidori.
Reprinted as Appendix in A325.

B298 Rieger, James. "Shelley's Paterin Beatrice," *Studies in Romanticism*, 4 (Spring 1965), 169-184 [169, 177-181].
Valperga as a source for *The Cenci*; the Beatrice of MS contrasted with Shelley's.
Reprinted in A325.
See also D16.

B299 Roman, Robert C. "Boris Karloff," *Films In Review*, 15 (August/September 1964), 389-412 [394-395, 398-399].
Brief contrast of the novel *Frankenstein* with the 1931 and 1935 film versions.

B300 Rosenberg, Samuel. "'Frankenstein.' Literature's most celebrated monster is revived for another airing," *TV Guide*, 21 (November 24, 1973), 29-30, 32, 34, 36.
"Background" for the NBC Television adaptation of the novel: sketchy and familiar, mentioning that Shelley and Byron were working "on a much higher intellectual plateau" than MS.
Condensed version of B301.
For response, see B209. See also A363.

B301 Rosenberg, Samuel. "The Horrible Truth About Frankenstein," *Life*, 64 (March 15, 1968), 74B-74D, 77-82, 84.
Superficial biography of MS and critical comments: "Are you now asking the question: Was Mary Shelley the Frankenstein Creature of her own book? Was her book a device for self-and-mother purgation? The answers are: yes, of course."
Alternate title on p. 74D reads "Happy Sesquicentennial, Dear Monster."
See also A363, B300.

B302 Russell, Bertrand. "Byron and the Modern World," *The Journal of the History of Ideas*, 1 (January 1940), 24-37 [32-33].
Frankenstein contains "an allegorical history of the development of romanticism" in the Monster, "a gentle being, longing for human affection."

B303 Sambrook, A. J. "A Romantic Theme: The Last Man," *Forum for Modern Language Studies*, 2 (January 1966), 25-33 [31-32, 33].
Biographical elements noted in MS *The Last Man*, which is briefly compared with Beddoes and Hood's versions.

B304 "Says Doctor Thought Shelley Henpecked. Miss Furnivall, 100, Tells of Her Father's Experiences with the Poet," The New York *Times*, April 1, 1926, p. 6 cols. 4-5.
"The physician thought the poet was henpecked by his second wife, whom he quoted as continually saying, 'Shelley, fetch this, or that.'"

B305 Schulz, H. C. "English Literary Manuscripts in the Huntington
      Library," *Huntington Library Quarterly*, 31 (May 1968), 251-302
      [291].
          Included is the notation of 167 MS letters (1817-1849) in the
      library.†

B306 Schwarz, Sheila. "The World of Science Fiction," *English Record*,
      21 (February 1971), 27-40 [29-31].
          Superficial treatment of *Frankenstein*: "The question of the
      relationship between the scientist and his invention is one of the
      most critical ones of our time."

B307 Scortia, Thomas N. "Woman's Rib," *Galaxy*, 33 (July-August 1972),
      144-154 [151].
          Short story about a woman's creation of a love-mate named
      Frank, in which "that abomination" by MS is mentioned.

B308 Scott, Sir Walter. "On the Supernatural in Fictitious Composition;
      and particularly on the Works of Ernest Theodore William Hoffman,"
      Foreign Quarterly Review, 1 (July 1827), 60-98 [72-73].
          Brief, favorable remarks on *Frankenstein*: "a powerful romance."
      Reprinted in A375.

B309 Seccombe, Thomas. "H. G. Wells," *The Bookman* (London), 46 (April
      1914), 13-24 [16].
          In Wells' *The Island of Dr. Moreau*, "*membra disjecta* from
      'Gulliver's Fourth Voyage,' 'Jekyll and Hyde,' and 'Frankenstein,'
      could, perhaps, be detected . . . by one of that new species, the
      thesis-fiend."†

B310 Sencourt, Robert. "Byron and Shelley at the Lake of Geneva," *The
      Quarterly Review*, 284 (April 1946), 209-221.
          Review of *Works of Lord Byron* [A83]; John Murray, ed., *Lord
      Byron's Correspondence* (London: John Murray, 1922); *Moore's Life
      of Byron* [A291, A293]; E. C. Mayne, *Byron* (London: Methuen, 1912);
      André Maurois, *Byron* (London: Jonathan Cape, 1930); and Peck's
      Life of Shelley [A328]. Traces the movements of Byron, Shelley,
      and MS in Geneva; mentions *Frankenstein* as MS "one remarkable
      novel."

B311 Sencourt, Robert. "Mary Wollstonecroft Shelley," *Contemporary
      Review*, 192 (October 1957), 215-218.
          Apparently a centennial "tribute" to MS: Shelley was blameless
      in the matter of the elopement and desertion of Harriet; MS seduced
      him and "involved one of our finest poets in the most lurid scan-
      dal." Understanding of facts slight: MS actually died in 1851,
      misspelling of her matronymic, reliance on anecdotes.

B312 Shales, Tom. "Frankenstein," in "The Weekend: From Monsters to
      Ballet," Washington *Post*, December 3, 1973, p. B10.
          The novel is "essentially sloppy," with a "murky Gothic
      spirit."

B313   Shaw, George Bernard. "Shaming the Devil about Shelley," *The
        Albemarle. A Monthly Review*, 2 (September 1892), 91-98 [93].
        MS did not appreciate Shelley's suggestion that Harriet come
        to live with them.
        Reprinted as A381.
        Note to Library of Congress users: *The Albemarle*, as of
        February 1975, is being microfilmed.

B314   Shelley, Percy Bysshe. "On 'Frankenstein,'" *The Athenæum*, No. 263
        (November 10, 1832), 730.
        Extremely favorable remarks on the novel. "We are led breath-
        less with suspense and sympathy, and the heaping up of incident
        upon incident, and the working of passion out of passion. We cry,
        'hold, hold! enough!'—but there is yet something to come."
        Presented by Thomas Medwin as part of the "Shelley Papers"
        series.
        See A386 for first publication in book form, and subsequent
        reprintings.
        See also B270.

B315   "Shelley," under "Spirit of the Times," *Philadelphia Album and
        Ladies' Literary Gazette*, March 13, 1830, pp. 86-87 [87].
        Defends MS actions, but confuses her with Harriet.
        Robert Morris possibly the author.

B316   "Shelley and Dundee," Dundee *Advertiser* (Dundee, Scotland), March
        8, 1892, p. 2.
        History of the Baxters, with mention of MS connection.

B317   "Shelley Memorials," *Saturday Review* (London), 85 (July 30, 1859),
        134-135.
        Complimentary remarks on MS: "Her writings have long ago
        established her literary reputation, but these new documents will
        confirm and add to it."
        Review of A382.
        See also B17.

B318   "Shelley's Early Years," *Cornhill Magazine*, 31 (February 1875),
        184-206 [199-202].
        MS was not to blame in Shelley's desertion of Harriet.

B319   Shivas, Mark. "Is There a Doctor in the House? Yes, and His Name
        is Frankenstein," The New York *Times*, June 24, 1973, Section II,
        p. 15.
        Preview of the NBC Television adaptation of *Frankenstein*.
        Author of the teleplay, Christopher Isherwood, "always liked the
        Mary Shelley story and felt it had never really been done properly.
        Victor Frankenstein is a young man and he's usually shown as a 50-
        year-old."

B320   [Simms, William Gilmore.] "Modern Prose Fiction," *Southern
        Quarterly Review*, 15 (April 1849), 41-83 [72-73].
        Review of A206. Mixed comments on *Frankenstein*: the "vital

defect" is its unbelievability, and although it is "emphatically a work of power . . . it is a power too frequently exercised at random, and lacking that symmetry of parts which denotes a subdued judgment, and a presiding taste."
See also A320.

B321 Smith, Harry B[ache]. "Books and Autograph Letters of Shelley," *Scribner's Magazine*, 72 (July 1922), 73-87.
Reproduces and discusses facsimiles of MS letters and Shelley letters concerning her.

B322 Smith, John Harrington. "Shelley and Claire Again," *Studies in Philology*, 41 (January 1944), 94-105.
Suggests Claire, not MS, as "the cruel lady" in Shelley's *Julian and Maddalo*.

B323 Smith, John Harrington. "Shelley and Claire Clairmont," *PMLA*, 54 (September 1939), 785-814.
Suggests that Claire, not MS, is referred to in passages of Shelley's "Epipsychidion," *Alastor*, and *Julian and Maddalo*. Supposes Shelley unfaithful to MS with Claire, the reason MS "forced" Claire's exile.
See also B137.

B324 Spark, Muriel. "Mary Shelley: a Prophetic Novelist," *The Listener*, 45 (February 22, 1951), 305-306.
Frankenstein is prophetic in that it anticipates "the ultimate conclusions to which the ideas of her epoch were heading—an epoch in which religious beliefs had been shaken by eighteenth-century rationalism, and were now being challenged by science and progress"; *The Last Man* "has a solemnity that often defeats itself," but in it MS "had a grip on social ideas, and though she could never comfortably bring off a domestic scene, she was able to manipulate people in a mass; she could depict a social trend."

B325 Spears, Jack. "Robert Florey," *Films In Review*, 11 (April 1960), 210-231 [220-221].
Brief contrast of *Frankenstein* and the 1931 film version: "Many of the basic incidents of this picture—lacking in the novel—were born in Florey's imagination."

B326 *The Spectator* (London), No. 97 (May 8, 1830), 295.
"Mrs. Shelley's [*Perkin Warbeck*], which this announcement is intended to favour by insinuation, we have not seen. But we have read a part . . . of Mr. Newman's publication."†

B327 Steffan, Truman Guy. "Seven Accounts of the Cenci and Shelley's Drama," *Studies in English Literature 1500-1900*, 9 (Autumn 1969), 601-618 [602-603, 609].
MS connection with three versions of the "Relation of the Death of the Cenci Family," now in the Miriam Lutcher Stark Library of the University of Texas at Austin.

B328 Stockwell, La Tourette. "Two Unpublished Letters of Mary Wollstone-
      craft Shelley," *Dublin Magazine*, n.s. 8 (April 1933), 41-45.
      MS letters to Thomas Crofton Croker (Oct. 30, 1829; Nov. 4,
      1829).
      See also B66.

B329 "The Strange Sequel to Shelley's Romantic Career," The New York
      Times, October 15, 1911, part 6, p. 10.
      Pulp account of MS "affairs," based on A178.

B330 Strout, Alan Lang. *"Maga*, Champion of Shelley," *Studies in Philol-
      ogy*, 29 (January 1932), 95-119 [96 n. 6].
      Notes the history of Scott's review of *Frankenstein* [cf. C9].

B331 S[tuart], I[sobel]. "New Light on Shelley," *The Star* (London),
      March 12, 1894, p. 1 col. 7.
      Gives MS addition to a Shelley letter addressed to William
      Baxter (Dec. 30, 1817).

B332 Swingle, L. J. "Frankenstein's Monster and Its Romantic Relatives:
      Problems of Knowledge in English Romanticism," *Texas Studies in
      Literature and Language*, 15 (Spring 1973), 51-65.
      In *Frankenstein*, MS pursues "the question of the human mind's
      ability to grasp the essential nature of things"—as do Wordsworth
      and Keats, the latter in "The Eve of St. Agnes."

B333 *The Tatler*, No. 185 (April 7, 1831), 737.
      MS is the author of the memoir in Godwin's *Caleb Williams*,
      which is to appear soon.

B334 Taylor, Charles H[enry], Jr. "The Errata Leaf to Shelley's *Post-
      humous Poems* and Some Surprising Relationships Between the Earliest
      Collected Editions," *PMLA*, 70 (June 1955), 408-416.
      In connection with the Errata Leaf, observes that "perhaps one
      reason that the more recent (and most highly respected) textual
      editors have neglected to examine [it] is that Mrs. Shelley incor-
      porated the majority of the corrections in her collected editions."

B335 Thomas, Donald. "The First Poetess of Romantic Fiction: Ann
      Radcliffe, 1764-1823," *English* (London), 15 (Autumn 1964), 91-95
      [91].
      Frankenstein belongs to both the science fiction and Gothic
      genres.

B336 "$3 For Shelley-Payne Letter. Congratulatory Note Sold in an
      Auction Room in This City," The New York *Times*, March 17, 1904,
      p. 9 col. 2.
      Two-page MS letter to Payne sold.

B337 Trelawny, E[dward] J[ohn]. Letter, "Shelley's Last Days. (A Reply to R. Garnett's Article in the 'Fortnightly')," *The Athenæum*, No. 2649 (August 3, 1878), 144.

Reply to B90. Claims MS refused Shelley's heart, did not ask him for her portrait until very late, and did not help in the writing of his *Adventures of a Younger Son*. Also asserts that *Frankenstein* was "the creation of her husband's brain."

B338 Twain, Mark [pseud. of Samuel Langhorne Clemens]. "In Defense of Harriet Shelley," *North American Review*, 159 (July 1894), 108-119 [109, 110].

Concerning A126: "This is perhaps the strangest book that has seen the light since Frankenstein. Indeed it is a Frankenstein itself; a Frankenstein with the original infirmity supplemented by a new one; a Frankenstein with the reasoning faculty wanting."
See also B339, B340.

B339 Twain, Mark. "In Defense of Harriet Shelley," *North American Review*, 159 (August 1894), 240-251 [246].

Part II. Complains that Dowden does not censure MS [in A126] for forcing Shelley to pay her father's debts.
See also B338, B340.

B340 Twain, Mark. "In Defense of Harriet Shelley," *North American Review*, 159 (September 1894), 353-368 [353, 356, 359-360, 361-362, 364, 365, 367, 368].

Part III. Brusque comments on MS in conclusion: "She was a child in years only. From the day that she set her masculine grip on Shelley he was to frisk no more."
See also B338, B339.

B341 Tyler, Henry. Letter, "Hunt and Shelley," *Times Literary Supplement*, November 8, 1947, p. 577.

MS letter to Leigh Hunt (April 8, 1825) shows her reaction to an article by him for *Westminster Review*—she asks if he would remove all references to Claire.

B342 "An Unpublished Letter. Mary Wollstonecraft Shelley to T. B. Cooper," The New York *Times*, February 2, 1890, p. 20 col. 2.

In a letter to actor Thomas Cooper (August 24, 1836), MS asks for Godwin letters.

B343 "Unpublished Poems by Mary Shelley," *Littell's Living Age*, 316 (January 20, 1923), 183.

Notice of the publication of *Proserpine and Midas*, so that lovers of Shelley "are at last able to read 'Arethusa' and other lyrics in the settings for which they were originally written." Little mention of MS, except the doubt that she wrote the two dramas.

B344 "Velluti," *The Atlas* (London), June 18, 1826, pp. 74-75.

Response to and criticism of MS letter to *The Examiner* (June 11, 1826). Dislikes Velluti's singing, but feels the "tone of his [MS] production is so good, that we feel tempted to notice it"—"though we hold his arguments light, and his facts questionable, we respect his feelings."

B345   Vernon, John. "Melville's 'The Bell-Tower,'" *Studies in Short Fiction*, 7 (Spring 1970), 264-276 [271-273].
       Notes the connection between *Frankenstein*, "The Bell-Tower," and Hawthorne's "The Birthmark": "The similarities between the three stories reveal the basic structure Melville was working with, and the effect of both [Mary] Shelley and Hawthorne on his imagination. *Frankenstein, Aylmer*, and *Bannadonna* are all scientists displeased with the imperfections of mankind."

B346   Vincent, E[ric] R[eginald] P[earce]. "Two Letters from Mary Shelley to Gabriele Rossetti," *Modern Language Review*, 27 (October 1932), 459-461.
       In the letters, written in Italian (April 3 & 20, 1835), MS asks for help in her biographies of Alfieri and Monti.

B347   *The Wasp*, 1 (October 28, 1826), 79.
       Announces "The Last Woman; by Mrs. Shelley."†

B348   Webb, Timothy. "Shelley and the Cyclops," *Keats-Shelley Memorial Bulletin*, No. 23 (1972), 31-37 [34-36].
       Somewhat forced comparison of Polyphemus, the Monster in *Frankenstein*, and Shelley.
       For a similar comparison, see D12 (pp. 112-114).

B349   White, Newman I[vey]. "*The Shelley Legend* Examined," *Studies in Philology*, 43 (July 1946), 522-544.
       Rebuttal to the allegations made in A19, concentrating on the forged Shelley letters and the attacks on Shelley scholarship.
       Reprinted as A437.
       See also B43 [and A87], B141 [and A226].

B350   White, Ted. "Editorial," *Fantastic Stories*, 23 (March 1974), 4, 125-128 [4, 125].
       Brian Aldiss' *Frankenstein Unbound* [cf. F2] "provides a work of critical exegisis on *Frankenstein* as a novel."

B351   Woof, R. S. Review of *The Diaries and Correspondence of James Losh*, *Notes and Queries*, 210 (November 1965), 433-436 [435].
       "Here is Losh's entry for June 11, 1819 (the words in italics are those omitted by the editor):
       'June 11. *Business 7. Frankenstein 2 and* looked *in that time* through 3 vols. of this monstrous and disgusting work—A mixture of Atheism *and false sensibility*, the genuine production of the German, French and Godwinian principles and morality.'"†

*B352 *The World of Fashion and Continental Feuilleton* [*Monde elegant*], 12 (June 1835), 128.
       de Palacio [E1, p. 670, Item 131] quotes the passage, a casual

reference to *The Last Man*: "It is beautifully observed by Mrs. Shelley, that 'it is one of the most beneficient dispensations of the Creator, that there is nothing so attractive and attaching as affection.'"

Not at the Library of Congress, Bodleian, British Library (unless lost), Yale, New York Public Library, University of Minnesota, or Toronto Public Library.

B353 Wylie, Elinor. "Shelley's Grandson and Some Others," *Bookman* (N.Y.), 57 (August 1923), 611-612.

The grandson of Shelley and Harriet is quoted as saying, "You know, in this family we don't think much of Mary."

B354 Zimmerman, Paul D. "Camp Frankenstein," *Newsweek*, 83 (May 20, 1974), 105-106.

Review of 1974 film *Andy Warhol's Frankenstein*, in which the X-rated, part-satire, part-serious, overground film is termed "the first original variation on 'Frankenstein' in years."

C REVIEWS

1. *Novels*

a) Frankenstein; or, The Modern Prometheus

1. *Frankenstein; or, The Modern Prometheus.* 3 vols.
   London: Printed for Lackington, Hughes, Harding,
   Mayor, & Jones, 1818.

C1   *La Belle Assemblée, or Court and Fashionable Magazine,* 2nd series,
     17 (March 1818), 139-142.
          Favorable, and perceptive. "[It] has, as well as originality,
     extreme interest to recommend it, and an easy, yet energetic style";
     its moral "that the *presumptive* works of man must be frightful,
     vile, and horrible; ending only in discomfort and misery to him-
     self."
          Reprinted in A349 (Vol. I, pp. 42-45).

C2   *The British Critic,* n.s. 9 (April 1818), 432-438.
          Unfavorable; "these volumes have neither principle, object, nor
     moral; the horror which abounds in them is too grotesque and *bizarre*
     ever to approach the sublime." However, "there are occasional
     symptoms of no common powers of mind, struggling through a mass of
     absurdity."
          Reprinted as C8.

C3   [Croker, John Wilson.] *The Quarterly Review,* 18 (January 1818),
     379-385.
          Mainly unfavorable. "Our taste and our judgment alike revolt
     at this kind of writing, and the greater the ability with which
     it may be executed the worse it is—it inculcates no lesson of
     conduct, manners, or morality; it cannot mend, and will not even
     amuse its readers, unless their taste have been deplorably
     vitiated."
          Reprinted in A349 (Vol. II, pp. 764-767).

C4   *The Edinburgh Magazine and Literary Miscellany, A new Series of the
     Scots Magazine,* 2 (March 1818), 249-253.
          Favorable. "There never yet was a wilder story imagined, yet
     like most of the fictions of this age, it has an air of reality
     attached to it, by being connected with the favourite projects and
     passions of the times."
          Reprinted in A349 (Vol. II, pp. 819-823).

C5   *The Gentleman's Magazine: and Historical Chronicle*, 88 (April 1818), 334-335.

    "This Tale is evidently the production of no ordinary Writer; and though we are shocked at the idea of the event on which the fiction is founded, many parts of it are strikingly good, and the description of the scenery excellent.

    "In the pride of Science, the Hero of the Tale presumes to take upon himself the structure of a human being; in which, though he in some degree is supposed to have succeeded, he forfeits every comfort of life, and finally even life itself.

    . . .

    "If we mistake not, this friend [mentioned in the novel's Preface, and quoted here] was a Noble Poet."†

*C6   *The Literary Panorama, and National Register*, n.s. 8 (June 1818), 411-414.

    de Palacio (El, p. 652, Item 24) terms it "Hostile."

C7   *The Monthly Review, or Literary Journal*, n.s. 85 (April 1818), 439.

    "An uncouth story, in the taste of the German novelists, trenching in some degree on delicacy, setting probability at defiance, and leading to no conclusion either moral or philosophical. In some passages, the writer appears to favour the doctrines of materialism: but a serious examination is scarcely necessary for so excentric a vagary of the imagination as this tale presents."†

C8   *Port Folio* (Philadelphia), 6 (August 1818), 200-207.

    Reprinting of C2.

C9   [Scott, Sir Walter.] *Blackwood's Edinburgh Magazine*, 2 (March 1818), 613-620.

    Favorable and detailed. "It is no slight merit in our eyes, that the tale, though wild in incident, is written in plain and forcible English, without exhibiting that mixture of hyperbolical Germanisms with which tales of wonder are usually told." Perhaps the most famous review, certainly the most quoted, in which Scott assumed Shelley to be the author of the novel.

    Reprinted in A349 (Vol. I, pp. 73-80), A375 (pp. 260-272).

    See also A134, A228, B191, B330.

        2. *Frankenstein; or, The Modern Prometheus*. Philadelphia: Carey, Lea & Blanchard, 1833.

C10   *The New York Mirror: A Weekly Journal, Devoted to Literature and the Fine Arts*, 10 (June 1, 1833), 378.

    "This is widely known as a work of intense interest, and, with the 'Last Man,' and 'Perkin Warbeck,' identifies the name of Mrs. Shelley with the literature of the present age. It is probable that there are many, in this country, who have never perused it, and who will gladly avail themselves of the present opportunity. We promise to such no ordinary pleasure."†

    Continued in C11.

C11   *The New York Mirror: A Weekly Journal, Devoted to Literature and the Fine Arts*, 10 (June 8, 1833), 390.
       Second notice; continuation of C10. Mixed; praises the work as a whole, but examines its "absurdities" and "improbabilities." "It is not impossible, that the author was aware of these inconsistencies, and presumed upon the license necessary to the illustration of so poetical a story; but . . . it is a matter of regret that they have not been corrected."

           3. *Frankenstein; or, The Modern Prometheus.* Boston: Sever & Francis, 1869.

C12   *Harvard Advocate*, 7 (March 16, 1869), 28-29.
       Unfavorable. "The principal moral to be derived by Harvard boys from this book is that dangerous proficiency in chemistry should be carefully avoided."
       Reprinted as A354.

           4. *Frankenstein; or, The Modern Prometheus.* N.Y.: James Pott & Co., 1901.

C13   "Classics in Leather," *The New York Times Saturday Review of Books and Art*, September 28, 1901, p. 672.
       "Apparently no series of English classics, however limited, is considered distinctive or representative unless it includes a copy of 'Frankenstein,' why, we are unable to say. It is purely a work of the imagination, written in a Teutonic style that leaves little for speculation and plenty for discovery in the field of anachronisms and the natural sciences. Still, the intermittent republication of this book is not without excuse. The popular fallacies that have been augmented around it can only be laid low by its perusal. The number of writers who should have read 'Frankenstein,' and yet have not read it, is appalling. Rarely is any reference made to the book but we hear about 'that monster Frankenstein.' Now, poor Frankenstein was not the monster at all, yet for years he has done rhetorical service as such. It can only be fervently hoped that the successive editions of Mrs. Shelley's fantastic and tiresome tale may at last stamp out the fallacy." Also briefly describes the binding of the book.†

           5. *Frankenstein.* Everyman's Library, No. 616. London, Toronto: J. M. Dent & Sons/N.Y.: E. P. Dutton [1922].

*C14   Constant Reader [pseud.]. *Literary Review* [of the New York *Evening Post*], September 2, 1922, p. 919.
       Cited in the *Annual Bibliography of English Language and Literature* of the Modern Humanities Research Association for 1922, but this issue not at the Library of Congress, New York Public Library, or Yale.

6. *Frankenstein, or the Modern Prometheus.* N.Y.:
Harrison Smith and Robert Haas, 1934.

C15 McMahon, A. *Parnassus. A Magazine of the Arts of All Countries*
(N.Y.), 7 (March 1935), 26.
Consists mainly of favorable remarks on Lynd Ward's wood en-
gravings, which accompany the text, with brief mention of the
novel: "This grisly, mysterious tale of horror, whose title gave
a new word to the English language, is one that might be neglected
by most readers today, although some of the established conventions
of that branch of fiction were first revealed in it."

7. *Frankenstein.* Adapted by Dale Carlson. A Golden
Book. N.Y.: Golden Press, 1968.

C16 Levitas, Gloria. "Shudders of Delight," *The New York Times Book
Review. Children's Books*, November 3, 1968, p. 52.
Unfavorable to this edition. "Miss Carlson seems to have
missed the entire point of the Gothic novel. Stripping the narrative to its bare essentials, she has succeeded in transforming the
romantic horror of 'Frankenstein' into a clumsy, didactic, and
bloodless bore."

8. *Frankenstein or The Modern Prometheus.* M[ichael]
J[oseph] Kennedy, ed. Oxford English Novels series.
London, Oxford, N.Y.: Oxford University Press, 1969.

*C17 Birmingham *Post*, November 19, 1969.
Source: publicity department of the Oxford University Press,
New York.

C18 *Choice*, 7 (March 1970), 80.
Favorable comments upon the edition ("the best for both the
casual reader and the serious scholar of Romanticism or gothicism").

C19 *English Studies. A Journal of English Language and Literature*
(Amsterdam), 53 (August 1972), 385.
"A more striking expression [than in Jane Austen] of what the
emancipated woman's imagination was capable of [is] in Mary
Shelley's *Frankenstein*, although truly this book's power to disturb
is no greater than Jane Austen's at her most formidable."†

C20 Graves, Charles. "Mrs. Shelley's Monster," *The Scotsman*, September
20, 1969, p. 3.
Favorable. MS may have wanted a moral in the story, but "it is
as a superthriller that it lives," despite "overtones relevant to
modern times."

C21 Gribble, Jennifer. *AUMLA. Journal of the Australasian Universities & Literature Association*, No. 34 (November 1970), 328-329.
     Mixed. The novel "is an individual and an active response to the phenomenon of the romantic imagination," but "The scientific and philosophical ideas on which [MS] draws are not sufficiently controlled to be compelling, and the sketchy plot, schematic structure and flatness of the prose must surely prevent its being taken seriously as a novel."

C22 Kosok, Heinz. *Notes and Queries*, n.s. 17 (October 1970), 391-392.
     Favorable. "What makes this book particularly modern . . . is the idea of man creating, with the help of the most advanced techniques of science and with the purest of intentions, the terrifying means of his own destruction." Briefly notes textual errors.

C23 "Meeting his maker," *Times Literary Supplement*, October 16, 1969, p. 1215.
     Favorable review of both the novel and the edition. "At the heart of Mary Shelley's visionary book lies a Godwinian visionary book about social relationships."

C24 Payne, Mervyn. "Mary Shelley's Monster," *Eastern Daily Press*, October 20, 1969, p. 9 col. 3.
     Favorable, but mainly superficial comments. "This novel has many of the weaknesses of immaturity, but the central idea is carried through with skillful determination."

C25 S., C. "Mary Shelley's Monster," Glasgow *Herald*, September 13, 1969, p. 7.
     Favorable. Both Victor Frankenstein and the Monster are portraits of Shelley, and the Promethean theme is a warning to him and to modern science.

         b) Valperga: Or, the Life and Adventures of Castruccio, Prince of Lucca.

             1. *Valperga: Or, the Life and Adventures of Castruccio, Prince of Lucca*. 3 vols. London: Printed for G. and W. B. Whittaker, 1823.

C26 *La Belle Assemblée, or Court and Fashionable Magazine*, n.s. 28 (August 1823), 82-84.
     Favorable: "occasionally tinged with a sombre hue . . . yet contains numerous passages of powerful interest, and displays not only an intimate acquaintance with the history and manners of the times . . . but also a perfect knowledge of the passions by which the human breast is agitated."

C27 *Blackwood's Edinburgh Magazine*, 13 (March 1823), 283-293.
     Mixed; objects to the portrait of Castruccio not being "done justice," but recommends the novel as "clever." "The work . . .

undoubtedly reflects no *discredit* even on the authoress of Frankenstein—although we must once more repeat our opinion, that Valperga
is, for a second romance, by no means what its predecessor was for
a first one."
Reprinted in *The Athenæum*, 13 (June 16, 1823), 209-221.

C28   *The British Luminary and Weekly Intelligencer*, March 9, 1823, p. 74.
Mixed. The novel is quite different from *Frankenstein*, the
construction of the narrative inartificial and irregular, with
little attention to unity, although the latter part is well wrought
up and written "with much elegance and pathos." Still, it is "evidently the production of superior talent."

*C29   *The British Magazine; or Miscellany of Polite Literature*, (March
1823), 33-41.
de Palacio [El, p. 655, Item 61) notes the review as being very
favorable, and quotes, "For power, eloquence, and sentiment, the
work is unrivalled among co[n]temporary publications." Burton R.
Pollin, in *Godwin Criticism: A Synoptic Bibliography* ([Toronto:]
University of Toronto Press, 1967), p. 39, paraphrases the review
as noting that the novel is without the liberal flaws of *Frankenstein*, and has power, eloquence, and sentiment.
According to my correspondence with the British Library, the
above issue of this periodical was destroyed in the Blitz. However,
see C38 for an apparent reprinting.

C30   *The Country Literary Chronicle and Weekly Review*, February 22,
1823, pp. 113-116.
Favorable, but highly descriptive only. Promises to notice
the merits of "this excellent work" after summarizing the plot,
but merely mentions that the novel "is a work which only requires
to be read, in order to be ardently admired."

C31   *The Examiner*, No. 788 (March 2, 1823), 154.
Brief and favorable. "The story is full of action, and the
spirit of the narrative keeps up with it in animation."

C32   *The Ladies' Monthly Museum; or, Polite Repository of Amusement and
Instruction*, Improved Series, 17 (April 1823), 216-218.
Favorable. "In Frankenstein the author suffered imagination
to riot unchecked amidst the regions of romance; in Valperga, the
excursive faculty is restrained within moderate limits, and
judgment asserts her legitimate authority."

C33   *The Literary Gazette, and Journal of Belles Lettres, Arts, Sciences,
Etc.*, No. 319 (March 1, 1823), 132-133.
Favorable. "In this work the most powerful passions are called
into action; and love, enthusiasm, and ambition, appear on the can-
vass, stamped with the same wild imagination that characterized
Frankenstein." Much plot synopsis.

C34   *The Literary Register of the Fine Arts, Sciences, and Belles
      Lettres*, No. 36 (March 8, 1823), 151-152.
          Favorable; the novel is better even than *Frankenstein*. "The
      principal merit of this novel consists . . . in its faithful de-
      lineation of the character and manners of the people of the age of
      which it treats, and the chaste and elegant style in which it is
      written."

C35   *The London Chronicle*, 133 (March 8-10, 1823), 240.
          Favorable, especially commending the character of Beatrice as
      "a fine piece of painting of the Rembrandt School."

C36   *The Monthly Review, or Literary Journal*, 101 (May 1823), 105.
          Mixed: "Clearly written, and the characters are not ill-
      developed: but the subject is not well-chosen, and the tale is
      tedious." Pronounces it "more tolerable" than *Frankenstein*.

*C37 *Morning Herald* (London), March 12, 1823, p. 3.
          de Palacio (El, p. 656, Item 70), terms it very favorable.
      This issue not in the British Library.

C38   *The Weekly Magazine, or the Repository of Modern Literature*, 1
      (1823), 112-120.
          Favorable. Applauds the novel for reverting to the "old style"
      of novel-writing, in which a history of men's lives was traced
      "from the cradle to the tomb," and admits being pleasantly sur-
      prised, despite a "petticoat prejudice." "For power, eloquence,
      and sentiment, the work is unrivalled among contemporary publi-
      cations."
          de Palacio (El, p. 657, Item 73) notes that this is a word-for-
      word reprinting of C29. The above quotation would seem to reinforce
      this.

          c) The Last Man

          1. *The Last Man*. 3 vols. London: Henry Colburn, 1826.

C39   *The Ladies' Monthly Museum; or, Polite Repository of Amusement and
      Instruction*, 23 (March 1826), 169.
          "The highly-talented writer of this romance has manifested an
      ability to communicate interest too extravagant for common con-
      ception, and which attract attention solely from the skill with
      which they are treated. We should be better pleased to see her
      exercise her powers of intellect on subjects less removed from
      nature and probability. The present work has all the beauties and
      defects of her former production."†

C40   *The Literary Gazette and Journal of Belles Lettres, Arts, Sciences,
      &c.*, No. 473 (February 18, 1826), 102-103.
          Unfavorable. "After the first volume, it is a sickening repe-
      tition of horrors." After admitting that some readers may find the
      novel to their liking, wonders why the author did not choose "*the*

last Woman? she would have known better how to paint her distress at having nobody left to talk to."

C41   *The Monthly Review, or Literary Journal*, n.s. 1 (March 1826), 333-335.

Hostile and rambling. In choosing this kind of work, MS "has merely made herself ridiculous"; the work is "The offspring of a diseased imagination, and of a most polluted taste." On MS: "the whole course of her ambition has been to pourtray monsters which could have existed only in her own conceptions."

C42   *The Panoramic Miscellany, or Monthly Magazine and Review of Literature, Science, Arts, Inventions, and Occurrences*, 1 (March 1826), 380-386.

Unfavorable. "With respect to the work before us, we are free to declare—that we have rarely met with an instance in which a subject so promising was more lamely or incompetently treated." Notes the biographical portrayals of Byron and Shelley.
Reprinted in A349 (Vol. II, pp. 742-748).

*C43   *The St. James Royal Magazine.*

Exact date unknown; destroyed at the British Library during the Blitz, as also noted by de Palacio (El, pp. 663-664, Item 93).

2. *The Last Man.* Philadelphia: Carey, Lea & Blanchard, 1833.

C44   *The Knickerbocker Magazine*, 2 (October 1833), 315.

"We suppose this lady to be the widow of the far famed poet and atheist Shelly [*sic*]. She has constructed a thrilling tale of much pathos, power, and horror; wilder, more extravagant, and remoter from probability, than ever entered the fevered brain of an expiring man, held back on this side the invisible country by the momentary stimulus of alcohol and laudanum. It is a sort of detailed and prose copy of Byron's terrible painting of darkness. Gloomy indeed must be the musings of the widow of a man so gifted and so horribly dark in his creed as Shelly, imagining herself alone in the universe. A love tale, and the usual incidents of a novel, the era of which is supposed in 2098, conduct Verney to the aid of earthquake, pestilence and shipwreck, to his dreary catastrophe of being THE LAST MAN—an unfortunate title, which we are sure ladies will not admire; for though men are filthy, smoking, spitting animals, with rough chins, yet they are useful in keeping off the dogs from ladies, and divers other offices of indispensable utility. Yet there is genius in these volumes, and many a sad mind will be arrested by the sombre eloquence and force of these paintings."†

3. *The Last Man*. Hugh J. Luke, Jr., ed. Lincoln, Neb.: University of Nebraska Press, 1965.

C45 Adkinson, R. V. *Revue des langues vivantes*, 33 (1967), 441-442.
Unfavorable; of "little interest beyond the historical and biographical" and "unlikely to detain the attention" of anyone besides students of the period.
Included with reviews of William Godwin's *Italian Letters* and Sir Walter Scott's *The Fortunes of Nigel*.

C46 C[ameron], K[enneth] N[eill]. *English Language Notes*, 4, Supplement (September 1966), 37.
Brief. "It is curious in view of the preoccupations of the present with racial annihilation that [it] has not been reprinted since 1833."
Reprinted in A. C. Elkins, Jr. and L. J. Forstner, eds. *The Romantic Movement Bibliography 1936-1970. A Master Cumulation from ELH, Philological Quarterly and English Language Notes.* Ann Arbor, Mich.: The Pierian Press, in association with the R. R. Bowker Co., 1973, Vol. V, p. 1937.

C47 *Choice*, 3 (November 1966), 773.
Brief, and favorable. "Certainly the theme of civilization wiped out save for a solitary individual is a modern one and hence, its likely appeal to contemporary readers."

C48 Guzzardi, Walter, Jr. "Romantic Vision of Destruction," *The Saturday Review of Literature*, 49 (January 8, 1966), 86.
Brief, and mixed. Comment, after giving the history of the novel: "Such an apocalyptic vision requires a style beyond the author's reach, although it is difficult to name many writers who would be up to it."

C49 Hartman, Geoffrey. In "Recent Studies in the Nineteenth Century," *Studies in English Literature 1500-1900*, 6 (Autumn 1966), 758.
"Mary Shelley's *The Last Man* (1826) is reprinted for the first time since 1833 by Hugh J. Luke, Jr. (Nebraska). It is a fascinating if somewhat longwinded novel-romance on a timely subject. In some ways, as the editor argues, it elaborates 'the great recurring myth of the Solitary' found in Wordsworth."†

C50 Lovell, Ernest J[ames], Jr. *College English*, 27 (May 1966), 646.
Brief, and favorable: "of interest" and "well worth reprinting."

C51 Mann, Charles W. *Library Journal*, 91 (January 1, 1966), 163.
"Whatever interest the book retains, and it must be admitted, that there is very little, is in the portraits of Byron and Shelley, and other members of their circle, who appear in easily recognizable fictive guise. The story is, unfortunately, an offshoot of the Gothic novel, and the style is turgid. The concept of a great plague decimating the world toward the end of the 21st century, the period in which the novel is set, while arresting, is not arresting enough. Mrs. Shelley remains the author of a single book, and that

book, of course, is *Frankenstein*. However the editor and publisher have done an exemplary job of getting this scarce book back in print, and *The Last Man* is a recommended research choice for university and larger public libraries."†

C52   *Nineteenth Century Fiction*, 21 (December 1966), 298.
        "Whatever this novel's literary merits—it is a rather morbid forerunner of *On the Beach*, with the catastrophe supplied by plague rather than fall-out—it has considerable biographical and historical interest, since Mary constructed it as a monument to her dead husband's ideas, and wrote also something of a *roman à clef*, with yet another portrait of Lord Byron. It is unfortunate that the economies of printing have required Mary Shelley's three volumes to be compressed into 342 pages of almost microscopic print (as is also the case with the Bison reprint of Maturin's *Melmoth*); with eyestrain added to the strain of Mary Shelley's rather exalted prose, the last page becomes too much an achievement. Professor H. J. Luke, Jr.'s introduction, on the other hand, is scolarly, informative, and, unlike the novel, mercifully brief."†

C53   Tompkins, J. M. S. *Keats-Shelley Journal*, 16 (Winter 1967), 108-109.
        Favorable, with brief examination of themes. "The heart of the book is the devastation of her private world and the value of what was lost."

C54   Yarker, P. M., and Brian Lee. In "The Nineteenth Century." In *The Year's Work in English Studies. 1965.* London: John Murray, 1967, Vol. 46, p. 279.
        Brief mention of the novel as "an absorbing *roman à clef* [which] develops one of the major themes of romantic art, that of spiritual isolation."

        d)   The Fortunes of Perkin Warbeck

              1.   *The Fortunes of Perkin Warbeck, A Romance.* 3 vols.
                    London: Henry Colburn and Richard Bentley, 1830.

C55   *The Athenæum*, No. 135 (May 29, 1830), 323-335.
        Favorable. "In spite, however, of our objection to historical romances, we are bound to confess that the volumes before us are the productions of no ordinary pen. It is manifest that a richly-endowed and vigorous intellect has directed the hand which traced them. They are written with a noble energy of thought—a deep concentration of feeling—a sentiment, which display in their author the very highest capabilities. The reader is hurried on from action to action with a spirit-stirring impulse, which never for a moment allows his excitement to abate; and the scenes which follow each other in such rapid succession, are wrought out with all the distinctness of a present reality. The characters are drawn with great vividness, and in some of them, especially, there is an originality which strikingly marks the powerfully-creative

mind of the author of 'Frankenstein.'" This is the main comment;
review mainly consists of lengthy extracts.

*C56   *The Edinburgh Literary Gazette*, 2 (June 12, 1830), 369-372.
       de Palacio (El, p. 665, Item 102) terms the review favorable.

C57   *The Edinburgh Literary Journal; or, Weekly Register of Criticism
       and Belles Lettres*, No. 83 (June 12, 1830), 339.
       Notes that the novel is an "interesting work," gives a lengthy
       extract, and promises a notice next week [cf. C58].

C58   *The Edinburgh Literary Journal; or, Weekly Register of Criticism
       and Belles Lettres*, No. 84 (June 19, 1830), 350-352.
       Continuation of C57. Mixed, but mainly unfavorable. "The
       chief fault we have to find with her production is, that it does
       not blend together with sufficient skill what is fictitious and
       what is true."

C59   *The Intelligence* (London), May 30, 1830, p. 83 col. 4.
       Favorable. Although historical inaccuracies are present, and
       the truth stretched a bit, the novel will be a Godsend to romance
       readers, and the style "is at once elegant and perspicuous."

C60   *The Literary Gazette, and Journal of the Belles Lettres*, No. 696
       (May 22, 1830), 335.
       "Full of strange incident and mysterious interest, Perkin War-
       beck, either as the last of the Plantagenet's ill-fated race, or
       else as the most picturesque of impostors, led a life admirably
       adapted for the novelist; and Mrs. Shelley, taking up the belief
       that he really was Duke of York, flings over her subject all the
       attraction belonging to the innocent and unfortunate. The story
       is so ill calculated for extract, that we must content ourselves by
       commending the good use our fair author has made of her *matériel*,
       which she has invested with the grace and excitement of her own
       poetical imagination. The character of Monia is a conception as
       original as it is exquisite."†

C61   *Monthly Magazine, or British Register of Literature, Sciences, and
       the Belles Lettres*, 10 (October 1830), 470-471 [470].
       A review of "*Perkin Warbeck*. 3 *vols*. 12*mo*" that treats both
       MS novel and Newman's: "Which Perkin? Mr. Newman's—not Colburn
       and Bentley's; and though we have not seen the latter—Mrs.
       Shelley's, we believe—so little confidence have we that a tolerable
       story . . . can come from her hands, that we have no hesitation in
       matching this before us with it."

C62   *New Monthly Magazine and Literary Journal*, 30 (November 1830), 457.
       Brief, and favorable. "The characters are skillfully pour-
       trayed, and well-contrasted with each other, while the descriptions
       are full, clear, and powerful. Throughout, indeed, the book is
       written with great energy, both of thought and expression, as well
       as with all that feminine delicacy of feeling and perception which
       throws such a peculiar charm over the fictions penned by an accom-
       plished woman."

C63   *Sunday Times* (London), June 20, 1830, p. 1 col. 5.
      "Not always adopting the sentiments of Mrs. Shelley, and
      thinking she is sometimes too profuse of her reflections, we are
      captivated with the situations she has imagined. Part of the
      ground had been ably gone over by the author of 'Richard Plantag-
      enet;' but the 'Fortunes of Perkin Warbeck' is still rich in
      attraction. The descriptions of character are often very fine."†
      Lengthy extract follows.

      e)   Lodore

           1. *Lodore*. 3 vols. London: Richard Bentley, 1835.

C64   *The Age*, May 3, 1835, p. 138 col. 2.
      Extract from C79 (2nd and last paragraphs).

C65   *The Athenæum*, No. 387 (March 28, 1835), 238-239.
      Mainly favorable. "The tale of 'Lodore' is consistent in its
      own peculiar colouring, so that we do not feel that it contains un-
      solved improbabilities, and difficulties and hindrances, too finely
      drawn for reality."

C66   *The Atlas* (London), May 10, 1835, pp. 294-295.
      Favorable. Unlike "the wild and fantastic spirit" of *Franken-
      stein* and *The Last Man*, "the paramount spell of this delightful
      work lies in its minute and faithful delineation of the feelings
      of love." The narrative is linked and interwoven—"fact with
      feeling, causes and their influences"—and has "great power and
      poetical truth."

C67   *The Courier* (London), April 16, 1835, p. 3 col. 4.
      Favorable. *Lodore*, unlike the previous novels of MS, deals
      with familiar situations, its style "quiet, easy, and flowing, and
      the sentiments natural." As a result, "we can promise her a more
      pleasing, as well as a more during reputation from her present
      work than from the wild fictions she has before handled."
      See also C71.

C68   *The Examiner*, No. 1425 (May 24, 1835), 323-324.
      Favorable. "*Lodore*, though rather tedious in parts, is a novel
      of great beauty, and will add to the reputation of Mrs. Shelley."

C69   *Fraser's Magazine for Town and Country*, 11 (May 1835), 600-605.
      Favorable. From this novel, the reviewer is now almost con-
      vinced that MS wrote *Frankenstein*. "The execution of the work is,
      upon the whole, extremely good—it is quite worthy of the design.
      The impress of an original and thoughtful mind is visible through-
      out, and there are many passages of exceeding gracefulness, of
      touching eloquence, and of intense feeling."
      See also C72, C73.

C70   *The Globe* (London), April 11, 1835, p. 4 col. 4.
       Extract from C77.

C71   *The Globe* (London), April 20, 1835, p. 4 col. 4.
       Extract from C67.

C72   *The Globe* (London), May 5, 1835, p. 4 col. 5.
       Extract from C69.
       See also C73.

C73   *The Globe* (London), May 11, 1835, p. 4 col. 5.
       Extract from C69.
       See also C72.

C74   *The Globe* (London), May 19, 1835, p. 4 col. 5.
       Extract from C78.

C75   *Leigh Hunt's London Journal*, No. 58 (May 6, 1835), 138-139.
       Favorable. "It has not the inventive genius of 'Frankenstein.'
       That is a thing to happen only once in many years. But then it is
       not mixed up, like that work, with matter of doubtful attraction;
       neither has it the uneasiness of her subsequent novels, either in
       story or style."
       Continued as C76.

C76   *Leigh Hunt's London Journal*, No. 60 (May 20, 1835), 156.
       Continuation of C75, with extracts and little comment.

C77   *The Literary Gazette, and Journal of the Belles Lettres*, No. 949
       (March 28, 1835), 194-195.
       Favorable, with an overview of MS past works. Little comment,
       besides description, of *Lodore*, except to note that "as a whole,
       [it] is full of talent and feeling, and, we must add, of knowledge."
       See also C70.

C78   *Morning Herald* (London), May 14, 1835, p. 5.
       Favorable; the work "deserves to be considered a work of deep
       feeling and delicate moral scrutiny," with singular incidents,
       beautiful descriptions, and an indebtedness to Godwin.
       See also C74.

C79   *Morning Post* (London), April 16, 1835, p. 3 col. 6.
       Favorable. Briefly contrasts the present novel with *Franken-
       stein*: "We cannot choose but admire the author of 'Frankenstein,'
       but we cannot help loving the author of 'Lodore.' Love, indeed,
       in one or other of its glorious *avatars* is the pervading spirit,
       the genius, of the book."
       See also C64.

C80   *New Monthly Magazine and Literary Journal*, 44, Part the Second
       (June 1835), 236-237.
       Brief, and favorable. "This is exquisite romance—the romance—
       as a friend of ours well expressed it—the romance of *sentiment*,

not of *incident*; and in the highly-imaginative walk of literature Mrs. Shelley has few competitors."

C81   *The Sun* (London), April 15, 1835, p. 2 col. 5.
      Favorable, comparing MS work briefly with Godwin's, noting that in the present novel "truth and pathos, springing up warm from the heart, abound quite as much in the verse of the novelist, as the verse of the poet" and that the moral, "though not remarkable for originality, is worked out with consummate skill."

C82   *Sunday Times* (London), April 19, 1835, p. 1 col. 5.
      "This is an affecting tale of domestic wants and of every-day life. The plot is simple, nor is there any great development of character, excepting in Ethel, who is a beautiful specimen of her loving sex; but there is a simplicity and quiet natural charm about the novel, together with a grace of diction in the language, worthy of Mrs. Shelley, which is well adapted to the home occurrences principally delineated."†

C83   *Weekly Dispatch* (London), April 12, 1835, p. 138 cols. 1-2.
      Favorable. *Frankenstein* was unbelievable, *The Last Man* unpopular, and *Perkin Warbeck* a failure, but *Lodore* narrates "the affairs of real life, and [MS] characters, although highly interesting, do not outrage either nature or probability."

      f) Falkner

          1. *Falkner. A Novel.* 3 vols. London: Saunders and Otley, 1837.

C84   *The Athenæum*, No. 484 (February 4, 1837), 74-75.
      Favorable. "We have always admired Mrs. Shelley's novels, as breathing more of the spirit of romance than the generality of works which see the light in these matter-of-fact days. Even when their scene is laid in our country—when their actors are drawn from the class to which we ourselves belong—we recognize an elevation of tone in their conception—a constant appeal to our more generous sympathies—a constant display of the finer affections, which raise them above the common level of tales of every-day life, though they be somewhat deficient, perhaps, in that vitality which characterizes other contemporary works. They are, in short, stories of thought and feeling, rather than of manners and character; and the one before us is among the best, if not quite the best, of the number." Plot synopsis follows.

C85   *Bell's Weekly Messenger*, February 12, 1837, p. 55 col. 1.
      Subtly unfavorable; the story, its moral, and the character development are all according "to the true French taste."

C86   *The Court Journal*, No. 407 (February 11, 1837), 90-91.
      Favorable. "The story of 'Falkner' is one of absorbing interest, of infinite and varied beauty, and great power of

delineation and development in the principal characters." Promises
further comment, but none published.

C87   *The Examiner*, No. 1515 (February 12, 1837), 101.
      Unfavorable. The design of the book "is to obtain a spurious
sympathy for a criminal," and the novel as a whole "is swollen out
with tedious reflections, and prosing explanations of motives and
feelings"—although "Some of the fine writing . . . is rather in
millinery style."

C88   *The Literary Gazette, and Journal of the Belles Lettres*, No. 1046
      (February 4, 1837), 66-68.
      Favorable. "Falkner bears a near resemblance to Sir Edward
Mortimer; and Elizabeth Raby, the heroine, his adopted daughter,
reminds us (cept that she is of another sex) of the general construction of the plot and the incidents of the 'Iron Chest.' The
principal characters, as well as the leading events of the story,
belong rather to the regions of romance than to that representation
of actual life which we understand by the term, 'Novel;' and the
reader, without being much at a loss to guess the mystery enveloped
in the narrative, or the way in which affairs will end, is led
along by the talent of the writer through certain walks of imagination, till her task is completed, and the *dénoûment* allowed."
Lengthy extracts follow.

C89   M. *The Monthly Repository*, n.s. No. 124 (April 1837), 228-236.
      Favorable; MS "finest work." "It possesses deep interest, and
fine development of character. The descriptions are vivid and
graphic, and . . . the style . . . is formed on the model of that
of Godwin." However, "not a few stumbling blocks have been thrown
in the way by the authoress herself, who interweaves with her finest
passages the most trite conventionalisms, in the shape of moral reflections."
      See also B240.

C90   *The Metropolitan*, 18 (March 1837), 65-67.
      Favorable; its principal characteristic power, its moral im-
pressive, painting remorse in vivid colors, although its tone "is
too universally sombre."

C91   *The Monthly Review*, 1 (March 1837), 376-380.
      Very favorable. "Her colouring for the most part is sombre
. . . her themes gloomy. . . . But it is to the honour of her
genius, and to the force as well as delicate beauty of her minute
delineations, that this gloominess is never felt to be unwelcome,
but of a soft and melancholy cast."

*C92 *The Observer* (London), February 5, 1837, p. 3.
      de Palacio (El, p. 672, Item 143) terms the review favorable.
This issue not in the British Library.

C93   *The Satirist*, February 26, 1837, p. 482 col. 3.
       Unfavorable. "Each page of her books is a tombstone, with a
skull and cross-bones upon it. Her effort is at startling effect,
but she overlays her object with excess of means—*superat materiem
opus*—she keeps us so long trampling the rank grass of the church-
yard, that its odour of sactity is lost in foul air." "Therefore
we presume the book a failure—a lame, if not an altogether impotent
attempt."

C94   *The Spectator*, No. 449 (February 4, 1837), 111.
       Mainly unfavorable. "In spirit this novel is an imitation of
Caleb Williams, but without its consistency of gloom, and with a
good deal more of its inconsistency of character"—although it is
"occasionally dashed by the vice of good writing."

C95   *The Weekly Chronicle* (London), February 12, 1837, p. 5 col. 3.
       "Sentiment run mad, and madness without a strait waistcoat, are
the plot and characters of this novel. We cannot indeed say that
decency is outraged by the writer, but all common sense is entirely
thrown overboard."†

       g) Mathilda

            1. *Mathilda*. Elizabeth Nitchie, ed. Chapel Hill, N.C.:
                University of North Carolina Press [1959].

C96   Cameron, Kenneth Neill. *Keats-Shelley Journal*, 10 (Winter 1961),
       111-113.
       Favorable, with attention to biographical significance. "Its
theme is remarkably advanced for the time, and it has some excellent scenes."

C97   C[ameron], K[enneth] N[eill]. *Philological Quarterly*, 39 (April
       1960), 159.
       Brief, descriptive, and non-committal. "The first part is
clearly based on Mary's interpretation of her father's feelings
towards her, and is surely one of the first such psychological
studies, just as *Frankenstein* was the first major work of science
fiction."
       Reprinted in A. C. Elkins, Jr. and L. J. Forstner, eds. *The
Romantic Movement Bibliography 1936-1970. A Master Cumulation
from* ELH, Philological Quarterly *and* English Language Notes. Ann
Arbor, Mich.: The Pierian Press, in association with the R. R.
Bowker Co., 1973, Vol. III, p. 1320.

C98   Milne, W. Gordon. *Books Abroad*, 34 (Spring 1960), 181.
       Two paragraphs; mainly unfavorable. The book "has a tenuous
plot, stock characters, and a number of incredibly romantic effu-
sions."

*C99   Milne, W. Gordon. *Creative Writing*, 11 (March 1960), 32.
        Listed in the annual bibliography of the *Keats-Shelley Journal*,
        but periodical not located (not listed in the *Union List of
        Serials.*)

C100   *Nineteenth-Century Fiction*, 14 (March 1960), 373.
        "The story is admittedly 'bizarre,' and the most devoted
        Shelleyans are not likely to discover much merit in the strained
        and pretentious style; yet the autobiographical nature of the
        piece, with its implications about Mary's relations with her hus-
        band and father, justifies its publication."†

C101   Reiman, Donald H. *Journal of English and Germanic Philology*, 59
        (April 1960), 306-308.
        Favorable, with examination of the autobiographical signifi-
        cance and Nitchie's Introduction. "As a work of fiction *Mathilda*
        shows Mary Shelley to be scrupulously aware of the problems of
        realistic psychological motivation. This awareness is, indeed,
        the greatest virtue of the work."

C102   Tompkins, J. M. S. *Modern Language Review*, 56 (April 1961), 303.
        Brief, and mixed. "[It] is superficially a compound of sen-
        sationalism, analysis, landscape and lamentations, displaying
        Mary Shelley's genuine but unsufficing talent."

C103   W[erkmeister], L[ucyle]. *The Personalist*, 41 (Autumn 1960), 535.
        Two paragraphs; mixed. "The fact remains that the morbidity
        of the theme, combined with the intensity of passion of the lan-
        guage, obscures many of the flaws, so that, although *Mathilda* is
        not a great novel, it is also not an uninteresting one."

        2. Dramas

            a) Proserpine & Midas

                1. *Proserpine & Midas. Two Unpublished Mythological
                    Dramas by Mary Shelley.* A[ndré] [Henri] Koszul, ed.
                    London: Humphrey Milford, 1922.

C104   A., N. *The Freeman*, 8 (October 3, 1923), 95.
        Favorable, although "the lapse of a hundred years has given [the
        dramas] a faded and old-fashioned air."

C105   Murry, J. Middleton. *The Nation & The Athenæum*, 32 (December 16,
        1922), 461.
        Very favorable. "These little dramas supply the connecting
        link between the two manifestations [the author of 'Frankenstein'
        and the measured commentator on her husband's poetry]. Their res-
        traint, their purity is unmistakable; and it is a natural restraint."

C106 *Times Literary Supplement*, February 15, 1923, p. 105.
      Mainly favorable: "henceforward we must add to Mary Shelley's
      acknowledged intellectual power a tenderer and more emotional side."

3. *Collected Stories*

a) *Tales and Stories*. Richard Garnett, ed. London: William
   Paterson, 1891.

C107 *The Athenæum*, 97 (January 3, 1891), 12-13.
      Mixed. "There is no introspection in these stories, no
      searching study of character, but there is some imaginative power
      and generous sympathy with all that is noble. Their merit, of
      course, varies; the romantic stories are much the best."

C108 *The Spectator*, 66 (January 3, 1891), 18-19.
      Mixed. Apparently resents the reprinting of MS stories just
      because of her connection with Shelley, yet offers a few insightful
      comments on "The Mortal Immortal" and "Transformation." "Here and
      there we find evidences of a feeling for natural beauty and a
      power of rendering it, which are bot⁺ beautiful and Shelley-like."
      However, "That these stories will attract the general reader of
      to-day, is unlikely. They are interesting mainly as the work of
      the author of *Frankenstein*."

4. *Travel Works*

a) [with Percy Bysshe Shelley.] *History of a Six Weeks' Tour
   through a Part of France, Switzerland, Germany, and Holland: with Letters Descriptive of a Sail around the Lake
   of Geneva, and of the Glaciers of Chamouni*. London: T.
   Hookham, Jun.; and C. and J. Ollier, 1817.

C109 *Blackwood's Edinburgh Magazine*, 3 (July 1818), 412-416.
      Mainly favorable. "There is little information, no reflection,
      and very few incidents, in this volume, and yet it somehow or other
      produces considerable amusement and interest." Compliments the
      "lady" author on her "ease, gracefulness, and vivacity."
      See also B147.

b) *Rambles in Germany and Italy, in 1840, 1842, and 1843*.
   2 vols. London: Edward Moxon, 1844.

C110 *The Athenæum*, No. 876 (August 10, 1844), 725-727.
      Favorable, with lengthy extracts. "[The volumes] have the charm
      of taste, sincerity, and individuality: and may be read and re-
      turned to with pleasure."

C111 *The Atlas* (London), August 17, 1844, pp. 556-557.
Favorable, and lengthy, though with few critical comments. MS
is an enchantress of fiction, her monster still not dead—"it only
sleepeth." The volumes of this novel are delightful; their pages
"glow with the brightness and fervour of the clime and the country
which they describe, and are replete with information both interesting and instructive."

C112 *Bell's Weekly Messenger*, August 17, 1844, p. 262 col. 3.
"The writer takes two subjects; a tour through Germany, and a
more descriptive account of Italy. We pass over the German portion
of these travels; with the exception of the banks of the Rhine and
Baden Baden, there is scarcely a town in Germany which can seduce
the British traveller to remain over a day. Mrs. S. commences her
Italian tour from the neighbourhood of the Lake of Como. She saw a
good deal of the peasantry, and describes them well."†

*C113 *The Critic, Journal of British and Foreign Literature and the Arts*,
n.s. 1 (September 2, 1844), 36-39.
de Palacio (El, p. 677, Item 198) ·terms the review favorable.
This issue not at the British Library; according to the card
catalogue at Yale, the Sterling Library is supposed to have this
issue, but it is temporarily lost, or the card incorrectly notated.

C114 *The Eclectic Review* (London), n.s. 16 (December 1844), 693-706.
Favorable, with lengthy extracts. "The contents are varied, the
descriptions often picturesque, and the observations upon manners,
art, and literature in many instances instructive."

C115 *The Examiner*, No. 1904 (July 27, 1844), 467-468.
Favorable, and descriptive. "[Of these volumes] every word
. . . we have read, and can cordially recommend to the politician,
the man of letters, and the whole reading world."

C116 *The Globe* (London), August 15, 1844, p. 1 col. 4.
Favorable. "Her accounts of manners, literature, and the
present state of politics, are given with a vivacity, force, and
graphic interest which cannot fail to inspire an abiding interest."

C117 "Lady Travellers in Italy and Germany," *New Monthly Magazine and
Humorist*, 72 (October 1844), 284-286.
Favorable, also reviewing Mrs. Ashton Yates' *A Winter in Italy*.
"[Mrs. Shelley] is a woman who thinks for herself, and who dares to
say what she thinks. . . . The travelling reflections and feelings
of such a woman will therefore be peculiarly acceptable to that
'fit audience though few,' who give the tone to intellectual society
in this country."

C118 "Mrs. Shelley's Rambles in Germany and Italy," *Tait's Edinburgh
Magazine*, 11 (November 1844), 729-740.
Mixed, with lengthy extracts. "To some readers it may be an
objection that beyond beauty of style and sentiment, and a few
scattered profound thoughts, the work does not contain much of

either the precise information or philosophical discussion . . .
expected from a writer of Mrs. Shelley's compass of mind."

C119   *Morning Chronicle* (London), August 23, 1844, p. 3.
       Favorable, and brief, terming the volumes "delightful" and
"written in the true spirit which ought to distinguish travellers."

*C120 *Morning Herald* (London), August 21, 1844, p. 6.
       de Palacio (El, pp. 678-679, Item 204) indicates the review
is favorable, quoting "Two light, amusing, and readable volumes."
This issue not at the British Library.

C121   *Morning Post* (London), August 19, 1844, p. 6 col. 6.
       Mixed. The letters contain annoying repetitions, and the art
criticism is common, but the practical advice to travellers is in-
valuable. "As to the philosophising and the political observations
of Mrs. Shelley, the less said about them the better."

*C122 *New Edinburgh Review* (Part I, 1844), 33-38.
       Mentioned by Nitchie (A12, p. 178); not by de Palacio (El).
Not at the British Library, or, I believe, at any U.S. libraries.
Possibly a confusion with another "Edinburgh Review," although I
have not found the review in any of them.

*C123 *The Observer* (London), August 11, 1844), p. 3.
       de Palacio (El, p. 679, Item 207) terms the review favorable
with reservations.
       This issue not at the British Library.

C124   *The Spectator*, No. 842 (August 17, 1844), 782-783.
       Mainly favorable. The work "far surpasses the majority of
books of travels. Her style is buoyant, lively & agreeable."
Complains about the number of times MS tells of her physical condition.

C125   *The Sun* (London), August 22, 1844, p. 3 col. 5.
       Favorable. "What her volumes want in the novelty of matter,
they make up for in the vivacity of their manner. On every subject which she discusses, the authoress writes with an eloquence
and animation that lure the reader on, in spite of himself."

C126   *Sunday Times* (London), August 25, 1844, p. 2 col. 4.
       Extremely favorable. Not merely a travel book, but one in
which the objects described have "the power to give utterance to a
pleasing melancholy, to sentiments tender and devoted, to recollections of sorrows hushed a little by time, but still with a sharp
and vital sting in them."

C127   *Weekly Dispatch* (London), August 18, 1844, p. 394 cols. 1-2.
       Mixed. MS wishes to see too much, and describes it too pom-
pously, and seems to dislike Germany; but "The book abounds with
vivid and tasteful descriptions."

5. *Biographies*

a) Lives of the most Eminent Literary and Scientific Men of Italy, Spain, and Portugal (3 vols.)

1. [with James Montgomery.] *Lives of the most Eminent Literary and Scientific Men of Italy, Spain, and Portugal.* Vol. I. Vol. 86 of The Cabinet of Biography, Conducted by the Rev. Dionysius Lardner (Lardner's Cabinet Cyclopedia). London: Printed for Longman, Orme, Brown, Green, & Longman, and John Taylor, 1835.

C128 *The Athenæum*, No. 383 (February 28, 1835), 168.
     After a list of the subjects: "all interesting subjects, but the writer never goes directly to his purpose, and his style wants simplicity."†

C129 *The Monthly Review*, 1 (March 1835), 297-315.
     Mainly unfavorable, with detailed examination of the subjects, especially Petrarch. The lives bear "such marks of a mechanical composition, that the spirit belonging to each of the characters is lost."

C130 "Petrarch and Boccaccio," *Leigh Hunt's London Journal*, No. 52 (March 25, 1835), 96.
     Very brief comment on the volume: "the present writer of their lives has judiciously shown them in that connexion [Petrarch as the *Lover*; Boccaccio as the *Story-Teller*] as much as possible."

C131 *The Spectator*, No. 345 (February 7, 1835), 138-139.
     Mixed; admires impartiality of the author, but "arrangement is defective" and "method inartificial."

C132 *Sunday Times* (London), February 8, 1835, p. 1 col. 5.
     "We have been especially pleased with this volume, which contains sketches of the lives and incidental remarks upon the works of Dante, Petrarch, Ariosto, Boccaccio, and others who have made their names renowned throughout the world. The style is pleasing, and the translated extracts from some of the works yield an additional interest."

2. [with James Montgomery and Sir David Brewster.] Vol. II [Vol. 87]. 1835.

C133 *The Literary Gazette, and Journal of the Belles Lettres*, No. 976 (October 3, 1835), 634.
     "Most of the figures in this volume have often been exhibited at full length, and in every possible light; so that we need only mention the names of Galileo, Tasso, Felicaja, Mestastasio [*sic*], Goldoni, Alfieri, &C&C. There are fourteen memoirs very neatly compiled."†

C134 *The Monthly Magazine of Politics, Literature, and Belles Lettres*,
20 (November 1835), 480.
　　No opinion really given: "we shall feel disappointed if [this
volume] fail to give less satisfaction, if not pleasure and
delight, than its precursors." (Previous review of the volume on
Greeks and Romans [20 (October 1835), 396] was favorable.)

C135 *The Monthly Review*, 3 (November 1835), 317-332.
　　Favorable, but mainly a discussion of Alfieri, Monti, and
Foscolo. "As a compilation, it is full but concise, perspicuous
and not destitute of that enthusiasm, which commands for the narrative a warm and welcome reception in the mind of the reader."

　　　　3. [with others?] Vol. III [Vol. 88.] 1837.

C136 *Sunday Times* (London), November 5, 1837, p. 1 col. 6.
　　Brief, noting that "the chapter on the early dramatists is
full of interest."

　　b) Lives of the most Eminent Literary and Scientific Men of
　　　France (2 vols.)

　　　　1. *Lives of the most Eminent Literary and Scientific
　　　　　Men of France*. Vol. I. Vol. 102 of The Cabinet of
　　　　　Biography, Conducted by the Rev. Dionysius Lardner
　　　　　(Lardner's Cabinet Cyclopedia). London: Printed for
　　　　　Longman, Orme, Brown, Green, & Longmans; and John
　　　　　Taylor, 1838.

C137 *The Literary Gazette, and Journal of the Belles Lettres*, No. 1126
(August 18, 1838), 524.
　　The memoirs "seem to be attentively compiled."†

C138 *Sunday Times* (London), August 5, 1838, p. 5 col. 1.
　　"The biographies are given with fairness and conciseness."†

　　　　2. *Lives of the Most Eminent French Writers*. 2 vols.
　　　　　Philadelphia: Lea and Blanchard, 1840.

C139 [Poe, Edgar Allan.] *Graham's Magazine*, 18 (January 1841), 48.
　　Brief, and mainly favorable. "The design is praiseworthy,"
but does not believe MS was "the principal author of these
sketches, as it would neither be truth, nor, in fact, add to her
reputation."
　　Burton R. Pollin attributes the review to Poe, and reprints
and discusses it, in his A339 (pp. 89, 256 n. 46).

D   GRADUATE RESEARCH

1.   *Ph.D. Dissertations*

*D1   Alterman, Peter Steven. "A Study of Four Science Fiction Themes
       and Their Function in Two Contemporary Novels." University of
       Denver, 1974. [Abstracted in *Dissertation Abstracts Interna-
       tional*, 35: 2976-A to 2977-A.]
            Abstract mentions a discussion of Victor Frankenstein as a
       mad scientist.
            Not yet in the microfilm collection of the Library of Congress.

D2   Bailey, James O[sler]. "Scientific Fiction in English: 1817-1914.
       A Study of Trends and Forms." University of North Carolina, 1934.
            Published as A39.

D3   Baker, Donald Whitelaw. "Themes of Terror in Nineteenth Century
       English Fiction: The Shift to the Internal." Brown University,
       1955, pp. 6, 28, 36-38, 48, 99, 100, 108, 124. [Abstracted in
       Dissertation Abstracts, 16: 118-119.]
            The pseudo-science of *Frankenstein* bridges those works dealing
       with magic and the occult sciences and the more sophisticated
       pseudo-science of H. G. Wells; Victor Frankenstein combines the
       medieval scientist and the modern scientist.

D4   Callaghan, Cecily M. "Mary Shelley's Frankenstein. A Compendium
       of Romanticism." Leland Stanford Junior University, 1936. [Ab-
       stracted in *Stanford University Abstracts of Dissertations*, 1935-
       1936, Vol. 11; and *Stanford University Bulletin*, Sixth Series
       (1936), 45-46.]
            Biographical and critical study of *Frankenstein*, noticing the
       influence of Godwin, Shelley, Rousseau, and Schiller upon the
       novel. The novel is "attuned to all the winds of Romanticism
       sweeping through her world."

D5   Coleman, William Emmet. "On the Discrimination of Gothicisms."
       City University of New York, 1970, pp. 2, 36, 40, 41, 42, 71, 129,
       236, 238-239, 254-255, 256-259. [Abstracted in *Dissertation Ab-
       stracts International*, 31: 2871-A.]
            Frankenstein "explores the characteristic theme of the natu-
       ralistic goodness of man"; the "mysterious love-hate relationship
       between Victor Frankenstein and the Monster is a symbiotic rela-
       tionship."

D6   Feldman, Paula R. "The Journals of Mary Wollstonecraft Shelley:
      An Annotated Edition." Northwestern University, 1974.
      The five journal books of MS, edited from the manuscript, and
      considerably more complete than Frederick L. Jones' edition [cf.
      IA1]. Editor notes that "My editorial decisions have been guided
      by my desire to have the text visually convey the sense of the
      journal as a private, casual, uncorrected manuscript rather than
      as a finished product. Thus, with only few exceptions, I have
      preserved idiosyncrasies of spelling, punctuation, paragraphing
      and abbreviation as exactly as limitations of type permit. This
      edition also includes extensive textual and factual annotation."
      (From abstract sent to me by the editor, not yet included in
      Dissertation Abstracts International.)
      Revised version of this dissertation will appear in the near
      future, in published form.

D7   Greene, D. Randolf. "Chapter V, The Horror of Imagination: Mary
      Shelley's *Frankenstein*." In his "The Romantic Prometheus: Varie-
      ties of the Heroic Quest." University of Wisconsin, 1973, pp. 179-
      205; and ii-iii, iv, 3, 10, 64, 80, 90, 94, 169, 206. [Abstracted
      in *Dissertation Abstracts International*, 35: 403-A.]
      Discussion of the Monster as an allegory of "what happens when
      the artist's vision turns back upon the artist, drives him to mad-
      ness, and destroys all that he loves," and of the frame technique,
      which "allows the reader to sense the horror of the tale without
      being able to penetrate the mystery."

D8   Harson, Robert R. "A Profile of John Polidori, with a new edition
      of *The Vampyre*." Ohio University, 1966, pp. 55-65, 99, 102, 108-
      109. [Abstracted in *Dissertation Abstracts*, 27: 3010.]
      Emphasizes Polidori's role in MS creation of *Frankenstein*: his
      discussions with Shelley on June 15, 1816 were "the germ from which
      Frankenstein grew."

D9   Hoffman, Harold L[eroy]. "An Odyssey of the Soul, Shelley's
      'Alastor.'" Columbia University, 1933.
      Published as A204.

D10   Mansfield, Joseph Gerard. "Chapter II, Muriel Spark's Gothic
      Novels." In his "Another World Than This: The Gothic and the
      Catholic in the Novels of Muriel Spark." University of Iowa, 1973,
      pp. 22-43 [28-43]. [Abstracted in *Dissertation Abstracts Interna-
      tional*, 34: 5890-A.]
      Illumination of Muriel Spark's criticism of MS [cf. A20], and
      discussion of the influence of *Frankenstein* upon Spark's novels.

D11   Miller, Arthur McA. "Chapter 5, The Last Man of Mary Shelley."
In his "The Last Man: A Study of the Eschatological Theme in
English Poetry and Fiction From 1806 through 1839." Duke University, 1966, pp. 112-178; and 11-12, 19, 21, 26 n. 3, 36, 40, 41,
46, 47, 91, 104, 105, 110-111, 179-180, 183, 203, 223, 226, 242-
243, 244, 247, 249, 258, 262-3 [the last only one page]. [Ab-
stracted in *Dissertation Abstracts*, 28: 687.]
    Close examination of the major themes and events in the novel;
mention of works influencing and influenced by the novel.

D12   Neumann, Bonnie Rayford. "Mary Shelley." University of New
Mexico, 1972. [Abstracted in *Dissertation Abstracts International*,
33: 5689-A.]
    Focuses on the loneliness in MS life as reflected in her works.

D13   Ozolins, Aija. "The Novels of Mary Shelley: From Frankenstein to
Falkner." University of Maryland, 1972. [Abstracted in *Dissertation Abstracts International*, 33: 2389-A.]
    Thorough examination of recurrent elements in the novels, with
particular attention to *Frankenstein*.

D14   Philmus, Robert Michael. "Into the Unknown: The Evolution of
Science Fiction in England from Francis Godwin to H. G. Wells."
University of California at San Diego, 1968. [Abstracted in
Dissertation Abstracts, 29: 1545.]
    Published as A333.

D15   Powers, Katherine Richardson. "The Influence of William Godwin on
the Novels of Mary Shelley." University of Tennessee, 1972. [Ab-
stracted in *Dissertation Abstracts International*, 33: 4359-A.]
    The ideas of Godwin as set forth in *Political Justice* and in
his novels as influences upon MS novels, particularly *Frankenstein*.

D16   Rieger, James Henry. "The Gnostic Prometheus: A Study of Godwin
and the Shelleys." Harvard University, 1963.
    Chapters 1, 3, 4, and part of 5 published in revised form in
A357.

D17   Senseman, Wilfred Minnich. "Chapter IV, The Treatment of Alchemy
in Some English Novels of the period from 1790 to 1840." Part 6.
"Mrs. Shelley's Frankenstein." In his "Demi-Science and Fiction:
The Utilization of the Pseudo-Scientific in Some English Novels of
the Period from 1790 to 1840." University of Michigan, 1950, pp.
95-224 [140-151]. [Abstracted in *Dissertation Abstracts*, 10:
150.]
    Mainly re-telling of the novel, pointing out MS attempts to
make the story believable and the variations on the usual theme
of "acquisition and manipulation of 'forbidden' knowledge." On
the whole, the novel is "a precocious performance."

D18   Taylor, Charles H[enry], Jr.   "The Early Collected Editions of
       Shelley's Poems." Yale University, 1955.
           Published as A21.

D19   Tropp, Martin. "Mary Shelley's Monster: A Study of Frankenstein."
       Boston University Graduate School, 1973. [Abstracted in *Disserta-
       tion Abstracts International*, 34: 1871-A.]
           Intelligent multi-level examination of the novel, including
       psychological criticism and evaluation of the work as a revitali-
       zation of the Gothic novel.

D20   Van Luchene, Stephen Robert. "Chapter V, Frankenstein." In his
       "Essays in Gothic Fiction: From Horace Walpole to Mary Shelley."
       University of Notre Dame, 1973, pp. 149-221. [Abstracted in *Disser-
       tation Abstracts International*, 34: 4220-A to 4221-A.]
           The novel "incorporates, exploits, and in certain cases rejects
       conventions established by the early Gothicists," and establishes
       "a new form, with a new ethical and philosophical substructure."
       The central question in the novel concerns Victor Frankenstein's
       responsibility towards his creation and the nature of scientific
       knowledge.

D21   Wade, Philip Tyree. "Influence and Intent in the Prose Fiction of
       Percy and Mary Shelley." University of North Carolina at Chapel
       Hill, 1966. [Abstracted in *Dissertation Abstracts*, 27: 3021-A.]
           Primarily Chapters 3, 4, 5, and 6, which concern the six MS
       novels. Appendix summarizes 21 MS short stories, but with little
       comment.

D22   Zirker, Joan McTigue. "The Gothic Tradition in English Fiction,
       1764-1824." Indiana University, 1974, pp. 10, 21, 22, 24, 31, 33,
       43, 78-83, 87, 124-128, 137, 175-177, 180, 191. [Abstracted in
       Dissertation Abstracts International, 35: 422-A.]
           As part of a re-evaluation and re-definition of the Gothic
       novel, the theme of the vision of disjunction is treated briefly
       in *Frankenstein* and *The Last Man*, and the role of the narrator
       discussed in the former.

       2. M.A. Theses

D23   Atkinson, Marthalee. "Mary Shelley's Frankenstein: Its Art and
       Thought." Western Kentucky University, 1972.
           Treated are the genesis of the novel, the narrative, Gothic
       elements, and as a "novel of ideas." Brief mention of theatrical
       and film versions in Chapter 5.

*D24   Gilliland, Norman Paul. "An Inquiry into the Longevity of Franken-
       stein." University of Florida, 1972.
           Temporarily unavailable, as of early 1975.

D25   Hood, Forrest Leslie. "Mary Shelley." University of Colorado, 1941.
        Mainly summarization of biographical material from A6 and A8. On microfilm at the Library of Congress.

*D26   Sharpe, Barbara H. "Social Criticism in William Godwin's <u>Caleb Williams</u> and Mary G. Shelley's <u>Frankenstein</u>." University of South Carolina, 1970.

D27   el-Shater, Safaa Mohammed. "The Novels of Mary Shelley." University of Liverpool, 1963.
        MS "not a first-class novelist"—she is at her best in the first three, but the last three "have no great value." Much plot synopsis of all the novels, with emphasis on the central characters of each and on the autobiographical significance of the works.

E FOREIGN WORKS

1. Books

a) Entire Books

E1 Palacio, Jean de. *Mary Shelley dans son œuvre: Contributions aux études shelleyennes*. Paris: Editions Klincksieck, 1969.

Exhaustive critical study of MS writings; evaluation of MS not merely for her connection with Shelley and other figures, but as an author, although a minor one, in her own right. Combination of critical approaches, including historical, biographical, and psychological. Appendices include publication of 22 MS notes and letters for the first time, MS corrections from her annotation copy of *Perkin Warbeck*, and three stanzas of unpublished MS verse. 55-page bibliography lists both primary and secondary works, detailed on reviews of MS works, but highly selective regarding criticism of MS. The most thorough critical study of MS yet to appear.

For review, see B89.

b) Portions of Books

*E2 Bergier, Jacques. "Préface" to Mary Shelley. *Frankenstein*. [Belgium:] Verviers, Gérard, 1964.

Listed in the catalogue of the Bibliothéque Nationale, Supplement, tome 9, p. 572.

See also IB93a.

*E3 Biagi, Guido. *Gli ultimi giorni di Percy Bysshe Shelley, nuovi documenti*. Florence: Società an. edit. "La Voce," 1892.

Published in English as A53.

E4 Boujut, Michel. "Préface" to Mary Shelley. *Frankenstein*. Lausanne: Editions Recontre, 1964, pp. 7-25.

Brief criticism of the novel and biography of MS, noting the Golem legend and Pygmalion as influences on the myth begun by *Frankenstein*, and the film versions which continued it.

See also IB92a, and B98a, B116a, and B127a for reprintings.

*E5 Briganti, Gabriele. *Maria Shelley e il suo romanzo su Castruccio Castracani*. Lucca: Scuola Tip. Artigianelli, 1934.

Alternate publication of E47.

E6   Capanna, Pablo. *El Sentido de la Ciencia Ficción*. Buenos Aires:
Editorial Columbia, 1966, pp. 74-75.
The myth of *Frankenstein* has been so influential that "it is
almost impossible to imagine a mechanical being without character-
istics similar [to those of the Monster]."

E7   Carneiro, André. *Introdução ao Estudo da "Science-Fiction."* São
Paulo: Conselho Estadual de Cultura, Comissão de Literatura, 1967,
pp. 32-33.
Brief remarks on *Frankenstein* as science fiction.

*E8   Cochetti, Ranieri. "Introduzione" to Mary Shelley. *Frankenstein*.
Rome: Donatello de Luigi, 1944, pp. 9-16.
In the Library of Congress card catalogue, but searches by the
present author have failed to uncover it.
See also ĪB55a.

E9   Dédéyan, Charles. *Le Thème de Faust dans la littérature européenes:
Le Préromantisme*. 4 vols. Paris: Lettres modernes, 1954-1967,
Vol. 2, Part 2, pp. 276-286, 287.

               _____. Vol. 3, Part 1, pp. 58, 120.
Notice of Victor Frankenstein as a Faust figure, and the Monster
as a figure of evil, with brief mention of sources and influences of
Frankenstein. "Mrs. Shelley disposes in a personal and happy
manner of sources and elements already registered, and presents an
original Faust."

E10   Dischner, Gisela [Bezzel-]. "Mary Shelley." In her *Ursprünge der
Rheinromantik in England. Zur Geschichte der romantischen Asthetik*.
Frankfurt am Main: Vittorio Klosterman [ca. 1922], pp. 168-191; and
48, 132, 196ff, 241ff, 248, 251ff, 258, 260, 277.
Evaluation of the landscape, especially the Rhine area, in
Frankenstein (which is "almost the hero of the novel"), and Freudian
analysis of the personality split between Victor and his creation,
the latter representing Victor's "'demonic' drive-id."

*E11   Ebeling, Hermann. "Nachwort" in Mary Shelley. *Frankenstein: oder
der neue Prometheus*. Munich: Carl Hanser Verlag, 1970, pp. 317-339.
Source: Annual Bibliography of the *Keats-Shelley Journal*.
See also ĪB130a and B132a.

*E12   Eimer, Manfred. *Die persönlichen Beziehungen zwischer Byron und
der Shelleys; eine Kritische Studie*. Heft 32 of *Anglistiche
Forschungen*, Johannes Hoops, ed. Heidelberg: Carl Winter, 1910.
In the British Museum Catalog of Printed Books.
Possibly similar to E49.

E13   Elistratova, A[nna] A[rkad'evna]. Foreword and Notes to Mary
       Shelley. *Frankenstein, ili Sovremennyi Promethei.* Moscow: Khudo-
       zhestvennaia literatura, 1965, pp. 3-23, 243-245.
           Consideration of the moral implications of the novel as it
       relates to problems caused by modern technology, with some back-
       ground of Mary Shelley.
           See also IB99a.

E14   Ferreras, Juan Ignacio. *La Novela de ciencia ficción. Interpre-
       tacion de una Novela Marginal.* Madrid: España Editores, 1972,
       p. 35.
           In *Frankenstein* there appeared for the first time a typical
       theme of science fiction, that of robots and androids.

E15   Gasca, Luis. Chapter 2, Part 2, "La Criatura del Dr. Frankenstein."
       In his *Cine y Ciencia-ficción.* Barcelona: Llibres de Sinera, 1969,
       pp. 122-132.
           Superficial comments on the novel *Frankenstein* in connection
       with film and comic-book adaptations.

E16   Gasca, Luis. *Imagen y Ciencia Ficción.* San Sebastian: XIV Festi-
       val Internacional del Cine, 1966, pp. 12-13.
           List of theatrical and film versions of *Frankenstein.*

E17   Gattégno. Jean. *La Science-fiction.* Paris: Presses Universitaires
       de France, 1971, pp. 25, 29.
           Mention of *Frankenstein* as the beginning of the robot myth
       carried on by Karel Capek's *R.U.R.*

*E18   Hargest, G. d'. "Introduction" to Mary Shelley. *Frankenstein, ou
       le Prométhée moderne.* Paris: La Renaissance du livre, 1922.
           Listed in the catalogue of the Bibliothéque Nationale, tome
       172, p. 11.
           See also IB37a.

E19   Hartland, Reginald [William]. *Walter Scott et le Roman "frénétique."*
       Paris: Librairie Ancienne Honoré Champion, 1928, pp. 54-55.
           Mainly plot synopsis of *Frankenstein,* with mention of the
       novel's influence upon French romanticism.

E20   Hienger, Jörg. *Literarische Zukunftsphantastik. Eine Studie über
       Science Fiction.* Göttingen: Vandenhoeck & Ruprecht [ca. 1972],
       pp. 133-134, 137, 255 n. 3 (to Chapter 4).
           Compared to Goethe's *Faust, Frankenstein* is an "inferior work";
       a comparison of Wagner's homunculus and the Monster shows "an unna-
       tural form of man in an abnormal format," with the Monster seeking
       "a shorter path (to becoming a man)."

*E21   "Inledning" to Mary Shelley. *Frankenstein.* [Stockholm:] Delta
       Förlags AB, 1974, pp. 7-12 [7].
           Brief biographical sketch (untranslated by the present author)
       preceeding portion of MS 1831 Introduction to the novel.
           See also IB150a; IIE24.

*E22   Ivănescu, Mircea. "Postfața" to Mary Shelley. *Frankenstein sau
       Prometeul Modern*. Bucharest: Editura Albatros (Fantastic Club),
       1973, pp. 239-245.
       Copy in the Bodleian Library.
       See also IB146a.

*E23   Juin, Hubert. "Au Pays des Monstres." In Mary Shelley. *Franken-
       stein*. Paris: Les Editions de La Renaissance, "Club Géant," 1967,
       pp. 473-483.
       Source: Annual Bibliography of the *Keats-Shelley Journal*.

ᴬE24   Karlott, Boris [William Henry Pratt]. Prefatory Note to Mary
       Shelley. *Frankenstein*. [Stockholm:] Delta Förlags AB, 1974, p. 5.
       Possibly translated from an interview or article about Karloff
       (no source given), but more than likely not written by Karloff for
       this edition, since he died in 1969. Item untranslated by the
       present author.
       See also IB150a; IIE21.

E25   Kosok, Heinz. *Die Bedeutung der Gothic Novel für das Erzählwerk
       Herman Melvilles*. Vol. 12 of *Britannica et Americana*. Hamburg:
       Cram, de Gruyter, 1963, pp. 25, 26, 75, 89, 90, 91, 112.
       Frankenstein as one of the Gothic novels that influenced
       Herman Melville, with brief consideration of MS use of the sea
       corresponding to Melville's in *Moby Dick*.

E26   Koszul, A[ndré] [Henri]. *La Jeunesse de Shelley*. Paris: Librairie
       Bloud & Cie, 1910, pp. xvi, 117, 207-213, 215-219, 230, 232-245
       passim, 253, 277-278, 279-282, 286 n. 2, 287, 310, 311-314, 321,
       329, 331-332, 343, 428, 431, 432, 433.
       MS treated in connection with Shelley and his poetry; she was
       "capable of great effort and perseverance, [and] lively and en-
       thusiastic for her years," and *Frankenstein* is the best work of all
       the horror novels.

E27   Kreutz, Christian. "Mary Wollstonecraft Shelleys Prometheusbild."
       In his *Das Prometheussymbol in der Dichtung der Englischen Romantik*.
       Band 236 of *Palaestra. Untersuchungen aus der Eutschen und Engli-
       schen Philologie und Literaturgeschichte*. Göttingen: Vandenhoeck &
       Ruprecht, 1963, pp. 136-152.
       Examines the Monster's narrative in *Frankenstein*, stressing as
       sources Ovid's *Metamorphoses*, Francis Bacon's essay on Prometheus,
       and Shaftesbury's *Moralists*, notes the main thematic concern of MS
       as "how and with what purpose should man use his intellectual capa-
       cities without trangressing against divine perogative or to the
       detriment of other men and himself," and concludes that she is much
       more classical in her world view—more conservative and antiroman-
       tic--than one would think.

E28   Laclos, Michel. *Le Fantastique au cinema.* Paris: Jean-Jacques
      Pauvert, 1958, pp. xii-xv.
      Very brief description of *Frankenstein* and summary of film
      versions from 1910 to 1956.

*E29 Legouis, Émile [Hyacinthe]. *Histoire de la littérature anglaise.*
      Paris: Hachette, 1924.
      Original publication of A242.

*E30 Lundwall, Sam J. *Science Fiction, från begynnelsen till våra
      dagar.* Stockholm: Sveriges Radios förlag, 1969, pp. 61-62, 63,
      110, 113.
      Concerning *Frankenstein.*
      See also A254.

*E31 Maurer, Otto. *Shelley und die Frauen.* Berlin-Schöneberg: Emil
      Felber/Jena: Hermann Constable, 1906.
      Untranslated, but assume it discusses MS in some detail.
      Orginally dissertation; see E70.

E32   Maurois, André. *Ariel ou la vie de Shelley.* Paris: Bernard
      Grasset, 1923, pp. 107, 124, 159-168, 171-187, 188-190, 193-194,
      197-199, 207-208, 210, 214, 216, 219-223, 228-229, 231, 237-241,
      244, 250-252, 258, 260-263, 264-266, 268-275, 281-282, 285, 290-
      297, 298, 300-302, 306-307, 313-315, 318-322, 325-328, 332-333,
      340-347 *passim,* 351-353.
      Translated as A276.

E33   Mérimée, Prosper. *Correspondence générale.* 18 vols. Maurice
      Parturier *et al,* eds. Paris: Le Divan/Toulose: Privat, 1941-1964,
      Vol. I, pp. 29 n. 2, 44, 386.
      MS letter to Victor Jacquemont.

E34   Milner, Max. *Le Diable dans la littérature française de Cazotte
      à Baudelaire (1772-1861).* Paris: José Corti, 1960, Vol. I, pp.
      315-316, 317, 320 n. 12.
      Victor Hugo's *Hans d'Islande* was inspired by *Frankenstein.*

*E35 Neumann, Robert. *Passion, sechs dichter-ehen.* Vienna: Phaidon-
      verlag, 1930.
      Translated as A300.

E36   Plank, Robert. "Golems und Roboter." In Franz Rottensteiner,
      comp. *Pfade ins Unendliche.* Frankfurt am Main: Insel-Verlag,
      1971, pp. 73-99 [81-82].
      Translation of B275.

E37   Reavis, Edward. Introduction, "Frankenstein etc." In his comp.
      *Frankenstein. Wie er mordet und lacht. 17 Klassiche und moderne
      Horrorstories.* Frankfurt am Main: Barmeier & Nikel, 1968, pp. 7-9.
      The Monster's confession is "dreary." Two modern stories,
      W. C. Morrow's "The Monster-Maker" and Harry Harrison's "At Last,
      The True Story of Frankenstein" [cf. B114], "refrain from the

psychological and philosophical accessories" of MS novel, and are concerned with "panic and shock for their own sake."

*E38   Robbia, Enrica Viviani della [Maria Bianca Viviani della Robbia, marchesa]. *Vita di una donna (L'Emily di Shelley)*. Florence: G. C. Sansoni, 1936.
     Biography of Emilia Viviani, listed in Grylls' bibliography [cf. A6]; untranslated, but assumes it treats MS in connection with Viviani and Shelley.

E39   Swoboda, Helmut. *Der Künstliche Mensch*. Munich: Ernst Heimeran, 1967, pp. 220-222.
     Recapitulation of MS life in connection with the composition of *Frankenstein*, summarizing the novel and noting the film versions. The novel is not just another ghost story, for in it MS was too concerned with the responsibility of society to outsiders.

E40   Trousson, Raymond. *Le Thème de Prométhée dans la littérature européene*. 2 vols. Geneva: Librairie Droz, 1964, Vol. I, pp. 305-306.
     Frankenstein "illustrates the theme of *Faust* as well as that of Prometheus."

E41   Vax, Louis. *Le Séduction de l'Étrange. Étude sur la littérature fantastique*. Paris: Presses Universitaires de France, 1965, pp. 72, 217.
     Passing mention of *Frankenstein*, which is "ambiguous because the central figure presents two faces, that which is offered to the public, and that which is devoted to himself." (Note: MS is indexed as "Shelley [A. M.].")

*E42   Viola, Gianni Eugenio. "Introduzione al Frankenstein del Living." In his *Frankenstein. Interpretazione del Living*. Catania [Italy]: Underground-La Fiaccola, 1972, pp. 37-47.
     Introduction to discussion of the Living Theatre's version of *Frankenstein*.
     In the Library of Congress.

*E43   Vohl, Maria. *Die Erzählungen der Mary Shelley und ihre Urbilder*. Heidelberg: Carl Winter, 1913.
     Not translated; in "Portions of Books" section of this bibliography since it may deal as much or more with Shelley as MS.

E44   Voisine, Jacques-René. *J.-J. Rousseau en Angleterre à l'époque romantique: Les Écrits autobiographiques et la légende*. Paris: Marcel Didier, 1956, pp. 175-176, 262, 279-282, 284, 288, 289 n. 17, 291, 318.
     Passing mention of MS in connection with Godwin, Mary Wollstonecraft, and Shelley.

*E45   Volta, Ornella. *Frankenstein y Cie.* [Italy:] Sugar Editore, 1965.
        Glut [A4, pp. 303-304] notes that this contains the text of
        Frankenstein as well as commentary upon theatrical and film versions.

2. Periodicals

E46   André-Maurois, Simone. "La Femme de l'écrivain," *Les Annales*, 63
        (Mars 1956), 23-38.
        Brief mention of MS as an "exemplary widow" because she was
        "dedicated to the memory of Ariel."

*E47   Briganti, Gabriele. "Maria Shelley e il suo romanzo su Castruccio
        Castracani," *Bolletino Storico Lucchese*, 6 (1934), 85-105.
        de Palacio [E1, p. 657, Item 74] cites this article.
        Also published as E5.

E48   Ebeling, Hermann. "Die Stunde Frankensteins. Eine Lektion über
        die Welt des Horrors," *Der Monat. (Internationale Zeitschrift für
        Politik und gestiges Leben)* (Frankfurt am Main), 19 (März 1967),
        31-36, 38-40.
        Superficial descriptive comments on *Frankenstein* (the characters
        are as unrealistically sketched as are the geography and climate),
        which lead to a discussion of horror literature in general and a
        denunciation of teenage interest in horror films.

E49   Eimer, Manfred. "Einflüsse deutscher räuber—und Schauerromantik
        auf Shelley, Mrs. Shelley, und Byron," *Englische Studien*, 48 (1915),
        231-245 [238-241].
        The influence of the *Fantasmagoriana* stories upon *Frankenstein*,
        with description of the partial contents of the former.

*E50   Fleisher, Frederic. "Kvinnan som skapade Frankenstein," *Svenska
        Dagbladet* (Stockholm), October 24, 1954.
        Source: Annual Bibliography of the *Keats-Shelley Journal*.

E51   Forgues, E.-D. "Poètes et romanciers moderne de la Grande Bretagne.
        XI. Percy Bysshe Shelley," *Revue des deux mondes*, 21 (15 janvier
        1848), 250-277 [261].
        Mention of MS, "the boldness of her character and her opinions
        on a level with her family and with Shelley."
        See also B62.

E52   Gérard, Albert. "Prométhée a l'envers: ou le mythe de Franken-
        stein," *Synthèses, Revue mensuelle internationale* (Brussels), 7
        (Janvier 1953), 353-360.
        Concerns the Promethean myth in the novel, and Victor Franken-
        stein as a Faust figure. "But Mary Shelley's novel is by no means
        a parable of scientific messianism. . . . It is infinitely less
        superficial, more complex, more tragic."

E53   Helmar, Helmut S. "Frankensteins Mutter. Eine Neunzehnjährige erfand das vielverfilmte Monster," *Die Weltwoche* (Zurich), 12 Februar 1965, p. 37.

     Casual biography of MS and synopsis of *Frankenstein*, considering the novel as the beginning of the robot myth, and briefly mentioning MS other novels. (Also prints a portrait of Claire Clairmont as "Mary Shelley Wollstonecraft.")

*E54   Kagarlitskii, Iu. "Roman Meri Shelli" ["Mary Shelley's Novel"], *Inostrannaia literatura*, No. 1 (1966), 262-263.

     In Russian. Source: Annual Bibliography of the *Keats-Shelley Journal*.

*E55   Lorenz, Gunnar. "Frankensteins födelse," *Skånska Dagbladet* (Malmö, Sweden), March 3, 1954.

     Source: Annual Bibliography of the *Keats-Shelley Journal*.

E56   Ludwig, Albert. "Homunculi und Androiden. Part II. Homunculi und Androiden in der Zeit der Romantik," *Archiv für das Studium der neuen Sprachen und Literatur*, n.s. 38 [138] (Juli 1919), 141-155 [150-151].

     Brief mention of *Frankenstein* as part of the literature of androids.

*E57   Maanen, W. van. "Kroniek der Engelse Letterkunde. I. Over *Frankenstein or the Modern Prometheus*," *De Gids* (Amsterdam), 4 (November 1949), 133-138.

     Cited in Wade's dissertation [cf. D21], but with incorrect date. Untranslated.

*E58   May, Frederick. "Mary Wolstonecraft [sic] Shelley e il sonetto autoritratto del Foscolo," *Giornale storico della letteratura italiana* (Torino), 141 (3rd Trimestre 1964), 390-393.

     Concerns MS sonnet, "Portrait of Ugo Foscolo/By Himself." Source: the Annual Bibliography of the *Keats-Shelley Journal* and *Internationale Bibliographie der Zeitschriftenliteratur, aus allen gebieten des wisseus*. Untranslated.

*E59   Moeckli, Gustave. "Un Genevois méconnu: Frankenstein," *Musées de Genève*, 3 (Novembre-Décembre 1962), 10-13.

     Source: the Annual Bibliography of the *Keats-Shelley Journal*. This issue not at Yale.

*E60   Schöler, Franz. "Die Erben des Marquis de Sade. Horrorfilm Part III: Frankenstein, Jekyll, and the Gothic Horror," *Film*, 5 (October 1967), 12-19.

     Cited in the Bibliography of Roy Huss and T. J. Ross, eds. *Focus on the Horror Film* (Englewood Cliffs, N.J.: Prentice-Hall, 1972), p. 183, as "a scholarly and insightful critique," which I assume also discusses MS novel.

     Journal not located; not listed in *Union List of Serials*.

*E61   Stahuljak, Milan. "Pismo Gdje Shelley Gdji Gisborne," *Republika*
        (Zagreb), 11 (1955), 435-440.
            According to the Annual Bibliography of the *Keats-Shelley
        Journal*, a translation and discussion of MS letter to Maria Gis-
        borne. Untranslated by the present author.

E62   Thomsen, Christian W. "Die Verantwortung des Naturwissenschaftlers
        in Mary Shelleys *Frankenstein* und Heinar Kipphardts *In der Sache J.
        Robert Oppenheimer*: Zur literarischen Gestaltung eines Problemes,"
        Literatur in Wissenschaft und Unterricht (Kiel), 4 (1971), 16-26.
            Discussion of the responsibility of the scientist in both
        works, emphasizing that Frankenstein's motives were noble—for the
        progress of humanity—but that in exposing the Monster, he took a
        terrible risk, one comparable to a modern-day researcher working
        with radioactive materials.

        3. Reviews

            1. *Frankenstein*. Monica Stolpe, trans. Stockholm: Christo-
               fers, 1959.

*E63   Alderberth, Roland. *Göteborgs-Tidningen*, July 21, 1959.
            Source for this and the following Swedish reviews: the Annual
        Bibliography of the *Keats-Shelley Journal*.

*E64   Gustafsson, Lars. *Dagens Nyheter*, September 26, 1959.

*E65   Gustafsson, Lars. *Vestmanlands Läns Tidning*, June 23, 1959.

*E66   L[indma]n, S[tig]. *Vösterbottens Folkblad*, July 9, 1959.

*E67   L[ohmande]r, U[lla]. *Göteborgs-Posten*, July 7, 1959.

            2. *Frankenstein, ili Sovremenyi Promethei*. Z. Aleksandrova,
               trans. Moscow: Khudozhestvennaia literatura, 1965.

E68   Gorbunov, A. *Novyi Mir*, 42 (May 1966), 283.
            Favorable. Brief discussion of Promethean theme and topical
        relevance. "In our day *Frankenstein* strikes out with its gloom
        and abundance of dark colors, almost without end."

            3. *Mathilda*. Elizabeth Nitchie, ed. Chapel Hill, N.C.:
               University of North Carolina Press [1959].

E69   Huscher, Herbert. *Anglia Zeitschrift für Englische Philologie*, 79
        (1961), 125-128.
            Favorable. Summarizes Nitchie's Introduction and the plot of
        the work, with particular emphasis upon the incest motif.

4. Graduate Research—Ph.D. Dissertations

E70   Maurer, Otto. "Shelley und die Frauen." Universität zu Tubingen, 1904.
      Published as E31.

F MARY SHELLEY IN FICTION

1. Stories

F1 Hunt, John H. "Luigi Rivarola: a Tale of Modern Italy," *The Young Lady's Magazine. A Monthly Journal of Theology, Philosophy, History, and General Knowledge; Embracing Literature, Science, and Art*, No. 10 (February 1838), 71-80 [71, 72].
MS is "Mrs. Godwin Percy." The narrator expects her to be "an awful-looking creature, with a large, dark, restless eye, and a strong voice, and a bold manner"—but he does not meet her as expected.
See also B168.

2. Novels

F2 Aldiss, Brian. *Frankenstein Unbound*. London: Jonathan Cape, 1973.
Joe Bodenland travels from the future to 1816 Geneva, and meets MS, Victor Frankenstein, and the Monster ("the living model for the protagonist in . . . *Frankenstein*"), all of whom co-exist in a mythical time-mixture. In the characters' dialogue, the theme of machines' domination of man from the MS novel is stressed. MS is represented quite sympathetically, but often with lacklustre dialogue ("You know I can't leave dear Shelley. He means to mend the world, but he needs me to mend his clothes . . . Do you like me, Joe?").
Also published, N.Y.: Random House, 1974. Serialized in *Fantastic Stories*, 23 (March 1974), 6-61, 108-110; 23 (May 1974), 38-103.
See also B350.

F3 Artmann, H. C. *Frankenstein in Sussex*. In his *Frankenstein in Sussex. Fleiss und Industrie*. [Berlin?:] Suhrkamp Verlag, 1969, pp. 7-39.
Involves the Golem, MS, and a "Doktor Wilbur von Frankenstein."

F4 Bolton, Guy. *The Olympians*. Cleveland: The World Publishing Company, 1961.
Mainly concerns the MS-Shelley elopement and aftermath.

F5   Dodd, Catherine I[sabel]. *Eagle Feather*. N.Y.: D. Appleton and
     company, 1933.
          Novelistic treatment of the lives of Mary Wollstonecraft,
     Godwin, Byron, Shelley, MS, and their circle.
          Often cited in early bibliographies as a biography of MS.

F6   Edwards, Anne. *Haunted Summer*. N.Y.: Coward, McCann & Geoghagen,
     1972.
          Told in first person, from MS point of view, covering the
     period immediately after the elopement until Shelley's death, and
     concentrating on the 1916 summer in Geneva.

F7   Hughes, Rupert. *The Man Without a Home*. N.Y., London: Harper &
     Brothers, 1935.
          The MS-Payne affair: "Only a cynic could have assumed that the
     grimmest, most blood-freezing story in the language . . . would be
     created, as a sort of parlor pastime, by a delicately lovely young
     girl of nineteen.
          "Only the fantastic adventures of both [MS and Payne] could
     have brought them together in a love-affair."

F8   Kenyon, Frank Wilson. *The Golden Years: A Novel Based on the Life
     and Loves of Percy Bysshe Shelley*. N.Y.: Crowell, 1959.
          Mainly concerns Shelley's relationships with MS, Harriet, Jane
     Williams, and Claire.

F9   [Peacock, Thomas Love.] *Nightmare Abbey*. London: T. Hookham, Jun.,
     1818.
          MS is presented as the mysterious "Stella," with whom Scythrop
     [Shelley] falls in love, and as having "a highly cultivated and
     energetic mind, full of impassioned schemes of liberty, and im-
     patience of masculine usurpation." Her real identity is Celinda
     Toobad, later Celinda Flosky. MS mainly in Chapters 10 and 13.
          Also published in *Headlong Hall and Nightmare Abbey*. London,
     Toronto: J. M. Dent & Sons/N.Y.: E. P. Dutton, 1929; *Nightmare
     Abbey. Crotchet Castle*. Raymond Wright, ed. Harmondsworth,
     Middlesex: Penguin Books, 1969—reprinted, 1974.
          See also A120.

F10 Wylie, Elinor. *The Orphan Angel*. N.Y.: Alfred A. Knopf, 1926.
          Instead of drowning, Shelley is rescued and travels to the U.S.
     His reflections on MS are on p. 223.
          Also published as *Mortal Image*. London: William Heinemann,
     1927.

     3. Novels Based on Films

F11 Egremont, Michael. *The Bride of Frankenstein*. London: The Queens-
     way Press [1936].
          Based on the 1935 film of the same title, with MS, Shelley, and
     Byron in the "prologue" discussing *Frankenstein*. Closely follows
     the film.

4. *Plays*

*F12   Bate, Sam. *Shelley and Mary: A Romantic Play in One Act.* London: Deane, 1956.

       Also published, Boston: Baker, 1956.

5. *Teleplays*

F13   Isherwood, Christopher, and Don Bachardy. *Frankenstein: The True Story.* N.Y.: Avon Books, 1973.

       First part (pp. 7-15) involves MS, Shelley, Byron, and Polidori in the Geneva of 1816, as Shelley and MS become characters in the drama to follow (Shelley as Victor Frankenstein, MS as Elizabeth Fanshawe). This sequence was omitted from the 1974 television production.

       See also B40, B55, B300, B319.

ADDENDA

PART I

B155a "From *Frankenstein or The Modern Prometheus.*" In Gregory Fitz
Gerald and Jack C. Wolf, eds. *Past, Present, and Future Perfect.*
A Text Anthology of Speculative and Science Fiction. A Fawcett
Premier Book. Greenwich, Conn.: Fawcett Publications, 1973,
pp. 390-400.
Excerpts from Chapters 4 and 5 of the 1831 edition.

B9c "From *The Last Man.*" In Gregory Fitz Gerald and Jack C. Wolf,
eds. *Past, Present, and Future Perfect.* *A Text Anthology of
Speculative and Science Fiction.* A Fawcett Premier Book. Greenwich, Conn.: Fawcett Publications, 1973, pp. 367-389.
Excerpt from the final chapter.

PART II

A457 Jensen, Paul M. *Boris Karloff and His Films.* South Brunswick,
N.J.; N.Y.: A. S. Barnes/London: The Tantivy Press [1975], pp.
10, 26-29, 33 n., 81, 88.
The novel in connection with the 1931 and 1935 film versions
of *Frankenstein*, lamenting the fact that the 1931 film was based
not on the MS work but on Peggy Webling's play.

A458 Moss, Howard. "Mary Wollstonecraft Shelley." In his *Instant
Lives.* N.Y.: Saturday Review Press/E. P. Dutton, 1974, pp. 72-
74.
Humorous sketch of MS.

B355 Lanchester, Elsa. Letter, *Life*, 64 (April 5, 1968), 21.
The actress portraying MS in the film *Bride of Frankenstein*
confirms the deduction of Rosenberg [cf. B301] that director
James Whale used her to play both MS and the "Bride" to stress
the connection of MS and the Monster.
For other responses to Rosenberg's article, see B358, B359.
See also B357.

B356 [Peacock, Thomas Love.] "Unpublished Letters of Percy Bysshe
Shelley. From Italy—1818 to 1822," *Fraser's Magazine for Town
and Country*, 61 (March 1860), 301-319 [318-319].
MS letter to Shelley (Sept. 29, 1822).

B357　Rosenberg [Samuel]. Reply to letter by David T. Russell, *Life*,
　　　 64 (April 5, 1968), 21.
　　　　 Reply to B358: MS and Shelley may have known the legend con-
　　　 cerning the Frankenstein castle; the name "Frankenstein" may be
　　　 a combination of "Wolfstein" in Shelley's *St. Irvyne* and Benjamin
　　　 Franklin.

B358　Russell, David T. Letter, *Life*, 64 (April 5, 1968), 21.
　　　　 Wonders if the legend surrounding the Frankenstein castle
　　　 might have influenced MS in her novel.
　　　　 See B357 for reply.

B359　Uzzle, Bill. Letter, *Life*, 64 (April 5, 1968), 21.
　　　　 Frankenstein "is an incredibly dull book"; in it MS "passed
　　　 up nearly every opportunity to create suspense."

UNDERGRADUATE RESEARCH

*G1　Boyd, A. N. "The Treatment of Crime in Some Novels between 1794
　　　 and 1845, with Special Reference to *Caleb Williams*, *Frankenstein*,
　　　 The Heart of Midlothian, *Paul Clifford*, and *Lucretia*." Oxford
　　　 University, 1969.

APPENDICES

APPENDIX I

MARY SHELLEY'S WORKS,
CHRONOLOGICALLY ARRANGED

1817 [with Percy Bysshe Shelley.] *History of a Six Weeks' Tour through a Part of France, Switzerland, Germany, and Holland: with Letters Descriptive of a Sail round the Lake of Geneva, and of the Glaciers of Chamouni.* [Fla]

1818 *Frankenstein; Or, The Modern Prometheus.* [Bla]

1822 "A Tale of the Passions, or, the Death of Despina." [Dla]

1823 *Valperga: Or, the Life and Adventures of Castruccio, Prince of Lucca.* [Blb]

      "Madame D'Houtetôt." [Hl]

      "Giovanni Villani." [H2]

      "Narrative of a Tour round the Lake of Geneva, and of an Excursion through the Valley of Chamouni." [H3]

1824 (Ed.) Percy Bysshe Shelley. *Posthumous Poems of Percy Bysshe Shelley.* [Il]

      "Recollections of Italy." [H4]

      "On Ghosts." [H5]

      "The Bride of Modern Italy." [Dlb]

1826 *The Last Man.* [Blc]

      "Defense of Velluti" [I]. [H6]

      "The English in Italy." [H7].

1828 "The Sisters of Albano." [Dlc]

      "Ferdinando Eboli." [Dld]

1829   "Illyrian Poems—Feudal Scenes." [H8]

        "Modern Italy." [H9]

        review of *The Loves of the Poets*. [H10]

        "Recollections of the Lake of Geneva." [H11]

        "The Mourner." [D1e]

        "The Evil Eye." [D1f]

        "The False Rhyme." [D1g]

1830   review of *Cloudesley*. [H12]

        ?review of *1572 Chronique du Temps de Charles IX*. [H13]

        The Fortunes of Perkin Warbeck. [B1d]

        "Transformation." [D1h]

        "Absence" (poem). [E1]

        "A Dirge" (poem). [E2]

        "The Swiss Peasant" [D1i]

        "A Night Scene" (poem). [E4]

        ?"Song; 'When I'm no more, this harp that rings.'" [E5]

1831   "Memoir of Godwin." [H14]

        revised edition of *Frankenstein*. [B4a]

        (Ed.) [Edward John Trelawny.] *Adventures of a Younger Son*. [I2]

        ?review of Thomas Moore. *The Life and Death of Lord Edward Fitz-gerald*. [H15]

        ?"Living Literary Characters, No. II. *The Honourable Mrs. Norton*." [H16]

        ?"Living Literary Characters, No. IV. *James Fenimore Cooper*." [H17]

        "Proserpine." [C1a]

        "The Dream." [D1j]

1832   "The Pole." [D1k & D2k]

1832 "The Brother and Sister, An Italian Story." [Dl*l*]

"The Invisible Girl." [Dlm]

1833 "The Mortal Immortal." [Dln]

1834 "Ode to Ignorance." [E6]

?"Fame" (poem). [E7]

"The Elder Son." [Dlo]

"The Trial of Love." [Dlp]

1835 [with James Montgomery.] *Lives of the most Eminent Literary and Scientific Men of Italy, Spain, and Portugal.* Vol. I [Gla]

Lodore. [Ble]

[with James Montgomery and Sir David Brewster.] *Lives of the most Eminent Literary and Scientific Men of Italy, Spain, and Portugal.* Vol. II. [G2a]

(Ed.) William Godwin, Jun. *Transfusion; or, The Orphan of Unwalden.* [I3]

1836 "The Parvenue." [Dlq]

1837 *Falkner.* [Blf]

[with others?] *Lives of the most Eminent Literary and Scientific Men of Italy, Spain, and Portugal.* Vol. III. [G3a]

"The Pilgrims." [Dlr]

1838 *Lives of the most Eminent Literary and Scientific Men of France.* Vol. I. [Glb]

"Euphrasia." [Dls]

"Stanzas; 'How like a star you rose upon my life.'" [E8]

"Stanzas; 'O come to me in dreams, my love!'" [E9]

1839 (Ed.) Percy Bysshe Shelley. *The Poetical Works of Percy Bysshe Shelley.* [I4]

Lives of the most Eminent Literary and Scientific Men of France. Vol. II. [G2b]

(Ed.) Percy Bysshe Shelley. *Essays, Letters from Abroad, Translations and Fragments.* [I7]

ca.
1842 *Oh Listen While I Sing to Thee* (poem). [E10]

1844 *Rambles in Germany and Italy, in 1840, 1842, and 1843.* [F1b]

1876 *The Choice* (poem). [E11]

1877 "The Heir of Mondolpho." [D1t]

1891 *Tales and Stories.* [D1u]

1918 *Letters of Mary W. Shelley (Mostly Unpublished).* [Henry Howard Harper, ed.] [A2]

1922 *Proserpine & Midas.* A[ndré] [Henri] Koszul, ed. [C2a & C1b]

1938 "On Reading Wordsworth's Lines of Peel [sic] Castle." [E12]

"Fragment; 'Tribute for thee, dear solace of my life.'" [E13]

1944 *The Letters of Mary W. Shelley.* Frederick L[afayette] Jones, ed. [A7]

1947 *Mary Shelley's Journal.* Frederick L[afayette] Jones, ed. [A1]

1953 *My Best Mary* [selected letters]. Muriel Spark and Derek Stanford, eds. [A8]

"*Tempo e' piu du Morire*" (poem). [E15]

"La vida es sueño" (poem). [E16]

"[Fragment] Alas I weep my life away." [E17]

"[Fragment] Struggle no more, my Soul with the sad chains." [E18]

1959 *Mathilda.* Elizabeth Nitchie, ed. [B1g & B2g]

APPENDIX II

THE LEGEND OF GEORGE OF FRANKENSTEIN

The following recounting of the heroic George of Frankenstein and
the salamander-like monster is reprinted from F. J. Kiefer's The Legends
of the Rhine from Basle to Rotterdam. L. W. Garnham, trans. (Mayence:
David Kapp [1868]), pp. 72-75, first printed in German ca. 1847, translated into French in 1847, and last reprinted, as far as I have been able
to determine, in 1892, in English. Whether Mary Shelley knew of the
legend or not is highly debatable—she may have merely chosen the name,
Frankenstein, on a whim, or she may have had ulterior motives, as at least
two writers suspect. (See A231, B103, B104, B116, and Addenda in this
bibliography, for speculation concerning the name and the castle at
Niederbeerbach.) But the legend has interest in its own right, and in a
possible but unlikely connection with Mary Shelley's novel. I reprint
it to make it more available to anyone pursuing the connection. The text
is from the 1868 edition, at the Sterling Library of Yale University.

In ancient times the neighbourhood of Frankenstein on the mountain-
way was infested by a huge monster, which had chosen for its sojourn the
vale of Modaubachs, covered with reeds and underwood. The monster had a
serpent-like figure of powerful length, having a regularly formed thick
head and jaws that could have swallowed an ox. The terror which was
spread among the inhabitants of the country by the presence of such a
monster was so much the greater, because it not only regarded their
flocks and herds, but even men as its booty; and almost daily a human
being was its sacrifice.

Uselessly some bold champions had made the attempt to destroy the
dragon, they were obliged to pay, with their lives, their temerity, and
soon nobody more was to be found who had the least wish for a combat with
the monster; complete pusillanimity overpowered all spirits, and whoever
could, removed far from the country as if the plague ravaged there.

Not far from this place of terror, however on the other side of
Eberstadt; lived at that time, George of Frankenstein at a castle, the
ruins of which still look down upon the beautiful Rhine valley, from its
far seen woody eminence. He was a brave knight, and celebrated champion,
his gigantic bodily form, and the strength of his arm had always procured
his arms the victory, so that also in gymnastics nobody ventured to enter
the lists with him.

George heard the lamentation of the poor inhabitants of the Modau-
bach valley, who wandered about homeless, their necessity affected him,
and he resolved to try a combat with the monster however furious and
terrific it might be.

On a war-horse suitable to the size of the champion, armed with
sword club, and armour, he rode into the abandoned valley, and soon he
saw the monster in the willow-ground, rolled together and comfortably
sunning itself. Awakened by the noise of the approaching knight, it rose
hissing, and in making a long spring, at the hoped for booty; opened its
immense jaws as if he would swallow, at once, man and horse. But of firm
courage, although his horse reared, the knight waited for his monstrous
enemy, and as it was near enough, the courageous made a dexterous side
spring, and avoided the greedy snapping of the dragon, and seeing his
advantage, he thrust his sword into the neck of the salamander. Then he
seized his heavy club, and struck the monster (that attacked him again
grazing him with its bloody teeth), so violently on the head, that it
fell stunned to the earth, and could be killed without trouble.

In the meanwhile the squires of the knight, and many people waited
in the distance the announcement of the hero's enterprise, and the result
of the struggle, and as now one blew the hunter's horn as joyful sign of
the victory, and the hurrying persons saw the monster lying in its blood,
a joyous cry arose, and thousands of voices praised the heroic act. But
suddenly the knight's face was deadly pale, he sank to the earth, and
could only say, with weak voice that he felt himself deadly wounded, by
the poisonous teeth of the animal. Terrified, the knight's armour was
loosened, and not to be mistaken was seen a slight wound on the hip, into
which the terrible serpent's poison had penetrated.

The general joy for the obtained victory, was now changed into
mourning for the hero, like that celebrated Saintly hero George, treading
on the dragon's neck, died after some minutes. His memory is still with
the grateful inhabitants.

In the village of Nieder-Beerbach, one sees near the church-door,
still to this day; a grave stone on which is represented by an artistic
hand, the knight triumphantly advancing to the dragon.

APPENDIX III

THEATRICAL, FILM, AND TELEVISION
VERSIONS OF FRANKENSTEIN

A THEATRICAL VERSIONS

1   Richard Brinsley Peake. *Presumption; or, The Fate of Frankenstein.*
     1823.
     MS mentions seeing this version in a letter to Leigh Hunt of
     September 9, 1823 [cf. IA7, Vol. I, p. 259], which was first pre-
     sented in July at the English Opera House.
     A playbill for the sixth performance, on August 2, gives an
     extract from the first paragraph of Shelley's Preface to the MS
     novel, and gives the following cast: Frankenstein, Mr. Wallack;
     De Lacey (a banished gentleman), Mr. Rowbotham ; Felix De Lacey
     (his Son), Mr. Pearman; Fritz, Mr. Keeley; Clerval, Mr. J. Bland;
     William, Master Boden; Hammerpan, Mr. Salter; Tanskin, Mr. Shield;
     Guide, Mr. R. Phillips; Gypsey, Mr. H. Phillips; (------), Mr. T.
     P. Cooke, Elizabeth (Sister of Frankenstein), Mrs. Austin; Agatha
     De Lacey, Miss L. Dance; Safie (an Arabian Girl), Miss Holdaway;
     Madame Ninon (Wife of Fritz), Mrs. J. Weippert; Chorus of Gypsies,
     Peasants.
     A playbill for September 29 mentions the "unabated attraction"
     of the play. Revived in 1824 at the English Opera House and Covent
     Garden, and in 1826 at the English Opera House, with a new scene.
     This new version also ran at the Theatre-Royal, Liverpool, from
     June 9 to June 13, 1828, with especial billing for Thomas Potter
     Cooke as the unnamed Monster. A playbill for June 11 gives the
     following cast: (*********), Mr. T. P. Cooke; Frankenstein, Mr.
     Elton; Clerval (his friend, in love with Elizabeth), Mr. King;
     William (Brother of Frankenstein), Master F. Lloyds; De Lacey (a
     banished Gentleman), Mr. Webster; Felix (his son), Mr. Raymond;
     Fritz (Servant of Frankenstein), Mr. W. J. Hammond; Tanskin (a
     Gipsy), Mr. Barrett; Hammerpan (a Tinker), Mr. Smith; A Guide, Mr.
     Gardiner; Gipsies, Messrs. Herbert, Benwell, Wilton, Thornhill, &
     Morelli; Elizabeth (Frankenstein's Sister), Miss Eyre; Agatha
     (Daughter of De Lacey), Miss Taylor; Safie (an Arabian girl, be-
     trothed to Felix), Miss Holdaway; Madame Ninon (Housekeeper to
     Elizabeth, and Wife of Fritz), Mrs. Clarke; Gipsies, Villagers.
     The playbill also notes the following:
     "Incidental to the Piece, the following new and appropriate
     scenery—in Act First, Foreign Interior connected with Franken-
     stein's Laboratory. Frankenstein's Sleeping Room. In Act Second,

Romantic Country and Gipsies' Rendezvous. Interior of De Lacey's
Cottage destroyed by Fire. In Act Third, Mountains of Snow, with
the destruction of Frankenstein, and (******) by an Avalanche."
Reviewed in *The London Magazine*, 8 (September 1823), 322-323;
satirical reference in the *Episcopal Gazette: A Journal of Priest-
craft and Knavery*, No. 1 (March 1, 1832), 2; mention in *The Opera
Glass* (October 23,1826), 30-31. See also Elizabeth Nitchie [IIB250,
pp. 384, 385-386, 387-392], Clement Scott [A371], and Donald F.
Glut [A4, pp. 28-33], the last mentioning the manuscript of the
play in the Huntington Library.

2 Henry M. Milner. *Frankenstein; or, The Demon of Switzerland*.
   1823.

3 *Humgumption; or, Dr. Frankenstein and the Hobgoblin of Hoxton*.
   1823.

4 *Frankenstein; or, The Danger of Presumption*. 1823.

5 Richard Brinsley Peake. *Another Piece of Presumption*. 1823.
   A burlesque; opened at the Adelphi on October 20.

6 *Frank-In-Steam; or, The Modern Promise to Pay*. 1824.
   A burlesque. See Donald F. Glut [IIA4, pp. 33-34].

7 *The Devil Among the Players*. 1826.
   The Opera Glass (October 9, 1826), 14, contains a poem con-
   cerning the popularity of the play, stanzas VI and VII of which
   follow:
   "What shall I say of Frankenstein,
       Such crowds each night attracting?
   The devil's in it, I maintain;
   And as for Cooke—Why his, 'tis plain,
       Is *monstrous* clever acting!
   In Paris how he made them stare,
       While looking fierce this part in!
   'Twas voted by the gay Parterre
   Fit for the Barriere d'Enfer,
       Rather than Porte St. Martin!"
   See also Donald F. Glut [IIA4, pp. 38-39].

8 Merle and Anthony. *Le Monstre et le Magicien*. 1826.
   At the Porte St. Martin, Paris, with T. P. Cooke as the Mon-
   ster for a while.
   See also Items 7 and 10, and Donald F. Glut [IIA4, p. 34].

9 Henry M. Milner. *The Man and the Monster; or, The Fate of Frankenstein*. 1826.
   Partially based on Merle and Anthony's play; opened at the
   Royal Coburg, July 3. A playbill for that date gives the following
   cast: The Prince del Piombino (a Sicilian Nobleman, and Patron of
   the Arts and Sciences), Mr. Hemmings; Frankenstein (a Professor of
   Natural Philosophy, attached to the Prince's Household), Mr.

Rowbotham; Ritzberg (a German, Father to Emmeline), Mr. Meredith; Strutt (Servant to Frankenstein), Mr. E. L. Lewis; Quadro (Butler to the Prince), Mr. Goldsmith; Julio (the Prince's Son), Miss Burnett; (******), Mr. O. Smith; Rosaura (Sister of the Prince del Piombino), Mrs. Lewis; Emmeline (betrothed to Frankenstein), Mrs. Young; Lisetta (Daughter of Quadro), Mrs. Rowbotham. The playbill also summarizes the plot: Frankenstein creates the Monster in his study; the Monster, rejected by society, murders the Prince's son; Frankenstein is accused of the murder; the Monster sets the cottage of the Ritzbergs' on fire, taking away Emmeline and her child to the summit of Mount Aetna; the Monster falls into the volcano ("the first attempt ever made to display this tremendous Spectacle [the volcano] on the Stage").

Also titled *Frankenstein! or, The Man and the Monster*; revived under this title at the Theatre Royal, Birmingham. A playbill for this performance, on December 2, 1857, gives the following cast: The Monster, Sir William Don; The Prince, Mr. Ashley; Frankenstein, Mr. Barton; Ritzberg, Mr. Munro; Quadro, Mr. Manders; Strutt, Mr. H. Leigh; Julio, Master Simonds; Emmeline, Miss S. Vivash; Lisetta, Miss Eliza Webb; Rosara, Miss Evans; Peasants, Soldiers.

Published as H. M. Milner. *Frankenstein: or The Man and the Monster. A Romantic Melo-Drama in Two Acts. Founded principally on Mrs. Shelley's singular work entitled Frankenstein; Or, The Modern Prometheus. And partly on the French piece, "Le Magicien et le Monstre"* [sic]. In *Lacy's Acting Edition of Plays: Dramas, Farces, Extravaganzas, etc.* London: Thomas Hailes Lacy [ca. 1830], Vol. 75, pp. 1-37 (separately paginated). In this version, the mute Monster, repulsed by everyone, kills the servant Julio, kidnaps Emmeline and her child, but is softened by her soft sweet music. He is captured once, but escapes to the summit of Mount Aetna. There, already wounded, he is fired upon by angry peasants, but before dying manages to stab Frankenstein and to throw his creator from the mountain (who is caught, lifeless, by Emmeline). Mortally wounded, the Monster hurls himself into the lava-belching crater of the volcano.

See also Donald F. Glut [IIA4, pp. 34-38], who prints part of the play.

10   J. Kerr. *The Monster and the Magician.* 1826.
Based on Merle and Anthony's play; opened at the New Royal West London Theatre, October 9.

11   *Frankenstein; or, The Vampire's Victim.* 1849.
Mentioned by Donald F. Glut [IIA4, p. 39].

12   William Brough and Robert Barnabas Brough. *Frankenstein; or, The Model Man.* 1849.
Opened at the Adelphi, ca. December. A playbill for January 14, 1850, advertises the play (somewhat cheerfully) as "a Gross Piece of 'Presumption' on the part of the Authors . . . In the Shape of an Entirely New Composite Polytechnic Extravaganza," under the direction of Madame Celeste. The elaborate and amusing cast list is as follows:

"The Characters may be classed under Three heads, viz: I.—
Characters which, properly speaking, belong to the Story, being
in the Original Legend. · Frankenstein (The Student Senior Wrangler
of Brazenface College, in the University of Krackenjausen, an eminent manufacturer causing the deepest distress in his own immediate
district), Mr. Wright; The What Is It? (a singular being who may be
most aptly and expressively described as '——' a curious compound
of many qualities—an animated character), Mr. Paul Bedford.
      "II.—Characters which do not exactly belong to the Story, but
which, being creations of the Authors' own, they maintain they have
a right to do what they like with   Baron Von Donnerundblitzen (a
genuine German Baron of the old school slightly modified by the
advanced spirit of the age), Mr. C. J. Smith; Otto of Rosenberg (a
very nice Fellow of a first-rate College at the University of
Krackenjausen), Miss Woolgar; Tiddliwincz (a Fellow (much) Commoner
of the same), Miss Ellen Chaplin; Ratzbaen (an Evil as well as a
Pantomimic Genius), Mr. Hitchenson; Frightz (a 'Baron's Retainer'),
Mr. J. Sanders; Master of the Ceremonies, Mr. Freeborn; Agatha (the
Baron's beautiful (of course) Daughter, beloved by every body (but
Frankenstein) & by Otto of Rosenberg particularly), Miss Harriet
Coveney; Bobinetta (her (it is needless to say) faithful Attendant),
Miss Turner; Students, Peasants, Guests, Populace.
      "III.—Characters with which, honestly speaking, the Authors
have no business at all, and like their impudence to make use of
them, being other people's property. Zamiel (The Demon of the
Hartz and Sciences—a victim to the March of Intellect), Mr. O.
Smith (Who is supposed to have played something of the sort
before—if it could only be known); Undine (the Spirit of the
Flood & Managing Directress of the Water-works), Miss E. Harding;
Fire Water Spirits."
      The playbill also briefly summarizes the seven scenes of the
play.

13   Ferdinand Dugué. *Le Monstre et le Magicien.* 1861.
      New version of Merle and Anthony's play.

14   Richard Henry [pseud. of Richard Butler and H. Chance Newton].
      Frankenstein, A Melodramatic Burlesque in 3 Acts. 1887.
      Opened at the Gaiety on December 24, with Fred Leslie as the
      Monster, who was created by a young girl named Mary Ann (played
      by Nellie Farren), and without Frankenstein.
      See also Elizabeth Nitchie [IIB250, pp. 396-397], Donald F.
      Glut [A4, pp. 39-42]; and W. Macqueen-Pope [A262].

15   *The Last Laugh.* 1915.
      In New York. Mentioned by Donald F. Glut [IIA4, p. 42] and
      Edmund Lester Pearson [A327, p. xii].

16   Peggy Webling. *Frankenstein: An Adventure in the Macabre.* 1927.
      Opened at the Preston in London; re-opened at London's Little
      Theatre on February 10, 1930, with Henry Hallat as Henry Franken-
      stein and Hamilton Deane as the Monster. The basis for the 1931

film by James Whale.
Reviewed in *The Nation & Athenæum*, 46 (February 22, 1930), 703. See also Elizabeth Nitchie [IIB250, pp. 393-394]; Donald F. Glut [A4, pp. 42-45]; Ivan Butler [A81, p. 46]; Harry Ludlam, *A Biography of Dracula. The Life Story of Bram Stoker* (London: The Quality Book Club, 1962), p. 166; and Paul M. Jensen, *Boris Karloff and His Films* (South Brunswick, N.J.; N.Y.: A. S. Barnes/London: The Tantivy Press [1975]), pp. 21 n., 28.

17   Gladys Hastings-Walton. *Frankenstein*. 1933.
In Glasgow. Mentioned by Elizabeth Nitchie [IIB250, p. 394].

18   Alfred Kreymborg. *Frank and Mr. Frankenstein*. 1935.

19   The Living Theatre. *Frankenstein*. 1965.
A bizarre, freewheeling adaptation in three acts, incorporating the Golem, Paracelsus, Norbert Wiener, the Four Horsemen of the Apocalypse, and police repression of everyone involved.
For photographs from the production, quotations from reviews, and a sketch of the basic, though always changing in actual performances, script, see Aldo Rostagno, Julian Beck, and Judith Malina, *We, The Living Theatre. A pictorial documentation by Gianfranco Mantegna of the life and the pilgrimage of The Living Theatre in Europe and in the U.S. and of the productions of* Mysteries *and* Smaller Pieces. Antigone. Frankenstein. Paradise Now. *Introduced by a panel discussion on* Theatre as Revolution *coordinated by Aldo Rostagno with the participation of Julian Beck and Judith Malina. With an Appendix of selected documents and reviews from the American Press* (N.Y.: Ballantine Books, 1970), pp. 110-135. See also Donald F. Glut [IIA4, pp. 49-52] and Gianni Eugenio Viola, *Frankenstein. Interpretazione del Living* (Catania, Italy: Underground-La Fiaccola, 1972).

20   The San Francisco Mime Troupe. *Frankenstein*. 1967.
Mentioned by Donald F. Glut [IIA4, p. 46].

B FILM VERSIONS

1   *Frankenstein*. Thomas Edison Studios, 1910.
Director: J. Searle Dawley. Producer: Thomas Edison.
Cast: Charles Ogle (*the Monster*).
For many years, a film entitled *Frankenstein's Trestle* (1899) was thought to be the first film version of the MS novel, but that film, of a locomotive passing over a bridge, was only shot in the town of Frankenstein, New Hampshire—thus the title. Edison's film is the first adaptation, but unfortunately no longer survives. A synopsis of the film may be found in "The Return of Frankenstein," *Famous Monsters of Filmland*, No. 110 (September 1974), 61, reprinted from the March 15, 1910 issue of the Edison *Kinetogram*; Denis Gifford reproduces three photographic stills from the film in his

Movie Monsters (London: Studio Vista/N.Y.: E. P. Dutton, 1969),
pp. 8, 10; and the scenario is reprinted as "Frankenstein Meets
the Edison Company," in Roy Huss and T. J. Ross, eds., *Focus on
the Horror Film* (Englewood Cliffs, N.J.: Prentice-Hall, 1972),
pp. 66-69. See also Lewis Jacobs, *The Rise of the American Film,
A Critical History* (N.Y.: Harcourt, Brace, 1939), p. 126.

2   *Life Without Soul.* Ocean Film Corporation, 1915.
     Director: Joseph W. Smiley. Producer: George DeCarlton.
     Scenario: Jesse J. Goldburg.
     Cast: Percy Darrell Standing (*the Monster*), William A. Cohill
     (*Frankenstein*), Lucy Cotton (*Elizabeth*), George DeCarlton (*father
     of Frankenstein*), Pauline Curley, Jack Hopkins, Violet De Biccari,
     David McCauley.
     The film, like Edison's version, no longer survives. For dis-
     cussion, see Donald F. Glut [IIA4, pp. 63-67]; for a photographic
     still, see Denis Gifford, *Movie Monsters* (London: Studio Vista/
     N.Y.: E. P. Dutton, 1969), p. 11.

3   *Il Mostro di Frankenstein.* Italy, 1920.
     Director: Eugenio Testa. Scenario: Giovanni Drovetti.
     Cast: Umberto Guarracino (*the Monster*), Luciano Alberti.
     Little is known of this film; the present author's correspon-
     dence with the Cineteca Nazionale in Rome and the Museo Nazionale
     del Cinema in Torino has verified the existence of the film only;
     no synopsis or photographic stills apparently survive.

4   *Frankenstein.* Universal Studios, 1931.
     Director: James Whale. Producer: Carl Laemmle, Jr. Scenar-
     io: Garrett Fort, Francis Edward Faragoh, and John L. Balderston,
     from Peggy Webling's play. Photography: Arthur Edeson. Art
     Designer: Charles D. Hall. Sets: Herman Rosse. Special Effects:
     John P. Fulton. Make-up: Jack Pierce. Editor: Clarence Kolster.
     Cast: Colin Clive (*Henry Frankenstein*), Boris Karloff (*the
     Monster*), Mae Clarke (*Elizabeth*), Edward Van Sloan (*Dr. Waldman*),
     John Boles (*Sir Victor Morris*), Dwight Frye (*Fritz, assistant to
     Frankenstein*), Frederick Kerr (*Baron Frankenstein*), Lionel Belmore
     (*Burgomaster*), Marilyn Harris (*Maria*), Michael Mark (*Ludwig, father
     of Maria*), Arletta Duncan and Pauline Moore (*Bridesmaids*), Otis
     Harlan and Francis Ford (*Villagers*).
     Robert Florey was originally scheduled to direct the film;
     Leslie Howard to portray Henry Frankenstein, and Bette Davis the
     part of Elizabeth.
     The filmscript, with numerous photographic stills, has been
     published [cf. IIA30]; see also Donald F. Glut [A4, pp. 90-120];
     Forrest J. Ackerman, ed., *Boris Karloff: The Frankenscience
     Monster* (N.Y.: Ace Books, 1969); Denis Gifford, *Karloff: The Man,
     The Monster, The Movies* (N.Y.: Curtis Books, 1973); Jack Pierce,
     "Character Make-up," *American Cinematographer* (May 1932), 8-9, 43;
     and A219, B127, B85, B189.
     The popularity of this film, released in December, gave rise to
     seven sequels: *Bride of Frankenstein, Son of Frankenstein, Ghost*

*of Frankenstein, Frankenstein Meets the Wolf Man, House of Franken-
stein, House of Dracula,* and *Abbott and Costello Meet Frankenstein.*

5   *Bride of Frankenstein.* Universal Studios, 1935.
        Director: James Whale. Producer: Carl Laemmle, Jr. Scenar-
     io: William Hurlbut and John L. Balderston. Photography: John
     Mescall. Art Director: Charles D. Hall. Special Properties:
     Kenneth Strickfaden. Special Effects: John P. Fulton. Make-up:
     Jack Pierce. Music: Franz Waxman. Design of "Bride" Make-up:
     James Whale, Ernest Thesiger, and Jack Pierce.
        Cast: Boris Karloff *(the Monster),* Colin Clive *(Henry Franken-
     stein),* Valerie Hobson *(Elizabeth),* Elsa Lanchester *(Mary Shelley/
     the "Bride"),* O. P. Heggie *(Hermit),* Ernest Thesiger *(Dr. Prae-
     torius),* Gavin Gordon *(Lord Byron),* Douglas Walton *(Percy Bysshe
     Shelley),* Dwight Frye *(Karl, assistant to Praetorius),* Lucien
     Prival *(Otto, the Butler),* Una O'Connor *(Minnie, servant to Frank-
     enstein),* E. E. Clive *(Burgomaster),* Reginald Barlowe *(Hans, father
     of Maria* [in the 1931 film]*),* Mary Gordon *(Wife of Hans),* Ann
     Darling *(Shepherdess),* Ted Billings *(Ludwig, assistant to Prae-
     torius),* John Carradine *(Hunter),* Neil Fitzgerald, Tempe Piggott,
     Grace Cunard, Rollo Lloyd, Walter Brennan. HOMUNCULI: Monty
     Montague *("Henry VIII" King),* Joan Woodbury *(Queen),* Norman Aisley
     (Archbishop), Peter Shaw *(Devil),* Kansas De Forest *(Ballerina),*
     Josephine McKim *(Mermaid),* Billy Barty *(Baby* [omitted from final
     print of film]*).*
        A semi-satirical sequel to the 1931 film, not unlike (at least
     in the cast list) the early theatrical burlesques. Mary Shelley,
     Shelley, and Byron are featured in the Prologue to the film, the
     latter recounting the "story" of the novel as portions of the 1931
     film are shown on the screen.
        For reviews, see *Illustrated London News,* 186 (June 29, 1935),
     1170; *Newsweek,* 5 (May 4, 1935), 25; and *Time,* 25 (April 29, 1935),
     52. See also Donald F. Glut [IIA4, pp. 121-132]; Denis Gifford
     [A167]; Roy Huss [A113]; and Chris Steinbrunner and Burt Goldblatt,
     Cinema of the Fantastic (N.Y.: Saturday Review Press, 1972), pp.
     89-106. For a novelization of the film, see Michael Egremont
     [F11].

6   *Son of Frankenstein.* Universal Studios, 1939.
        Director & Producer: Rowland V. Lee. Scenario: Willis
     Cooper. Photography: George Robinson. Art Director: Jack
     Otterson and Richard Reidel. Sets: R. A. Gausman. Make-up:
     Jack Pierce. Music: Frank Skinner. Editor: Ted Kent.
        Cast: Boris Karloff *(the Monster),* Basil Rathbone *(Wolf von
     Frankenstein),* Bela Lugosi *(Ygor),* Lionel Atwill *(Police Inspector
     Krogh),* Josephine Hutchinson *(Elsa, wife of Wolf),* Donnie Dunnagan
     (Peter, son of Wolf), Edgar Norton *(Benson, the Butler),* Emma Dunn
     (Amelia, servant to the Frankensteins), Lawrence Grant *(Burgo-
     master),* Perry Ivins *(Fritz),* Michael Mark *(Ewald Neumiller),*
     Caroline Cook *(Frau Neumiller),* Lionel Belmore *(Emil Lang),* Gustav
     von Seyfferitz, Lorimer Johnson, and Tom Rickets *(Burghers).*
        In this, the second sequel to the 1931 film, the son of Henry
     Frankenstein returns to his ancestral home, encounters the Monster,

who has found the friendship of a badly-hanged shepherd named Ygor, and "re-animates" his father's creation.
See Donald F. Glut [IIA4, pp. 134-144].

7   *Ghost of Frankenstein*. Universal Studios, 1942.
    Director: Erle C. Kenton. Producer: George Waggner. Scenario: W. Scott Darling, from a story by Eric Taylor. Photography: Milton Krasner and Woody Bredell. Art Director: Jack Otterson. Make-up: Jack Pierce and Ellis Burman. Music: Hans J. Salter and Charles Previn. Editor: Ted Kent.
    Cast: Lon Chaney, Jr. (*the Monster*), Bela Lugosi (*Ygor*), Cedric Hardwicke (*Ludwig Frankenstein*), Evelyn Ankers (*Elsa Frankenstein*), Barton Yarborough (*Dr. Kettering*), Lionel Atwill (*Dr. Bohmer*), Ralph Bellamy (*Eric*), Janet Ann Gallow (*Celestine*), Doris Lloyd (*Martha*), Eddie Parker (*double for Lon Chaney, Jr.*), Leyland Hodgson, Olaf Hytten, Holmes Herbert, Lawrence Grant, Brandon Hurst, Dwight Frye, Julius Tannen, Otto Hoffmann, Lionel Belmore, Harry Cording, Michael Mark, Dick Alexander, George Eldredge, Ernie Stanton.
    The third sequel features Ludwig, the second son of Henry Frankenstein, his daughter Elsa, the crazed and neglected Dr. Bohmer, Ygor, and a temporarily-weakened and permanently-subhuman Monster.
    See Donald F. Glut [IIA4, pp. 153-160].

8   *Frankenstein Meets the Wolf Man*. Universal Studios, 1943.
    Director: Roy William Neill. Producer: George Waggner. Scenario: Curt Siodmak. Photography: George Robinson. Art Director: John B. Goodman. Special Effects: John P. Fulton. Music: Hans J. Salter. Editor: Edward Curtiss.
    Cast: Lon Chaney, Jr. (*Lawrence Talbot, the Wolf Man*), Patric Knowles (*Dr. Frank Mannering*), Ilona Massey (*Baroness Elsa Frankenstein*), Bela Lugosi (*the Monster*), Eddie Parker (*double for Bela Lugosi*), Lionel Atwill (*Mayor*), Maria Ouspenskaya (*Maleva*), Dennis Hoey (*Inspector Owen*), Don Barclay (*Franzec*), Dwight Frye (*Rudi*), Rex Evans (*Vazek*), Harry Stubbs (*Guno*), Torben Meyer, Doris Lloyd, Jeff Corey, David Clyde, Tom Stevenson, Cyril Delevanti.
    A combination sequel to both the 1931 film and to *The Wolf Man* (1941). Lawrence Talbot, trying to escape the lycanthropic curse, and pursued by the curious Dr. Mannering, meets the Monster in the town of Vasaria, where the granddaughter of Henry Frankenstein, Elsa, is visiting. Originally the Monster was intended to be blind in the film (a result of a hasty blood transfusion at the conclusion of *Ghost of Frankenstein*); the omission of references to this created an often-confusing film, in the final sequence of which the Monster and the metempsychotic Talbot/Wolf Man battled in a dissolving laboratory.
    See also Donald F. Glut [IIA4, pp. 160-166].

9   *House of Frankenstein*. Universal Studios, 1945.
    Director: Erle C. Kenton. Producer: Paul Malvern. Scenario: Edward T. Loewe, from a story by Curt Siodmak. Photography: George Robinson. Art Director: John B. Goodman and Martin Obzina.

Make-up: Jack Pierce. Special Effects: John P. Fulton. Music: Hans J. Salter.
Cast: Boris Karloff (*Dr. Gustav Niemann*), Lon Chaney, Jr. (*Lawrence Talbot, the Wolf Man*), John Carradine (*"Baron Latos"—Count Dracula*), J. Carroll Naish (*Daniel, assistant to Niemann*), Glenn Strange (*the Monster*), George Zucco (*Prof. Lampini*), Anne Gwynne (*Rita Hussman*), Peter Coe (*Carl Hussman*), Lionel Atwill (*Inspector Arnz*), Elena Verdugo (*Ilonka, a Gypsy*), Sig Rumann (*Burgermaster Hussman*), William Edmunds (*Fejos*), Julius Tannen (*Hertz*), Charles Miller (*Toberman*), Philip Van Zandt (*Muller*), Hans Herbert (*Meier*), Dick Dickinson (*Born*), George Lynn (*Gerlach*), Michael Mark (*Strauss*), Frank Reicher (*Ullman*), Olaf Hytten (*Hoffman*), Brandon Hurst (*Dr. Geissler*), Belle Mitchell, Eddie Cobb.

A combination sequel to the 1931 film, *The Wolf Man* (1941), and *Dracula* (1931). Mad doctor Niemann meets Lawrence Talbot, Dracula, and the Monster (the last in a minor role), along the way to his laboratory-home, where, pursued by irritated villagers, he is carried off to a swamp full of quicksand by the resuscitated Monster.

See also Donald F. Glut [IIA4, pp. 167-175].

10   *House of Dracula*. Universal Studios, 1945.
Director: Erle C. Kenton. Executive Producer: Joe Gershenson. Producer: Paul Malvern. Scenario: Edward T. Loewe, from a story by George Bricker and Dwight V. Babcock. Photography: George Robinson. Art Director: Joe B. Goodman and Martin Obzina. Special Effects: John P. Fulton. Make-up: Jack Pierce and Joe Hadley. Music: Hans J. Salter and Edgar Fairchild. Hair Styles: Carmen Dirigo. Editor: Russell Schoengarth.
Cast: Lon Chaney, Jr. (*Lawrence Talbot, the Wolf Man*), John Carradine (*"Baron Latos"—Count Dracula*), Onslow Stevens (*Dr. Franz Edelmann*), Glenn Strange (*the Monster*), Lionel Atwill (*Inspector Holtz*), Martha O'Driscoll (*Miliza Morrell*), Jane Adams (*Nina, assistant to Edelmann*), Ludwig Stossel (*Ziegfried*), Skelton Knaggs (*Steinmuhl*), Joseph E. Bernard (*Brahms*), Gregory Muradian (*Johannes*), Beatrice Gray (*Mother*), Fred Cordova and Carey Harrison (*Policemen*), Dick Dickinson (*Villager*), Harry Lamont.

As with *House of Frankenstein*, a combination sequel to the 1931 film, *The Wolf Man* (1941), and *Dracula* (1931). Kindly, respected, and skilled Dr. Edelmann encounters and attempts to cure, by 1945-scientific methods, Dracula, the Wolf Man, and the Frankenstein Monster. Dracula infects the doctor, who becomes a Jekyll/Hyde character, the Wolf Man is cured, and the Monster is glimpsed near the film's conclusion, destroyed in a burning laboratory.

See also Donald F. Glut [IIA4, pp. 175-178].

11   *Abbott and Costello Meet Frankenstein*. Universal Studios, 1948.
Director: Charles T. Barton. Producer: Robert Arthur. Scenario: Robert Lees, Frederic Rinaldo, and John Frant. Photography: Charles Van Enger. Art Director: Bernard Herzbrun and Hilyard Brown. Special Effects: David S. Horsely and Jerome H. Ash. Make-up: Jack Kewan and Bud Westmore. Music: Frank Skinner. Editor: Frank Gross.

Cast: Lou Costello (*Wilbur Gray*), Bud Abbott (*Chick Young*), Lon Chaney, Jr. (*Lawrence Talbot, the Wolf Man*), Bela Lugosi ("*Dr. Latos*"—*Count Dracula*), Glenn Strange (*the Monster*), Frank Ferguson (*MacDougall*), Jane Randolph (*Joan Raymond*), Lenore Aubert (*Dr. Sandra Mornay*), Charles Bradstreet (*Dr. Stevens*), Vincent Price (*the voice of "The Invisible Man"*), Joe Kirk, Bobby Barber, Harry Brown.

Very loosely based on the characters from the *Frankenstein* series and incorporating the title character from *The Invisible Man* (1933). Abbott and Costello are involved in a series of farcical episodes with the "monsters."

See also Donald F. Glut [IIA4, pp. 179-186.

12   *Torticola contre Frankensberger*. Marceau Films (France), 1952.
Director: Paul Paviot. Scenario: Luis Sapin and Albert Vidalie. Photography: André Thomas. Sets: Jamé Allan and Alexandre Trauner. Scenery: Charles Bretoneiche. Make-up: Hagop Arakélian. Music: Joseph Kosma.

Cast: Michel Piccoli (*Torticola*), Roger Blin (*Dr. Frankensberger*), Vera Norman (*Lorelei*), François Patrice (*Eric von Meusenberger*), Marc Boussac (*Fürrenspiegel*), Héléna Menson (Housekeeper), Daniel Gélin.

Consists of three 10-minute episodes: "Le Laboratoire de l'epouvante," "La Proie du maudit," and "Le Monstre avait un cœur." A parody of the Universal films, involving a stiff-necked monster named Torticola.

See also Luis Gasca [IIE15].

13   "Una de Miedo" in *Tres Eran Tres*. Cooperativa del Cinema (Spain), 1955.
Director & Scenarist: Eduardo García Maroto. Photography: Heinrich Gaertner and Carlos Pahissa Lopez. Sets: Tadeo Villalba Ruiz. Scenery: Bienvenida Sanz. Music: Augosto Algueró Algueró and Daniel Montorio Fajo.

Cast: Manuel Arbó del Val (*the Frankenstein Monster*), Manolo Moran (*Sr. Ulpiano*), Antonio Riquelme (*Dr. Salsamendi*), Gustavo Re (*Don Sisebuto*), Luis Sanchez Polack ["Tip"] (*Estanislao*), Joaquín Portillo ["Top"] (*Epaminondas*), Matilde de Múgica (*Carmen*), Antonio Casas (*Nicolás*), Jacinto San Emeterio (*Pepe*), Rosita Palomar.

See Luis Gasca [IIE15].

14   *I Was a Teenage Frankenstein*. American-International, 1957.
Director: Herbert L. Strock. Producer: Herman Cohen. Scenario & Story: Kenneth Langtry. Photography: Lathrop Worth. Art Director: Leslie Thomas. Make-up: Philip Scheel. Music: Paul Dunlap. Editor: Jerry Young.

Cast: Whit Bissell (*Dr. Frankenstein*), Gary Conway (the "*teenage Monster*"), Phyllis Coates (*Margaret*), Robert Burton (*Dr. Karlton*), George Lynn (*Sgt. Burns*), John Cliff (*Sgt. McAffee*), Marshall Bradford (*Dr. Randolph*), Claudia Bryar (*Arlene's mother*), Angela Blake (*sexy girl*), Russ Whiteman (*Dr. Elwood*), Gretchen Thomas (*woman in corridor*), Joy Stoner (*Arlene*), Larry Carr (*young man*),

Paul Keast (*man at automobile crash*), Charles Seel (*Jeweler*), Pat
Miller (*Police Officer*).
Partial satire involving a 20th-century descendant of Victor
Frankenstein.

15 *Curse of Frankenstein*. Hammer Films (Great Britain), 1957.
Director: Terence Fisher. Executive Producer: Michael
Carreras. Associate Producer: Anthony Nelson-Keys. Producer:
Anthony Hinds. Scenario: Jimmy Sangster. Photography: Jack
Asher. Art Director: Ted Marshall. Make-up: Phil Leakey.
Music: James Bernard. Editor: James Needs.
Cast: Peter Cushing (*Baron Victor Frankenstein*), Christopher
Lee (*the Creature*), Hazel Court (*Elizabeth*), Robert Urquhart
(*Paul Krempe, tutor and later assistant to Frankenstein*), Valerie
Gaunt (*Justine*), Melvyn Hayes (*the young Victor*), Paul Hardtmuth
(*Prof. Bernstein*), Fred Johnson (*Grandfather*), Noël Hood (*Aunt
Sofie*), Alex Gallier (*Priest*), Michael Mulcaster (*Warden*), Claude
Kingston (*child in woods*), Ann Blake (*Mayor's Wife*), Sally Walsh
(*Elizabeth, as a young girl*), Marjorie Hume (*Mother*), Henry Caine
(*Teacher*), Patric Troughton (*Kurt*), Joseph Behrman (*Fritz*), Hugh
Dempster (*Mayor*), Raymond Rollet (*Father Felix*), Ernest Jay (*Under-
taker's Employee*), J. Trevor Davis (*Uncle*), Bartlett Mullins
(*Lecturer*), Raymond Ray (*Uncle*), Andrew Leigh (*Burgermaster*).
The first of the British *Frankenstein* series, featuring an
obsessed and coldhearted Victor, a Justine made pregnant by the
master, a "Doctor" Krempe who quotes the Faustian moral, and a
doglike Monster—and a variety of anatomical close-ups, which would
become common in the sequels: *Revenge of Frankenstein, Evil of
Frankenstein, Frankenstein Created Woman, Frankenstein Must Be
Destroyed*, and *Frankenstein and the Monster from Hell*. As Universal Studios used the Monster as a continuing character, the Hammer
series used Victor Frankenstein.
See also Donald F. Glut [IIA4, pp. 189-195], Allen Eyles
[A139], and David Pirie [A336].

16 *El Castillo de los Monstruos*. Producciones Sotomayer (Mexico),
1957.
Director: Julián Soler. Scenario: Fernando Galiana and Carlos
Orellana. Photography: Victor Herrera. Sets: Gunther Gerszo.
Music: Cristavo César Carrión. Editor: Carlos Savage.
Cast: Clavillazo, Evangelina Elizondo, Carlos Orellana, German
Robles, Guillermo Orea, Antonio Espino.
Involves "Frentestein," a vampire, a mummy, a werewolf, and a
gorilla.

17 *Revenge of Frankenstein*. Hammer Films (Great Britain), 1958.
Director: Terence Fisher. Executive Producer: Michael
Carreras. Associate Producer: Anthony Nelson-Keys. Producer:
Anthony Hinds. Scenario: Jimmy Sangster and H. Hurford Janes.
Photography: Jack Asher. Production Designer: Bernard Robinson.
Music: Leonard Salzedo. Make-up: Phil Leakey. Editors: James
Needs and Alfred Cox.
Cast: Peter Cushing (*"Dr. Victor Stein"/"Dr. Frank"—Victor*

Frankenstein), Francis Matthews (*Hans Kleve*), Michael Gwynn (*the "new" Karl*), Eunice Grayson (*Margaret*), John Welsh (*Bergman*), Lionel Jeffries (*Fritz*), Oscar Quitak (*Karl*), John Stuart (*Inspector*), Arnold Diamond (*Molke*), Charles Lloyd Pack (*President of Medical Society*), Richard Wordsworth (*Patient*), George Woodbridge (*Custodian*), Margaret Cresley (*Countess Barscynska*), Anna Walmsley (*Vera Barscynska*), Michael Ripper (*Kurt*), Ian Whittaker (*Boy*), Avril Leslie (*Girl*).

In this sequel to *Curse of Frankenstein*, Victor Frankenstein, with a new identity, transplants the brain of a deformed dwarf into a healthy body, but the "new man" turns cannibalistic.

18   *Frankenstein—1970.* Allied Artists, 1958.
Director: Howard W. Koch. Producer: Aubrey Schenck. Scenario: Richard Landau and George W. Yates, from a story by Charles A. Moses and Aubrey Schenck. Photography: Carl E. Guthrie. Art Director: George Vieira. Sets: George Sweeney. Production Design: Jack T. Collis. Make-up: Gordon Bau. Music: Paul A. Dunlap. Editor: John A. Bushelman.
Cast: Boris Karloff (*Dr. Victor Frankenstein*), Mike Lane (*Hans/the Monster*), Jana Lund (*Carolyn Hayes*), Tom Duggan (*Mike Shaw*), Donald Barry (*Douglas Row*), Charlotte Austin (*Judy Stevens*), Rudolph Anders (*Wilhelm Gottfried*), John C. Dennis (*Morgan Haley*), Norbert Schiller (*Shuter*), Irwin Berke (*Inspector Raab*).
Appropriately, Boris Karloff portrays the 20th-century descendant of Victor Frankenstein, who plays host to a troupe of television personnel while he creates a monster (a double of himself, as revealed in the film's end) using atomic energy.

19   *Frankenstein's Daughter.* Layton (Astor), 1958.
Director: Richard E. Cunha. Producer: Marc Frederick. Scenario: H. E. Barrie. Photography: Meredith Nicholson. Special Effects: Ira Anderson. Make-up: Harry Thomas. Production Manager: Ralph Brooke. Music: Nicholas Carras. Editor: Everett Dodd.
Cast: Donald Murphy (*"Oliver Frank"—Oliver Frankenstein*), John Ashley (*Johnny Bruder*), Harold Lloyd, Jr. (*Don*), Sandra Knight (*Trudy Morton*), Sally Todd (*Suzie*), Felix Locher (*Dr. Carter Morton*), Wolfe Barzell (*Elsu*), John Zaremba, Robert Dix, Harry Wilson, Voltaire Perkins, Charlotte Portney, Bill Coontz, George Barrows, Page Cavanaugh and His Trio.
The deranged grandson of Victor Frankenstein creates a female monster.

20   *Frankenstein, El Vampiro y Cia.* Cinematográfica Calderón (Mexico), 1961.
Director: Benito Alzraki. Producer: Guillermo Calderón Stell. Scenario: Alfredo Salazar, from his story. Photography: Enrique Wallace. Art Director: José Rodriguez Granada. Music: Gustavo Cesár Carrión. Editor: Jorge Bustos.
Cast: Manuel "Loco" Valdés, José Jasso, Nora Veyrán, Martha Elendra Cervantes, Joaquin García Vargas, Arturo Castro, Roberto G.

Rivera, Quintin Bulnes.
Comedy involving the Frankenstein Monster, a vampire, and a werewolf.

21   *The House on Bare Mountain.* Olympic International, 1962.
     Director: R. L. Frost.   Producers: David Andrew and Wes Don.
     Scenario: Denver Scott.   Photography: Greg Sandor.   Scenery:
     Gary Lindsay.   Music: Pierre Martel.
     Cast: Warren Ames (*the Frankenstein Monster*), Jeffrey Smithers
     (*Dracula*), Bob Cresse (*Granny Good*), Laura Eden (*Prudence*), Hugh
     Cannon (*Krakow/Werewolf*), Angela Webster (*Honey*), Ann Meyers
     (*Sally*), Laine Carlin, Letitia Cooper, Connie Hudson, Ingrid Lind,
     Virginia Mark, Betty Peters, Laura Sanders, Millie Stewart, Dan
     Hyland, William Kirk, John Nada, Doc Shannon, J. J. Watson.
     Mildly pornographic film involving a man disguised as the
     Frankenstein Monster at a costume party.

22   *Orlak, El Infierno de Frankenstein.* Independiente (Mexico), 1962.
     Director & Producer: Rafael Baledon.   Scenario: Alfreda
     Ruanova and Carlos E. Taboada.   Photography: Fernando Colin.
     Music: Fondo Jorge Perez.
     Cast: Joaquin Cordero, Armado Calva, Rose de Castilla, Irma
     Dorantes, Andres Soler, Pedro D'Aguillar.
     Involves a Dr. Carlos Frankenstein and a resuscitated corpse.

23   *El Testmento del Frankenstein.* Spain, 1964.
     Director: José Luis Madrid.
     Cast: Gerald Landry (*Dr. Frankenstein*), George Vallis (*the
     Monster*).

24   *Lurk.* Film-makers' Coop; Canyon Cinema, 1964.
     Directors: Red Groom and Rudy Burckhardt.   Scenarist & Nar-
     rator: Edwin Denby.
     Cast: Red Grooms (*the "Frankenstein Monster"*), Edwin Denby
     (*Mad Professor*), Mimi Grooms, Yvonne Burckhardt, Jacob Burckhardt,
     Neil Welliver.
     An "underground" version, shot in Belfast, Maine.

25   *Evil of Frankenstein.* Hammer Films (Great Britain), 1964.
     Director: Freddie Francis.   Producer: Anthony Hinds.   Scenar-
     io: John Elder [pseud. of Anthony Hinds].   Photography: John
     Wilcox.   Special Effects: Les Bowie.   Art Director: Don Mingaye.
     Make-up: Roy Ashton.   Music: Don Banks.   Editor: James Needs.
     Cast: Peter Cushing (*Victor Frankenstein*), Kiwi Kingston (*the
     Monster*), Peter Woodthorpe (*Zoltan*), Sandor Eles (*Hans*), Duncan
     Lamont (*Police Chief*), Katy Wild (*Beggar Girl*), James Maxwell
     (*Priest*), David Hutcheson (*Burgermaster*), Tony Arpino (*Body-
     snatcher*), Caron Gardner (*Burgermaster's Wife*), Howard Goorney
     (*Drunk*), Timothy Bateson (*Hypnotized Man*), Alister Williams (*Land-
     lord*).
     In this, the third Hammer film in the series, Victor returns
     to his ancestral home to find his first monstrous creation, whom

he revives.
Slightly different version released in the U.S.

26 *Jesse James Meets Frankenstein's Daughter.* Circle Productions, 1965.
Director: William Beaudine. Producer: Carroll Case. Scenario: Carl K. Hittleman. Photography: Lothrop Worth. Art Director: Paul Sylos. Music: Raoul Kraushaar. Assistant Director: Howard W. Koch.
Cast: Narda Onyx (*Maria Frankenstein*), Steven Geray (*Rudolf Frankenstein*), John Lupton (*Jesse James*), Carl Dulder (*Hank/"the Monster"/Ygor*), Estelita (*Juanita*), Raymond Barnes (*Lonny*), Jim Davis (*Marshal*), William Faucett (*Jensen*).
The film, accurately titled, was often double-billed with *Billy the Kid vs. Dracula.*

27 *Frankenstein Created Woman.* Hammer-Seven Arts (Great Britain), 1967.
Director: Terence Fisher. Producer: Anthony Nelson-Keys. Scenario: John Elder [pseud. of Anthony Hinds]. Photography: Arthur Grant. Art Director: Don Mingaye. Special Effects: Les Bowie. Make-up: George Partleton. Music: James Bernard. Production Designer: Bernard Robinson. Editor: James Needs.
Cast: Peter Cushing (*Victor Frankenstein*), Susan Denberg (*Christina*), Thorley Walters (*Dr. Hertz*), Robert Morris (*Hans*), Peter Blythe (*Anton*), Barry Warren (*Karl*), Derek Fowlds (*Johann*), Alan MacNaughton (*Kleve*), Peter Madden (*Police Chief*), Stuart Middleton (*Hans, as a boy*), Duncan Lamont (*Prisoner*), Colin Jeavens (*Priest*), Ivan Beavis (*New Landlord*), John Maxim (*Sergeant*), Philip Ray (*Mayor*), Kevin Flood (*Jailer*), Bartlett Mullins (*Bystander*), Alex Mango (*Spokesman*).
Victor Frankenstein transplants a man's soul into the body of a young woman.

28 *Mad Monster Party?* Embassy, 1967.
Director: Jules Bass. Producers: Jules Bass and Arthur Rankin, Jr. Presented by: Joseph Levine. Scenario: Len Korobkin and Harvey Kurtzman, from a story by Arthur Rankin, Jr. Music: Murray Lewis.
Voices: Boris Karloff (*Baron Boris von Frankenstein*), Phyllis Diller (*The Monster's Mate*), Gale Garnett (*Franceska*), Alan Swift (*The Frankenstein Monster; Dracula; The Creature [from the Black Lagoon]; Dr. Jekyll/Mr. Hyde; "It"; King Kong; the Mummy; Werewolf; Mr. Kronkeit; Felix Flanken; The Invisible Man; Quasimodo; Ship Captain; Mate; Yech [Peter Lorre]; Chef Machiavelli; the Skeleton Band; and assorted creatures*).
An animated feature, with puppets.

29 *Frankenstein Must Be Destroyed.* Hammer-Seven Arts (Great Britain), 1969.
Director: Terence Fisher. Producer: Anthony Nelson-Keys. Scenario: Bert Batt, from a story by Anthony Nelson-Keys and Bert

Batt. Photography: Arthur Grant. Art Director: Bernard Robin-
son. Special Effects: Studio Locations, Ltd. Make-up: Eddie
Knight. Music: James Bernard. Editor: Gordon Hales.
Cast: Peter Cushing (*"Mr. Fenner"—Victor Frankenstein*),
Veronica Carlson (*Anna*), Freddie Jones (*Prof. Richter/the "new"
Dr. Frederick Brandt*), Simon Ward (*Karl Holst*), Thorley Walters
(*Inspector Frisch*), Maxine Audley (*Ella Brandt*), George Pravda
(*Dr. Frederick Brandt*), Colette O'Neill (*Mad Woman*), Harold Good-
win (*Burglar*), Peter Copley, Frank Middlemass, Norma Shelley,
Michael Gover, George Belbin, Jim Collier, Allan Surtees, Windsor
Davies, Geoffrey Bayldon.
   Victor Frankenstein, with unusually good intentions, trans-
plants a "mad" brain into another body, in the process curing it.
The "new man" struggles, unsuccessfully, to regain his former
identity.

30   *Horror of Frankenstein.* Hammer-Seven Arts (Great Britain), 1970.
   Director & Producer: Jimmy Sangster. Scenario: Jimmy Sang-
ster and Jeremy Burnham. Photography: Moray Grant. Art Direc-
tor: Scott MacGregor. Make-up: Tom Smith. Music: Malcolm
Williamson. Editor: Chris Barnes.
   Cast: Ralph Bates (*Victor Frankenstein*), Dave Prowse (*the
Monster*), Kate O'Mara (*Alys*), Dennis Price (*Grave Robber*), Veronica
Carlson (*Elizabeth Heiss*), Graham James (*Wilhelm*), Bernard Archard
(*Elizabeth's father*), Joan Rice (*Grave Robber's Wife*), Jon Finch.
   A partial satire of the Hammer series, involving a student
Victor Frankenstein and a brutal, deer-eating Monster.

31   *El Hombre Que Vino del Ummo.* Jaimes Prades/Eichberg Film/Interna-
tional Jaguar (Spain/West Germany/Italy), 1970.
   Director: Julio Demicheli. Producer: Jaimes Prades. Sce-
nario: Jacinta Molina Alvarez. Photography: Godofredo Pachecho.
Art Director: Adolfo Corfiño. Make-up: Francisco R. Ferrer.
Music: Rafael Ferrer. Editor: Emilio Rodriguez.
   Cast: Paul Naschy [Jacinto Molina Alvarez] (*the Frankenstein
Monster/Werewolf*), Michael Rennie (*Alien*), Karin Dor, Craig Hill,
Patty Shepard, Angel del Pozo.
   A sequel to *Frankenstein's Bloody Terror* (which did not involve
Frankenstein or the Monster).
   Credits partially derived from Walt Lee, *Reference Guide to
Fantastic Films. Science Fiction, Fantasy, & Horror.* 3 vols. (Los
Angeles: Chelsea-Lee Books, 1972), Vol. I, p. 112 col. 4.

32   *Dr. Frankenstein on Campus.* [*Frankenstein on Campus; Flick.*]
Agincourt (Canada), 1970.
   Director: Gil Taylor. Producer: Bill Marshall. Scenario:
David Cobb, Bill Marshall, and Gil Taylor. Photography: Jackson
Samuels. Music: Paul Hoffert and Skip Prokop.
   Cast: Robin Ward (*Dr. Frankenstein*), Kathleen Sawyer, Austin
Willis, Sean Sullivan, Ty Haller, Tony Moffat-Lynch.
   A 20th-century Frankenstein creates a monster, whom he monitors
with a remote-control device.

33   *Dracula vs. Frankenstein*. Independent International, 1971.
     Director: Al Adamson. **Executive Producer:** Mardi Rustam.
     Producers: Al Adamson and John Van Horne. **Scenario:** William
     Pugsley and Samuel M. Sherman. **Photography:** Gary Craver and
     Paul Glickman. **Art Director:** Ray Markham. **Special Effects:**
     Kenneth Strickfaden. **Art Design:** Gray Morrow. **Make-up:** George
     Barr. **Music:** William Lava. **Editor:** Erwin Cadden.
     Cast: John Bloom (*the Frankenstein Monster*), Zandor Vorkov
     (*Dracula*), J. Carroll Naish, Lon Chaney, Jr., Anthony Eisley,
     Regina Carol, Angelo Rossitto, Russ Tamblyn, Jim Davis, Forrest J.
     Ackerman.
     Credits partially derived from Walt Lee, *Reference Guide to
     Fantastic Films. Science Fiction, Fantasy, & Horror.* 3 vols. (Los
     Angeles: Chelsea-Lee Books, 1972), Vol. I, p. 113 col. 1.

34   *Dracula contra El Dr. Frankenstein*. Fenix/Comptoir Français du
     Film (Spain/France), 1971.
     Director & Scenarist: Jesus Franco. **Executive Producer:**
     Arturo Marcos. **Photography:** José Climent. **Make-up:** Monique
     Adelaide and Elisenda Villanueva. **Music:** Daniel White and Bruno
     Nicolai.
     Cast: Fernando Bilbao (*the Frankenstein Monster*), Howard
     Vernon (*Dracula*), Dennis Price, Alberto Dalbes, Mary Francis, Brit
     Nicols, Luis Barboo.
     Credits partially derived from Walt Lee, *Reference Guide to
     Fantastic Films. Science Fiction, Fantasy, & Horror.* 3 vols. (Los
     Angeles: Chelsea-Lee Books, 1972), Vol. I, p. 112 col. 4.

35   *La Figlia di Frankenstein*. [U.S. title: *Lady Frankenstein*.]
     Italy; distributed in the U.S. by New World Pictures, 1971.
     Director: Mel Wells. **Producer:** Harry Cushing.
     Cast: Sarah Bay (*Lady Tanya Frankenstein*), Joseph Cotten
     (*Baron Frankenstein*), Paul Muller (*Charles Marshall*), Mickey Har-
     gitay (*Shepherd*).
     The Baron creates a monster, which destroys him; Lady Franken-
     stein does the same.

36   *Frankenstein and the Monster from Hell*. Hammer Films (Great
     Britain), 1973.
     Director: Terence Fisher. **Scenario:** John Elder [pseud. of
     Anthony Hinds]. **Photography:** Brian Probyn.
     Cast: Peter Cushing (*Victor Frankenstein*), Dave Prowse (*the
     Monster*), Shane Briant (*Dr. Helder*), Madeline Smith (*Angel/Sarah*),
     John Stratton (*the Director*), Bernard Lee (*Tarmut*), Clifford Mol-
     lison (*Judge*).
     To date, the last entry in the Hammer *Frankenstein* series.

37   *Andy Warhol's Frankenstein*. Carlo Ponti-Braunsberg-Rassam, 1974.
     Director: Paul Morrissey.
     Cast: Udo Kier (*Baron Frankenstein*), Monique Van Vooren (*Wife
     and Sister of Frankenstein*), Joe Dallesandro, Arno Juerging, Dalila
     Di Lazzaro, Srdjan Zelenovic.
     A camp parody, of a sexual and anatomical nature.

· For a review, see Paul D. Zimmerman [IIB354]. See also Melton S. Davis, "Morissey—From 'Flesh' and 'Trash' to 'Blood for Dracula,'" The New York Times, July 15, 1973, p. D9.

38 Young Frankenstein. 20th-Century Fox, 1974.
    Director: Mel Brooks. Scenario: Gene Wilder and Mel Brooks.
    Cast: Gene Wilder (Freddy Frankenstein), Peter Boyle (the Monster), Marty Feldman (Igor), Madeline Kahn (Elizabeth), Cloris Leachman (Frau Blücher), Teri Garr (Inga), Kenneth Mars (Inspector Kemp), Richard Hadyn (Herr Falkstein), Danny Goldman (Medical Student), Liam Dunn (Mr. Hilltop), Anne Beesley (Little Girl), Gene Hackman (Blindman).
    Semi-parody of the MS novel and the Universal films.
    For a review, see Jay Cocks [IIB49]. See also Arthur Cooper [B51]. Novelized by Gilbert Pearlman [cf. A326].

C TELEVISION VERSIONS

1 "Frankenstein" on Tales of Tomorrow. ABC, 1952.
    Make-up: Vincent Kehoe.
    Cast: Lon Chaney, Jr. (the Monster).
    See Donald F. Glut [IIA4, p. 266].

2 Frank N. Stein. Louis G. Gowan, Inc.
    Director: Mary Chase. Story: Everett Crosby. Photography: Drummond Drury.
    Voices: John Griggs, Gilbert Mack, Jean Carson.
    A puppet show with Fearless Fosdick and a "monster."
    Copy at the Motion Pictures Division of the Library of Congress.

3 "Frankenstein" on Matinee Theater. NBC, 1957.
    Cast: Primo Carnera (the Monster).
    See Donald F. Glut [IIA4, pp. 267-268].

4 "The Face in the Tombstone Mirror" on Tales of Frankenstein. Hammer Films/Screen Gems (Great Britain), 1958.
    Cast: Anton Diffring (Baron Frankenstein), Don Megowan (the Monster).
    See Donald F. Glut [IIA4, p. 268].

5 The Munsters. Kayro-Vue Productions; CBS, September 21, 1964 to May 9, 1966.
    Executive Producer: Irving Paley. Make-up: Bud Westmore.
    Cast: Fred Gwynne (Herman Munster), Yvonne de Carlo (Lily [a vampire]), Al Lewis (Grandpa [a vampire]), Butch Patrick (Eddie [a werewolf]), Pat Priest (Marilyn).
    Comedy series. One episode, "A Visit from Johann," featured the "creator" of Herman Munster, Dr. Victor Frankenstein III (played by John Abbott); directed by Gene Reynolds.
    A motion picture version was also released in 1966, entitled Munster, Go Home!—directed by Earl Bellamy.

6   *Frankenstein Jr. and the Impossibles.* Hanna Barbera; NBC, 1966.
     Animated series, created by Bill Hanna and Joe Barbera.
     The characters are featured in a "Big Little Book" noveliza-
     tion by Carl Fallberg, *Frankenstein, Jr. The Menace of the Heart-
     less Monster* (Racine, Wisc.: Whitman Publishing Company, 1968).

7   *Sur Les Traces de Frankenstein.* France, 1968.
     Director: Carlo di Carlo.
     Story of a young girl researching a thesis on Mary Shelley
     who finds herself followed by the spectre of the Monster.

8   "Frankenstein" on *Mystery and Imagination.* Thames Television Net-
     work (London), 1968.
     Director: Voytek. Producer: Reginald Collin. Teleplay:
     Robert Muller.
     Cast: Ian Holm (*Victor Frankenstein/the Monster*), Richard
     Vernon (*Prof. Krempe*), Ron Pember (*Fritz*), Sarah Bodel (*Eliza-
     beth*).
     A fairly close adaptation of the MS novel, with a few elements
     from the film *Bride of Frankenstein,* stressing the bond between
     Victor and his creation.
     Shown on CBS-Television in the U.S., November 18, 1973; for a
     review, see Alan M. Kriegsman [IIB154].

9   "Junior" on *Rod Serling's Night Gallery.* NBC, 1972.
     Director: Jeff Corey. Teleplay: Fred Kearney.
     Cast: Wally Cox.
     A five-minute comedy episode.

10   "The Mad, Mad Monsters" on *The Saturday Superstar Movie.* Rankin-
     Bass; ABC, 1972.
     Director: William Bradley.
     An animated farce adapted from *Mad Monster Party?* without the
     voice of Boris Karloff, re-naming the central character Henry von
     Frankenstein.

11   "Frankenstein" on *ABC's Wide World of Entertainment.* ABC, January
     16 and 17, 1973.
     Director: Glenn Jordan. Producer: Dan Curtis. Teleplay:
     Sam Hall and Dan Curtis. Art Director: Trevor Williams. Sets:
     Charles Pierce. Special Effects: Roger George. Music: Robert
     Cobert. Stunt Coordinator: Dick Ziker.
     Cast: Robert Foxworth (*Victor Frankenstein*), Bo Svenson (*The
     Giant*), Susan Strasberg (*Elizabeth Clerval*), Heidi Vaughn (*Agatha
     DeLacey*), Robert Gentry (*Henri Craval*), Philip Bourneuf (*Alphonse
     Frankenstein*), John Karlen (*Otto Roget*), Willie Ames (*William*),
     William Hansen (*Prof. Waldman*), Marie Saint-Deval (*Safie*), Jon
     Lormer.
     The adaptation intends faithfulness to the novel (quoting the
     Paradise Lost extract from the title page of the MS novel during
     the credits; having the "Giant" complain that "All men hate the
     wretched"), but provides a Frankenstein who is initially kind to

his creation and a "Giant" rather mild in appearance, with long golden hair. Still, the inevitable rejection occurs, the creation causes Frankenstein's death, lamenting it afterwards.

See also Alan M. Kriegsman [IIB153], and B86.

12 *Frankenstein: The True Story.* Universal Pictures Television Limited (Great Britain), 1973.

Director: Jack Smight. **Producer:** Hunt Stromberg, Jr. **Teleplay:** Christopher Isherwood and Don Bachardy. **Associate Producer:** Ian Lewis. **Photography:** Arthur Ibbetson. **Music:** Gil Melle.

Cast: James Mason (*Dr. Polidori*), Leonard Whiting (*Victor Frankenstein*), David McCallum (*Henry Clerval*), Jane Seymour (*Prima/ Agatha Lacey*), Nicola Pagett (*Elizabeth Fanshawe*), Michael Sarrazin (*The Creature*), Michael Wilding (*Sir Richard Fanshawe*), Clarissa Kaye (*Lady Fanshawe*), Agnes Moorehead (*Mrs. Blair, Housekeeper*), Margaret Leighton (*Frenchwoman*), Ralph Richardson (*Lacey*), Tom Baker (*Ship Captain*), Sir John Gielgud (*Chief Constable*).

Only the names of the characters are derived from the MS novel: the story concerns Victor and two creations, although he only assists Clerval and Polidori (respectively). The Creature is beautiful at first, entrancing Victor; when its physical appearance decays, so does Victor's interest.

See also Alan M. Kriegsman [IIB154], Tom Shales [B314], and Mark Shivas [B319]. Teleplay published in 1973 [cf. F13].

Shown in the U.S. on NBC in 1974 and early 1975.

APPENDIX IV

SELLING PRICES FOR SELECTED WORKS
BY AND ABOUT MARY CHOLLDY,
CULLED FROM BOOK AUCTION RECORDS
AND CATALOGUES OF SECONDHAND
BOOKDEALERS

This list depends mainly upon the following sources:

> ABPC = *American Book-Prices Current* (Indices and current
> volume)
> BAR = *Book-Auction Records* (1902 to present)
> BPC = *Book-Prices Current* (1887-1901)
> BPI = *Bookman's Price Index*

In addition, several of the prices given have been found in book-sellers' catalogues, and some from offers made privately to the present author. The list is as comprehensive as possible for editions of Mary Shelley's novels; highly selective for other works. The item number in the bibliography is cited first, then the year of the auction or offer, price, and nature of the reference.

PART I

A2   1945; $17 (*ABPC*, 1941-1945 Index, p. 844).
      1965; $7.50 (*BPI*, 3: 879).
      1968; $12.50 (*BPI*, 4: 776).
      1974; £15.75; private offer.

A8   1964; $4.20 (*BPI*, 2: 1085).

B1a   1890; 10s (*BPC*, 2: 396).
      1899; 16s (*BPC*, 13: 414).
      1910; £35 (*BAR*, 7: 284). The "Mrs. Thomas copy," sold to Bernard
      Quaritch; now in the Huntington Library.
      1911; £4 8s (*BAR*, 8: 320).
      1914; £6 5s (*BAR*, 11: 449).
      1920; $80 (*BAR*, 17: 478).
      1921; £50 (*BAR*, 18: 701). Presentation copy to Thomas Jefferson
      Hogg.
      —— £21 (*BAR*, 19: 162).

Bla   1922; £8 5s (*BAR*, 19: 565).
     1923; £2 2s (*BAR*, 20: 336).
     1924; £10 10s (*BAR*, 21: 310).
     —— £50 (*BAR*, 22: 148).
     1925; $185 (*ABPC*, 1923-1932 Index, p. 775).
     —— $180 (*ABPC*, 1923-1932 Index, p. 775).
     1926; $260 (*ABPC*, 1923-1932 Index, p. 775).
     —— $35 (*ABPC*, 1923-1932 Index, p. 775).
     —— $50 (*ABPC*, 1923-1932 Index, p. 775).
     1928; £7 (*BAR*, 25: 307).
     —— £40 (*BAR*, 25: 506).
     1929; £8 (*BAR*, 26: 343).
     —— $4,600 (*ABPC*, 1923-1932 Index, p. 775). The C. G. M. Gaskell
       copy, containing a Shelley letter to the publisher.
     1930; £78 (*BAR*, 27: 565).
     —— £32 (*BAR*, 27: 565). Worn copy.
     —— £40 (*BAR*, 28: 299).
     1932; $260 (*ABPC*, 1923-1932 Index, p. 775).
     —— $120 (*ABPC*, 1923-1932 Index, p. 775).
     —— $21 (*ABPC*, 1923-1932 Index, p. 775).
     1933; £170 (*BAR*, 30: 376).
     —— £29 (*BAR*, 30: 376).
     —— £18 (*BAR*, 30: 376). William Beckford's copy [cf. IIA173].
     —— $375 (*ABPC*, 1933-1940 Index, p. 545).
     1934; $45 (*ABPC*, 1933-1940 Index, p. 545).
     1935; $37 (*ABPC*, 1933-1940 Index, p. 545).
     —— £7 (*BAR*, 33: 115).
     1937; £7 10s (*BAR*, 34: 621).
     —— £15 10s (*BAR*, 35: 127).
     —— £2 12s (*BAR*, 35: 127).
     1938; £130 (*BAR*, 35: 363).
     1939; $425 (*ABPC*, 1933-1940 Index, p. 545).
     —— £2 2s (*BAR*, 36: 356).
     —— £1 14s (*BAR*, 36: 461).
     1940; £17 (*BAR*, 37: 194).
     —— £2 14s (*BAR*, 38: 78).
     1941; $115 (*BAR*, 39: 309). H. Buxton Forman's copy.
     1942; £3 3s (*BAR*, 39: 309).
     —— $90 (*BAR*, 39: 309). With A.L.s.
     —— $115 (*ABPC*, 1941-1945 Index, p. 844). Imperfect.
     1945; $475 (*BAR*, 42: 480-481).
     —— $37 (*ABPC*, 1941-1945 Index, p. 844). Imperfect.
     1946; £23 (*BAR*, 43: 538).
     1947; £40 (*BAR*, 44: 542).
     —— £1 10s (*BAR*, 44: 542). Poor condition.
     1948; $32 (*ABPC*, 1945-1950 Index, p. 1056).
     1949; $800 (*BAR*, 46: 437). The Capra copy.
     —— £12 10s (*BAR*, 46: 437).
     1951; $105 (*BAR*, 48: 468). With MS letter to Lady Manners-Sutton.
     —— $40 (*BAR*, 49: 451).
     1952; £18 (*BAR*, 49: 451).
     1953; £25 (*BAR*, 50: 362).
     1954; $775 (*BAR*, 51: 377). With Shelley letter.

Bla   1955; £13 (*BAR*, 52: 394).
       1958; £75 (*BAR*, 56: 431).
       ———— £46 (*BAR*, 55: 403).
       1959; $25 (*BAR*, 56: 431). Worn copy.
       ———— £75 (*ABPC*, 1955-1960 Index, p. 1127). Rebacked.
       1961; £48 (*BAR*, 58: 452).
       1962; $725 (*BAR*, 59: 499). With A.L.s by MS and Shelley.
       ———— £95 (*BAR*, 59: 499).
       1963; $210 (*BPI*, 1: 1017).
       ———— $425 (*BAR*, 61: 561).
       1970, 0230 (*BAR*, 67. 961).
       1973; £600 (*BPI*, 9: 596).

B2a   1933; $6 (*ABPC*, 1933-1940 Index, p. 545).

B6a   1960; $10 (*BAR*, 57: 501).
       1971; $16 (*BAR*, 69: 1140).
       1972; $32 (*BAR*, 70: 1085).

B9a   1974; £3.50; private offer.

B14a   1975; $9.50; private offer. F. E. Sotheby's copy.

B46a   1941; $5 (*ABPC*, 1941-1945 Index, p. 844).
       1948; $11 (*BAR*, 45: 525).
       1959; $11 (*BAR*, 56: 431).
       1961; $12 (*BAR*, 58: 452).
       1964; £15 (*BPI*, 2: 1084).
       ———— $12 (*BAR*, 62: 640).
       1969; $22 (*BAR*, 66: 755).
       1970; $19 (*BAR*, 68: 952).
       1971; $22 (*BAR*, 68: 952).
       1972; $16 (*BAR*, 69: 1140).

B1b   1914; £3 10s (*BAR*, 11: 449).
       1915; $8.50 (*BAR*, 12: 431).
       1918; 5s (*BAR*, 15: 249).
       1929; £24 (*BAR*, 26: 554). Godwin's copy.
       ———— $200 (*ABPC*, 1923-1932 Index, p. 775).
       1930; £16 10s (*BAR*, 27: 715).
       1931; £9 (*BAR*, 28: 299).
       1933; £3 3s (*BAR*, 30: 241).
       1940; £1 2s (*BAR*, 37: 194).
       ———— £1 15s (*BAR*, 37: 348).
       1941; $20 (*BAR*, 39: 309).
       1949; £16 (*BAR*, 46: 437).
       1955; £3 10s (*BAR*, 52: 394).
       ———— £17 (*BAR*, 52: 394).
       1962; £14 (*BAR*, 59: 499).
       1968; $30 (*BAR*, 65: 770).
       ———— $50 (*ABPC*, 1965-1970 Index, p. 1744).
       1973; £400 (*BPI*, 9: 596).

Blc 1913; 1s (*BAR*, 10: 520).
     1924; £1 10s (*BAR*, 21: 487).
     —— £10 (*BAR*, 22: 148).
     1927; £2 10s (*BAR*, 25: 161).
     1929; £5 5s (*BAR*, 26: 343).
     —— £10 10s (*BAR*, 26: 554).
     —— £52 (*BAR*, 26: 712).
     —— $150 (*ABPC*, 1923-1932 Index, p. 775).
     1931; £6 (*BAR*, 28: 299).
     —— £2 10s (*BAR*, 29: 125).
     —— $85 (*ABPC*, 1923-1932 Index, p. 775).
     1934; £4 5s (*BAR*, 31: 359).
     1936; £2 2s (*BAR*, 33: 219).
     —— £2 10s (*BAR*, 33: 354).
     1937; £2 15s (*BAR*, 35: 127).
     1939; £46 (*BAR*, 36: 461). Presentation copy to Maria Gisborne.
     1940; £1 12s (*BAR*, 37: 194).
     1942; $12 (*ABPC*, 1941-1945 Index, p. 844).
     1944; £5 (*BAR*, 41: 446).
     1946; $40 (*BAR*, 43: 538).
     —— $8 (*ABPC*, 1945-1950 Index, p. 1056).
     1949; £9 (*BAR*, 46: 437).
     1952; £2 12s (*BAR*, 49: 451). The Jerome Kern copy.
     —— $7 (*ABPC*, 1950-1955 Index, p. 1294).
     1955; £12 (*BAR*, 52: 394).
     —— $20 (*BAR*, 53: 396).
     1956; £13 (*BAR*, 53: 396).
     —— $20 (*ABPC*, 1955-1960 Index, p. 1127). With A.L.s.
     1960; £10 (*BAR*, 57: 501).
     1961; £16 (*BAR*, 58: 452).
     1962; £14 (*BAR*, 59: 499).
     1965; £13 (*BAR*, 62: 640).
     —— £13 (*ABPC*, 1961-1965 Index, p. 1521). First edition of Vols.
     I and III, second edition of Vol. II.
     1966; £82 (*BAR*, 64: 747).
     1971; £48 (*BAR*, 69: 1140).

B2c 1941; $12.50 (*BAR*, 39: 309).
     1963; $55 (*BAR*, 61: 561).
     1965; £13 (*ABPC*, 1961-1965 Index, p. 1521). Second edition of
     Vol. II, first edition of Vols. I and III.

Bld 1908; 5s (*BAR*, 6: 122).
     1919; 16s (*BAR*, 16: 384).
     1929; $75 (*ABPC*, 1923-1932 Index, p. 775).
     1930; £8 5s (*BAR*, 27: 715).
     1931; £5 10s (*BAR*, 28: 299).
     1945; $6 (*ABPC*, 1941-1945 Index, p. 844).
     1962; £20 (*BAR*, 59: 499).

B3d 1974; £3; private offer.

B1e   1923; $12 (*ABPC*, 1923-1932 Index, p. 775).
        1929; $80 (*ABPC*, 1923-1932 Index, p. 775).
        1962; £12 (*BAR*, 59: 499). With notes by Edward Dowden.
        1968; $30 (*BAR*, 65: 770).

B2e   1968; $12.50 (*BPI*, 4: 776).

B1f   1919; 12s (*BAR*, 17: 121).
        1929; $55 (*ABPC*, 1923-1932 Index, p. 775).
        1960; $19 (*BAR*, 57: 501).
        1962; £15 (*BAR*, 59: 499).

C2a
C1b   1974; $15; private offer. Koszul's edition of *Proserpine & Midas*.

D1a ⎫
H1 ⎬   1974; £50 (Blackwell's Antiquarian Books, catalogue 1012). The two
H2 ⎭   volumes of *The Liberal*.

D1c
D1d   1975; £6; private offer. The 1829 *Keepsake*.

D1e ⎫
D1f ⎬   1975; £6; private offer. The 1830 *Keepsake*.
D1g ⎭

D1h ⎫
D1i ⎪
E1 ⎪
E2 ⎬   1975; £6; private offer. The 1831 *Keepsake*.
E4 ⎪
E5 ⎭

D1k   1975; £6; private offer. The 1832 *Keepsake*.

D1p   1924; £18 (*BAR*, 21: 626). The manuscript of "The Trial of Love."

D1s ⎫
E8 ⎬   1975; £6; private offer. The 1839 *Keepsake*.
E9 ⎭

D1u   1967; £14 (*BPI*, 4: 776).

E11   1887; £1 5s (*BPC*, 1: 221).
        1963; $12.50 (*BPI*, 1: 1017).
        1971; 12 (*BAR*, 68: 952).

F1a   1887; £1 10s (*BPC*, 1: 80).
        1890; £2 (*BPC*, 4: 223).
        1893; £1 18s (*BPC*, 7: 475).
        1894; £1 (*BPC*, 8: 270).
        1895; £2 4s (*BPC*, 9: 48).
        1899; £1 12s (*BPC*, 13: 451).

Fla 1900; £1 (*BPC*, 14: 349).
1901; £2 14s (*BPC*, 15: 475).
1903; £3 15s (*BAR*, 1, Part I: 668).
1904; 2s (*BAR*, 1, Part II: 393).
1906; £1 19s (*BAR*, 3: 278).
1907; 12s (*BAR*, 4: 291).
———— 13s (*BAR*, 4: 469).
———— £1 11s (*BAR*, 5: 127).
1909; 12s (*BAR*, 6: 280).
1911; £1 (*BAR*, 8: 320).
1913; £2 5s (*BAR*, 10: 442).
1916; 12s (*BAR*, 13: 422).
———— 12s (*BAR*, 14: 122).
1918; £5 (*BAR*, 15: 495).
1919; £2 4s (*BAR*, 17: 121).
1920; £2 12s (*BAR*, 17: 478).
1921; £3 15s (*BAR*, 18: 347).
1923; £8 (*BAR*, 20: 336).
———— £6 (*BAR*, 20: 672).
———— $20 (*ABPC*, 1923-1932 Index, p. 775).
1924; £2 (*BAR*, 21: 310).
———— £11 (*BAR*, 21: 627).
———— $10 (*ABPC*, 1923-1932 Index, p. 775).
———— $7 (*ABPC*, 1923-1932 Index, p. 775).
1925; £6 15s (*BAR*, 22: 623).
1926; $12 (*ABPC*, 1923-1932 Index, p. 775).
1929; £39 (*BAR*, 26: 344, 555).
———— £4 10s (*BAR*, 26: 555).
———— £5 15s (*BAR*, 27: 168).
———— $175 (*ABPC*, 1923-1932 Index, p. 775).
———— $260 (*ABPC*, 1923-1932 Index, p. 775).
1930; £7 10s (*BAR*, 28: 148).
1932; £9 (*BAR*, 29: 490).
———— £21 (*BAR*, 30: 120).
1933; £3 12s 6d (*BAR*, 30: 241).
———— $20 (*ABPC*, 1933-1940 Index, p. 545).
———— $15 (*ABPC*, 1933-1940 Index, p. 545).
1934; £3 (*BAR*, 31: 359).
1935; £1 10s (*BAR*, 32: 470).
———— $17 (*ABPC*, 1933-1940 Index, p. 545).
———— $25 (*ABPC*, 1933-1940 Index, p. 545).
1936; £1 (*BAR*, 33: 219).
———— £6 (*BAR*, 33: 354).
———— £2 10s (*BAR*, 34: 157).
———— $32 (*ABPC*, 1933-1940 Index, p. 545).
———— $17 (*ABPC*, 1933-1940 Index, p. 545).
1937; £7 10s (*BAR*, 34: 622).
———— $80 (*ABPC*, 1933-1940 Index, p. 545).
———— $15 (*ABPC*, 1933-1940 Index, p. 545).
1938; £2 5s (*BAR*, 35: 363).
———— $10 (*ABPC*, 1933-1940 Index, p. 545).
———— $17 (*ABPC*, 1930-1940 Index, p. 545).

Fla   1939; $12 (*ABPC*, 1933-1940 Index, p. 545).
       —— $15 (*ABPC*, 1933-1940 Index, p. 545).
       1940; $15 (*BAR*, 38: 78).
       —— £1 15s (*BAR*, 37: 195).
       —— £3 10s (*BAR*, 38: 459).
       1941; $30 (*BAR*, 39: 310).
       —— £1 (*BAR*, 39: 310).
       1943; $22.50 (*BAR*, 41: 446).
       1944; $50 (*BAR*, 41: 446).
       1945; £7 10s (*BAR*, 42: 481).
       —— $17.50 (*BAR*, 42: 483).
       —— £6 17s 6d (*BAR*, 42: 483).
       —— £6 (*BAR*, 42: 483).
       —— £3 15s (*BAR*, 42: 483).
       —— $42.50 (*BAR*, 43: 538).
       1946; £8 10s (*BAR*, 44: 542).
       —— $40 (*BAR*, 44: 542).
       —— £6 10s (*BAR*, 44: 542).
       1948; £1 10s (*BAR*, 46: 438).
       1949; $70 (*BAR*, 46: 438).
       —— $10 (*BAR*, 47: 390).
       1951; $25 (*BAR*, 48: 469).
       —— £5 (*BAR*, 49: 451).
       1956; $5 (*ABPC*, 1950-1955 Index, p. 1127).
       1966; £60 (*ABPC*, 1965-1970 Index, p. 1744; *BAR*, 63: 683).
       1971; £140 (*BAR*, 68: 952).
       —— £160 (*BAR*, 69: 1140).
       1972; £160 (*BAR*, 68: 827).
       1974; $550; private offer.

Flb   1902; £2 10s (*BAR*, 1, Part I: 97).
       1904; 2s (*BAR*, 1, Part II: 395).
       1906; 17s (*BAR*, 4: 138).
       1917; £1 1s (*BAR*, 14: 255).
       1919; 8s (*BAR*, 17: 121).
       1925; $9 (*ABPC*, 1923-1932 Index, p. 775).
       1927; £3 (*BAR*, 25: 161).
       —— $75 (*ABPC*, 1923-1932 Index, p. 775).
       1929; £1 8s (*BAR*, 26: 712).
       —— $95 (*ABPC*, 1923-1932 Index, p. 775).
       1931; £1 1s (*BAR*, 28: 549). Worn copy.
       1945; $11 (*ABPC*, 1941-1945 Index, p. 844).
       1950; $9 (*ABPC*, 1945-1950 Index, p. 1056).
       1962; £6 (*BAR*, 59: 499).
       1973; £90 (*BPI*, 9: 596).

G3b   1972; £8 (*BPI*, 8: 545).
       1973; $12.50 (*BPI*, 9: 596).

H14   1973; $3.95; private offer. The 1831 edition of Godwin's *Caleb
       Williams*.

I1 1902; £7 10s (*BAR*, 1, Part I: 668). Uncut, with leaf of errata.
    1912; £6 (*BAR*, 10: 124).
    1915; $40 (*BAR*, 12: 431).
    1917; £10 (*BAR*, 15: 495). Presentation copy from MS to Cyrus
        Redding.
    1922; £6 10s (*BAR*, 19: 362). The MS-Redding copy.
    1928; £12 (*BAR*, 25: 308).
    1930; £28 (*BAR*, 27: 565).
    —— £42 (*BAR*, 27: 716). With MS letter.
    1932; £30 (*BAR*, 29: 389). With MS letter.
    1963; $125 (*BPI*, 1: 1018).
    —— £15 (*BPI*, 1: 1018).
    —— £25 (*BPI*, 1: 1018).
    1966; £10 (*ABPC*, 1965-1970 Index, p. 1745).
    1969; £42 (*ABPC*, 1965-1970 Index, p. 1745).
    1970; £36 (*ABPC*, 1965-1970 Index, p. 1745).
    —— $100 (*ABPC*, 1965-1970 Index, p. 1745).
    1971; £75 (*BPI*, 6: 572).
    1972; $2,700 (*ABPC*, 78: 827). Jeweled binding.

I4 1902; £2 6s (*BAR*, 1, Part I: 219).
    1910; £2 17s 6d (*BAR*, 8: 148).
    1923; £5 5s (*BAR*, 20: 532). G. H. Lewes' copy.
    1928; £11 (*BAR*, 25: 651).
    1931; £1 10s (*BAR*, 29: 125).
    1963; £11 (*BAR*, 61: 561).
    1964; $117.60 (*BPI*, 2: 1085).
    —— £20 (*BPI*, 2: 1085).
    —— £16 (*BAR*, 61: 561).
    1965; $40 (*BPI*, 3: 879).
    1966; £20 (*BAR*, 64: 746).
    1967; $42 (*BPI*, 4: 777).
    —— £48 (*BPI*, 4: 777).
    1968; £70 (*BPI*, 5: 840).
    1969; £15 (*ABPC*, 1965-1970 Index, p. 1745).
    1970; £90 (*ABPC*, 1965-1970 Index, p. 1745).
    1973; £30 (*BPI*, 9: 597).
    1974; £24 (Jarndyce Books, catalogue 8; "fine" condition).

I7 1902; £1 10s (*BAR*, 1, Part I: 289).
    1923; £2 15s (*BAR*, 20: 672).
    1929; £1 5s (*BAR*, 27: 168).
    1964; $17.50 (*BPI*, 2: 1085).
    1967; £18 (*BPI*, 4: 777).
    1970; £24/10 (*BPI*, 6: 572).
    1972; £28 (*BAR*, 70: 1085).
    1975; £10 (Richard Booth Booksellers [Hay-on-Wye], "A Catalogue of
        English Literature," p. 33, Item 525).

PART II

A2   1974; £1.50; private offer.

A5   1919; $16 (*BAR*, 17: 121).
        1974; $35 (George Robert Minkoff [Mass.], catalogue 24).

A6   1974; £4 (Blackwell's Antiquarian Books, catalogue 1012).
        —— £6.30; private offer.

A8   1904; 7s (*DNB*, 1, Part II. 305).
        1923; 15s (*BAR*, 21: 156).
        1970; $12.50 (Carnegie Bookshop, catalogue 325).
            NOTE: In 1973, the Haskell House facsimile reprint sold for
            $28.95.

A14   1972; $15 (*BPI*, 8: 545).
        1973; $40 (*BPI*, 9: 596).
        1974; $10 (Carnegie Bookshop, catalogue 345).

A15   1949; £3 10s (*BAR*, 46: 438).
        1964; £5/5 (*BPI*, 2: 1085).
        —— £7/10 (*BPI*, 2: 1085).
        1965; £20 (*BAR*, 62: 640).
        1969; $30 (*BPI*, 5: 840).
        1970; $36 (*BPI*, 6: 572).
        1971; £10.50 (*BPI*, 7: 542).
        1972; £35 (*BAR*, 70: 1085).

A16   1923; £59 (*BAR*, 20: 532).
        1928; £4 10s (*BAR*, 26: 154). Typescript of Vol. I.
        1930; £78 (*BAR*, 27: 566). 3 vols.; presentation copy from Lady
            Shelley to Hamilton Aidé.
        1935; £80 (*BAR*, 32: 358). 3 vols.; purchased by the University
            of Texas.
        1941; £8 10s (*BAR*, 39: 310). 4 vols.
        1948; £30 (*BAR*, 45: 526). 3 vols.
        1949; £31 (*BAR*, 46: 436). 3 vols.
        1960; £35 (*BAR*, 57: 502). 4 vols.
        1961; £38 (*BAR*, 58: 452). 4 vols.
        1962; £140 (*BAR*, 59: 499). 3 vols.
        1964; £280 (*BAR*, 62: 640).
        1966; £340 (*BAR*, 63: 683).
        1967; £242 (*BAR*, 64: 746).
        —— £475 (*BPI*, 4: 777). Uncut.
        1968; £250 (*BAR*, 65: 771).
        —— £350 (*BPI*, 5: 840).
        1971; £240 (*BAR*, 68: 952). 3 vols.
        1972; £120 (*BAR*, 69: 1141; *ABPC*, 78: 827). 3 vols., with 31 supple-
            mentary leaves.
        —— £260 (*BAR*, 70: 1086). 3 vols.
        1975; £650; private offer. 4 vols.

A20   1974; £3; private offer.

A50   1970; $10 (Carnegie Bookshop, catalogue 325).

A53   1974; £7 (Blackwell's Antiquarian Books, catalogue 1012).
       —— $22; private offer.

A126   1904; £1 (*BAR*, 1, Part II: 395).
       1905; £1 (*BAR*, 2: 309).
       —— £1 8s (*BAR*, 2: 309).
       1919; £2 2s (*BAR*, 16: 384).
       1970; £4.15 (Percy Dobell, catalogue 183).
       1974; £20 (Blackwell's Antiquarian Books, catalogue 1012).

A133   1974; $35; private offer.

A144   1921; £6 6s (*BAR*, 18: 584).   Presentation copy to William Michael
           Rossetti.
       1922; £3 17s (*BAR*, 19: 565).
       1928; £5 10s (*BAR*, 26: 154).
       1932; £3 15s (*BAR*, 30: 120).
       1934; £4 4s (*BAR*, 31: 359).
       1966; $19 (*BAR*, 63: 682).
       1972; $35 (*BPI*, 8: 545).

A145   1970; £195 (Charles J. Sawyer, catalogue 283).

A159   1914; $.50 (*BAR*, 12: 100).
       1918; £1 10s (*BAR*, 15: 122).
       1945; $10 (*BAR*, 42: 482).
       1955; $14 (*BAR*, 52: 394).
       1965; £14 (*BPI*, 3: 879).
       1967; £15 (*BPI*, 4: 777).
       1971; £6 (*BAR*, 69: 1141).

A179   1974; £2.50; private offer.

A180   1974; £3.50; private offer.

A205   1902; £1 16s (*BAR*, 1, Part I: 289).
       1921; £2 17s (*BAR*, 19: 163).
       1974; £30 (Blackwell's Antiquarian Books, catalogue 1012).

A212   1974; £55 (Blackwell's Antiquarian Books, catalogue 1012).   First
           edition.
       —— £25 (Blackwell's Antiquarian Books, catalogue 1012).   Second
           edition.

A281   1907; £1 5s (*BAR*, 4: 291).
       1974; £45 (Blackwell's Antiquarian Books, catalogue 1012).

A283   1907; 15s (*BAR*, 4: 291).
       1923; £2 5s (*BAR*, 20: 673).
       1934; £1 12s (*BAR*, 31: 359).
       1948; £2 (*BAR*, 45: 526).
       1952; £9 (*BAR*, 50: 362).
       1964; £6 (*BPI*, 2: 1085).
       1965; $45 (*BPI*, 3: 879).
       1968; $60 (*BPI*, 5: 840).

A291   1974; £45 (Blackwell's Antiquarian Books, catalogue 1012).

A359   1975; £5.50 (Smith's Bookshop [New Zealand]; cf. *The Bookdealer*,
       January 8, 1975).

A382   1907; 4s (*BAR*, 5: 127).
       1917; 2s (*BAR*, 14: 255).
       1924; £1 1s (*BAR*, 22: 148).
       1926; £8 10s (*BAR*, 24: 496).
       ——— £2 15s (*BAR*, 24: 496).
       1930; £1 1s (*BAR*, 27: 566).
       1931; 15s (*BAR*, 29: 125).
       1937; £1 10s (*BAR*, 34: 499).
       1944; £1 (*BAR*, 41: 446).
       1974; £2.50; private offer.

A383   1971; £37.50 (John Smith [Glasgow], catalogue 47).
       1973; £105 (Henry Sotheran, catalogue 958).

A385   1974; £2.75; private offer.
       1975; $8.50; private offer.

A389   1973?; £20 (Deighton Bell, catalogue 147).

A445   1975; £50 (Island Books [Guernsey]; cf. *The Bookdealer*, January
       29, 1975).

       In addition, MS copies of books occasionally are included in the
       Book Auction Records; for example, *Les Veillees du Chateau*, Vol. I,
       1816, sold for £30 in 1965 (*ABPC*, 1960-1965 Index, p. 1521); and
       *Poems, on Religious, Moral, and Descriptive Subjects. By an Offi-
       cer in the Army*, 1827, sold for $15 in 1967 (*ABPC*, 1965-1970 Index,
       p. 1744).

INDEX

This index includes all titles, periodicals, and persons mentioned in the annotations, as well as authors and titles in the main entries—except, in the latter case, those authors of works in sections A and B of Part II. Cast lists in Appendix III are also excluded. The only synthetic entry is that of Mary Shelley. Persons are indexed before titles (Shelley, Mary before "Shelley, Mary"), and the word-for-word method is used ("Shelley, Byron, and Hunt" before "Shelley and Byron"). Umlauts are ignored in alphabetization.

The entries are of three kinds:
1) Italics [A68] = main entry
2) Roman [B75] = annotation
3) Page numbers [245] = Preface and Appendices

Boldface numbers preceeding the entries [IB150a] denote Parts I and II of the bibliography.

The reader's attention is called to the "Addenda" following the "Z" listings, for which the author apologizes.

"Aziola" (Shelley), IIB34

"Baby" (Emshwiller), IIA182
Bachardy, Don, and Christopher
Isherwood, Frankenstein: The
True Story, IIF13; 237
"Back Numbers—LXXXV," IIB17
Bacon, Francis, IIE27
Bailey, James O., "Scientific
Fiction in English," IID2
Baker, Donald Whitelaw, "Themes of
Terror in Nineteenth Century
English Fiction," IID3
Ballantyne, James, IIA372
Bannadonna [Melville, "The Bell-
Tower"], IIA208
Barbarina, The Hon. Lady Grey,
IIA256, B345
Bartlett, Mrs., IA6, A7
Barton, Bernard, IIA396
"Basic Library of Trash" (Newman &
Benton), IIB239
Bate, Sam, Shelley and Mary, IIF12
Bateson, Frederick, ed., The Cam-
bridge Bibliography of English
Literature, IIA84
Baudelaire, Charles, IIA336
Baum, L. Frank, IIB96
Baxter, Christy, IA7; IIB186, B211,
B212, B316
Baxter, Isabella, IIB211, B316
Baxter, Robert, IIA406
Baxter, William, IA7; IIB331
Beatrice [Shelley, The Cenci],
IIA357, B298
Beatrice [Valperga], IIA357, B298,
C35
Beauclerk, Aubrey, IIB48
Beavan, Arthur Henry, James and
Horace Smith, IIA393
Beck, Julian, Aldo Rostagno, and
Judith Malina, We, The Living
Theatre, 223
Beckford, William, IIA173; 239
—Vathek, IB119a; IIA340
Beddoes, Thomas Lovell, IIA50,
A121, A122, A394
—"Death's Jest-Book," IIA171,
B276
—"Last Man," IIB303
—Poetical Works (Gosse, ed.),
IIA171

Bedeutung der Gothic Novel für das
Erzählwerk Herman Melvilles
(Kosok), IIE25
Beinecke Library, IIB30
"Bell-Tower" (Melville), IIA208,
B345
Belle Assemblée, IH3; IIB21, C1,
C26
Bell's Weekly Messenger, IIB22,
C85, C112
Benjamin, Lewis S. See Melville,
Lewis
Bennett, Betty T., viii
Bergier, Jacques, IB93a; IIE2
Berkeley, George, IIA344
Berni, Francesco, IG1a
Berry, Alexander, IA7; IIA179
Berry, Mrs Alexander, IA7
Berry, Francis, The Iron Christ,
IIA235
Bertin, H. Jean-Baptiste, IIA340
Best from Famous Monsters of Film-
land (Ackerman, ed.), IIA150
Betjeman, Hannah, IB60a, B92a,
B127a
Biagi, Guido, Gli ultimi giorni di
Percy Bysshe Shelley, nuovi doc-
umenti, IIE3
Bibliography of Shelley's Letters
(de Ricci), IIA355
Bibliothéque Nationale, IB43a,
B93a; IIE2, E18
Bierce, Ambrose, IIA106
Billion Year Spree (Aldiss), IIA24
"Billion Year Spree. I. Origin
of the Species" (Aldiss), IIB3
Binder, Eando, "I, Robot," IIA234,
B36
—See also Binder, Otto O.
Binder, Otto O., IB145a
—See also Binder, Eando
"Biographical Element in the Novels
of Mary Wollstonecraft Shelley"
(Peck), IIB267
Biography of Dracula (Ludlam), 223
Biological Time Bomb (Taylor),
IIA411
Birmingham Post, IIC17
"Birth of Frankenstein," IB52a
"Birthmark" (Hawthorne), IIB1,
B345
Bishopsgate, IIB20

Capanna, Pablo, *El Sentido de la Ciencia Ficción*, IIE6
Capek, Karel, *R.U.R.*, IIA106, A112, E17
Captain Medwin (Lovell), IIA251
Carbe, Nino, IB42a, B63a
Carlisle, Henry E., *A Selection from the Correspondence of Abraham Hayward*, IIA196
Carlson, Dale, IB120a; IIC16
Carmilla (Le Fanu), In?t
Carne, John, IIA91, B61
Carneiro, André, *Introdução ao Estudo da "Science-Fiction,"* IIE7
Cashell, Lady Mount, IIA257
Casquet of Literature (Gibbon, ed.), ID2n; IIA164
Cassell's Encyclopedia of World Literature (Steinberg, ed.), IIA187
Castillejo, Cristova, IG3a
Castillo de los Monstrous (film), 229
Castle Frankenstein, IIB103, B104, B116; B357 (p. 209), B358 (p. 209).
Castle of Frankenstein, IIB67
Castle of Otranto (Walpole), IB119a, D2t; IIA340, A452
Castracani, Castruccio [*Valperga*], IIC27, E5, E47
Cat, Claude-Nicolas Le, IIA340
Catalyst, IIB54
Cavalcade of the English Novel (Wagenknecht), IIA424
Cazamian, Louis, and Émile Legouis, *A History of English Literature*, IIA242
Cenci (Shelley), IIA44, A69, A105, A123, A177, B298, B327
Central Self (Ball), IIA44
Cervantes, IG3a
Chambers's Cyclopædia of English Literature, IIA272
Chamisso, Adelbert von, *Peter Schlemihls wunderbare Geschichte*, IIA206
"Character and Writing of Shelley" (Egeria), IIB70
"Character Make-up" (Pierce), 224
"Character of Literature from

Blake to Byron" (Harding), IIA185
"Charles Brockden Brown's *Ormond*" (Davies), IIB60
"Chats with Jane Clairmont" (Graham), IIB106
Chattopadhyay, Nripendra Krishna, IB69a
Chiabrera, Gabriello, IG2a
Child of Light (Spark), IB5c; IIA20, 247
Choice, IIC18, C47
Choice, The, IE1, E2, E11; IIA146; A445; 242
Chorley, *Helen*, IIB146
Christabel (Coleridge), IIB78
Cine y Ciencia-Ficción (Gasca), IIE15; 228
Cinema of the Fantastic (Steinbrunner & Goldblatt), 225
Cini, Nerina Mason, IA7
Claire Clairmont (Grylls), IIA179; 247
Clairmont, Charles, IIB27
Clairmont, Claire, IA7, A8, Dlk; IIA29, A66, A78, A97, A113, A170, A177, A179, A302, A304, A314, A403, B33, B37, B84, B106, B134, B137, B149, B163, B322, B323, B341, F15, F8
Clairmont, Mrs. Mary Jane, IIA1
Clareson, Thomas D., ed., *SF: The Other Side of Realism*, IIA228, A278
Clarke, Charles Cowden, IA7
Classics Illustrated, IB58a
"Classics in Leather," IIC13
Cloning, IIB91
Cloudesley (Godwin), rev., IH12
Coat of Many Colours (Read), IIA347
Cobbe, Frances Power, IIB31
Cochetti, Ranieri, IB55a; IIE8
Colburn, Henry, IA7
Coleman, William Emmet, "On the Discrimination of Gothicisms," IID5
Coleridge, Samuel Taylor:
—*Christabel*, IIB78
—*Letters, Conversations and Recollections*, IIA25
"Coliseum" (Shelley), IIB207

- 261 -

"Frankenstein's Castle" (Haydock),
IIB116
"Frankenstein's castle is no
horror show" (Goshko), IIB103
"Frankenstein's Children" (Ebs-
worth), IIB68
Frankenstein's Daughter (film),
230
"Frankenstein's Facelift" (Gosh-
ko), IIB104
"Frankensteins Füdelse" (Lorenz),
IIE55
"Frankenstein's Monster: Paragon
or Paranoiac?" (Arnold), IIB15
"Frankenstein's Monster and Its
Romantic Relatives" (Swingle),
IIB332
"Frankensteins Mutter" (Helmar),
IIE53
Frankenstein's Trestle (film), 223
Frank-In-Steam; or, The Modern
Promise to Pay, 220
Franklin, Benjamin, IIB116; B357
(p. 209)
Fraser's Magazine for Town and
Country, IIB144, B265, B266,
C69; B356 (p. 208)
Fred Newton Scott Anniversary
Papers, IIA395
Fredman, Alice Green, viii
Freeman, IIC104
Freethinker, IIB214
"French Literature. On the School
of the 'Romantiques'" (E. M.),
IIB180
"Frère et la Sœur, Le," ID21
Friend of Shelley (Massingham),
IIA275
"Fritz Leiber" (Moskowitz), IIA295
Furnivall, Miss, IIB304
"Further Comment on 'Music, When
Soft Voices Die'" (Hirsch),
IIB121
Fuseli, Henry, paintings:
—The Nightmare, IB119a
—The Rosicrucian Cavern, IIA415
Fuseli Studies (Antal), IIA31

Gabriele Rossetti in England
(Vincent), IIA424
Gaiety theatre, 222

Gaiety, The (Macqueen-Pope &
Murray), IIA262; 222
Galatea, IIB180
Galaxy, IIB307
Galignani, W., IA7; IIB19
"Galignani's and the Publication
of English Books in France from
1800 to 1852" (Barber), IIB19
Galileo, IG2a; IIC133
Galloni, Monsieur, IA7
Galvani, Luigi, IIA36
Garnett, R. S., ed., Letters about
Shelley, interchanged by three
friends, IIA245
Garnett, Richard, vi; IIA95, A197,
A245, B29
—ed., Tales and Stories (Mary
Shelley), ID4a, D2c, D2d, D2e,
D2f, D4g, D4h, D4i, D2j, D3k, D31,
D2m, D3n, D2o, D2q, D2r, D2s, Dlu;
IIA157, C107-C108
Garnett Family (Heilbrun), IIA197
Gasca, Luis:
—Cine y Ciencia-Ficción, IIE15
—Imagen y Ciencia Ficción, IIE16
Gaskell, C. G. M., 239
Gattégno, Jean, La Science-fiction,
IIE17
Geddie, J. Liddell, and J. C.
Smith, rev., Chambers's Cyclo-
pedia of English Literature,
IIA272
Geneva, IIA384, B78, B115, B310,
F2, F6, F13
Geneva, Lake of, IIB153
Genevese Background (Häusermann),
IIA194
"Genevois méconnu, Un: Franken-
stein" (Moeckli), IIE59
Gentleman's Magazine, IIB273
Gentleman's Magazine: and Histori-
cal Chronicle, IIC5
Gentlewomen of Evil (Haining, ed.),
ID5b
George IV, IIB110
"George of Frankenstein," 217-218
Gérard, Albert, "Prométhée a
l'envers," IIE52
Gerlis, Mme. de, Pygmalion et Gala-
tée, IIB282
German Influence in the English Ro-
mantic Period, 1788-1818 (Stokoe),
IIA404

Gerson, Noel B., *Daughter of Earth and Water*, IIB89
"Gets a Shelley Relic," IIB92
Ghost of Frankenstein (film), IIA242; 226
Ghosts, Castles, and Victims: Studies in Gothic Terror (Wolf & Wolf, eds.), IB151a; IIA446
Ghouls, The (Haining, ed.), IIA343
Gibbon, Charles, ed., *The Casquet of Literature*, ID2n; IIA164
Gids, De (Amsterdam), IIE57
Gifford, Denis, *Karloff: The Man, The Monster, The Movies*, 224
"Gift of Shelley Manuscripts" (R. W. H.), IIB113
Gilder, Jeanette L., and Helen Gray Cone, eds., *Pen-Portraits of Literary Women*, IIA105
Gillet, Marilyn, IB128a
Gilliland, Norman Paul, "An Inquiry into the Longevity of Franken-stein," IID24
Giménez, Rafael, IB57a
Giornale storico della Letteratura italiana (Torino), IIE58
"Giovanni Villani," IH2; IIB63; 242
Gisborne, John, IA7; IIB142
Gisborne, Maria, IA3-A5, A7-A9; IIA203, A306, B84, B119, B133, B138, B149, E61; 241
Glasgow Herald, IIC25
Gli ultimi giorni di Percy Bysshe Shelley, nuovi documenti (Biagi), IIE3
Glirastes, IIB281, B284
Globe (Boston). See Boston *Globe*
Globe (London), IIB98-B101, C70-C74, C116
Glut, Donald F., *The Frankenstein Legend*, IB91a; IIA4; 220-229 *passim*, 235
"Gnostic Prometheus, The: A Study of Godwin and the Shelleys" (Rieger), IID16
Gobernado, Antonio, IB79a, B106a
Goblin Market (C. Rossetti), IIB219
Godwin, Mrs. (byline), IE5
Godwin, Mary. See Shelley, Mary

Godwin, William, IA7, B3a; IIA5, A75, A77, A89, A115, A135, A187, A198, A215, A258, A259, A272, A345, A358, A393, A397, A402, A432, B47, B53, B65, B70, B102, B158, B163, B168, B175, B210, B224, B255, B277, B278, B280, B339, B342, B351, C23, C78, C81, C89, D4, E44, F5; 240
—*Caleb Williams*, IH14; IIA68, A357, B77, B222, B333, C94, D26; Gl (p. 209); 244
—*Cloudesley*, rev., IH12
—*Italian Letters*, IIA338, C45
—*Political Justice*, IIB282, D15
—*St. Leon*, IIA438
Godwin, William, Jun., *Transfusion*, I13
Godwin Criticism (Pollin), IH12; IIC29
"Godwin's Account of Shelley's Return in September, 1814" (Pollin), IIB277
"Godwin's Memoirs as a Source of Shelley's Phrase 'Intellectual Beauty'" (Pollin), IIB278
Goethe, IIE20
Goldblatt, Burt, and Chris Stein-brunner, *Cinema of the Fantastic*, 225
Golden Book Magazine, ID5g
Golden Years (Kenyon), IIF8
Goldmann, H., IB74a
Goldoni, Carlo, IG2a; IIC133, F3
Golem, legend of, IIA38, A103, A296, A343, B96, B275, E4
"Golem and the Robot" (Plank), IIB275
"Golems und Roboter" (Plank), IIE36
Gongora y Argote, Don Luis de, IG3a
Gorbunov, A., IIE68
Gordon, Gavin, IIA167
Gosse, Sir Edmund, IIB276, B194
—ed., *The Letters of Thomas Lovell Beddoes*, IIA50
"Gosse's Candid 'Snapshots'" (Mattheisen), IIB194
Göteborgs-Posten, IIE67
Göteborgs-Tidningen, IIE63

Literary Landmarks of London
(Hutton), IIA214
Literary Magnet or Monthly Journal
of the Belles Lettres, IIB165
Literary Panorama, and National
Register, IIC6
Literary Register of the Fine
Arts, Sciences, and Belles
Lettres, IIC34
Literary Review [of the New York
Evening Post], IIC14
Literary Souvenir (Watts, ed.),
IIA430
Literatur in Wissenschaft und
Unterricht, IIE62
Literature and Psychology, IIB275
Littell's Living Age, IIB95, B181,
B294, B343
Little Journeys to the Homes of
Famous Women (Hubbard), IIA209
Little Theatre (London), 222
Lives of Eminent French Authors
(1851), IG4b
Lives of Eminent Literary and
Scientific Men of Italy (1841),
IG4a
Lives of the Most Eminent French
Writers (1840), IG3b
Lives of the most Eminent Literary
and Scientific Men of France,
IG1b-G4b; IIC137-C139
Lives of the most Eminent Literary
and Scientific Men of Italy,
Spain, and Portugal, IG1a-G4a;
IIA337, A424, B214, C128-C136;
244
Living Age. See Littell's Living
Age
"Living Literary Characters, No.
III. The Honourable Mrs.
Norton," IH16
"Living Literary Characters, No.
IV. James Fenimore Cooper,"
IH17
Living Theatre, Frankenstein,
IIE42; 223
Locke, John, Essay Concerning
Human Understanding, IIB282
Lodore, IB1e-B7e; IIA94, A115,
A169, A216, A359, A365, A438,
A439, A445, B19, B52, B100,
B101, B132, B135, B158, B214,

Lodore—cont.
B229, C64-C83; 242
L[ohmande]r, U., IIE67
London Chronicle, IIC35
London Magazine, ID1b, H4, H5;
IIB166, B167; 220
"Lord Byron, Leigh Hunt, and The
Liberal: Some New Evidence"
(Brack), IIB35
"Lord Byron and his contempora-
ries, &c., by an intimate
Friend of his Lordship.—No.
III," IIB168
Lord Byron and Some of his Con-
temporaries (Hunt), IIA212; 247
Lord Byron's Correspondence
(Murray, ed.), IIB310
Lorenz, Gunnar, "Frankensteins
födelse," IIE55
Losh, James, The Diaries and Cor-
respondence of James Losh,
IIB351
Lost Travellers (Blackstone),
IIA58
"Lost Women. Mary Shelley: In
the Shadow of 'Frankenstein'"
(Kmetz), IIB150
"Lounger, The," IIB169
Love Letters of Mary Hays (1779-
1780) (Wedd, ed.), IIA432
Lovell, Ernest J., Jr., IIC50
"Lovers Who Meet in Churches"
(Grigson), IIB109
Loves of the Poets, rev., IH10
Ludlam, Harry, A Biography of
Dracula, 223
Ludwig, Albert, "Homunculi und
Androiden," IIE56
Lugosi, Bela, IIA229, A243
"Luigi Rivarola" (J. Hunt), IIF1
Luke, Hugh J., Jr., IB7c
Lundwall, Sam J., Science fiction,
från begynnelsen till våra
dagar, IIE30
Lurk (film), 231
Lyrics (Shelley), IIA85

MacKnight, Mary Limeburner,
IIA406
McMahon, A., IIC15
Macmillan's Magazine, IIB84

M., IIC89
"M. W. Shelley at Pisa," IIB181,
B182
Maanen, W. van, "Kroniek der En-
gelse Letterkunde," IIE57
Mabbott, Thomas Ollive, and Frank
Lester Pleadwell, The Life and
Works of Edward Coote Pinkney,
IIA335
Machiavelli, IG1a
"Mad, Mad Monsters" (TV), IIC6
Mad Monster Party? (film), 232,
236
"Madame d'Houtetôt," IH1; IIB63;
242
"Maga, Champion of Shelley"
(Strout), IIB330
Magazine of Art, IIB235, B236
Magic Plant (Grabo), IIA175
Magill, Frank N., ed., Cyclopedia
of World Authors, IIA271
Main Currents of English Litera-
ture (Houston), IIA207
Major Byron (Ehrsam), IIA130
"Making of a Monster," IB134a;
IIA267
Malina, Judith, Aldo Rostagno, and
Julian Beck, We, The Living
Theatre, 223
Man and the Monster, The; or, The
Fate of Frankenstein (Milner),
220-221
Man and the Movies (Robinson,
ed.), IIA117
Man Without a Home (Hughes), IIF7
Manley, Seon, and Gogo Lewis,
eds., Ladies of Horror, IB134a;
IIA267
Mann, Charles W., IIC51
Manners-Sutton, Mrs., IA7; 239
Mansfield, Joseph Gerard, "Another
World Than This: The Gothic and
the Catholic in the Novels of
Muriel Spark," IID10
Mantell, Gideon Algernon, IA7
Marazul, Laura, IB61a
Marcuse, Herbert, IIB54
Maria Shelley e il suo Romanzo su
Castruccio Castracani (Briganti),
IIE5, E47
Marini, Giambattista, IG2a
Marino Faliero (Byron), IIA69

Marshall, Mrs. Julian, The Life
and Letters of Mary Wollstone-
craft Shelley, IIA126
Marshall, William H., Byron, Shel-
ley, Hunt, and the Liberal,
ID1a, D2a; IIA269
"Martian Point of View" (Glick-
sohn), IIB97
"Mary Godwin Shelley and the Mon-
ster" (Lund), IIB174
"Mary Godwin to T. J. Hogg. The
1815 Letters" (Jones), IIA222
"Mary Shelley," IIB185
Mary Shelley (Bigland), IIA1
Mary Shelley (Church), IIA2, A96;
246
"Mary Shelley" (Hood), IID25
"Mary Shelley" (B. Neumann),
IIB348, D12
"Mary Shelley" (Nitchie), IIB244
Mary Shelley (Walling), IG1a, G3a;
IIA22, B89
Mary Shelley. A Biography
(Grylls), IE1, E2, E12, E13,
E14; IIA6, A180, B32, E38; 246
"Mary Shelley. A Local Reminis-
cence," IIB186
"Mary Shelley: a Prophetic Nove-
list" (Spark), IIB324
Mary Shelley, Author of Franken-
stein (Nitchie), ID21, E4, E7,
E15-E18, H5, H8, H15, I2, I3;
IIA12, B168, C122
"Mary Shelley, 1851" (Rossetti),
IIA129
"Mary Shelley: Novelist and
Dramatist" (Norman), IC1a, C1b,
D2s; IIA310
"Mary Shelley, 1797-1851" (Norman),
IIB253
"Mary Shelley. The Years After
the Tragedy," IIB187
"Mary Shelley, Traveler" (Nitchie),
IIB245
"Mary Shelley, Walter Scott, and
'Maga'" (Massey), IIB191
"Mary Shelley and Claire Clair-
mont" (Jones), IIB137
"Mary Shelley and Dundee" (Millar),
IIB212
"Mary Shelley and 'Frankenstein'"
(Lyles), IIB177

Novela de Ciencia ficción (Ferreras), IIE14
Novello, Vincent, IA7
Novello, Mrs. Vincent, IA7
"Novels of Mary Shelley" (el-Shater), IID27
"Novels of Mary Shelley: From Frankenstein to Falkner" (Ozolins), IID13
Novyi Mir, IIE68

O, Those Extraordinary Women! (Manley & Belcher), IIA266
Observer, IIB8, B255, C92, C123
"Ode to Ignorance," IE6
Odyssey of the Soul (Hoffman), IIA204, D9
Oh Listen While I Sing to Thee, IE10
"Old Love Stories Retold. V. Shelley and Mary Godwin" (Le Galliene), IIB157
"Old Time Literary Romance Disclosed" (Jackson), IIB126
Ollier, Charles, IA6, A7; IIA148, A169, B243
Olympians (Bolton), IIF4
"On 'Frankenstein'" (Shelley), IIA386, B143, B270, B314
"On Ghosts," IH5; IIA50
"On Mutability" (Shelley), IIB58
"On Reading Wordsworth's Lines on Peel Castle," IE12
On Shelley, IIA310
"On Shelley's 'The Triumph of Life'" (Matthews), IIB195
On the Beach (Shute), IIA161, C52
"On the Discrimination of Gothicisms" (Coleman), IID5
"On the Supernatural in Fictitious Compositions" (Sir W. Scott), IIB308
O'Neill, Eliza, IIA123
Opera Glass, 220
Orlak, El Infierno de Frankenstein (film), 231
Ormond (C. B. Brown), IIB60
Orphan Angel (Wylie), IIF10
"Orpheus," IIB287
Ossian, IIB4
Ovid, *Metamorphoses*, IIB282, E27
Owen, Robert Dale, IA7; IIA73

Oxford Companion to English Literature (Harvey), IIA193
Oxford University Press, IIC17
Ozolins, Aija, "The Novels of Mary Shelley: From Frankenstein to Falkner," IID13
"'Ozymandias' and the Dormouse" (Pollin), IIB281

PMLA, IIB34, B44, B123, B141, B267, B269, B295, B323, B334
Pachter, Charles, IIA37
Paine, Thomas, IIB102
Palacio, Jean de, *Mary Shelley dans son œuvre*, IB53a, D3g, D2i, D3i, D21, D2n, H2-H5, H12, H13, H15; IIB89, B98, B352, C6, C29, C37, C38, C43, C56, C92, C113, C120, C122, C123, E1, E47
Panoramic Miscellany, IIC42
Pantika (Howitt), IIA206
Papers of the Bibliographical Society of America, IIB156
Paracelsus, IIA281, B1
Paradise Lost (Milton), IIB140, B202, B282; 236
Paradiso (Dante), IIA152
Parke, John, IA7; IIA203
Parliamentary Debates, IIB7
Parnassus, IIC15
Partisan Review, IIB26
"Parvenue, The," ID1q-D3q; IIB11, B146, B280
Pascal, Blaise, IG1b
Passion, sechs dichter-ehen (Neumann), IIE35
Passion: Six Literary Marriages (Neumann), IIA300
Past, Present, and Future Perfect (Wolf & Wolf), IIA161; B155a & B9c (p. 208)
Patrick, David, ed., *Chambers's Cyclopedia of English Literature*, IIA272
Patterns of English and American Fiction (Gerould), IIA162
Payne, John Howard, IA7, A8; IIA14, A190, A224, A247, A443, B107, B126, B232, B336
Payne, Mervyn, IIC24
Peacock, Mary, IA7

- 284 -

Shelley, Mary—cont.
—descriptive bibliography of her
works, IIA445
—dwellings, IIA78, A214, A442,
B115
—and Elise, nursemaid, IIB256
—in fiction, IIA120, F1-F27
—translation of Ugo Foscolo,
IIB198
—and 1931 *Frankenstein* film,
IIA30
—influence of Lake of Geneva on,
IIB153
—and Godwin, IIA403, A432, B65,
B70, B168, B255; author of "Memoirs of Godwin," IIB222, B333;
contemplated biography of Godwin,
IG2c; influence on her, IIA89,
A115, A218; severe towards his
Italian Letters, IIA337; suppres-
sion of his religious essays,
IIA68
—mentioned in Edmund Gosse's
diary, IIB194
—as Gothic novelist, IIA33
—mentioned in Teresa Guiccioli's
letters, IIA315
—and Wilhelm Hamm, IIA248
—handwriting, IIA449, B59, B148
—and Mary Hays, IIA432
—and Thomas Jefferson Hogg,
IIB281; use of her notes on Shelley, IG1c; Hogg on, IIA205; mentioned in his letters, IIA308;
intimacy with, IIA218, A222, B234;
proposal to her, IIA276
—as housewife, IIA218
—and Leigh Hunt, IIB168; mentioned in his letters, IIA98,
A211; her financial contributions
to, IIA286
—and Marianne Hunt, IIA286
—and Washington Irving, IIA443.
See also Shelley, Mary; letters—
to and from John Howard Payne
—and Italy, IIA29. *See also* Pisa
—journal, I*A1*, A2, E17, E18;
IIA6, A8, A10, A16, A97, A126,
A174, A223, A416, B81, B110, B224,
B248, *D6*
—Keats on, IIA82
—and Alexander Knox, IIB279
—Latin exercises, IIB143

Shelley, Mary—cont.
—letters. *See* Shelley, Mary;
letters
—contributions to *The Liberal*,
I*D1a*, *H1*, *H2*; IIA269, A286, B63,
B163
—T. H. Lister on, IIA104
—intended contribution to the
Literary Souveneir, IIA430
—lodgings. *See* dwellings
—and Mary Limeburner MacKnight,
IIA406
—manuscript material, IIB261,
B264
—and Thomas Medwin, IIB205, B206
—and Prosper Mérimée, IH8; IIA346
—Thomas Moore on, IIA290
—motherhood, IIB220
—novels, IIA12, A13, A20, A22,
A310, A387, A388, A436, A445,
B150, D12, D15, D27, E1. *See
also* individual works
—obituaries, IIB158, B215, B216
—observer of art, literature,
drama, and opera, IIA188
—and "Orpheus," IIB287
—and Robert Dale Owen, IIA73,
A244, B258
—and John Howard Payne, IIA189,
A443, F7
—and Thomas Love Peacock, IIA184;
Peacock on, IIB39, B265, B266;
portrayed in his *Nightmare Abbey*,
IIA120, F9
—and Henry Hugh Pearson, IE10;
IIB279
—in Pisa, IIA102
—affinities with Poe, IIA20,
A339
—poetry, IIA310, B113, E1. *See
also* individual poems
—and Gaetano Polidori, IIA337
—and John William Polidori,
IIA35, A337
—pregnancies, IIB220
—Cyrus Redding on, IIA348; as a
go-between for her with the Galig-
nanis, IIB19
—mentioned in letters of Henry
Crabb Robinson, IIA358, A359
—Richard Rothwell portrait of,
IIB169, B235, B236
—and Gabriele Rossetti, IIA337

- 285 -

Shelley, Mary; letters—cont.
—from Charles Clairmont, IIB27
—to Claire Clairmont, IA7, A8;
IIA177, B37, B84
—to Charles Cowden Clarke, IA7;
IIA98
—to Henry Colburn, IA7
—to Thomas Cooper, IIB342
—to Thomas Crofton Croker,
IIB66, B328
—to Amelia Curran, IA4, A5, A7,
A8
—to Disraeli, IIB48
—to An Editor, IA6, A7
—to W. Galignani, IA7
—to Monsieur Galloni (?), IA7
—to John Gisborne, IA5, A7
—to Maria Gisborne, IA3, A4, A5,
A7, A8, A9; IIA203, A306, B84,
B119, B133, B138, E61
—to Godwin, IA7
—to John Gregson, IA7
—to Teresa Guiccioli, IIA315
—to Mr. Halford, IA7
—to Marianna Hammond, IA7
—to John Hanson, IA7; IIA79
—to Mary Hays, IA7; IIA432
—to Abraham Hayward, IA7, A8;
IIA196, A322
—to William Hazlitt, Jr., IA7
—to J. A. Hessey, IA7
—to George S. Hilliard, IIA334
—to Thomas Jefferson Hogg, IA7,
A8; IIA385
—from Thomas Jefferson Hogg,
IIA15, A86, A222, A361
—to Louisa Holcroft, IA7
—to Thomas Hookham, IA7
—to Mrs. R. B. Hoppner, IA7, A8
—to Lord Houghton, IA7
—to J. C. Hudson, IA7
—to Leigh Hunt, IA2, A6, A7, A8;
IIA92, A159, A211, A220, B181,
B182, B188, B271, B341; 219
—from Leigh Hunt, IIA63, A211
—to Marianne Hunt, IA2, A6, A7,
A8; IIA92, A159, A304, B181,
B182, B271
—to Victor Jacquemont, IA7;
IIB117, E33
—to Douglas Jerrold, IA7
—to Maria Jane Jewsbury, IA7
—to Mrs. Jones, IA7

Shelley, Mary; letters—cont.
—to Thomas Forbes Kelsall, IA7;
IIA121
—to James Kenney, IA7
—to Alexander Knox, IA7, A8
—to Mary Lamb, IA7; IIA239
—to Walter Savage Landor, IA7
—to George Henry Lewes, IA7
—to Mrs. Manners-Sutton, IA7;
239
—to Gideon Algernon Mantell (?),
IA7
—from Mrs. Mason, IIA257
—to Alexander Mavrocordato,
IIB125
—to Thomas Medwin, IA7, A8
—from Thomas Medwin, IIA251
—to Prosper Mérimée, IA7, A8;
IIB117
—to Mr. Mignot, IA7
—to Mrs. Milner-Gibson, IA7
—to Thomas Moore, IA7, A8
—from Thomas Moore, IIA292
—to Lady Morgan, IA7
—to Edward Moxon, IA7
—to John Murray, IA7, A8; IIA389
—to Mary Peacock Nicolls, IA7
—from Caroline Norton, IIA332
—to Vincent Novello, IA7, A8
—to Mrs. Vincent Novello, IA7
—to Charles Ollier, IA6, A7;
IIA148, A169, B243
—to Robert Dale Owen, IA7;
IIA243
—to John Parke, IA7; IIA203
—to and from John Howard Payne
(the Mary Shelley-Payne-Irving
letters), IA7, A8; IIA14, A190,
A203, A224, A247, B107, B126,
B232, B336
—to Mary Peacock, IA7
—to Thomas Love Peacock, IA7,
A8; IIA325, B142
—from Thomas Love Peacock,
IIA184
—to George W. Portman, IA7
—to Bryan Waller Procter (?),
IA7; IIA121
—to Cyrus Redding, IA7; IIA348
—to Frederic Mansel Reynolds,
IA7
—to Capt. Daniel Roberts, IA7
—to Charles Robinson, IA7, A8

Williams, Edward Ellerker, IIB136, B273
—*Journal*, IIA158
Williams, Jane, IA7; IIA63, A158, A184, A308, B273, B295, F8
Williams's (Dr.) Library, IIA359
Wiltshire Essays (Hewlett), IIA201
Winter in Italy (Mrs. Yates), rev., IIC117
Winter's Wreath (1832), IC1h; IIB10, B152
Wise, Thomas James, ed., *Letters from P. B. Shelley to Jane Clairmont*, IIB139
Witch of Atlas (Shelley), IIA85
Wolf, Jack C., and Barbara H. Wolf, eds., *Ghosts, Castles, and Victims*, IB151a; IIA446
Wolf Man (film), 227
Wolfstein [Shelley, *St. Irvyne*], B357 (p. 209)
Wollstonecraft, Everina, IA7
Wollstonecraft, Mary, IIA29, A84, A141, A153, A258, A259, A270, A358, A393, A427, B65, B70, B158, E44, F5
"Woman's Rib" (Scortia), IIB307
Woman's Work in English Fiction (Whitmore), IIA439
Women in Love (Lawrence), IIB82
Women Novelists (Johnson), IIA221
Women of Letters (Mayer), IIA277
Women of Wonder (Sargent, ed.), IIA369
Word Portraits of Famous Writers (Wotton), IIA451
Wordsworth, William, IIB332, C49
Works of Lord Byron (Prothero, ed.), IIA83, B310
Works of Percy Bysshe Shelley (Forman, ed.), IIA145, A384; 247
Works of Thomas Love Peacock, IIA325
World of Fashion and Continental Feuilleton (Monde elegant), IIB352
"World of Science Fiction" (Schwartz), IIB306
Worlds of Tomorrow, IIB96

Wortley, The Lady Emmeline Stuart, ed., *The Keepsake* (1837), ID1q
Wright, David, ed., *Records of Shelley, Byron, and the Author* (Trelawny), IIA420, A453
Wright, Frances, IIA73
Wright, Raymond:
—ed., *Nightmare Abbey. Crotchet Castle* (Peacock), IIF9
—ed., *Prose of the Romantic Period*, ID70a
Wright, S. Fowler, *Deluge*, IIA295
Writer, The, IIB160
"Writing Science Fiction Today" (Leinster), IIB160
Wylie, Elinor:
—*Mortal Image*, IIF10
—*The Orphan Angel*, IIF10
Wyndham, John, *Day of the Triffids*, IIA100

Yale Review, IIB238
Yale University Library, IIA16
Yale University Library Gazette, IIB27
Yano, Kozaburo, IB147a
Yarker, P. M., and Brian Lee, IIC54
Yates, Mrs. Ashton, *A Winter in Italy*, rev., IIC117
Year's Work in English Studies:
—*1922*, IIA200
—*1948*, IIA165
—*1965*, IIC54
Yesterday's Tomorrows (Armytage), IIA33
Young Frankenstein (film), IIA326, B49, B51; 235
Young Frankenstein (Pearlman), IIA326; 235
Young Lady's Magazine, IIF1
Young Shelley, The (Cameron), IIA88

Zastrozzi (Shelley), IIA93
Zirker, Joan McTigue, "The Gothic Tradition in English Fiction, 1764-1824," IID22

→ → → →